KAWASAKI

KZ400 & 440 TWINS · 1974-1982
SERVICE · REPAIR · PERFORMANCE

SYDNIE A. WAUSON
Editor

JEFF ROBINSON
Publisher

CLYMER PUBLICATIONS

World's largest publisher of books devoted exclusively to automobiles and motorcycles.

12860 MUSCATINE STREET · P.O. BOX 20 · ARLETA, CALIFORNIA 91331

FIRST EDITION
Published, February 1977

SECOND EDITION
Revised by Ed Scott to include 1978-1979 models
First Printing, May 1979
Second Printing, December 1979

THIRD EDITION
Revised by Anton Vesely to include 1980 models
First Printing, April 1981

FOURTH EDITION
Revised by Anton Vesely to include 1981-1982 models
First Printing, January 1983

Printed in U.S.A.

ISBN: 0-89287-138-5

Production Coordinator, Marina Lerique
Graphic Artist, Mark Plunkett

•

Technical illustrations by Mitzi McCarthy

COVER:
Photographed by Michael Brown Photographic Productions, Los Angeles, CA.
Motorcycle courtesy of Dale Lewis.

KZ400 & 440 TWINS · 1974-1982

SERVICE · REPAIR · PERFORMANCE

CONTENTS

QUICK REFERENCE DATA

TUNE-UP SPECIFICATIONS

Spark Plugs	
Type	
1978 and later	B7ES (NGK) or W22ES-U (ND)
1974-1977	B8ES (NGK) or W24ES (ND)
Gap	0.028-0.032 in. (0.7-0.8 mm)
Breaker Points	
Gap	0.014 in. (0.35 mm)
Dwell	53% (193 degrees)
Valve Clearance (Cold, Intake and Exhaust)	
1978 and later	0.007-0.009 in. (0.17-0.22 mm)
1977	0.005-0.006 in. (0.13-0.15 mm)
1974-1976	0.004-0.006 in. (0.10-0.15 mm)
Idle Speed	
All models	1,100-1,300 rpm
Idle Mixture (Turns Out From Seated)	
1982	2 3/4
1980-1981	2 1/4
1979 H	2 1/4
1979 B	1 1/4
1978	1 1/4
1977	1 1/2
1976	1 5/8
1975	1 1/2
1974	7/8

FASTENER TORQUES

Fastener	Ft.-lb.	Mkg
Oil drain plug		
1974-1977	16	2.25
1978 & later	22	3.0
Oil filter bolt	14.5	2.0
Rocker shaft locknuts (1974-1977)	18	2.5
Spark plugs	20	2.8
Valve adjuster locknuts (1978 and later)	11	1.5
Engine mounting bolts	30	4.0
Front axle pinch nuts	14.5	2.0
Front axle nut(s)		
1974-1979	60	8.0
1980 and later	45	6.5
Rear axle nut		
1974-1979	90	12.0
1980 and later	55	7.5
Swing arm pivot nut	65	9.0

MAINTENANCE SCHEDULE

Weekly/Gas Stop Maintenance	
	•Check tire pressure cold; adjust to suit load and speed •Check brakes for a solid feel •Check brake lever play; adjust if necessary (1974-1977 models) •Check brake pedal play; adjust if necessary •Check throttle grip for smooth opening and return •Check clutch lever play; adjust if necessary •Check for smooth but not loose steering •Lubricate drive chain every 200 miles (300 km); check and adjust play if necessary •Check axles, suspension, controls and linkage nuts, bolts and fasteners; tighten if necessary •Check engine oil level; add oil if necessary •Check lights and horn operation, especially brake light •Check for any abnormal engine noise and leaks •Check kill switch operation
Monthly/3,000 Mile (5,000 km) Maintenance	
	•Check battery electrolyte level (more frequently in hot weather); add water if necessary •Check disc brake fluid level; add if necessary
6-Month/3,000 mile (5,000 km) Maintenance	
	•All above checks and the following •Clean or replace air filter •Drain float bowls; clean fuel tap •Clean spark plugs, set gap; replace if necessary •Adjust cam chain tension (1974-1979 models) •Clean contact breaker points, adjust gap; replace if necessary (breaker-point models) •Check ignition timing; adjust if necessary (breaker-point models) •Check valve clearance; adjust if necessary •Check and adjust carburetor cable play, idle speed mixture; synchronize •Change engine oil and filter (filter at every other check) •Lube cables, levers, pedals, pivots and throttle grip •Adjust clutch release •Check tire wear •Check drive chain wear •Check brake lining wear •Check steering play; adjust if necessary •Check suspension •Check drive belt tension, adjust if necessary; inspect for wear (belt-driven models)
Yearly/6,000 Mile (10,000 km) Maintenance	
	•All above checks and the following •Change air filter element •Change disc brake fluid •Change fork oil •Lubricate ignition advance •Check and tighten all nuts, bolts and fasteners •Grease swing arm pivot
2-Year/12,000 Mile (20,000 km) Maintenance	
	•All above checks and the following •Grease speedometer gear housing •Grease wheel bearings •Grease steering bearings

(continued)

MAINTENANCE SCHEDULE (CONTINUED)

2-Year Maintenance	• Grease drum brake camshaft • Replace disc brake master cylinder cup and dust seal • Replace disc brake caliper piston seal and dust seal
4-Year Maintenance	• Replace brake hoses • Replace fuel hoses

STANDARD FORK OIL

Year/Model	Dry Capacity U.S. fl. oz.	cc	Oil Level* Inch	mm	Oil Grade SAE
1982 A, D	5.9	175	R 16.8	R 426	5W20
1982 G, H	5.1	150	R 18.5	R 470	5W20
1979-1981 A, D, H	5.1	150	R 18.7	R 475	5W20
1979-1981 B, C	5.1	150	R 17.1	R 435	5W20
1978	5.1	150	R 17.1	R 435	5W20
1977	5.4	160	I 13.5	I 343	5W20
1974-1976	5.4	160	I 13.8	I 350	5W20

* Fork oil level is checked with forks fully extended;

R: fork springs removed

I: fork springs installed

TIRES AND TIRE PRESSURE

Model/Tire Size	Pressure @ Load 0-215 lb. (0-97.5 kg)	Over 215 lb. (Over 97.5 kg)
1982 G, H		
Front - 3.60S-19 4PR	25 psi (175 kpa)	25 psi (175 kpa)
Rear - 4.10S-18 4PR	28 psi (200 kpa)	32 psi (225 kpa)
1980-1982 A, D and 1979 A, D, H		
Front - 3.25S-19 4PR	25 psi (175 kpa)	25 psi (175 kpa)
Rear - 130/90-16 67S	21 psi (150 kpa)	25 psi (175 kpa)
1979-1982 B, C		
Front - 3.00S-18 4PR	25 psi (175 kpa)	25 psi (175 kpa)
Rear - 3.50S-18 4PR	28 psi (200 kpa)	36 psi (250 kpa)

	Pressure @ Load 0-280 lb. (0-127 kg)	280-330 lb. (127-150 kg)	Over 330 lb. (Over 150 kg)
1977-1978 A			
Front - 3.25S-18 4PR	32 psi (225 kpa)	32 psi (225 kpa)	32 psi (225 kpa)
Rear - 3.50S-18 6PR	32 psi (225 kpa)	36 psi (250 kpa)	40 psi (276 kpa)

	Pressure @ Load 0-215 lb. (0-97.5 kg)	Over 215 lb. (97.5 kg)
1974-1977 D, S		
Front - 3.25S-18 4PR	25 psi (175 kpa)	25 psi (175 kpa)
Rear - 3.50S-18 4PR	28 psi (200 kpa)	36 psi (250 kpa)

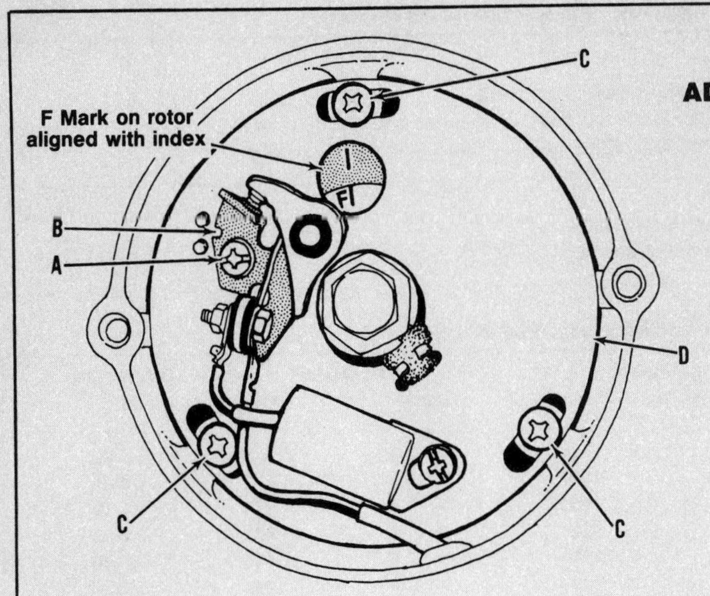

IGNITION TIMING ADJUSTMENTS (1974-1980)

A. Breaker point retaining screw
B. Point adjustment pry slots
C. Timing plate screws
D. Timing plate

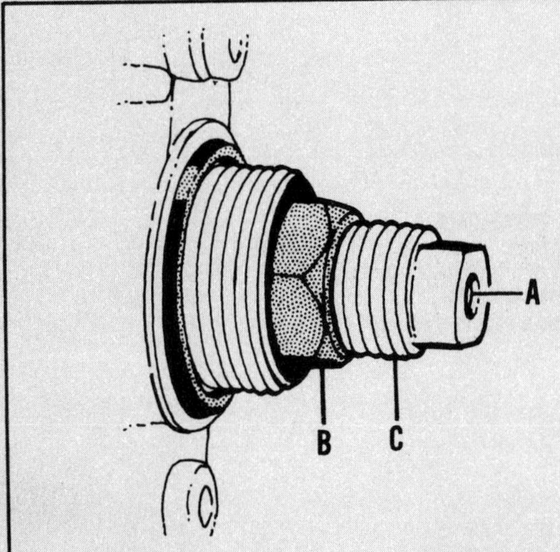

CAM CHAIN TENSIONER (1974-1977)

A. Pushrod
B. Locknut
C. Guide

RECOMMENDED LUBRICANTS AND FUEL

Engine oil	SAE 10W40, 10W50, 20W40, 20W50, rated "SE"
Front fork oil	SAE 5W20
Brake fluid	DOT 3
Fuel	87 pump octane (RON+MON)/2 91 research octane (RON)

CHASSIS ADJUSTMENTS

Disc brake lever play (1974-1977)	1/8-3/16 in. (3-5 mm) at tip of lever
Drum brake cable play	About 3/16 in. (4-5 mm) at cable end of lever
Brake pedal travel	3/4-1 1/4 in. (20-30 mm)
Clutch cable play	About 1/8 in. (2-3 mm) at cable end of lever
Drive chain play	
On centerstand	1-1 3/8 in. (25-35 mm)
On side stand	3/4-1 1/4 in. (20-30 mm)
Drive belt play	3/8-5/8 in. (8.5-17 mm)

KZ400 & 440 TWINS · 1974-1982

SERVICE • REPAIR • PERFORMANCE

INTRODUCTION

This detailed, comprehensive manual covers all 1974-1982 Kawasaki KZ400 and KZ440 Twins. The expert text gives complete information on maintenance, repair and overhaul. Hundreds of photos and drawings guide you through every step. The book includes all you need to know to keep your bike running right.

General information on all models and specific information on 1974-1979 models is contained in Chapters One through Seven. The Supplement at the end of the book contains specific information on 1980 and later models which differs from earlier models.

Where repairs are practical for the owner/mechanic, complete procedures are given. Equally important, difficult jobs are pointed out. Such operations are usually more economically performed by a dealer or independent garage.

A shop manual is a reference. You want to be able to find information fast. As in all Clymer books, this one is designed with this in mind. All chapters are thumb tabbed. Important items are indexed at the rear of the book. Finally, all the most frequently used specifications and capacities are summarized on the *Quick Reference* pages at the front of the book.

Keep the book handy. Carry it in your tool box. It will help you to better understand your bike, lower repair and maintenance costs and generally improve your satisfaction with your bike.

CHAPTER ONE

GENERAL INFORMATION

The troubleshooting, maintenance, tune-up, and step-by-step repair procedures in this book are written specifically for the owner and home mechanic. The text is accompanied by helpful photos and diagrams to make the job as clear and correct as possible.

Troubleshooting, maintenance, tune-up, and repair are not difficult if you know what to do and what tools and equipment to use. Anyone of average intelligence, with some mechanical ability, and not afraid to get their hands dirty can perform most of the procedures in this book.

In some cases, a repair job may require tools or skills not reasonably expected of the home mechanic. These procedures are noted in each chapter and it is recommended that you take the job to your dealer, a competent mechanic, or a machine shop.

MANUAL ORGANIZATION

This chapter provides general information, safety and service hints. Also included are lists of recommended shop and emergency tools as well as a brief description of troubleshooting and tune-up equipment.

Chapter Two provides methods and suggestions for quick and accurate diagnosis and repair of problems. Troubleshooting procedures discuss typical symptoms and logical methods to pinpoint the trouble.

Chapter Three explains all periodic lubrication and routine maintenance necessary to keep your motorcycle running well. Chapter Three also includes recommended tune-up procedures, eliminating the need to constantly consult chapters on the various subassemblies.

Subsequent chapters cover specific systems such as the engine, transmission, and electrical system. Each of these chapters provides disassembly, inspection, repair, and assembly procedures in a simple step-by-step format. If a repair is impractical for the home mechanic it is indicated. In these cases it is usually faster and less expensive to have the repairs made by a dealer or competent repair shop. Essential specifications are included in the appropriate chapters.

When special tools are required to perform a task included in this manual, the tools are illustrated. It may be possible to borrow or rent these tools. The inventive mechanic may also be able to find a suitable substitute in his tool box, or to fabricate one.

The terms NOTE, CAUTION, and WARNING have specific meanings in this manual. A NOTE provides additional or explanatory information. A

CAUTION is used to emphasize areas where equipment damage could result if proper precautions are not taken. A WARNING is used to stress those areas where personal injury or death could result from negligence, in addition to possible mechanical damage.

SERVICE HINTS

Time, effort, and frustration will be saved and possible injury will be prevented if you observe the following practices.

Most of the service procedures covered are straightforward and can be performed by anyone reasonably handy with tools. It is suggested, however, that you consider your own capabilities carefully before attempting any operation involving major disassembly of the engine.

Some operations, for example, require the use of a press. It would be wiser to have these performed by a shop equipped for such work, rather than to try to do the job yourself with makeshift equipment. Other procedures require precision measurements. Unless you have the skills and equipment required, it would be better to have a qualified repair shop make the measurements for you.

Repairs go much faster and easier if the parts that will be worked on are clean before you begin. There are special cleaners for washing the engine and related parts. Brush or spray on the cleaning solution, let stand, then rinse it away with a garden hose. Clean all oily or greasy parts with cleaning solvent as you remove them.

WARNING

Never use gasoline as a cleaning agent. It presents an extreme fire hazard. Be sure to work in a well-ventilated area when using cleaning solvent. Keep a fire extinguisher, rated for gasoline fires, handy in any case.

Much of the labor charge for repairs made by dealers is for the removal and disassembly of other parts to reach the defective unit. It is frequently possible to perform the preliminary operations yourself and then take the defective unit in to the dealer for repair, at considerable savings.

Once you have decided to tackle the job yourself, make sure you locate the appropriate section in this manual, and read it entirely. Study the illustrations and text until you have a good idea of what is involved in completing the job satisfactorily. If special tools are required, make arrangements to get them before you start. Also, purchase any known defective parts prior to starting on the procedure. It is frustrating and time-consuming to get partially into a job and then be unable to complete it.

Simple wiring checks can be easily made at home, but knowledge of electronics is almost a necessity for performing tests with complicated electronic testing gear.

During disassembly of parts keep a few general cautions in mind. Force is rarely needed to get things apart. If parts are a tight fit, like a bearing in a case, there is usually a tool designed to separate them. Never use a screwdriver to pry apart parts with machined surfaces such as cylinder head or crankcase halves. You will mar the surfaces and end up with leaks.

Make diagrams wherever similar-appearing parts are found. You may think you can remember where everything came from — but mistakes are costly. There is also the possibility you may get sidetracked and not return to work for days or even weeks — in which interval, carefully laid out parts may have become disturbed.

Tag all similar internal parts for location, and mark all mating parts for position. Record number and thickness of any shims as they are removed. Small parts such as bolts can be identified by placing them in plastic sandwich bags that are sealed and labeled with masking tape.

Wiring should be tagged with masking tape and marked as each wire is removed. Again, do not rely on memory alone.

Disconnect battery ground cable before working near electrical connections and before disconnecting wires. Never run the engine with the battery disconnected; the alternator could be seriously damaged.

Protect finished surfaces from physical damage or corrosion. Keep gasoline and brake fluid off painted surfaces.

Frozen or very tight bolts and screws can often be loosened by soaking with penetrating oil like Liquid Wrench or WD-40, then sharply striking the bolt head a few times with a hammer and punch (or screwdriver for screws). Avoid heat unless absolutely necessary, since it may melt, warp, or remove the temper from many parts.

Avoid flames or sparks when working near a charging battery or flammable liquids, such as gasoline.

No parts, except those assembled with a press fit, require unusual force during assembly. If a part is hard to remove or install, find out why before proceeding.

Cover all openings after removing parts to keep dirt, small tools, etc., from falling in.

When assembling two parts, start all fasteners, then tighten evenly.

Wiring connections and brake shoes, drums, pads, and discs and contact surfaces in dry clutches should be kept clean and free of grease and oil.

When assembling parts, be sure all shims and washers are replaced exactly as they came out.

Whenever a rotating part butts against a stationary part, look for a shim or washer. Use new gaskets if there is any doubt about the condition of old ones. Generally, you should apply gasket cement to one mating surface only, so the parts may be easily disassembled in the future. A thin coat of oil on gaskets helps them seal effectively.

Heavy grease can be used to hold small parts in place if they tend to fall out during assembly. However, keep grease and oil away from electrical, clutch, and brake components.

High spots may be sanded off a piston with sandpaper, but emery cloth and oil do a much more professional job.

Carburetors are best cleaned by disassembling them and soaking the parts in a commercial carburetor cleaner. Never soak gaskets and rubber parts in these cleaners. Never use wire to clean out jets and air passages; they are easily damaged. Use compressed air to blow out the carburetor, but only if the float has been removed first.

Take your time and do the job right. Do not forget that a newly rebuilt engine must be broken in the same as a new one. Refer to your owner's manual for the proper break-in procedures.

SAFETY FIRST

Professional mechanics can work for years and never sustain a serious injury. If you observe a few rules of common sense and safety, you can enjoy many safe hours servicing your motorcycle. You could hurt yourself or damage the motorcycle if you ignore these rules.

1. Never use gasoline as a cleaning solvent.

2. Never smoke or use a torch in the vicinity of flammable liquids such as cleaning solvent in open containers.

3. Never smoke or use a torch in an area where batteries are being charged. Highly explosive hydrogen gas is formed during the charging process.

4. Use the proper sized wrenches to avoid damage to nuts and injury to yourself.

5. When loosening a tight or stuck nut, be guided by what would happen if the wrench should slip. Protect yourself accordingly.

6. Keep your work area clean and uncluttered.

7. Wear safety goggles during all operations involving drilling, grinding, or use of a cold chisel.

8. Never use worn tools.

9. Keep a fire extinguisher handy and be sure it is rated for gasoline (Class B) and electrical (Class C) fires.

EXPENDABLE SUPPLIES

Certain expendable supplies are necessary. These include grease, oil, gasket cement, wiping rags, cleaning solvent, and distilled water. Also, special locking compounds, silicone lubricants, and engine and carburetor cleaners may be useful. Cleaning solvent is available at most service stations and distilled water for the battery is available at supermarkets.

SHOP TOOLS

For complete servicing and repair you will need an assortment of ordinary hand tools (**Figure 1**).

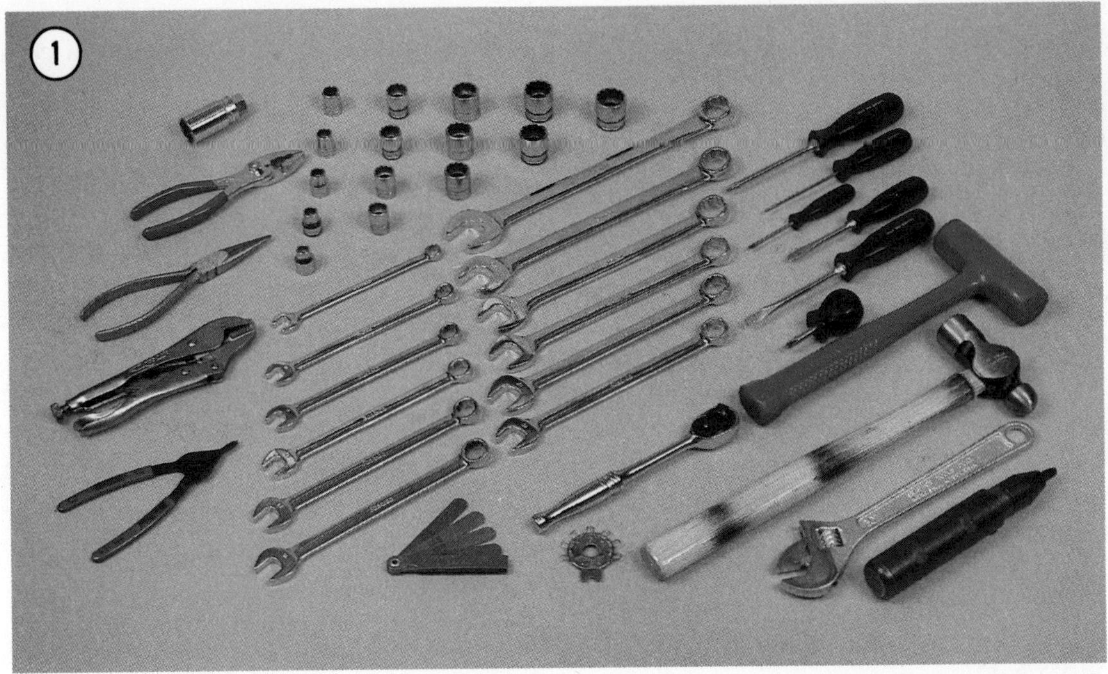

As a minimum, these include:

a. Combination wrenches
b. Sockets
c. Plastic mallet
d. Small hammer
e. Impact driver
f. Snap ring pliers
g. Gas pliers
h. Phillips screwdrivers
i. Slot (common) screwdrivers
j. Feeler gauges
k. Spark plug gauge
l. Spark plug wrench

Special tools required are shown in the chapters covering the particular repair in which they are used.

Engine tune-up and troubleshooting procedures require other special tools and equipment. These are described in detail in the following sections.

EMERGENCY TOOL KITS

Highway

A small emergency tool kit kept on the bike is handy for road emergencies which otherwise could leave you stranded. The tools and spares listed below and shown in **Figure 2** will let you handle most roadside repairs.

a. Motorcycle tool kit (original equipment)
b. Impact driver
c. Silver waterproof sealing tape (duct tape)
d. Hose clamps (3 sizes)
e. Silicone sealer
f. Lock 'N' Seal
g. Flashlight
h. Tire patch kit
i. Tire irons
j. Plastic pint bottle (for oil)
k. Waterless hand cleaner
l. Rags for clean up

Off-Road

A few simple tools and aids carried on the motorcycle can mean the difference between walking or riding back to camp or to where repairs can be made. See **Figure 3**.

A few essential spare parts carried in your truck or van can prevent a day or weekend of trail riding from being spoiled. See **Figure 4**.

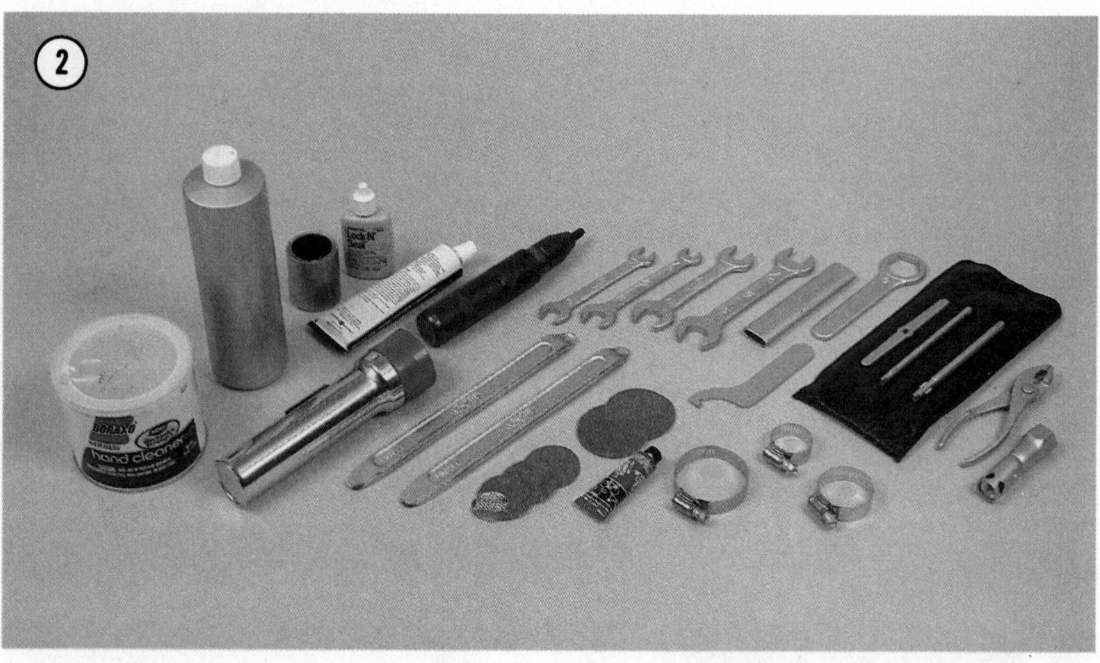

On the Motorcycle

a. Motorcycle tool kit (original equipment)
b. Drive chain master link
c. Tow line
d. Spark plug
e. Spark plug wrench
f. Shifter lever
g. Clutch/brake lever
h. Silver waterproof sealing tape (duct tape)
i. Loctite Lock 'N' Seal

In the Truck

a. Control cables (throttle, clutch, brake)
b. Silicone sealer
c. Tire patch kit
d. Tire irons
e. Tire pump
f. Impact driver
g. Oil

WARNING
Tools and spares should be carried on the motorcycle — not in clothing where a simple fall could result in serious injury from a sharp tool.

TROUBLESHOOTING AND TUNE-UP EQUIPMENT

Voltmeter, Ohmmeter, and Ammeter

For testing the ignition or electrical system, a good voltmeter is required. For motorcycle use, an instrument covering 0-20 volts is satisfactory. One which also has a 0-2 volt scale is necessary for testing relays, points, or individual contacts where voltage drops are much smaller. Accuracy should be ± ½ volt.

An ohmmeter measures electrical resistance. This instrument is useful for checking continuity (open and short circuits), and testing fuses and lights.

The ammeter measures electrical current. Ammeters for motorcycle use should cover 0-50 amperes and 0-250 amperes. These are useful for checking battery charging and starting current.

Several inexpensive VOM's (volt-ohm-milliammeter) combine all three instruments into one which fits easily in any tool box. See **Figure 5**. However, the ammeter ranges are usually too small for motorcycle work.

Hydrometer

The hydrometer gives a useful indication of battery condition and charge by measuring the

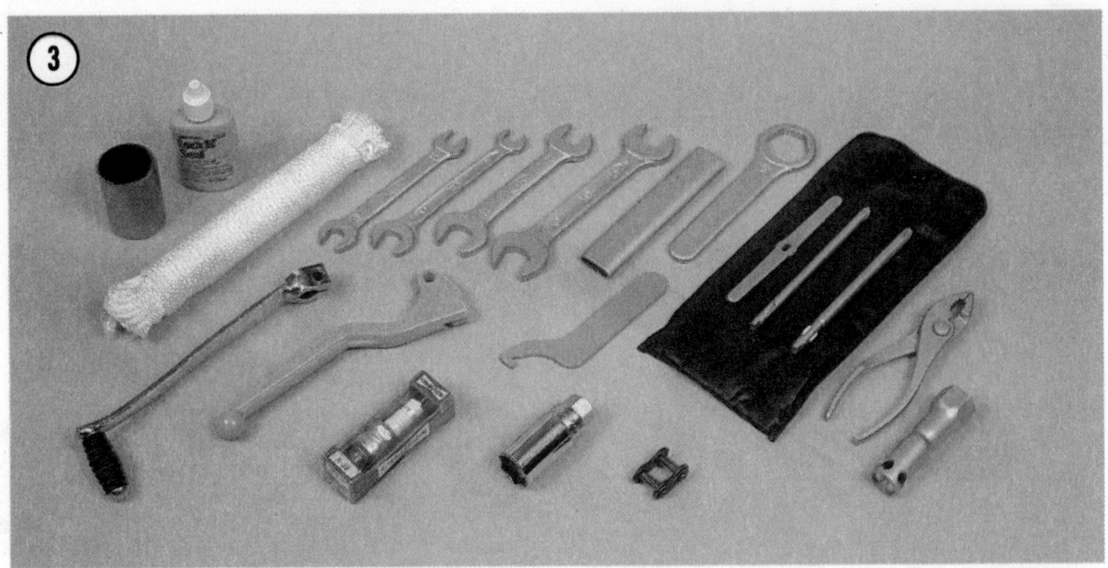

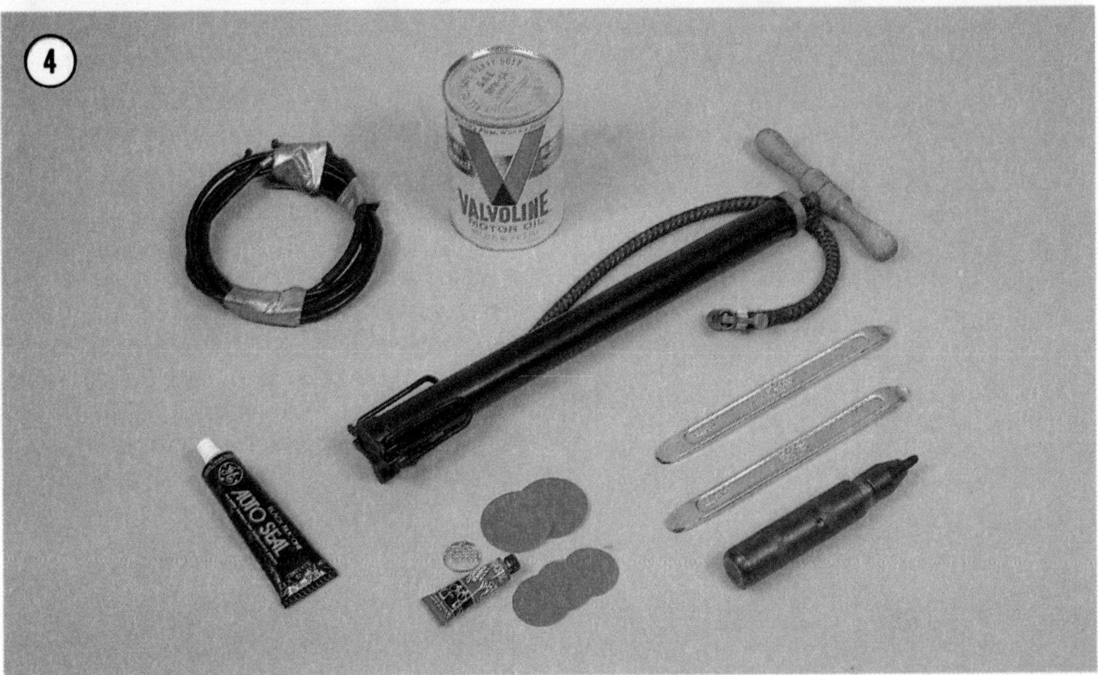

specific gravity of the electrolyte in each cell. See **Figure 6**. Complete details on use and interpretation of readings are provided in the electrical chapter.

Compression Tester

The compression tester measures the compression pressure built up in each cylinder. The results, when properly interpreted, can indicate general cylinder, ring, and valve condition. See **Figure 7**. Extension lines are available for hard-to-reach cylinders.

Dwell Meter (Contact Breaker Point Ignition Only)

A dwell meter measures the distance in degrees of cam rotation that the breaker points remain closed while the engine is running. Since

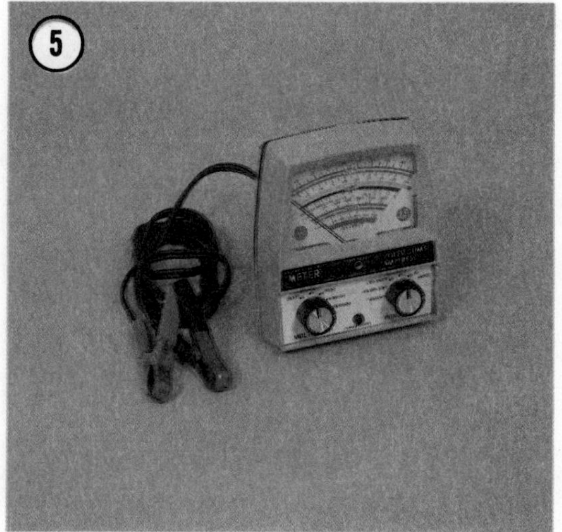

5

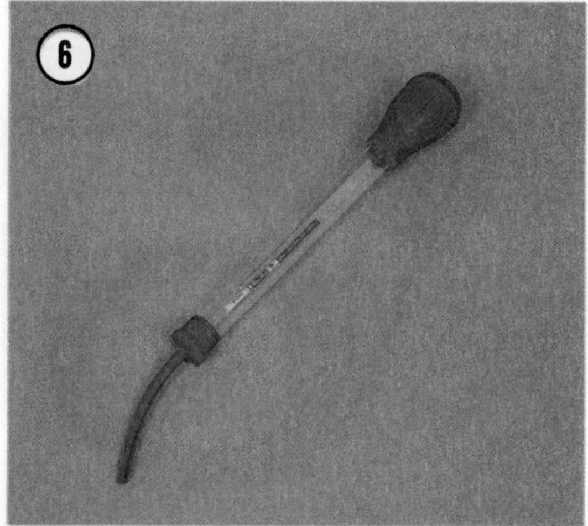

6

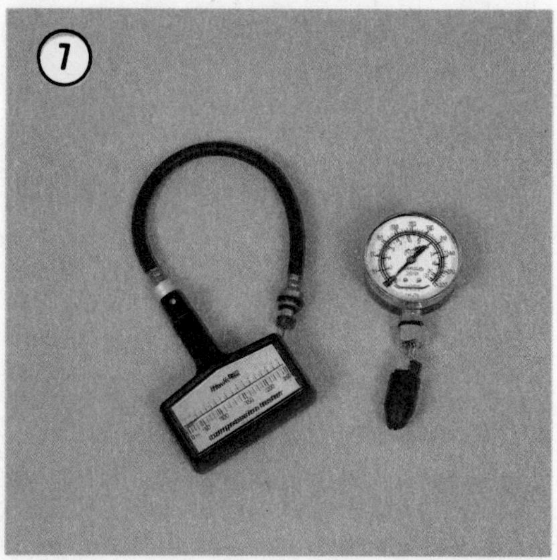

7

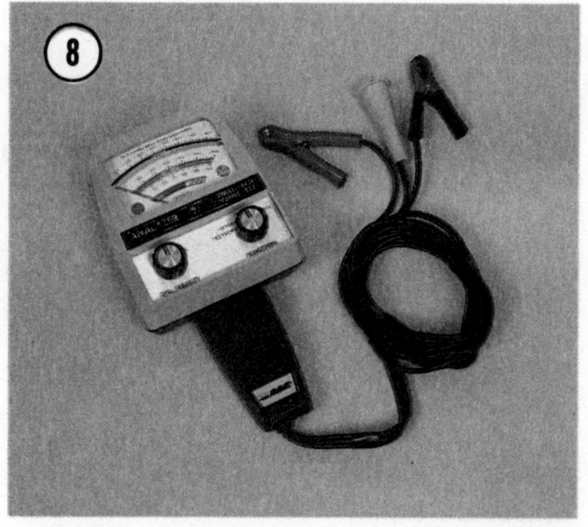

8

this angle is determined by breaker point gap, dwell angle is an accurate indication of breaker point gap.

Many tachometers intended for tuning and testing incorporate a dwell meter as well. See **Figure 8**. Follow the manufacturer's instructions to measure dwell.

Tachometer

A tachometer is necessary for tuning. See **Figure 8**. Ignition timing and carburetor adjustments must be performed at the specified idle speed. The best instrument for this purpose is one with a low range of 0-1,000 or 0-2,000 rpm for setting idle, and a high range of 0-4,000 or more for setting ignition timing at 3,000 rpm. Extended range (0-6,000 or 0-8,000 rpm) instruments lack accuracy at lower speeds. The instrument should be capable of detecting changes of 25 rpm on the low range.

> NOTE: *The motorcycle's tachometer is not accurate enough for correct idle adjustment.*

Strobe Timing Light

This instrument is necessary for tuning, as it permits very accurate ignition timing. The light flashes at precisely the same instant that No. 1 cylinder fires, at which time the timing marks on the engine should align. Refer to Chapter Three for exact location of the timing marks for your engine.

Suitable lights range from inexpensive neon bulb types ($2-3) to powerful xenon strobe lights ($20-40). See **Figure 9**. Neon timing lights are difficult to see and must be used in dimly lit areas. Xenon strobe timing lights can be used outside in bright sunlight.

Tune-up Kits

Many manufacturers offer kits that combine several useful instruments. Some come in a convenient carry case and are usually less expensive than purchasing one instrument at a time. **Figure 10** shows one of the kits that is available. The prices vary with the number of instruments included in the kit.

Manometer (Carburetor Synchronizer)

A manometer is essential for accurately synchronizing carburetors on multi-cylinder engines. The instrument detects intake pressure differences between carburetors and permits them to be adjusted equally. A suitable manometer costs about $25 and comes with detailed instructions for use. See **Figure 11**.

Fire Extinguisher

A fire extinguisher is a necessity when working on a vehicle. It should be rated for both *Class B* (flammable liquids — gasoline, oil, paint, etc.) and *Class C* (electrical — wiring, etc.) type fires. It should always be kept within reach. See **Figure 12**.

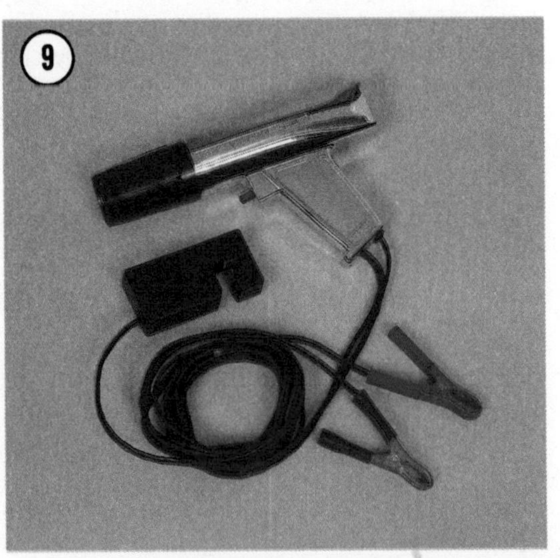
9

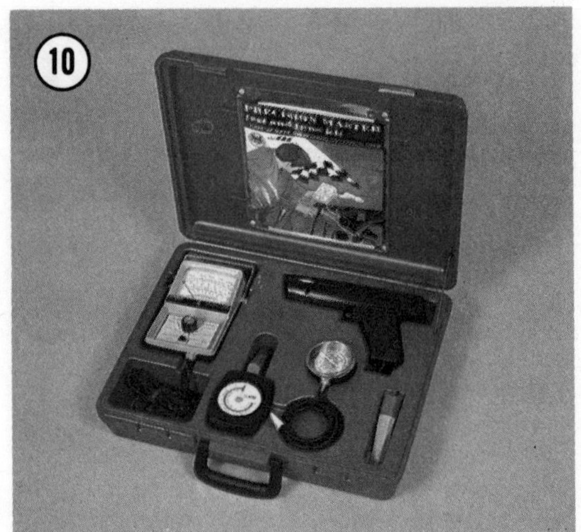
10

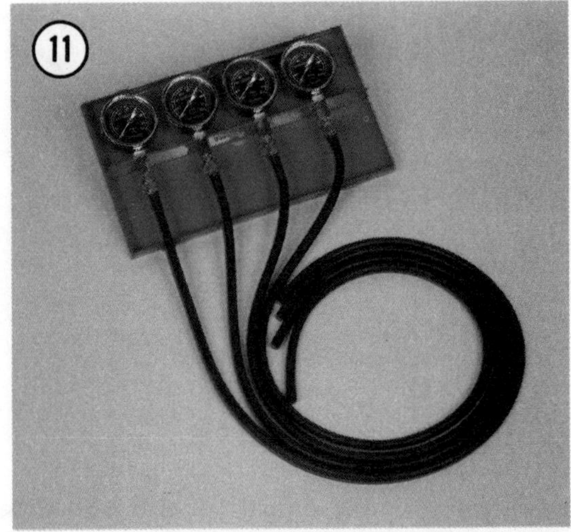
11

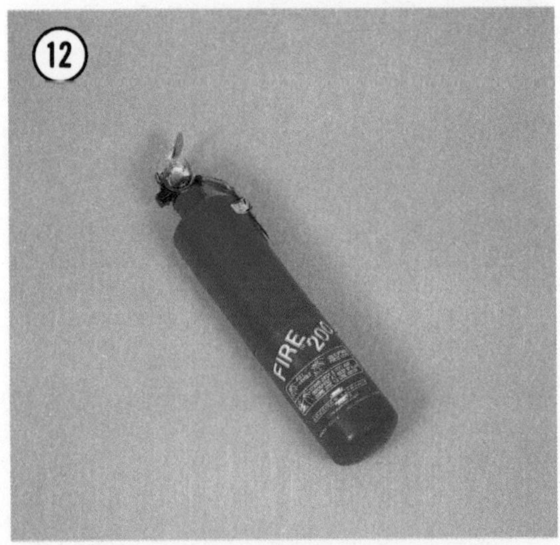
12

CHAPTER TWO

TROUBLESHOOTING

Troubleshooting motorcycle problems is relatively simple. To be effective and efficient, however, it must be done in a logical step-by-step manner. If it is not, a great deal of time may be wasted, good parts may be replaced unnecessarily, and the true problem may never be uncovered.

Always begin by defining the symptoms as closely as possible. Then, analyze the symptoms carefully so that you can make an intelligent guess at the probable cause. Next, test the probable cause and attempt to verify it; if it's not at fault, analyze the symptoms once again, this time eliminating the first probable cause. Continue on in this manner, a step at a time, until the problem is solved.

At first, this approach may seem to be time consuming, but you will soon discover that it's not nearly so wasteful as a hit-or-miss method that may never solve the problem. And just as important, the methodical approach to troubleshooting ensures that only those parts that are defective will be replaced.

The troubleshooting procedures in this chapter analyze typical symptoms and show logical methods for isolating and correcting trouble. They are not, however, the only methods; there may be several approaches to a given problem, but all good troubleshooting methods have one thing in common — a logical, systematic approach.

ENGINE

The entire engine must be considered when trouble arises that is experienced as poor performance or failure to start. The engine is more than a combustion chamber, piston, and crankshaft; it also includes a fuel delivery system, an ignition system, and an exhaust system.

Before beginning to troubleshoot any engine problems, it's important to understand an engine's operating requirements. First, it must have a correctly metered mixture of gasoline and air (**Figure 1**). Second, it must have an air-tight combustion chamber in which the mixture can be compressed. And finally, it requires a precisely timed spark to ignite the compressed mixture. If one or more is missing, the engine won't run, and if just one is deficient, the engine will run poorly at best.

Of the three requirements, the precisely timed spark — provided by the ignition system — is most likely to be the culprit, with gas/air mixture (carburetion) second, and poor compression the least likely.

STARTING DIFFICULTIES

Hard starting is probably the most common motorcycle ailment, with a wide range of problems likely. Before delving into a reluctant or non-starter, first determine what has changed

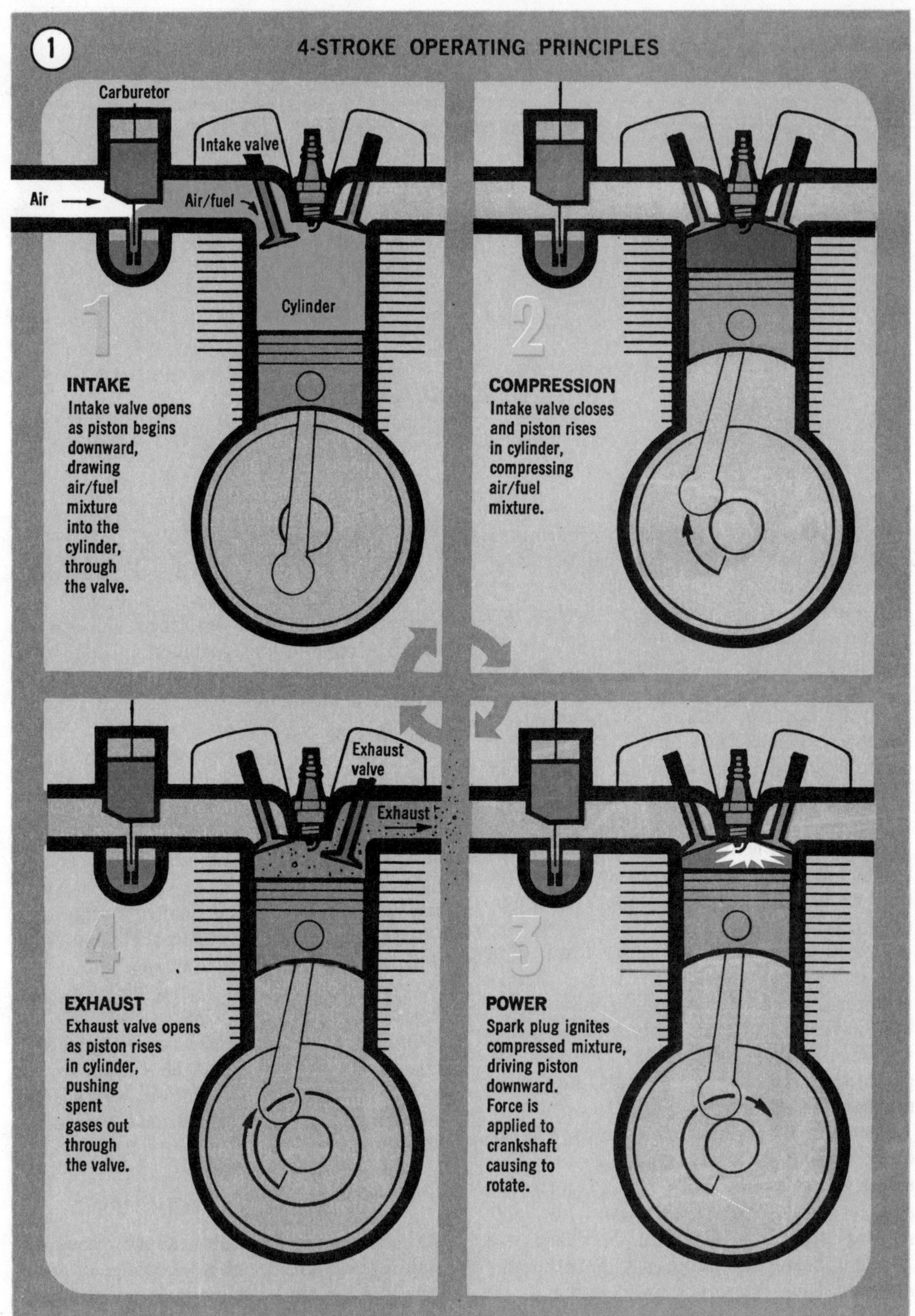
1
4-STROKE OPERATING PRINCIPLES
Carburetor
Intake valve
Air
Air/fuel
Cylinder
1
INTAKE
Intake valve opens as piston begins downward, drawing air/fuel mixture into the cylinder, through the valve.
2
COMPRESSION
Intake valve closes and piston rises in cylinder, compressing air/fuel mixture.
Exhaust valve
Exhaust
4
EXHAUST
Exhaust valve opens as piston rises in cylinder, pushing spent gases out through the valve.
3
POWER
Spark plug ignites compressed mixture, driving piston downward. Force is applied to crankshaft causing to rotate.

since the motorcycle last started easily. For instance, was the weather dry then and is it wet now? Has the motorcycle been sitting in the garage for a long time? Has it been ridden many miles since it was last fueled?

Has starting become increasingly more difficult? This alone could indicate a number of things that may be wrong but is usually associated with normal wear of ignition and engine components.

While it's not always possible to diagnose trouble simply from a change of conditions, this information can be helpful and at some future time may uncover a recurring problem.

Fuel Delivery

Although it is the second most likely cause of trouble, fuel delivery should be checked first simply because it is the easiest.

First, check the tank to make sure there is fuel in it. Then, disconnect the fuel hose at the carburetor, open the valve and check for flow (**Figure 2**). If fuel does not flow freely make sure the tank vent is clear. Next, check for blockage in the line or valve. Remove the valve and clean it as described in the fuel system chapter.

If fuel flows from the hose, reconnect it and remove the float bowl from the carburetor, open the valve and check for flow through the float needle valve. If it does not flow freely when the float is extended and then shut off when the flow is gently raised, clean the carburetor as described in the fuel system chapter.

When fuel delivery is satisfactory, go on to the ignition system.

Ignition

Remove the spark plug from the cylinder and check its condition. The appearance of the plug is a good indication of what's happening in the combustion chamber; for instance, if the plug is wet with gas, it's likely that engine is flooded. Compare the spark plug to **Figure 3**. Make certain the spark plug heat range is correct. A "cold" plug makes starting difficult.

After checking the spark plug, reconnect it to the high-tension lead and lay it on the cylinder head so it makes good contact (**Figure 4**). Then, with the ignition switched on, crank the engine several times and watch for a spark across the plug electrodes. A fat, blue spark should be visible. If there is no spark, or if the spark is weak, substitute a good plug for the old one and check again. If the spark has improved, the old plug is faulty. If there was no change, keep looking.

Make sure the ignition switch is not shorted to ground. Remove the spark plug cap from the end of the high-tension lead and hold the exposed end of the lead about ⅛ inch from the cylinder head. Crank the engine and watch for a spark arcing from the lead to the head. If it's satisfactory, the connection between the lead and the cap was faulty. If the spark hasn't improved, check the coil wire connections.

If the spark is still weak, remove the ignition cover and remove any dirt or moisture from the points or sensor. Check the point or air gap against the specifications in the *Quick Reference Data* at the beginning of the book.

If spark is still not satisfactory, a more serious problem exists than can be corrected with simple adjustments. Refer to the electrical system chapter for detailed information for correcting major ignition problems.

Compression

Compression — or the lack of it — is the least likely cause of starting trouble. However, if compression is unsatisfactory, more than a simple adjustment is required to correct it (see the engine chapter).

An accurate compression check reveals a lot about the condition of the engine. To perform this test you need a compression gauge (see Chapter One). The engine should be at operating temperature for a fully accurate test, but even a cold test will reveal if the starting problem is compression.

Remove the spark plug and screw in a compression gauge (**Figure 5**). With assistance, hold the throttle wide open and crank the engine several times, until the gauge ceases to rise. Normal compression should be 130-160 psi, but a reading as low as 100 psi is usually sufficient for the engine to start. If the reading is much lower than normal, remove the gauge and pour about a tablespoon of oil into the cylinder.

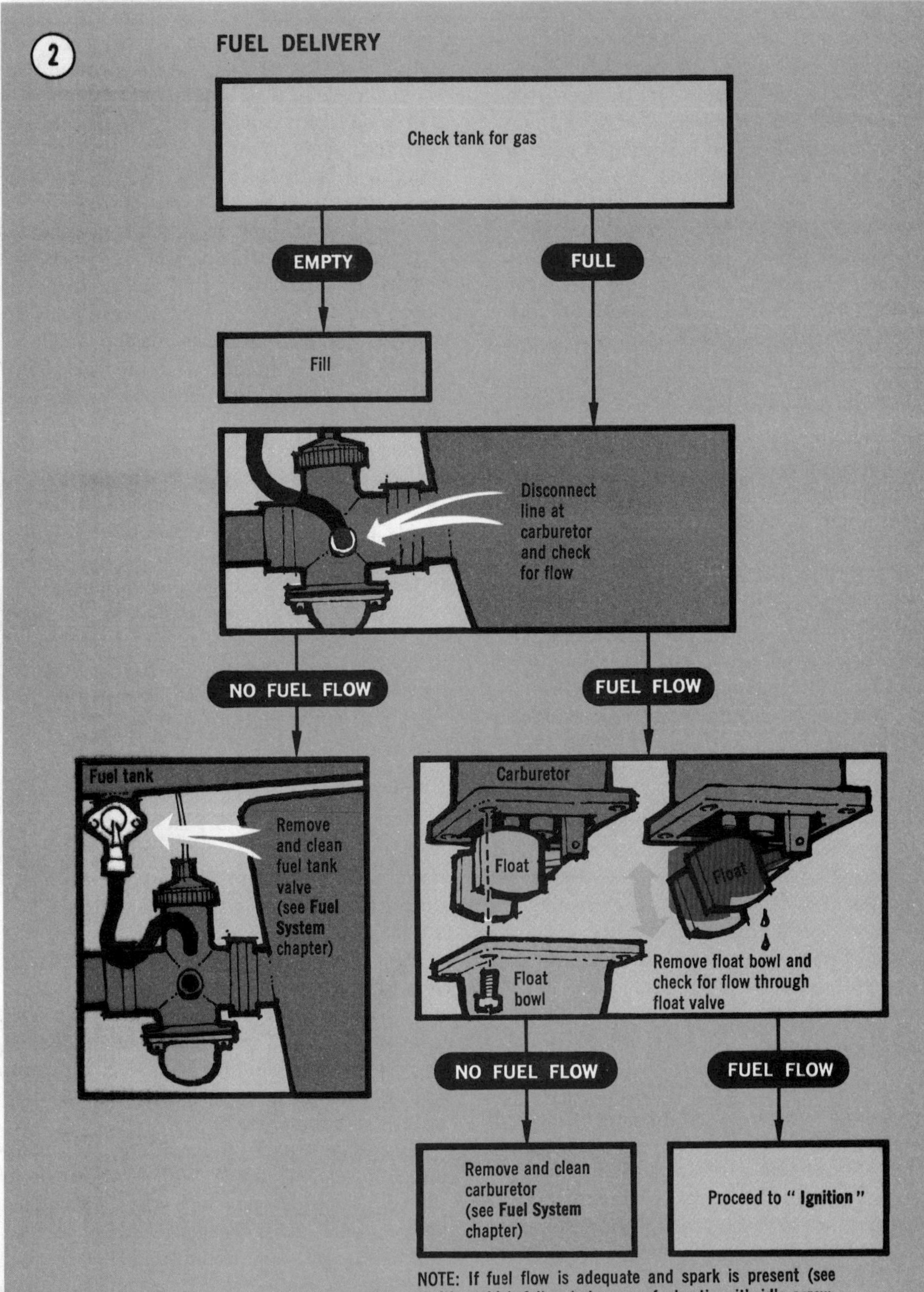
2
FUEL DELIVERY
Check tank for gas
EMPTY
FULL
Fill
Disconnect line at carburetor and check for flow
NO FUEL FLOW
FUEL FLOW
Fuel tank
Remove and clean fuel tank valve (see Fuel System chapter)
Carburetor
Float
Float
Float bowl
Remove float bowl and check for flow through float valve
NO FUEL FLOW
FUEL FLOW
Remove and clean carburetor (see Fuel System chapter)
Proceed to "Ignition"
NOTE: If fuel flow is adequate and spark is present (see Ignition which follows), increase fuel ratio with idle screw.

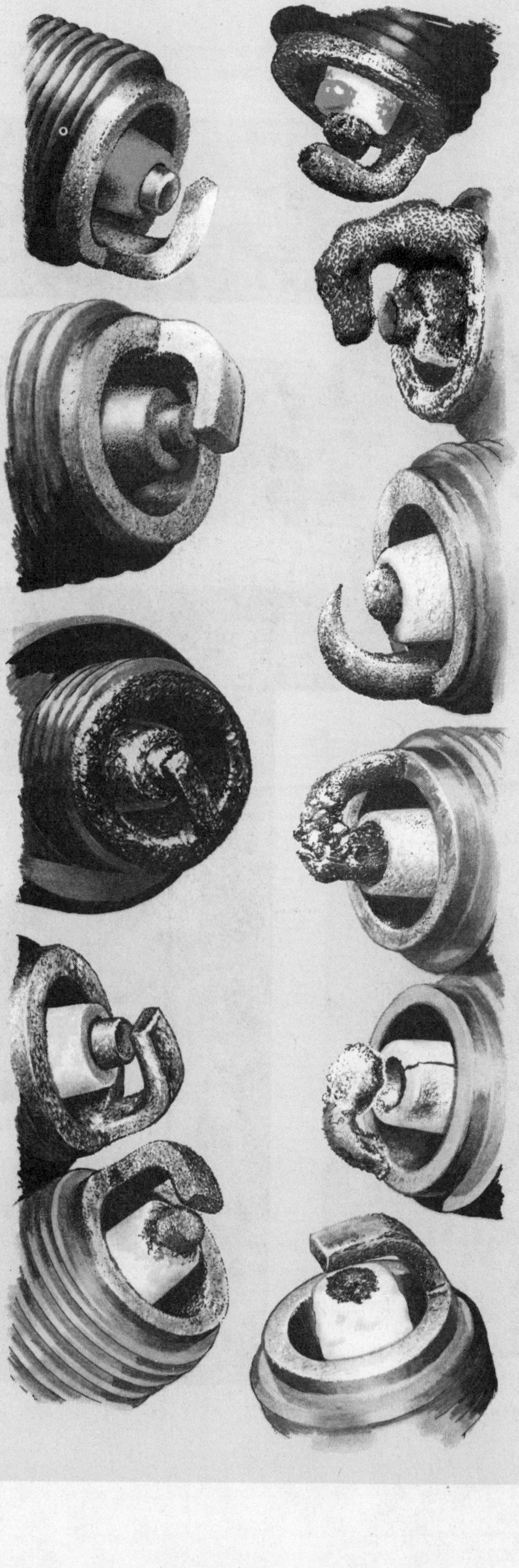

NORMAL
- Appearance—Firing tip has deposits of light gray to light tan.
- Can be cleaned, regapped and reused.

CARBON FOULED
- Appearance—Dull, dry black with fluffy carbon deposits on the insulator tip, electrode and exposed shell.
- Caused by—Fuel/air mixture too rich, plug heat range too cold, weak ignition system, dirty air cleaner, faulty automatic choke or excessive idling.
- Can be cleaned, regapped and reused.

OIL FOULED
- Appearance—Wet black deposits on insulator and exposed shell.
- Caused by—Excessive oil entering the combustion chamber through worn rings, pistons, valve guides or bearings.
- Replace with new plugs (use a hotter plug if engine is not repaired).

LEAD FOULED
- Appearance — Yellow insulator deposits (may sometimes be dark gray, black or tan in color) on the insulator tip.
- Caused by—Highly leaded gasoline.
- Replace with new plugs.

LEAD FOULED
- Appearance—Yellow glazed deposits indicating melted lead deposits due to hard acceleration.
- Caused by—Highly leaded gasoline.
- Replace with new plugs.

OIL AND LEAD FOULED
- Appearance—Glazed yellow deposits with a slight brownish tint on the insulator tip and ground electrode.
- Replace with new plugs.

FUEL ADDITIVE RESIDUE
- Appearance — Brown colored hardened ash deposits on the insulator tip and ground electrode.
- Caused by—Fuel and/or oil additives.
- Replace with new plugs.

WORN
- Appearance — Severely worn or eroded electrodes.
- Caused by—Normal wear or unusual oil and/or fuel additives.
- Replace with new plugs.

PREIGNITION
- Appearance — Melted ground electrode.
- Caused by—Overadvanced ignition timing, inoperative ignition advance mechanism, too low of a fuel octane rating, lean fuel/air mixture or carbon deposits in combustion chamber.

PREIGNITION
- Appearance—Melted center electrode.
- Caused by—Abnormal combustion due to overadvanced ignition timing or incorrect advance, too low of a fuel octane rating, lean fuel/air mixture, or carbon deposits in combustion chamber.
- Correct engine problem and replace with new plugs.

INCORRECT HEAT RANGE
- Appearance—Melted center electrode and white blistered insulator tip.
- Caused by—Incorrect plug heat range selection.
- Replace with new plugs.

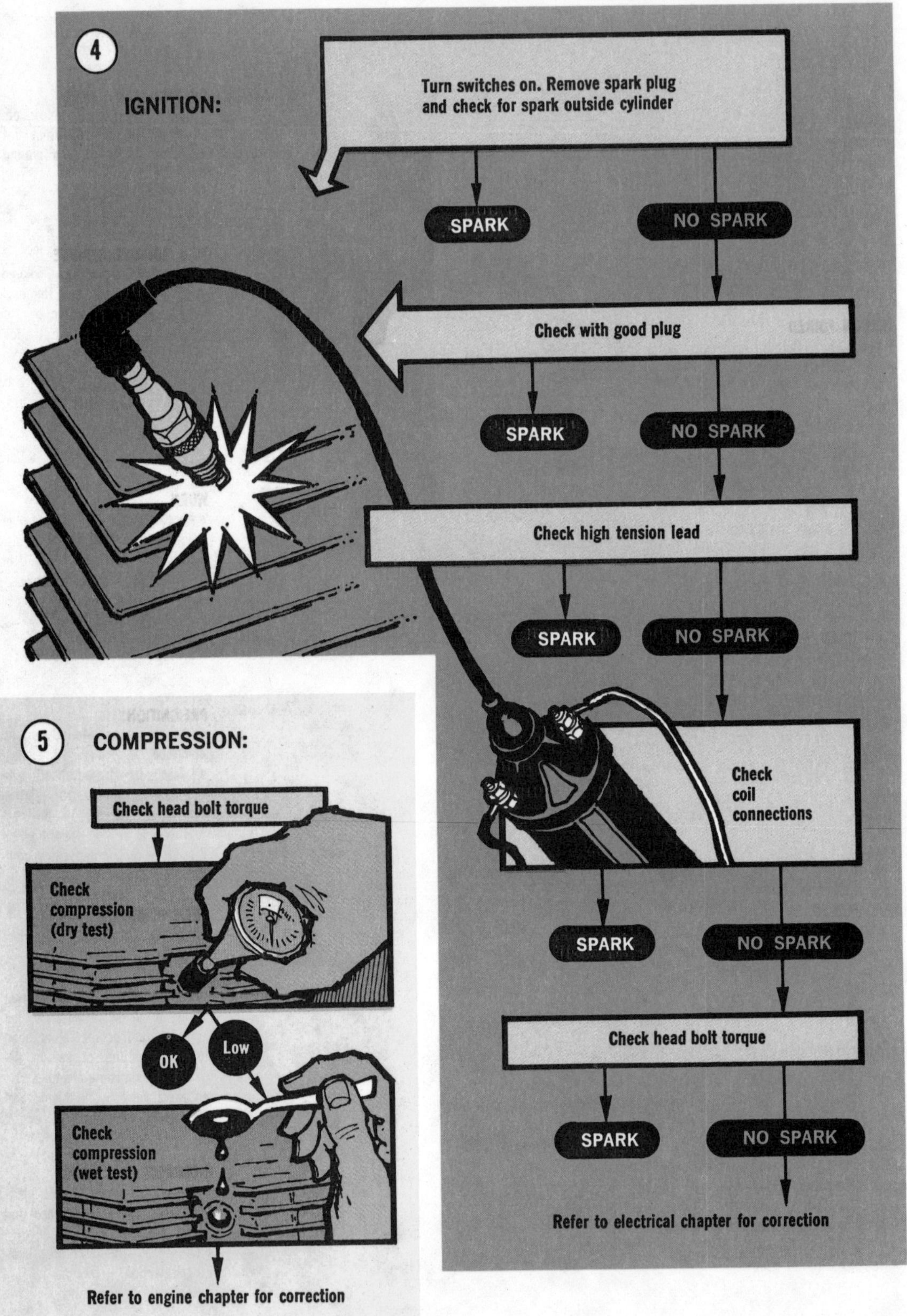
4
IGNITION:
Turn switches on. Remove spark plug and check for spark outside cylinder
SPARK
NO SPARK
Check with good plug
SPARK
NO SPARK
Check high tension lead
SPARK
NO SPARK
Check coil connections
SPARK
NO SPARK
Check head bolt torque
SPARK
NO SPARK
Refer to electrical chapter for correction
5
COMPRESSION:
Check head bolt torque
Check compression (dry test)
OK
Low
Check compression (wet test)
Refer to engine chapter for correction

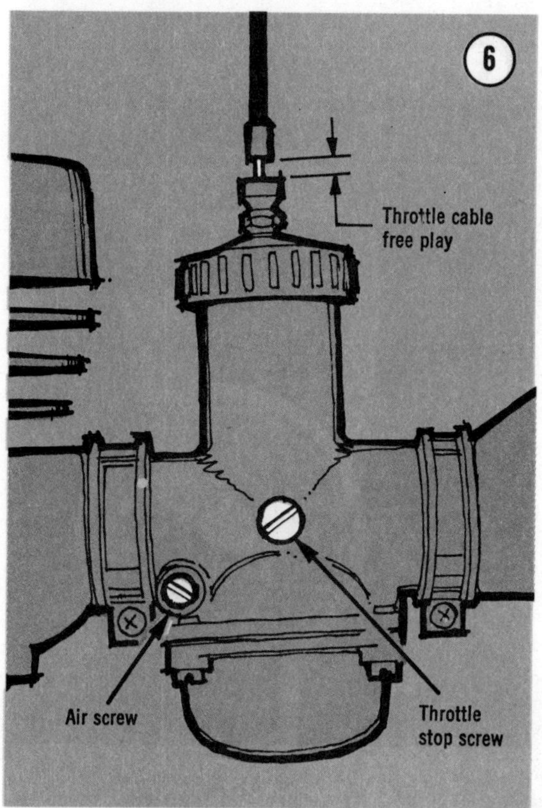

Crank the engine several times to distribute the oil and test the compression once again. If it is now significantly higher, the rings and bore are worn. If the compression did not change, the valves are not seating correctly. Adjust the valves and check again. If the compression is still low, refer to the engine chapter.

NOTE: *Low compression indicates a developing problem. The condition causing it should be corrected as soon as possible.*

POOR PERFORMANCE

Poor engine performance can be caused by any of a number of things related to carburetion, ignition, and the condition of the sliding and rotating components in the engine. In addition, components such as brakes, clutch, and transmission can cause problems that seem to be related to engine performance, even when the engine is in top running condition.

Poor Idling

Idling that is erratic, too high, or too low is most often caused by incorrect adjustment of the carburetor idle circuit. Also, a dirty air filter or an obstructed fuel tank vent can affect idle speed. Incorrect ignition timing or worn or faulty ignition components are also good possibilities.

First, make sure the air filter is clean and correctly installed. Then, adjust the throttle cable free play, the throttle stop screw, and the idle mixture air screw (**Figure 6**) as described in the routine maintenance chapter.

If idling is still poor, check the carburetor and manifold mounts for leaks; with the engine warmed up and running, spray WD-40 or a similar light lube around the flanges and joints of the carburetor and manifold (**Figure 7**). Listen for changes in engine speed. If a leak is present, the idle speed will drop as the lube "plugs" the leak and then pick up again as it is drawn into the engine. Tighten the nuts and clamps and test again. If a leak persists, check for a damaged gasket or a pinhole in the manifold. Minor leaks in manifold hoses can be repaired with silicone sealer, but if cracks or holes are extensive, the manifold should be replaced.

2

A worn throttle slide may cause erratic running and idling, but this is likely only after many thousands of miles of use. To check, remove the carburetor top and feel for back and forth movement of the slide in the bore; it should be barely perceptible. Inspect the slide for large worn areas and replace it if it is less than perfect (**Figure 8**).

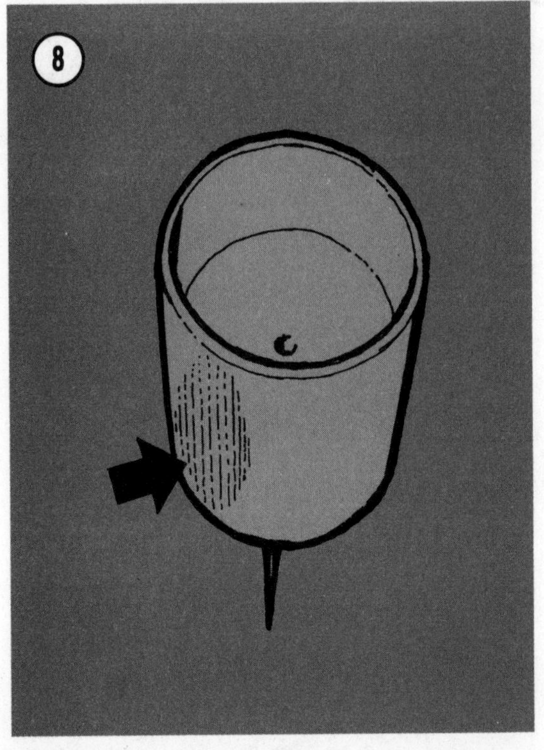

If the fuel system is satisfactory, check ignition timing and breaker point gap (air gap in electronic ignition). Check the condition of the system components as well. Ignition-caused idling problems such as erratic running can be the fault of marginal components. See the electrical system chapter for appropriate tests.

Rough Running or Misfiring

Misfiring (see **Figure 9**) is usually caused by an ignition problem. First, check all ignition connections (**Figure 10**). They should be clean, dry, and tight. Don't forget the kill switch; a loose connection can create an intermittent short.

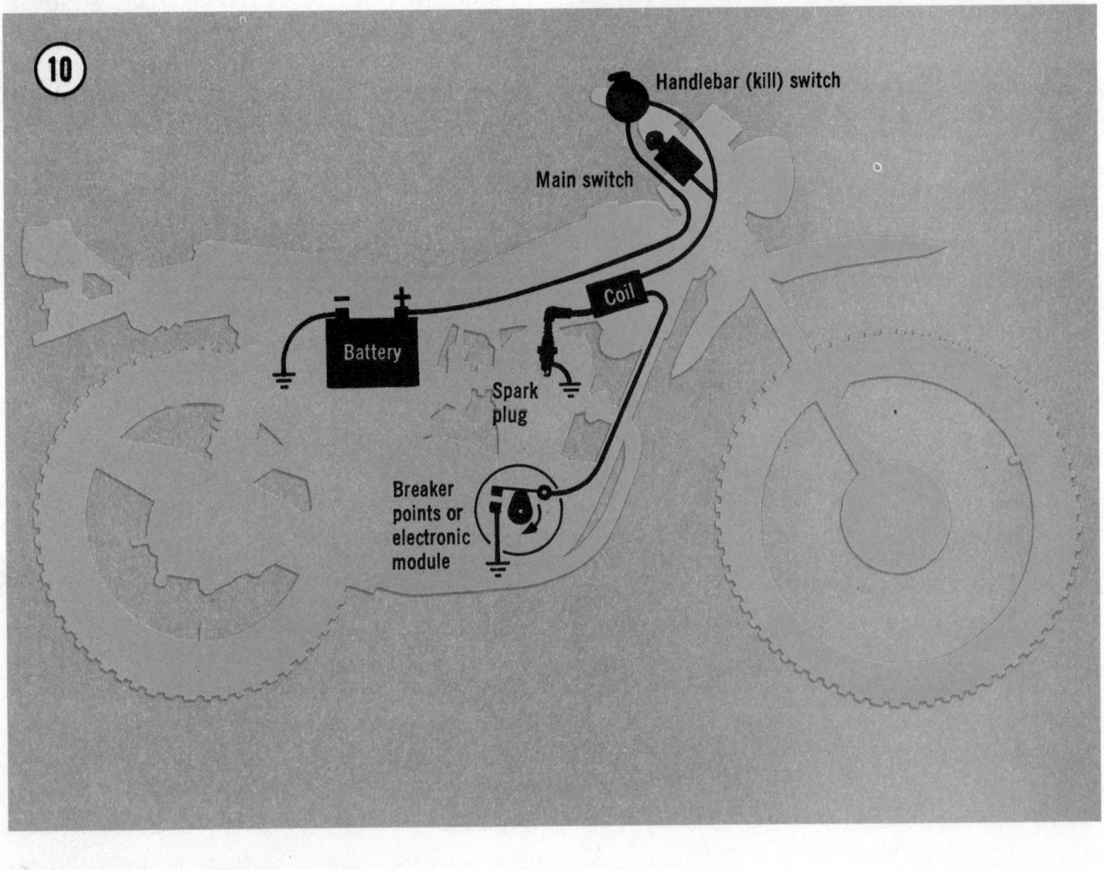

ENGINE RUNS ROUGH AND MISFIRES

9

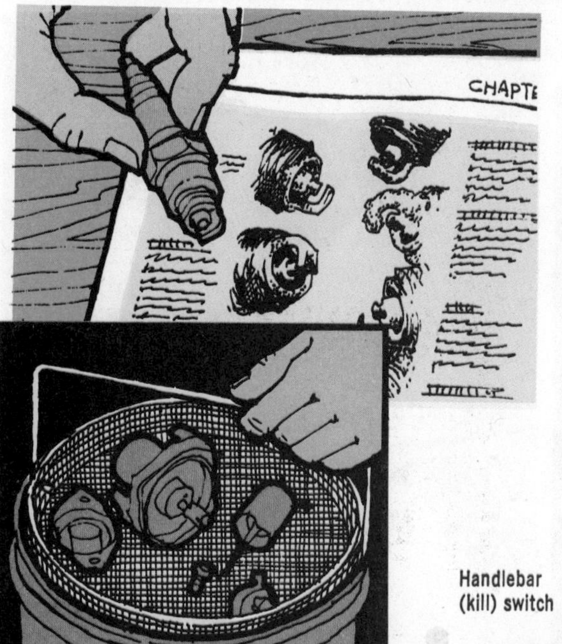

ENGINE MISSES—ALL SPEEDS

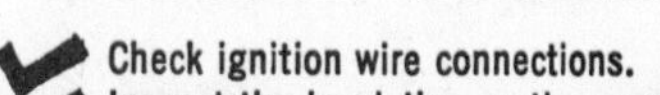

- Check ignition wire connections.
- Inspect the insulation on the spark plug high-tension lead for cracking and deterioration.
- Inspect the spark plug for correct heat range and condition.
- Check the point gap and the spring tension on the contact breaker or check electronic module on models with electronic ignition.

ENGINE MISSES AT LOW SPEED

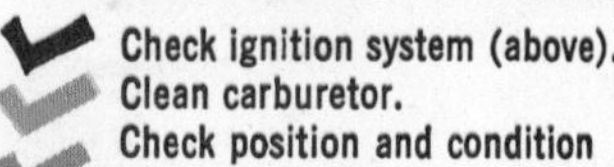

- Check ignition system (above).
- Clean carburetor—pay particular attention to low-speed jet and circuit.

ENGINE MISSES AT MID-RANGE

- Check ignition system (above).
- Clean carburetor.
- Check position and condition of slide needle.

ENGINE MISSES AT HIGH SPEED

- Check ignition system (above).
- Clean carburetor.
- Check jetting—main jet is likely too large.

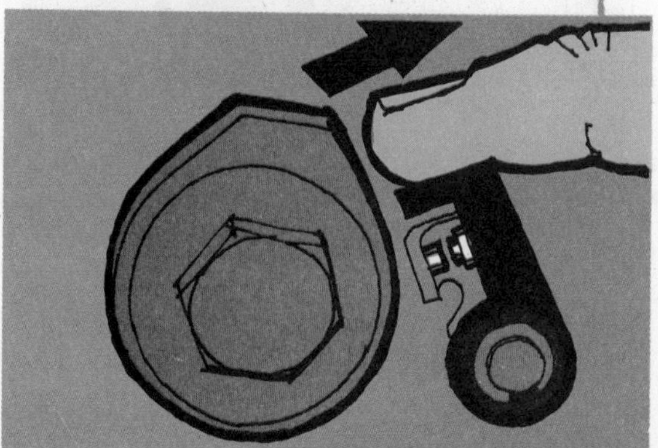

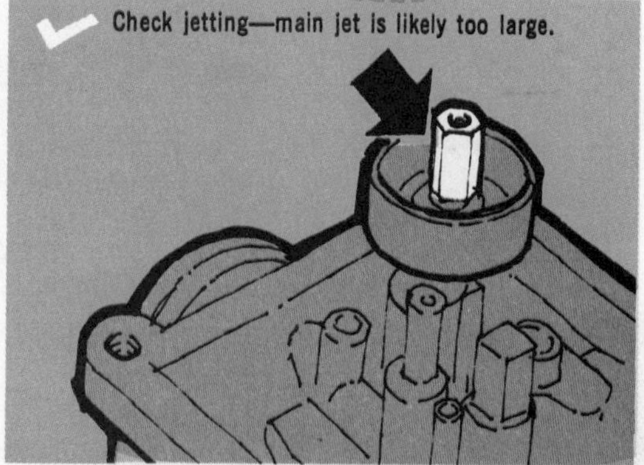

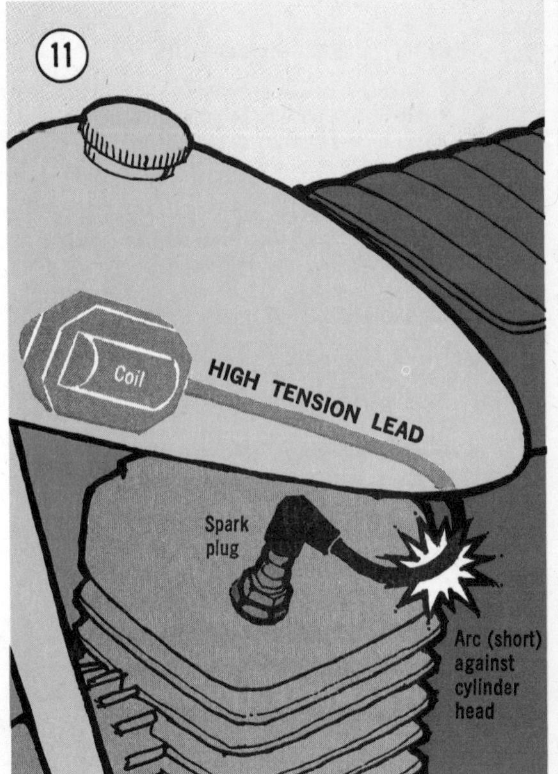

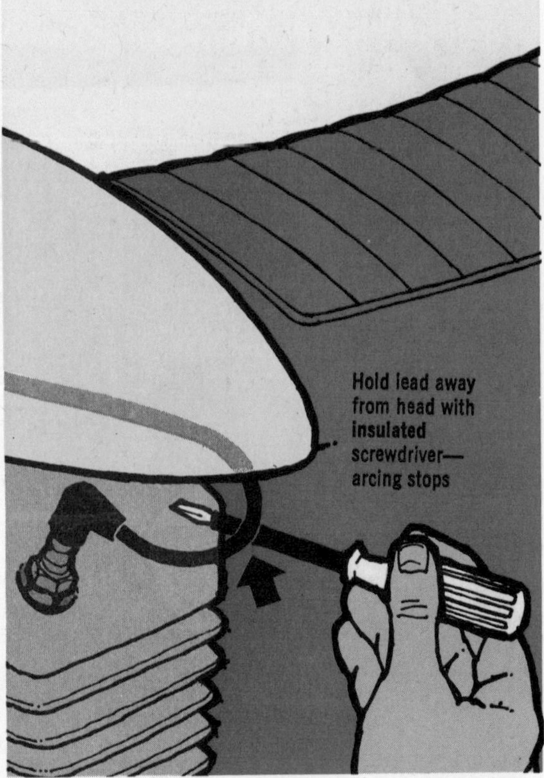

Check the insulation on the high-tension spark plug lead. If it is cracked or deteriorated it will allow the spark to short to ground when the engine is revved. This is easily seen at night. If arcing occurs, hold the affected area of the wire away from the metal to which it is arcing, using an insulated screwdriver (**Figure 11**), and see if the misfiring ceases. If it does, replace the high-tension lead. Also check the connection of the spark plug cap to the lead. If it is poor, the spark will break down at this point when the engine speed is increased.

The spark plug could also be poor. Test the system with a new plug.

Incorrect point gap or a weak contact breaker spring can cause misfiring. Check the gap and the alignment of the points. Push the moveable arm back and check for spring tension (**Figure 12**). It should feel stiff.

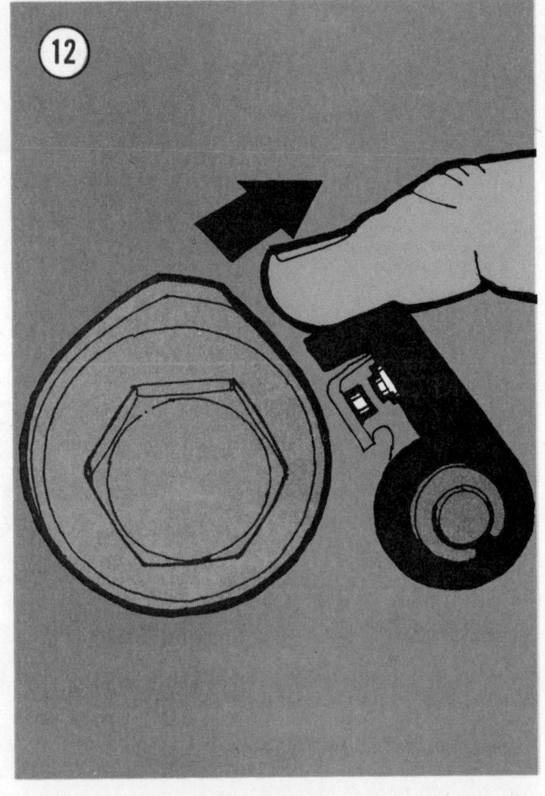

On models with electronic ignition, have the electronic module tested by a dealer or substitute a known good unit for a suspected one.

If misfiring occurs only at a certain point in engine speed, the problem may very likely be

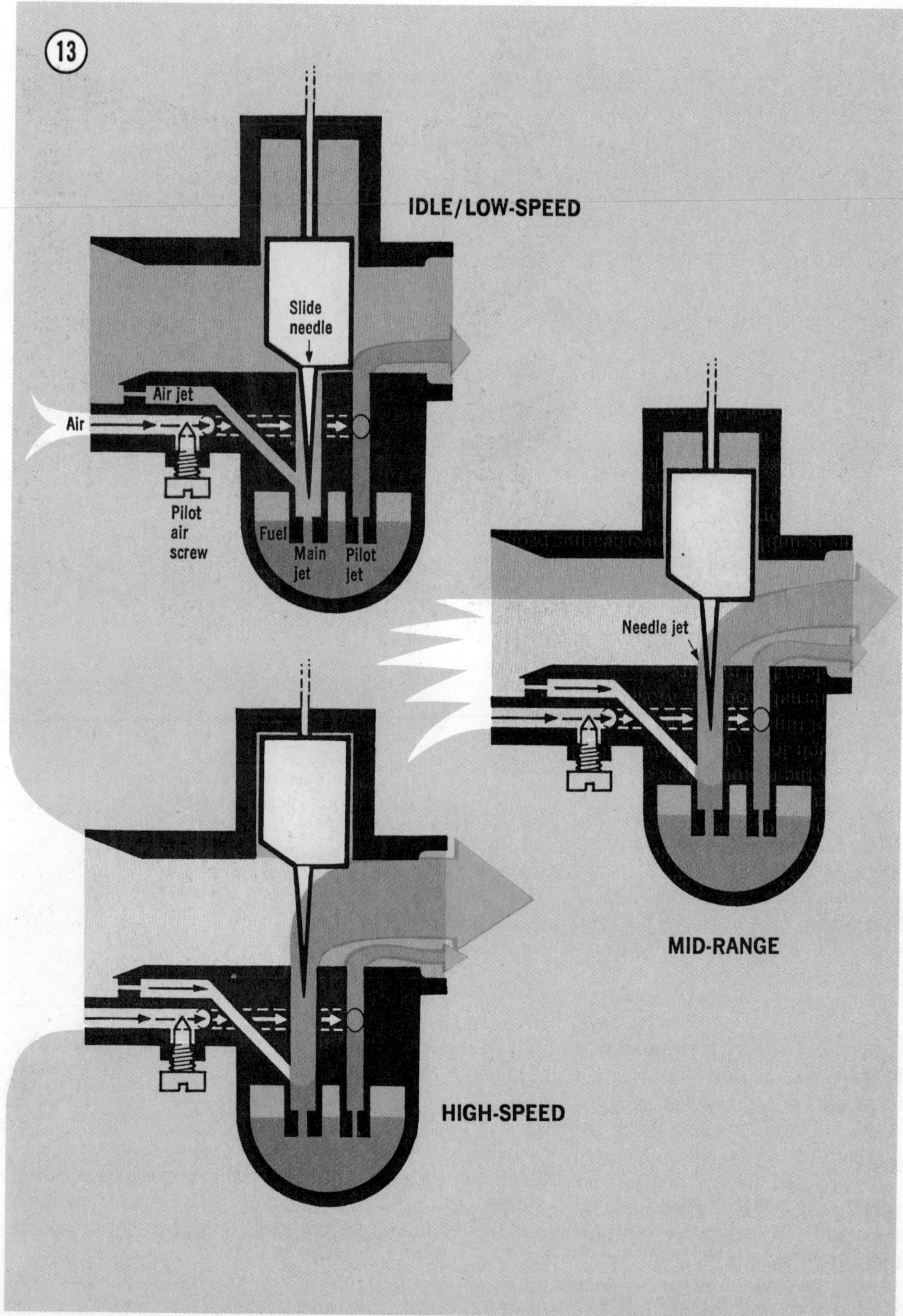
13
IDLE/LOW-SPEED
Slide needle
Air jet
Air
Pilot air screw
Fuel
Main jet
Pilot jet
Needle jet
MID-RANGE
HIGH-SPEED

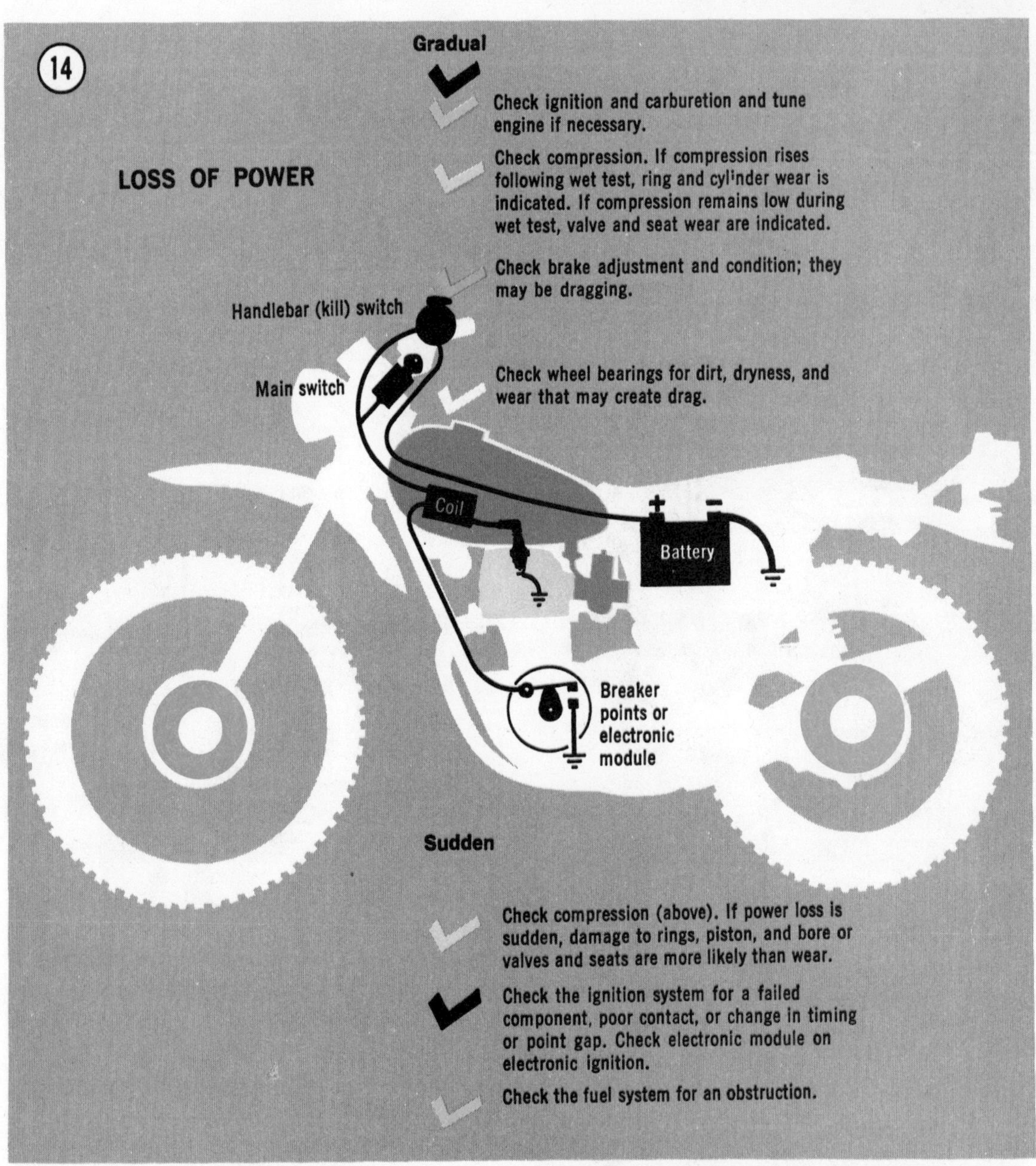

carburetion. Poor performance at idle is described earlier. Misfiring at low speed (just above idle) can be caused by a dirty low-speed circuit or jet (**Figure 13**). Poor midrange performance is attributable to a worn or incorrectly adjusted needle and needle jet. Misfiring at high speed (if not ignition related) is usually caused by a too-large main jet which causes the engine to run rich. Any of these carburetor-related conditions can be corrected by first cleaning the carburetor and then adjusting it as described in the tune-up and maintenance chapter.

Loss of Power

First determine how the power loss developed (**Figure 14**). Did it decline over a long period of time or did it drop abruptly? A gradual loss is normal, caused by deterioration of the engine's state of tune and the normal wear of the cylinder and piston rings and the valves and seats. In such case, check the condition of the

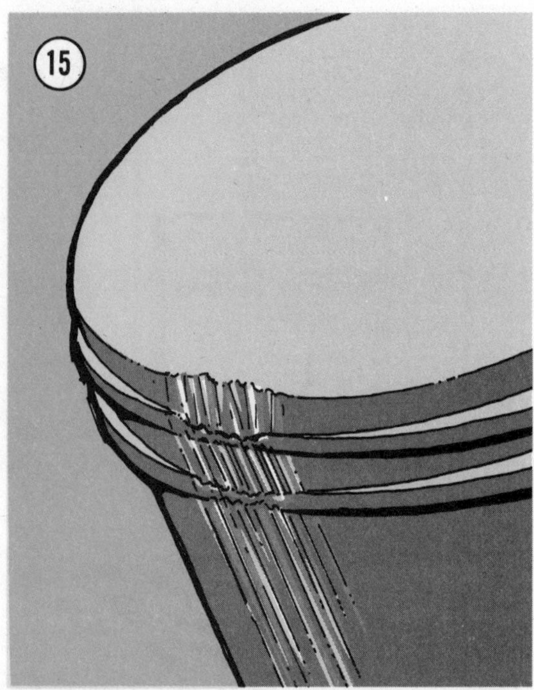

ignition and carburetion and measure the compression as described earlier.

A sudden power loss may be caused by a failed ignition component, obstruction in the fuel system, damaged valve or seat, or a broken piston ring or damaged piston (**Figure 15**).

If the engine is in good shape and tune, check the brake adjustment. If the brakes are dragging, they will consume considerable power. Also check the wheel bearings. If they are dry, extremely dirty, or badly worn they can create considerable drag.

Engine Runs Hot

A modern motorcycle engine, in good mechanical condition, correctly tuned, and operated as it was intended, will rarely experience overheating problems. However, out-of-spec conditions can create severe overheating that may result in serious engine damage. Refer to **Figure 16**.

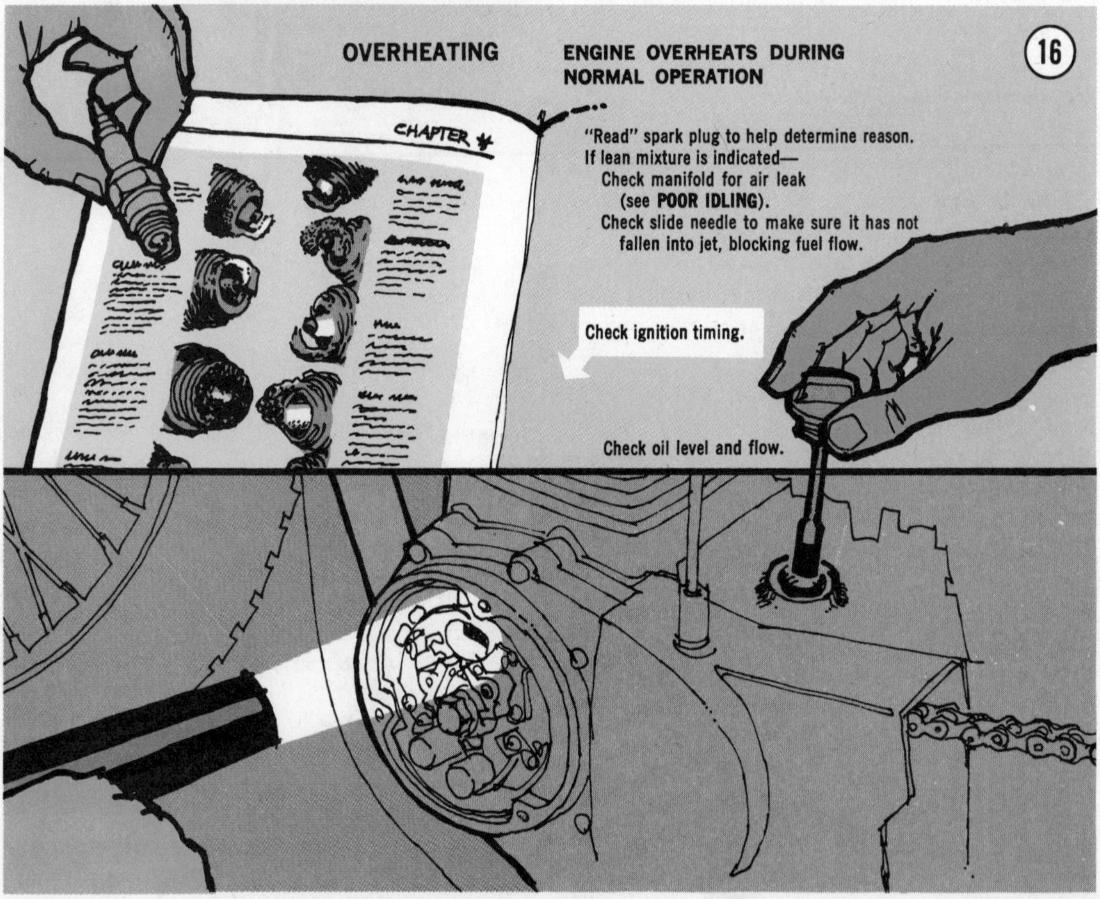

Overheating is difficult to detect unless it is extreme, in which case it will usually be apparent as excessive heat radiating from the engine, accompanied by the smell of hot oil and sharp, snapping noises when the engine is first shut off and begins to cool.

Unless the motorcycle is operated under sustained high load or is allowed to idle for long periods of time, overheating is usually the result of an internal problem. Most often it's caused by a too-lean fuel mixture.

Remove the spark plug and compare it to **Figure 3**. If a too-lean condition is indicated, check for leaks in the intake manifold (see *Poor Idling*). The carburetor jetting may be incorrect but this is unlikely if the overheating problem has just developed (unless, of course, the engine was jetted for high altitude and is now being run near sea level). Check the slide needle in the carburetor to make sure it hasn't come loose and is restricting the flow of gas through the mainjet and needle jet (**Figure 17**).

Check the ignition timing; extremes of either advance or retard can cause overheating.

Piston Seizure and Damage

Piston seizure is a common result of overheating (see above) because an aluminum piston expands at a greater rate than a steel cylinder. Seizure can also be caused by piston-to-cylinder clearance that is too small; ring end gap that is too small; insufficient oil; spark plug heat range too hot; and broken piston ring or ring land.

A major piston seizure can cause severe engine damage. A minor seizure — which usually subsides after the engine has cooled a few minutes — rarely does more than scuff the piston skirt the first time it occurs. Fortunately, this condition can be corrected by dressing the piston with crocus cloth, refitting the piston and rings to the bore with recommended clearances, and checking the timing to ensure overheating does not occur. Regard that first seizure as a warning and correct the problem before continuing to run the engine.

CLUTCH AND TRANSMISSION

1. ***Clutch slips***—Make sure lever free play is sufficient to allow the clutch to fully engage

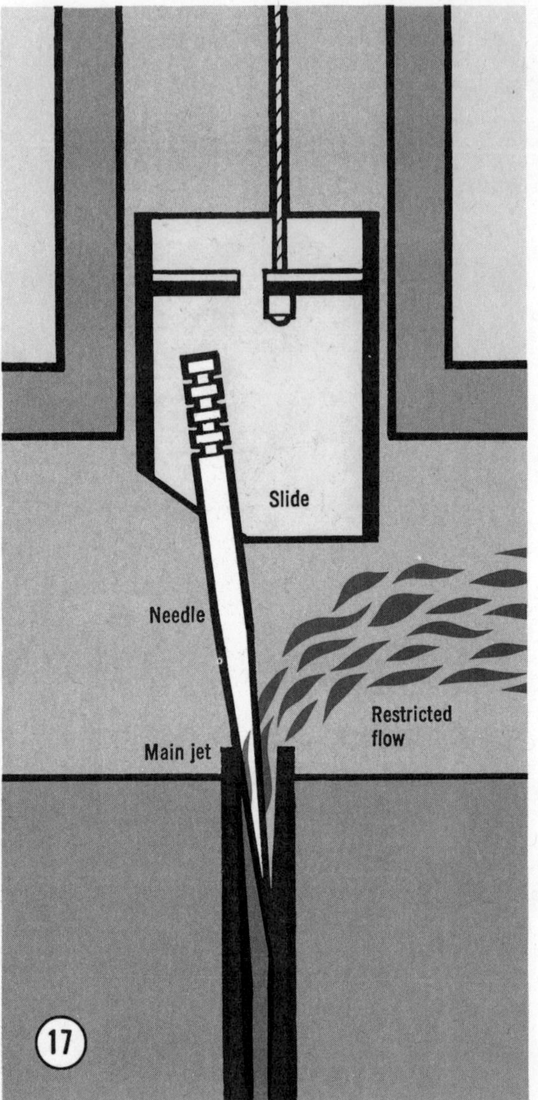

(**Figure 18**). Check the contact surfaces for wear and glazing. Transmission oil additives also can cause slippage in wet clutches. If slip occurs only under extreme load, check the condition of the springs or diaphragm and make sure the clutch bolts are snug and uniformly tightened.

2. ***Clutch drags***—Make sure lever free play isn't so great that it fails to disengage the clutch. Check for warped plates or disc. If the transmission oil (in wet clutch systems) is extremely dirty or heavy, it may inhibit the clutch from releasing.

3. ***Transmission shifts hard***—Extremely dirty oil can cause the transmission to shift hard.

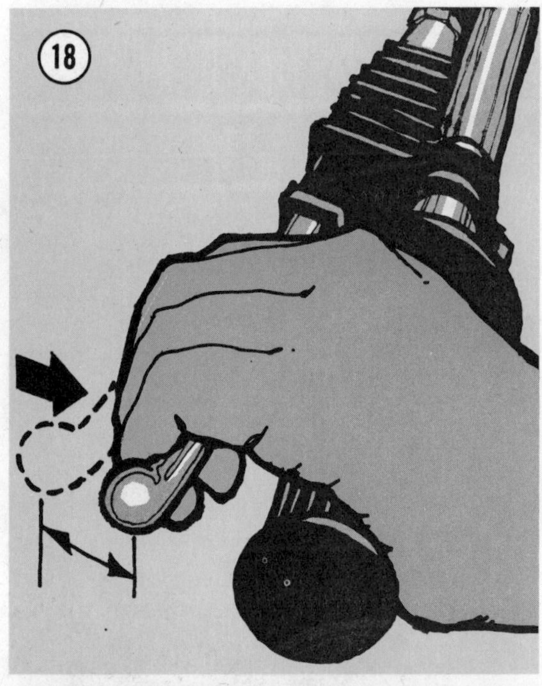

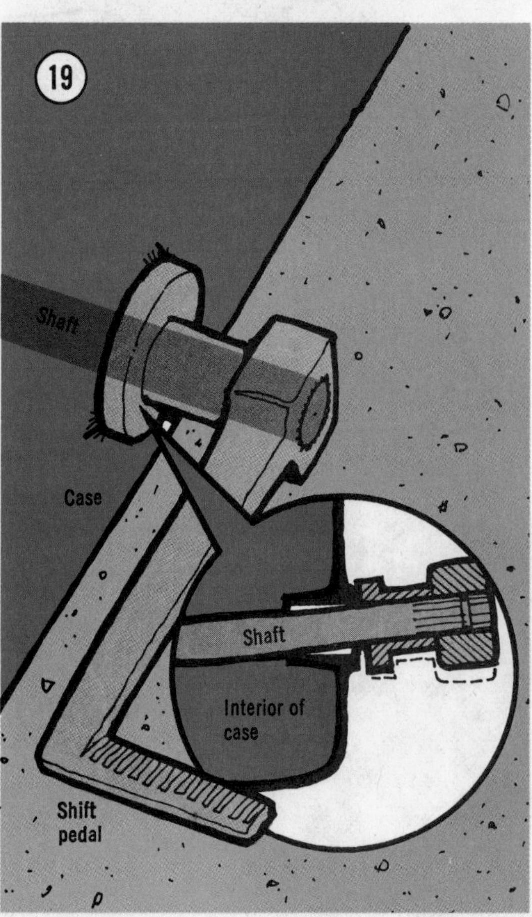

Check the selector shaft for bending (**Figure 19**). Inspect the shifter and gearsets for wear and damage.

4. ***Transmission slips out of gear***—This can be caused by worn engagement dogs or a worn or damaged shifter (**Figure 20**). The overshift travel on the selector may be misadjusted.

5. ***Transmission is noisy***—Noises usually indicate the absence of lubrication or wear and damage to gears, bearings, or shims. It's a good idea to disassemble the transmission and carefully inspect it when noise first occurs.

DRIVE TRAIN

Drive train problems (outlined in **Figure 21**) arise from normal wear and incorrect maintenance.

CHASSIS

Chassis problems are outlined in **Figure 22**.

1. ***Motorcycle pulls to one side***—Check for loose suspension components, axles, steering

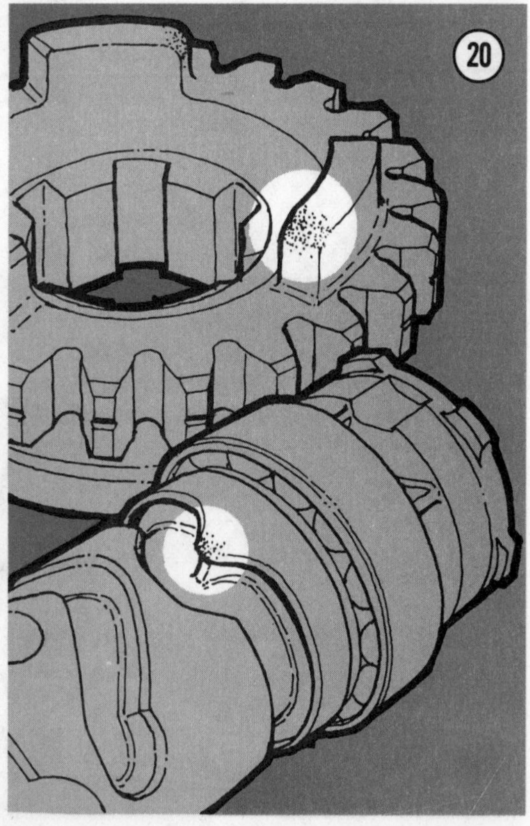

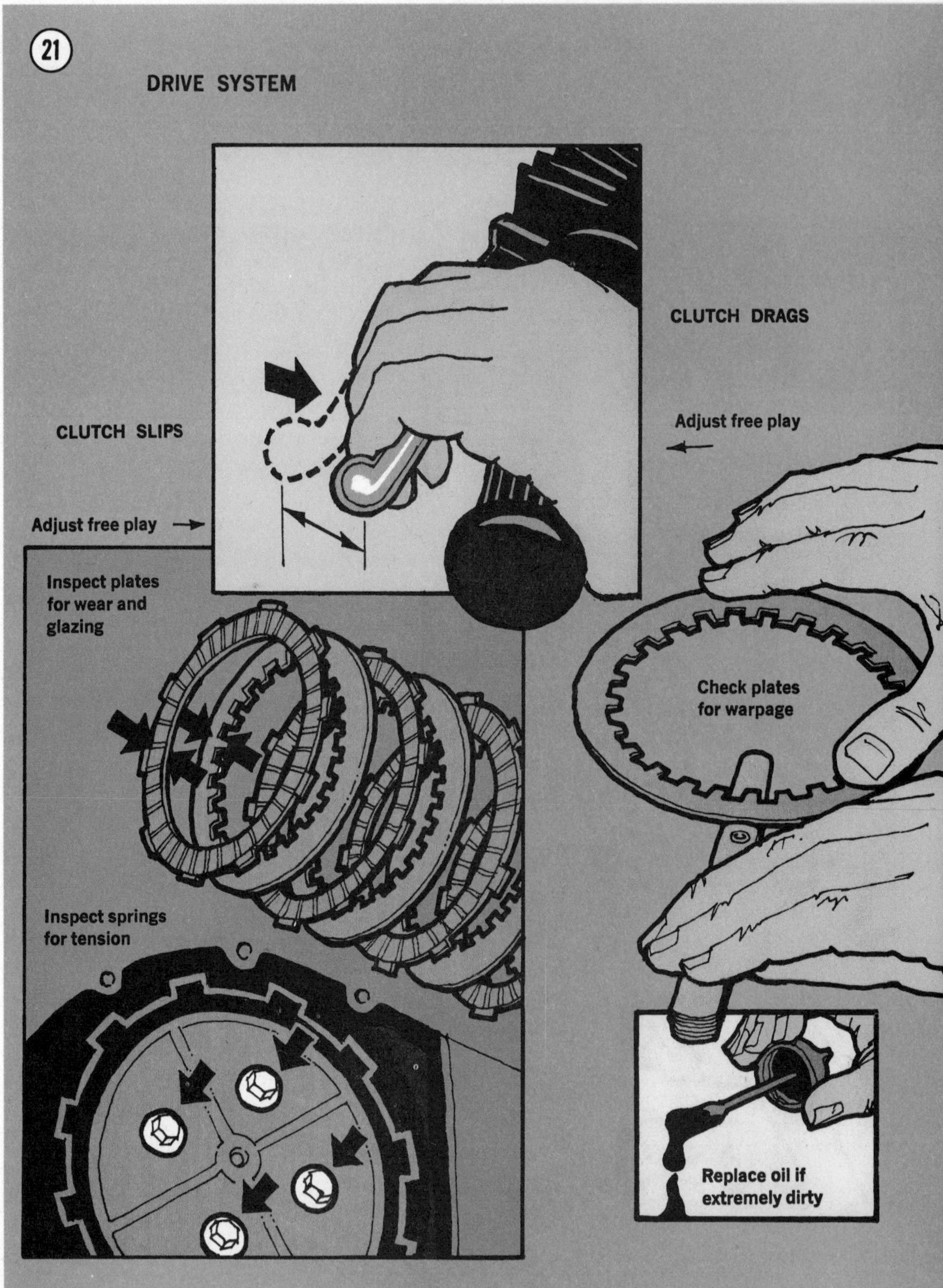
21
DRIVE SYSTEM
CLUTCH DRAGS
Adjust free play
CLUTCH SLIPS
Adjust free play
Inspect plates
for wear and
glazing
Check plates
for warpage
Inspect springs
for tension
Replace oil if
extremely dirty

TRANSMISSION SHIFTS HARD

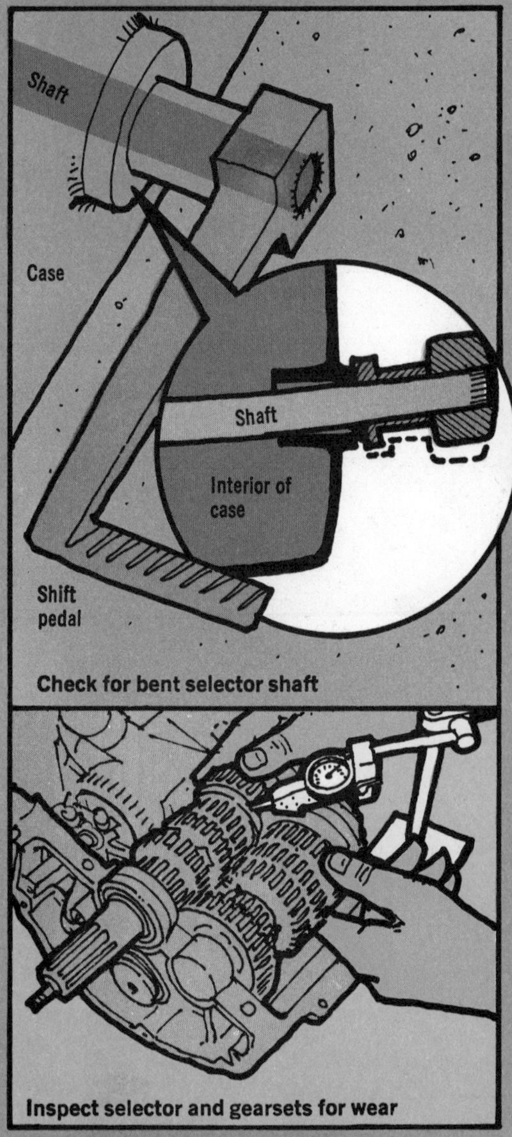

Check for bent selector shaft

Inspect selector and gearsets for wear

TRANSMISSION SLIPS OUT OF GEAR

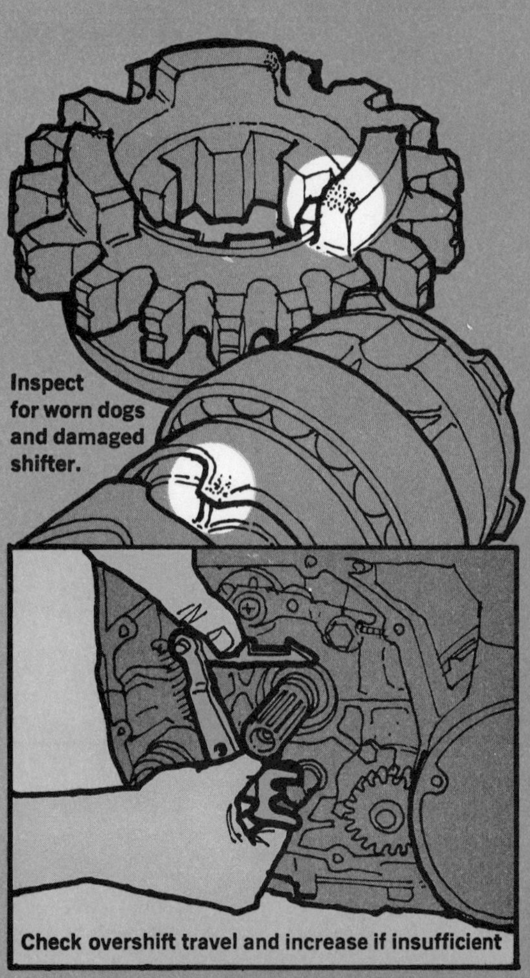

Check overshift travel and increase if insufficient

TRANSMISSION IS NOISY

Check oil level

Disassemble and inspect (see Transmission chapter)

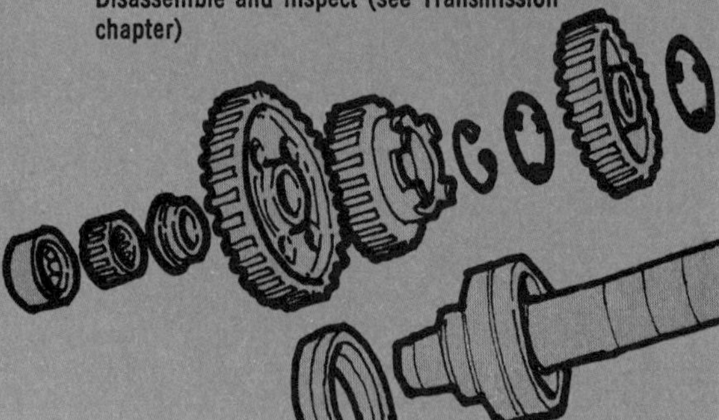

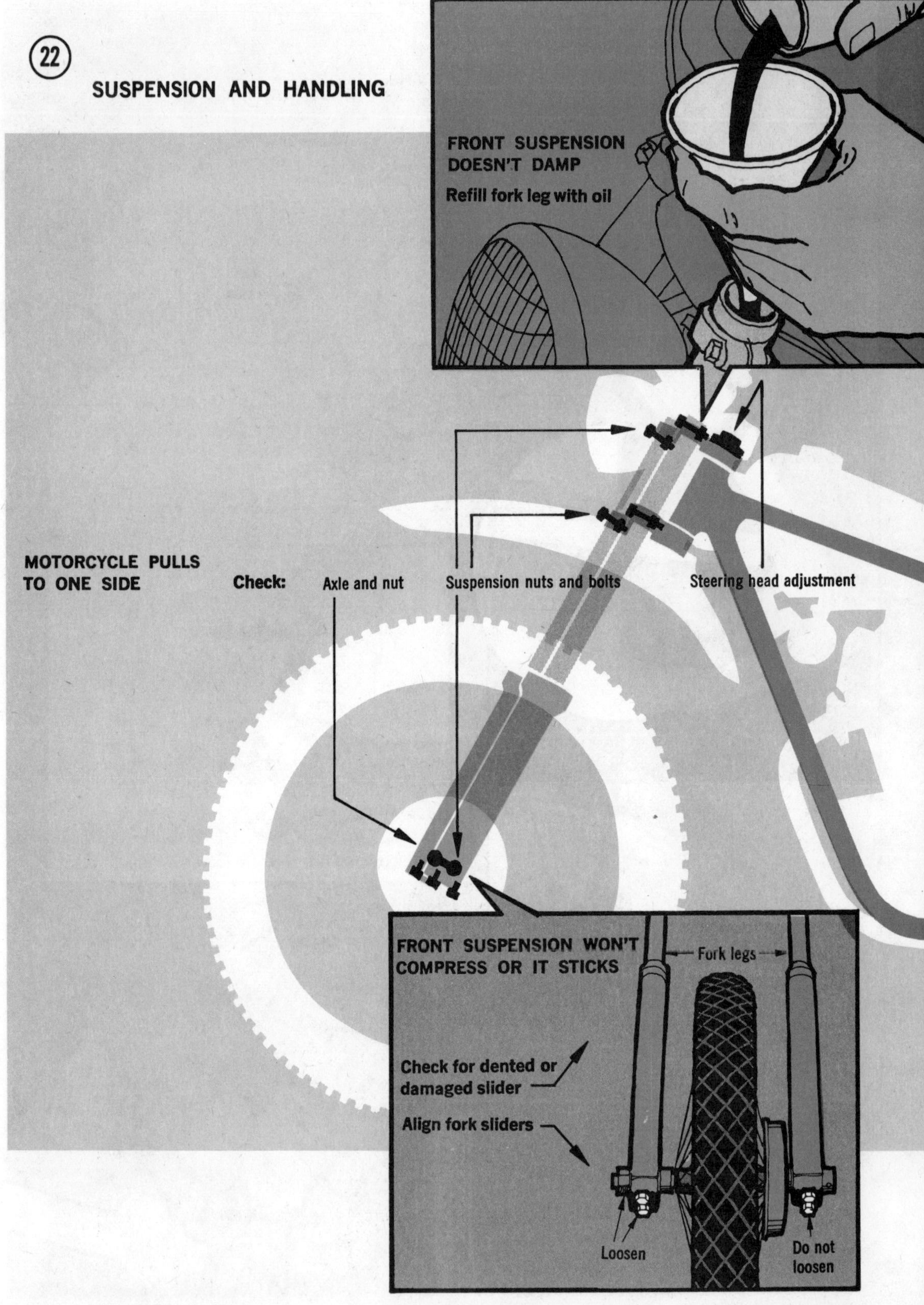
22
SUSPENSION AND HANDLING
FRONT SUSPENSION DOESN'T DAMP
Refill fork leg with oil
MOTORCYCLE PULLS TO ONE SIDE
Check:
Axle and nut
Suspension nuts and bolts
Steering head adjustment
FRONT SUSPENSION WON'T COMPRESS OR IT STICKS
Fork legs
Check for dented or damaged slider
Align fork sliders
Loosen
Do not loosen

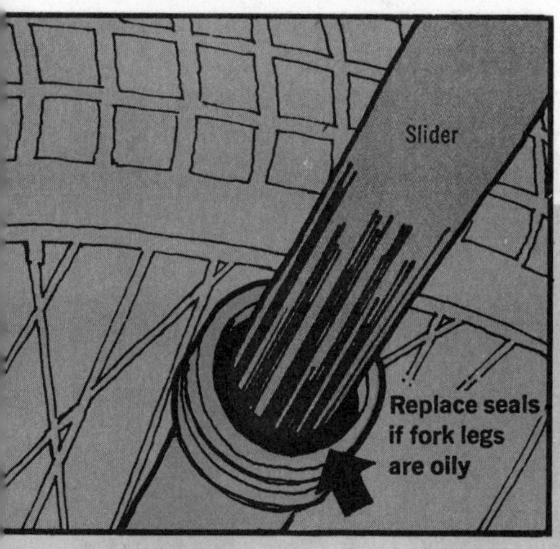

SUSPENSION AND HANDLING CONTINUED

2

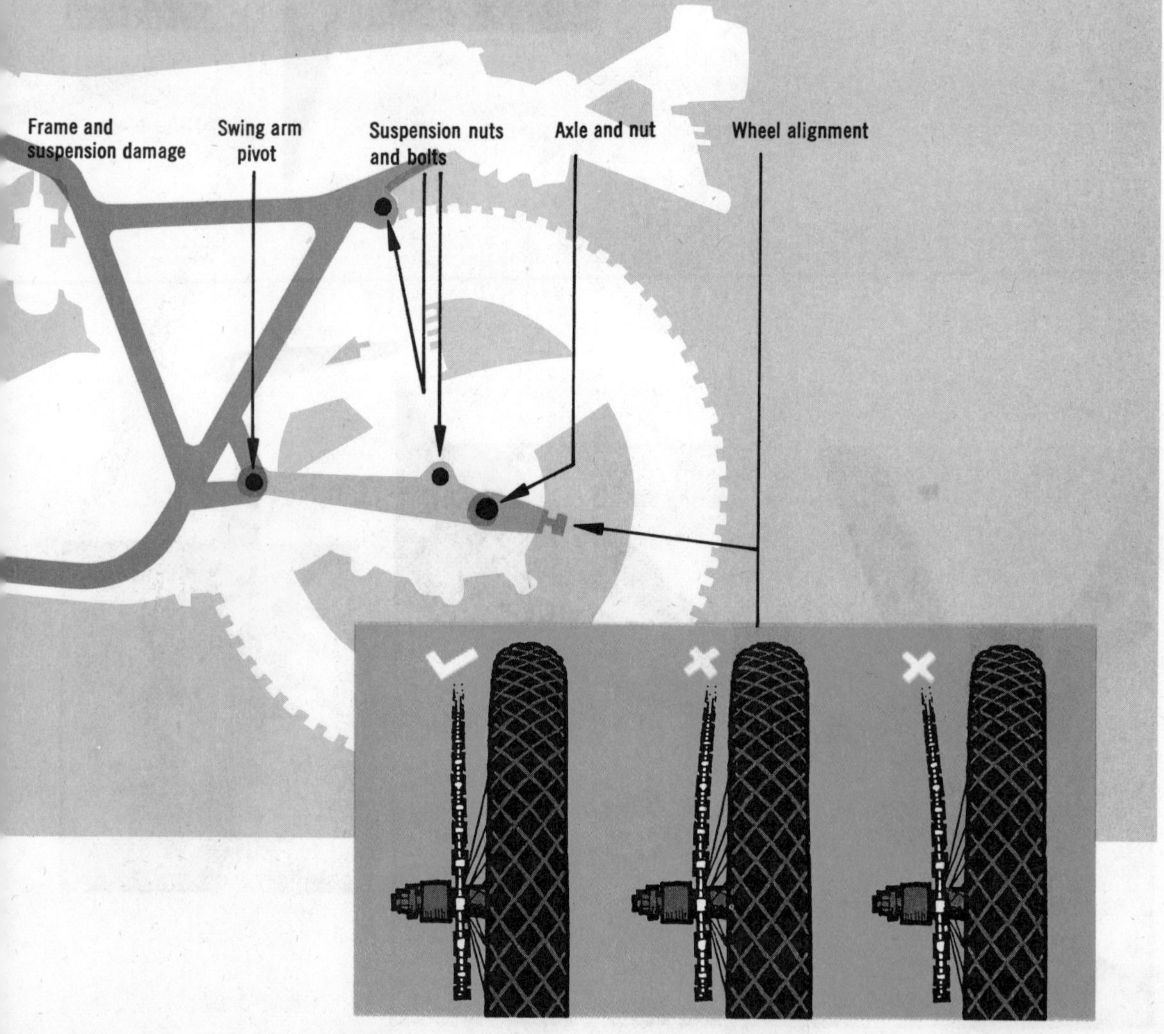

SUSPENSION AND HANDLING CONTINUED

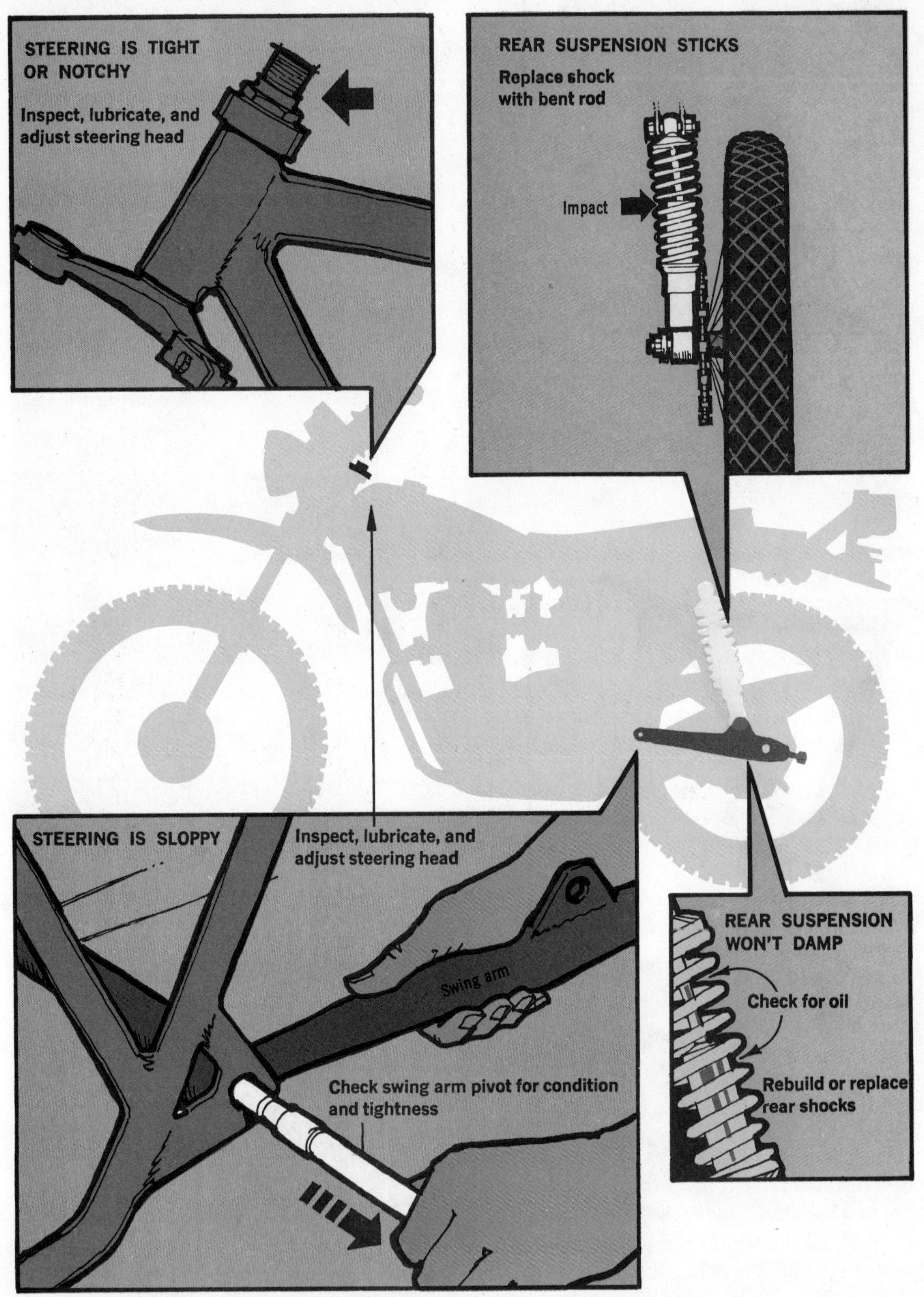

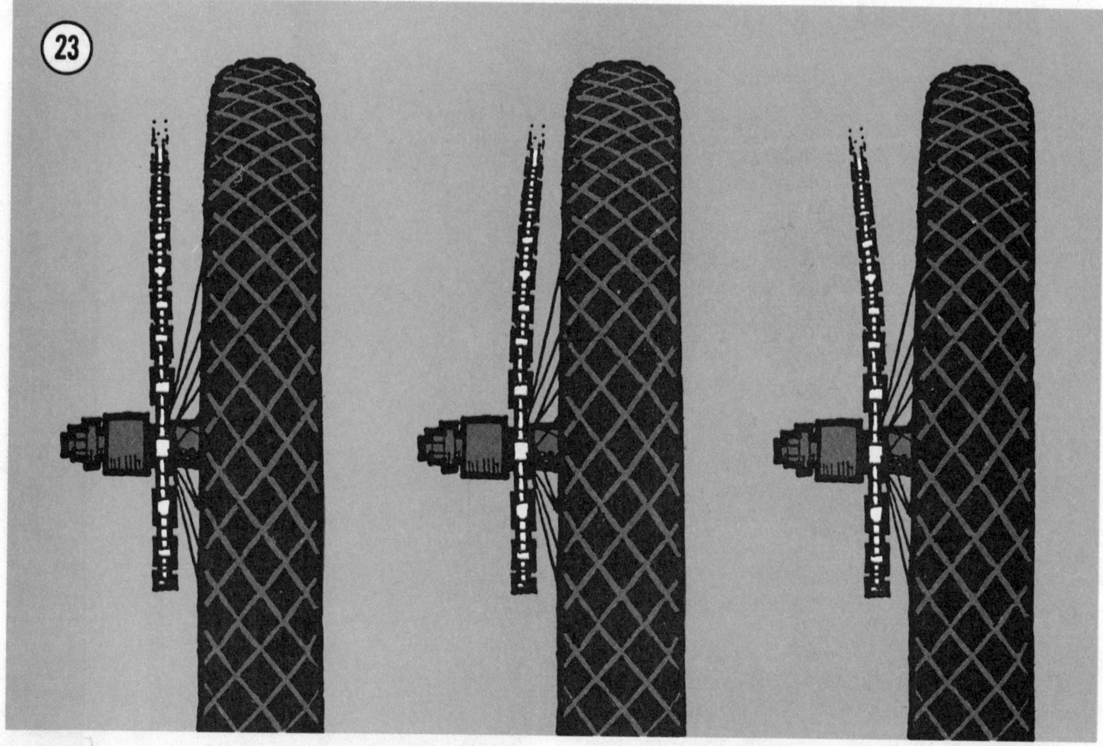

head, swing arm pivot. Check wheel alignment (**Figure 23**). Check for damage to the frame and suspension components.

2. ***Front suspension doesn't damp***—This is most often caused by a lack of damping oil in the fork legs. If the upper fork tubes are exceptionally oily, it's likely that the seals are worn out and should be replaced.

3. ***Front suspension sticks or won't fully compress***—Misalignment of the forks when the wheel is installed can cause this. Loosen the axle nut and the pinch bolt on the nut end of the axle (**Figure 24**). Lock the front wheel with the brake and compress the front suspension several times to align the fork legs. Then, tighten the pinch bolt and then the axle nut.

The trouble may also be caused by a bent or dented fork slider (**Figure 25**). The distortion required to lock up a fork tube is so slight that it is often impossible to visually detect. If this type of damage is suspected, remove the fork leg and remove the spring from it. Attempt to operate the fork leg. If it still binds, replace the slider; it's not practical to repair it.

4. ***Rear suspension does not damp***—This is usually caused by damping oil leaking past

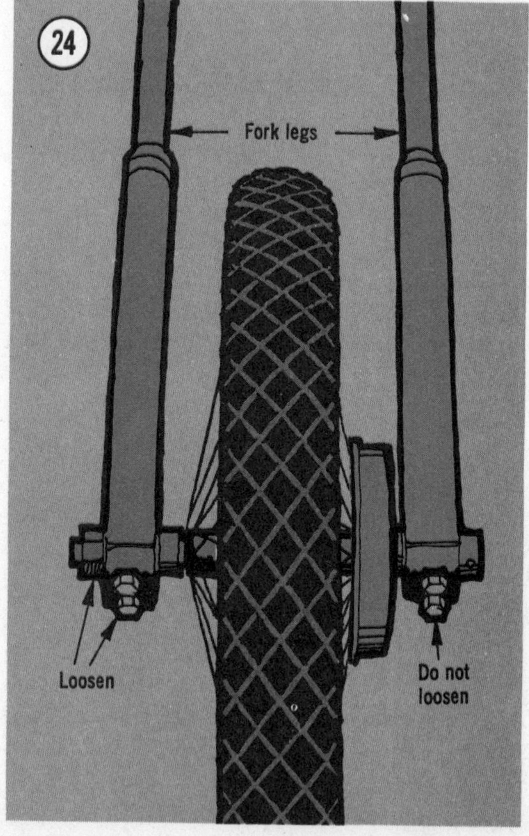

worn seals. Rebuildable shocks should be refitted with complete service kits and fresh oil. Non-rebuildable units should be replaced.

5. ***Rear suspension sticks***—This is commonly caused by a bent shock absorber piston rod (**Figure 26**). Replace the shock; the rod can't be satisfactorily straightened.

6. ***Steering is tight or "notchy"***—Steering head bearings may be dry, dirty, or worn. Adjustment of the steering head bearing pre-load may be too tight.

7. ***Steering is sloppy***—Steering head adjustment may be too loose. Also check the swing arm pivot; looseness or extreme wear at this point translate to the steering.

BRAKES

Brake problems arise from wear, lack of maintenance, and from sustained or repeated exposure to dirt and water.

1. ***Brakes are ineffective***—Ineffective brakes are most likely caused by incorrect adjustment. If adjustment will not correct the problem, remove the wheels and check for worn or glazed linings. If the linings are worn beyond the service limit, replace them. If they are simply glazed, rough them up with light sandpaper.

In hydraulic brake systems, low fluid levels can cause a loss of braking effectiveness, as can worn brake cylinder pistons and bores. Also check the pads to see if they are worn beyond the service limit.

2. ***Brakes lock or drag***—This may be caused by incorrect adjustment. Check also for foreign matter embedded in the lining and for dirty and dry wheel bearings.

ELECTRICAL SYSTEM

Many electrical system problems can be easily solved by ensuring that the affected connections are clean, dry, and tight. In battery equipped motorcycles, a neglected battery is the source of a great number of difficulties that could be prevented by simple, regular service to the battery.

A multimeter, like the volt/ohm/milliammeter described in Chapter One, is invaluable for efficient electrical system troubleshooting.

See **Figures 27 and 28** for schematics showing

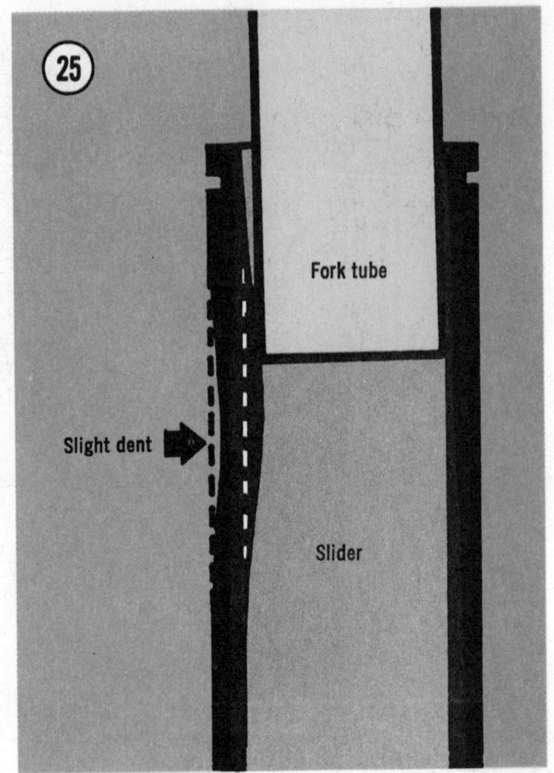

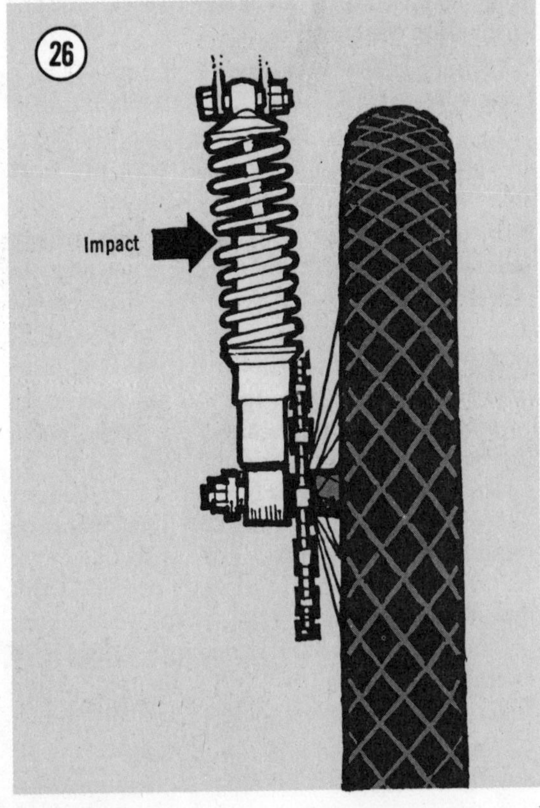

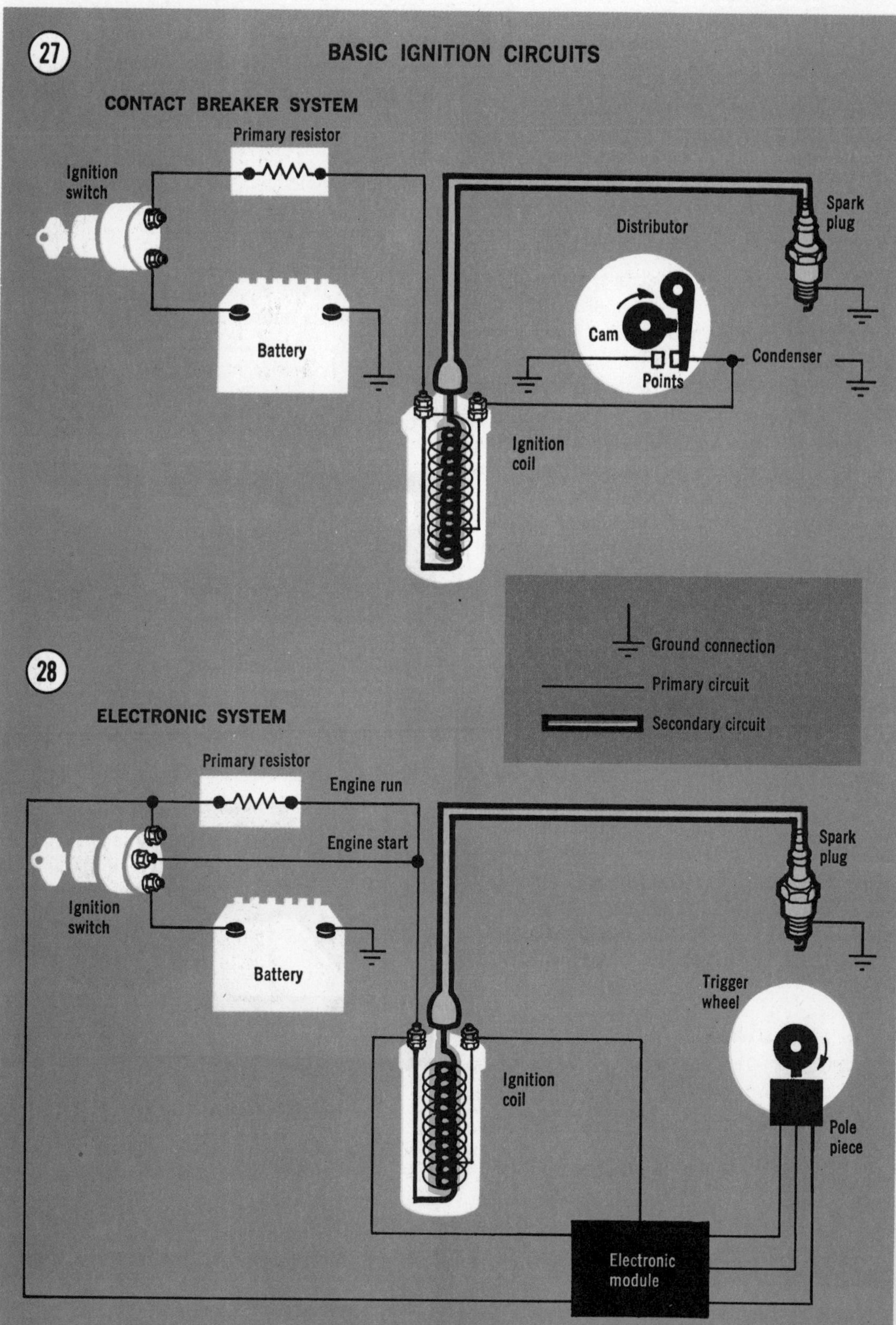
27
BASIC IGNITION CIRCUITS
CONTACT BREAKER SYSTEM
Primary resistor
Ignition switch
Battery
Distributor
Cam
Points
Condenser
Spark plug
Ignition coil
Ground connection
Primary circuit
Secondary circuit
28
ELECTRONIC SYSTEM
Primary resistor
Engine run
Engine start
Ignition switch
Battery
Spark plug
Trigger wheel
Ignition coil
Pole piece
Electronic module

simplified conventional and electronic ignition systems. Typical and most common electrical troubles are also described.

CHARGING SYSTEM

1. ***Battery will not accept a charge***—Make sure the electrolyte level in the battery is correct and that the terminal connections are tight and free of corrosion. Check for fuses in the battery circuit. If the battery is satisfactory, refer to the electrical system chapter for alternator tests. Finally, keep in mind that even a good alternator is not capable of restoring the charge to a severely discharged battery; it must first be charged by an external source.

2. ***Battery will not hold a charge***—Check the battery for sulfate deposits in the bottom of the case (**Figure 29**). Sulfation occurs naturally and the deposits will accumulate and eventually come in contact with the plates and short them out. Sulfation can be greatly retarded by keeping the battery well charged at all times. Test the battery to assess its condition.

If the battery is satisfactory, look for excessive draw, such as a short.

LIGHTING

Bulbs burn out frequently—All bulbs will eventually burn out, but if the bulb in one particular light burns out frequently check the light assembly for looseness that may permit excessive vibration; check for loose connections that could cause current surges; check also to make sure the bulb is of the correct rating.

FUSES

Fuse blows—When a fuse blows, don't just replace it; try to find the cause. Consider a fuse a warning device as well as a safety device. And never replace a fuse with one of greater amperage rating. It probably won't melt before the insulation on the wiring does.

WIRING

Wiring problems should be corrected as soon as they arise — before a short can cause a fire that may seriously damage or destroy the motorcycle.

A circuit tester of some type is essential for locating shorts and opens. Use the appropriate wiring diagram at the end of the book for reference. If a wire must be replaced make a notation on the wiring diagram of any changes in color coding.

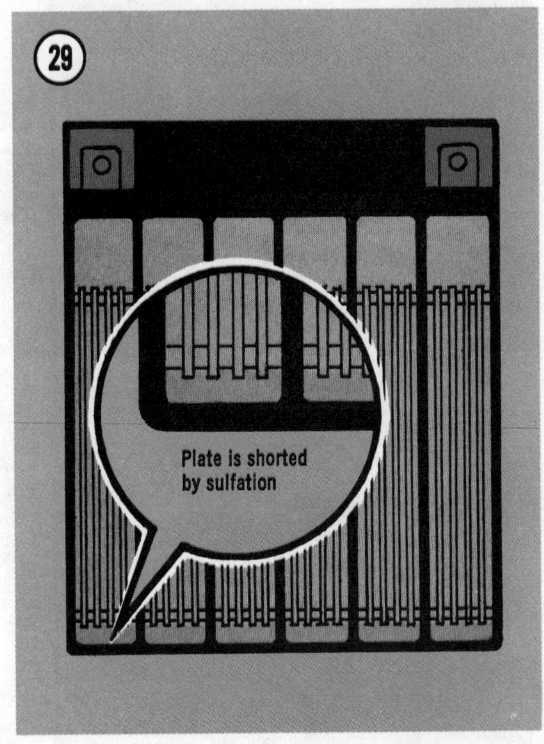

NOTE: If you own a 1980 or later model, first check the Supplement at the back of the book for any new service information.

CHAPTER THREE

3

LUBRICATION, MAINTENANCE, AND TUNE-UP

SCHEDULED MAINTENANCE

This chapter covers all the regular maintenance you have to perform to keep your machine in top shape.

Regular maintenance is the best guarantee of a trouble-free, long lasting motorcycle. In addition, while performing the routine jobs, you will probably notice any other developing problems at an early stage when they are simple and inexpensive to correct.

Table 1 is a recommended minimum maintenance schedule (**Tables 1-5** are at the end of the chapter). However, you will have to determine your own maintenance requirements based on the type of riding you do and the place you ride. If you ride in dusty areas or at high speeds or if you make a lot of short 5 or 10 minute rides, service the items more often. Perform the maintenance at each *Time* or *Mileage* interval, whichever comes first.

NOTE

If you have a brand new motorcycle, we recommend you take the bike to your dealer for the initial break-in maintenance at 500 miles (800 km).

Emission-controlled Motorcycles

This manual covers both emission-controlled motorcycles manufactured after January 1, 1978 and non-controlled motorcycles built before that date.

If your motorcycle is emission-controlled, we urge you to follow all procedures specifically designated for your bike. If you don't follow the maintenance schedule (**Table 1**) in this manual or if you alter engine parts or change their settings from the standard factory specifications (ignition timing, carburetor idle mixture, exhaust system, etc.), your bike may not comply with federal emissions standards.

In addition, since most emission-controlled bikes are carburetted on the lean side, any changes to emission-related parts (such as exhaust system modifications) could cause the engine to run so lean that piston seizure would result.

Model Identification

In the process of building motorcycles, the factory often introduces new models throughout the calendar year. New models, when introduced, are not necessarily identified by year but by model number suffix. See **Table 2** at the end of this chapter for model year and model suffix equivalents.

BATTERY

The battery electrolyte level should be checked regularly, particularly during hot weather. Motorcycle batteries are marked with electrolyte level limit lines (**Figure 1**). Always maintain the fluid level between the lines, adding distilled water as required. Distilled water is available at most supermarkets and its use will prolong the life of the battery, especially in areas where tap water is hard (has a high mineral content).

Inspect the fluid level in all the cells. On some models the battery must be removed to inspect it. Refer to *Battery* in Chapter Six before removing the battery from the motorcycle.

WARNING

Battery elecytrolyte contains sulfuric acid, which can destroy clothing and cause serious chemical burns. Electrolyte splashed into the eyes is extremely dangerous. Wear safety glasses. In case of contact, flood with water for about 5 minutes and call a doctor immediately if the eyes were exposed.

Don't overfill the battery or you'll lose some electrolyte, weakening the battery and causing corrosion. Never allow the electrolyte level to drop below the top of the plates or the plates may be permanently damaged.

CAUTION

If electrolyte is spilled on the motorcycle, wash it off immediately with plenty of water.

ENGINE TUNE-UP

The following list summarizes routine engine tune-up procedures. Detailed instructions follow the list. These tune-up procedures are arranged so that you start with the jobs that require a "cold" engine and finish with the jobs that call for a fully warmed-up engine. If you follow the sequence, you won't waste time waiting for your bike to cool down when required.

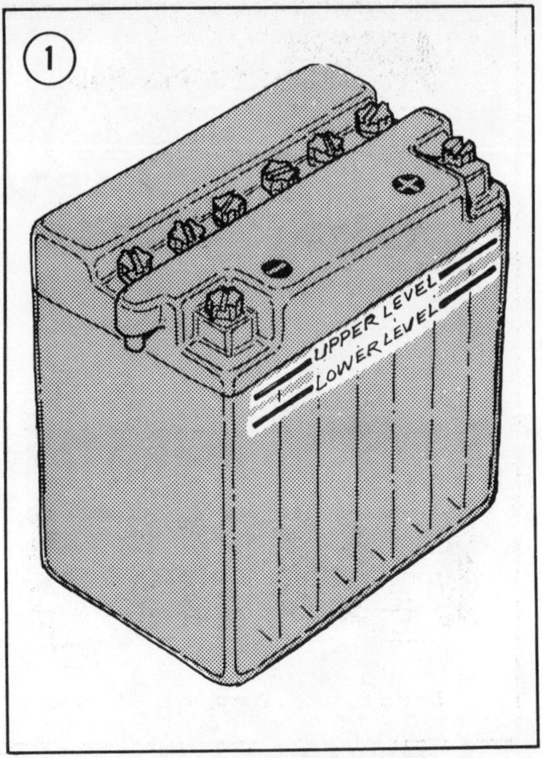

Consult Chapter Two for troubleshooting procedures when you suspect more serious trouble. Refer to **Table 3** at the end of the chapter for tune-up specifications.

1. Inspect the air filter and clean it or install a new one.
2. Clean the fuel system and fuel tap sediment bowl, if so equipped. Inspect the fuel lines for cracks or leakage.
3. Inspect the spark plugs. Clean them and adjust the gap or replace them if necessary. Leave the plugs out until after you inspect the cam chain tension and valve clearance.
4. Check cam chain tension and adjust if necessary.
5. Inspect valve clearance and adjust if necessary.
6. Inspect the contact breaker points, adjust the gap, or replace the points if necessary. Lubricate the point cam wick very lightly.
7. Inspect the ignition timing and adjust if necessary.
8. Adjust the carburetors if required: throttle cable play, idle mixture, idle speed, and synchronization.
9. Check and record cylinder compression.

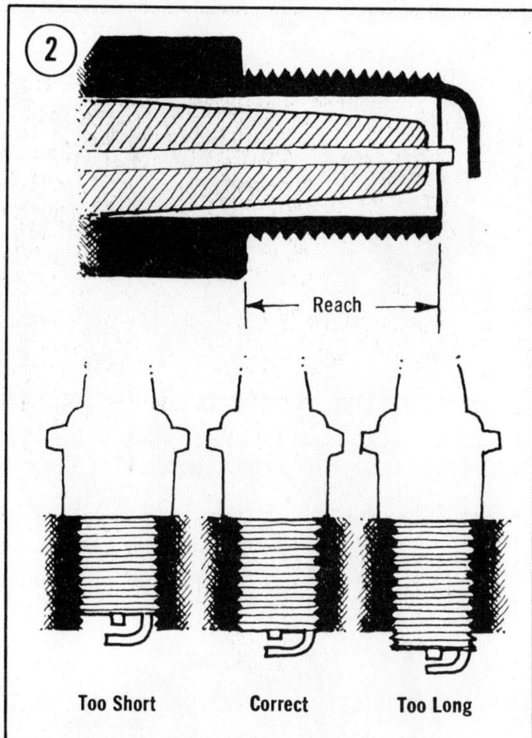

AIR FILTER

A clogged air filter will cause a rich fuel/air mixture, resulting in power loss and poor gas mileage. Never run the bike without an air filter. Even minute particles of dust can cause severe internal engine wear and clogging of carburetor passages.

Remove the filter element and tap it against a solid surface to remove the heavy particles, then blow it clean with compressed air, if available. Kawasaki recommends cleaning the paper-type filter in a non-oily solvent, then allowing it to dry. Install a new air filter every 5 cleanings or every 6,000 miles (10,000 km) or any time the element or gaskets are damaged. Clean the filter more frequently in dusty areas and after riding in the rain.

FUEL SYSTEM

As water and dirt accumulate in the fuel tank or carburetor float bowls, engine performance will deteriorate.

WARNING

Some fuel may spill during these procedures. Work in a well-ventilated area at least 50 feet from any sparks or flames, including gas appliance pilot lights. Do not smoke in the area.

Fuel Tap

1. Turn automatic (vacuum-operated) fuel taps to ON or manual fuel taps to OFF.
2. Remove the drain plug or sediment bowl from the bottom of the fuel tap and clean the sediment bowl and screen, if so equipped.
3. Install the drain plug or bowl and gasket, turn the fuel tap to PRI (automatic) or ON (manual), and make sure there are no leaks.

Carburetor Float Bowls

1. Turn automatic (vacuum-operated) fuel taps to PRI or manual fuel taps to RESERVE.
2. Remove the drain plug from the bottom of each carburetor float bowl and allow any accumulated water to drain out. Check that the drain plug O-rings are in good condition, and replace if necessary. Reinstall the drain plugs after any water has drained.
3. Make sure there are no leaks and that the fuel lines are not cracked or worn out.

SPARK PLUGS

Heat Range and Reach

The proper spark plug is very important for maximum performance and reliability. The proper heat range requires that a plug operate hot enough to burn off unwanted deposits, but not hot enough to burn up or cause preignition. A spark plug of the correct heat range will show a light tan color on the portion of the insulator within the cylinder after the plug has been in service.

The spark plugs recommended by the factory are usually the most suitable for your machine. For high speed riding in hot climates, a plug one step colder may be preferable. Refer to **Table 3** at the end of the chapter for the recommended spark plugs.

CAUTION

*Ensure the spark plug used has the correct thread reach (**Figure 2**). A thread reach too short will cause the exposed threads in the cylinder head to accumulate carbon, resulting in stripped cylinder head threads*

3

when the proper plug is installed. Too long a reach may cause plug/piston contact and serious damage.

Spark Plug Inspection

1. Grasp the spark plug leads as near to the plug as possible and pull them off the plugs. Clear away any dirt that has accumulated in the spark plug wells.

CAUTION

Dirt could fall into the cylinders when the plugs are removed, causing serious engine damage.

2. Remove the spark plugs with a 13/16 inch spark plug wrench.
3. Inspect the spark plugs carefully. Look for plugs with broken center porcelain, excessively eroded electrodes and excessive carbon or oil fouling. Refer to Figure 3, Chapter Two as a plug-reading aid. If deposits are light, the plugs may be cleaned with a wire brush or in a spark plug sandblast cleaner. However, a new plug is cheap assurance of higher power and gas mileage. Check the spark plug gasket. If it is completely flattened, install a new one.

CAUTION

Never sandblast an oily or wet plug. The grit will stick to the plug and later drop into the engine. After sandblasting plugs, clean them thoroughly.

4. If the plug is reusable, file center and side electrodes so their corners are not rounded. Less voltage is required to jump the gap when the electrode corners are sharp.
5. Measure the gap with a round wire spark plug gauge (**Figure 3**). Adjust the gap by bending the side electrode only, as specified in **Table 3**.
6. Apply a small amount of anti-sieze compound to the plug threads. Don't use oil or grease-they'll turn to pure carbon and make the plug harder to get out the next time.

NOTE

If you're going to adjust the cam chain and valve clearance, leave the spark plugs out until you're finished. It will be easier to turn the engine over precisely.

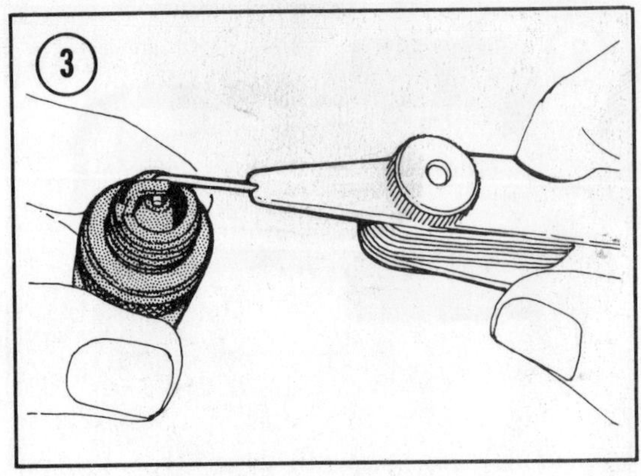

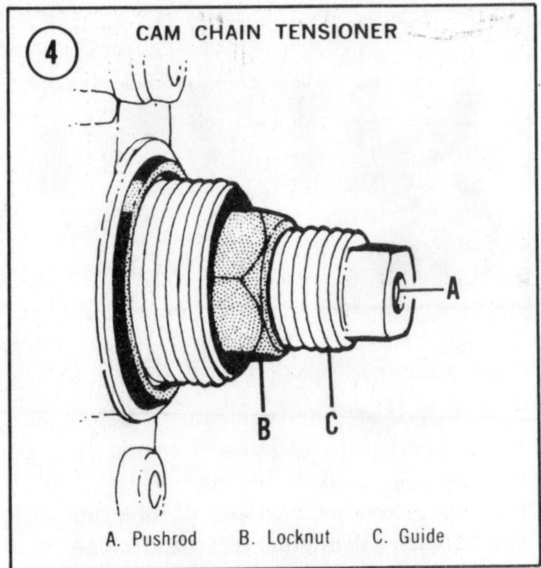

A. Pushrod B. Locknut C. Guide

7. Clean the seating area on the cylinder head and thread the plug in by hand until it seats. Then tighten the plug 1/8 to 1/2 turn with a spark plug wrench. If you use a torque wrench, the proper torque is 20 ft.-lb. (2.8 mkg).

CAM CHAIN TENSION

In time the cam chain and guides will wear and develop slack. If neglected too long, the cam chain could break and cause serious engine damage.

When chain tensioner adjustment no longer quiets the cam chain, the cam chain guides and tensioner may require replacement.

1. Check that the ignition switch is OFF.
2. Remove the spark plugs.
3. Remove the ignition timing cover and gasket from the lower right side of the engine.

4. Remove the tensioner cap.
5. Turn the crankshaft to the left (counterclockwise), with the 17 mm bolt on the right end of the crankshaft. At the same time, watch the tensioner pushrod move in the end of the tensioner (A, **Figure 4**).

CAUTION
Do not use the small inner bolt to turn the engine or you will damage the ignition advance mechanism.

6. Watch the pushrod move in and out as you turn the engine; stop turning when the pushrod moves to its innermost position.

NOTE
Do not turn the crankshaft to the right (clockwise), or you will cause improper tension adjustment.

7. Loosen the locknut (B, **Figure 4**), then turn the pushrod guide (C) by its flats until the end of the guide is flush with the end of the pushrod inside it.
8. Tighten the locknut and install the tensioner cap and O-ring.

NOTE
If you are going to adjust the valves, leave the ignition timing cover and gasket off the engine.

VALVE CLEARANCE

Normal wear of the valves and valve seats decreases valve clearance and alters valve timing slightly. Insufficient valve clearance can lead to burnt valves and seats and will eventually cause serious engine damage. Excessive clearance causes noisy operation and more rapid valve train wear.

NOTE
Check and adjust valve clearance with the engine cool (at room temperature).

Valve Clearance (1974-1977)

1. Check that the ignition switch is OFF.
2. Remove the spark plugs.
3. Remove the ignition timing cover and gasket from the lower right side of the engine.
4. See **Figure 5**. Remove the cylinder head side cover (A) and the valve adjuster plugs (B) from the engine.
5. Position the right piston at top dead center (TDC) on its compression stroke. To do this, turn the crankshaft to the left (counter-clockwise) with the 17 mm bolt on the end of the crankshaft and at the same time watch the right cylinder intake (rear) valve through the side cover. After that valve has opened and closed (moved down then up), continue to

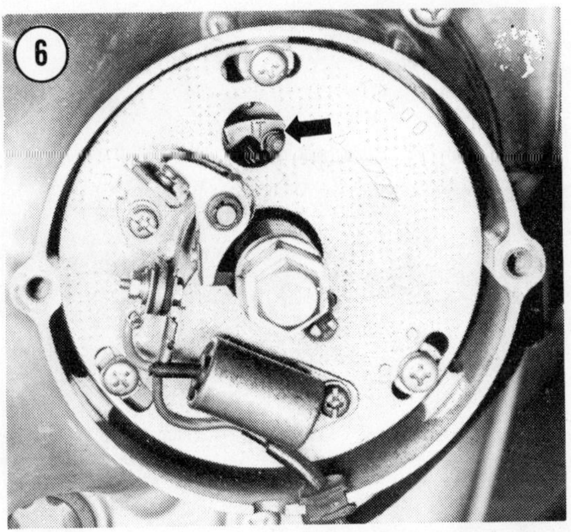

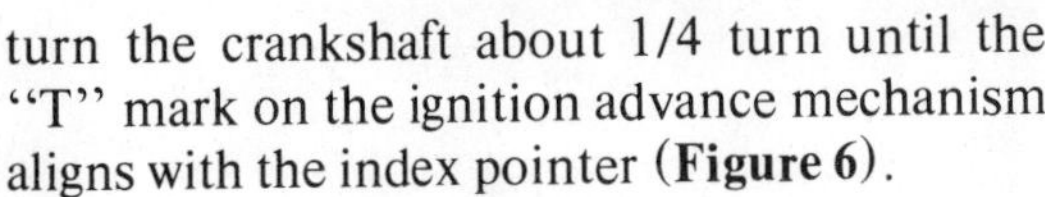

turn the crankshaft about 1/4 turn until the "T" mark on the ignition advance mechanism aligns with the index pointer (**Figure 6**).

CAUTION
Do not use the small inner bolt to turn the engine or you will damage the ignition advance mechanism.

6. Insert a feeler gauge between each right cylinder valve stem and its rocker arm. The clearance should be as specified in **Table 3** at the end of the chapter. The clearance is measured correctly when there is a slight drag on the feeler gauge when it is inserted and withdrawn. If the clearance is within tolerance, go on to Step 9. If adjustment is required, continue with Step 7.
7. Loosen the locknut (A, **Figure 7**), then turn the shaft (B) with a screwdriver as required to get the proper clearance.
8. Hold the shaft (B) steady and torque the locknut (A) to 20 ft.-lb. (2.8 mkg).

NOTE
When adjusting valve clearance, always keep the punch mark on each shaft facing inward, toward the (+) and (-) marks.

9. Turn the crankshaft one full turn to the left (counterclockwise), so that the "T" mark again lines up with the index pointer, and repeat Steps 6 through 8 for the left cylinder.

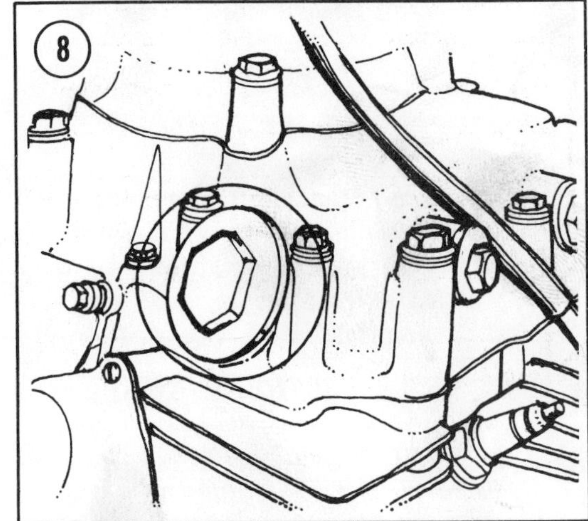

Valve Clearance (1978-1979)

1. Check that the ignition switch is OFF.
2. Remove the fuel tank.
3. Remove the spark plugs.
4. Remove the ignition timing cover and gasket from the lower right side of the engine.
5. Remove the 4 valve adjusting caps (**Figure 8**).
6. Position the right piston at top dead center (TDC) on its compression stroke. To do this, turn the crankshaft to the left (counterclockwise) with the 17 mm bolt on the end of the crankshaft and at the same time watch the right cylinder intake (rear) valve through the side cover. After that valve has opened and closed (moved down then up), continue to turn the crankshaft about 1/4 turn until the

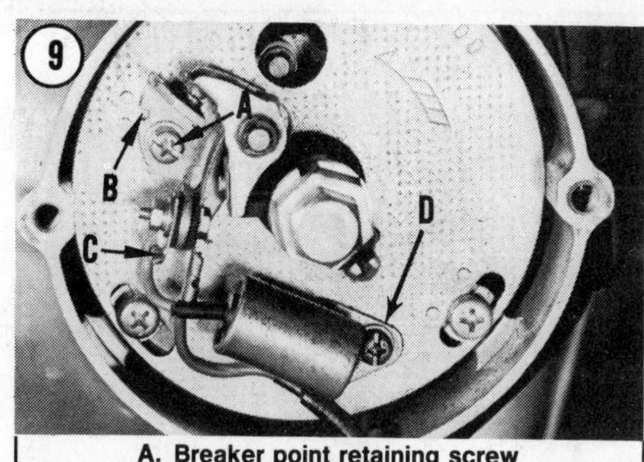

A. Breaker point retaining screw
B. Adjustment slot
C. Condenser lead
D. Condenser retaining screw

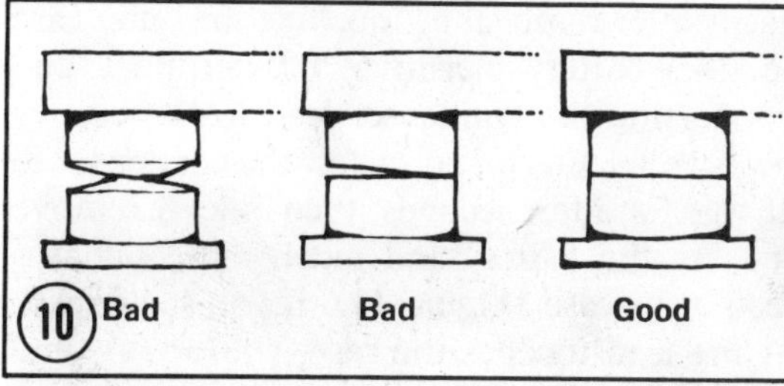

"T" mark on the ignition advance mechanism aligns with the index pointer (**Figure 6**).

CAUTION
Do not use the small inner bolt to turn the engine or you will damage the ignition advance mechanism.

7. Insert a feeler gauge between each right cylinder valve stem and its rocker arm. The clearance should be as specified in **Table 3** at the end of the chapter. The clearance is measured correctly when there is a slight drag on the feeler gauge when it is inserted and withdrawn.
8. Adjust by loosening the adjuster locknut and turning the adjuster as required to get the proper clearance. Hold the adjuster steady and tighten the locknut securely. Check that the locknut is tightened to 11 ft.-lb. (1.5 mkg).
9. Turn the crankshaft one full turn to the left (counterclockwise), so that the "T" mark again lines up with the index pointer, and repeat Steps 7 and 8 for the left cylinder's valves.

CONTACT BREAKER POINTS

The breaker points are shown in **Figure 9**. During normal operation, the contact surfaces of the points gradually erode and become contaminated. The point rubbing block also wears, retarding ignition timing. Periodic cleaning and gap adjustment are required to keep the engine operating at peak efficiency.

Contact Point Inspection

1. Turn the ignition switch OFF.
2. Remove the ignition timing cover and gasket from the lower right side of the engine.
3. Inspect the contact surfaces. If the points are not badly pitted they can be removed and dressed with a few strokes from a point file; "Flexstone" is a good brand to use. If the contact surfaces are badly pitted, replace the breaker point assembly and the condenser.

NOTE
Don't use sandpaper or emery cloth for dressing the points. They will leave abrasive particles embedded in the points and cause arcing.

4. Clean the contact surfaces by closing the points on a piece of clean paper, such as a business card, and pulling the paper through the points. Do this until no discoloration or residue remains on the card. Check the points when closed. If they do not meet squarely (**Figure 10**), replace them.
5. Inspect the breaker spring tension by hand. A weak breaker spring will allow the points to bounce at high engine speeds and cause misfiring. Usually the spring will last for the life of the contacts.
6. Apply a small amount of point cam lubricant or high temperature grease to the felt that bears against the point cam. If you use too much grease, the cam will sling it onto the contacts, fouling them.
7. Check the point gap and ignition timing.

Contact Point Gap (With Feeler Gauge)

1. Turn the crankshaft to the left (counterclockwise) with the 17 mm bolt on the end of the crankshaft, until the points are open to their widest gap.

3

CAUTION
Do not use the small inner bolt to turn the engine or you will damage the ignition advance mechanism.

2. Measure the point gap with a clean feeler gauge. The gap should be as specified in **Table 3** at the end of the chapter.

NOTE
There should be a slight drag on the feeler gauge as it is inserted and removed. Hold the gauge loosely in your fingers to make sure you're not prying the points open.

3. To adjust the point gap, loosen the locking screw slightly (A, **Figure 9**), then insert a screwdriver into the pry slots (B) and move the base contact as required to set the gap. Tighten the screw (A) and recheck the gap.
4. Inspect the ignition timing.

Contact Point Gap (With Dwell Angle Meter)

The dwell angle is the number of degrees (or the percentage of 360°) of point cam rotation during which the points are closed and current can flow through them to the primary winding of the ignition coil. The breaker point gap can be adjusted with greater accuracy with a dwell angle meter than with feeler gauges.

1. Connect a dwell angle meter according to the manufacturer's instructions.
2. Start the engine and allow it to idle.
3. Note the reading on the meter. The reading for the correct gap on a meter calibrated in percentages is 53%; the correct reading for a meter calibrated in degrees is 190° when set for "2 cylinders."
4. If the reading is incorrect, adjust the point gap. Loosen the locking screw slightly (A, **Figure 9**), then insert a screwdriver into the pry slots (B) and move the stationary contact as required to obtain the correct meter reading. Tighten the screw (A) and recheck the meter reading.
5. Check the ignition timing.

Contact Point and Condenser Replacement

It is a good idea to replace the condenser every time you replace the points, but if you

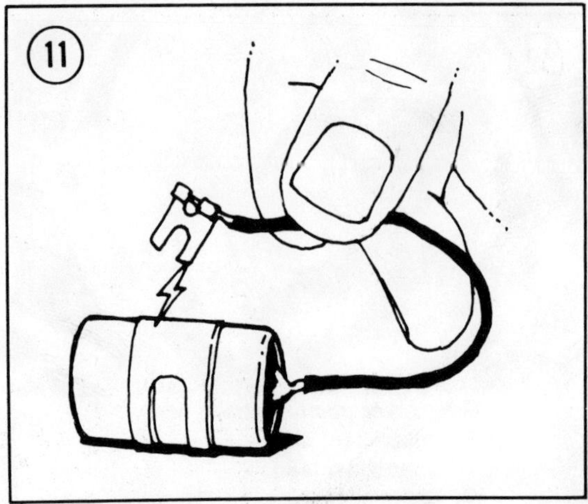

want to use the old condenser, you can test it easily after removal by touching the outer case to the battery negative (-) terminal and connecting the condenser lead to the battery positive (+) terminal. Allow the condenser to charge for a few seconds, then quickly remove it from the battery and touch the condenser lead to its case (**Figure 11**). If you see a spark as the lead touches the case, you can assume the condenser is OK.

1. Turn the ignition switch OFF.
2. Remove the screw that mounts the breaker point assembly to its backing plate (A, **Figure 9**).
3. Lift the point assembly from its pivot, loosen the nut and remove the ignition coil wire and condenser wire from the point terminal (C, **Figure 9**).
4. To remove the condenser, remove its mounting screw from the backing plate (D, **Figure 9**).
5. Remove all old lubricant from the point cam and apply a sparing coat of fresh breaker cam lubricant. Do not use too much.
6. Install a new condenser and set of points, making sure the new contacts are clean and that the backing plate is clean for a good ground connection.
7. Adjust the point gap and ignition timing.

IGNITION TIMING

Periodic inspection and adjustment of ignition timing is necessary to compensate for point and rubbing block wear. Failure to do so will result in incorrect ignition timing which in

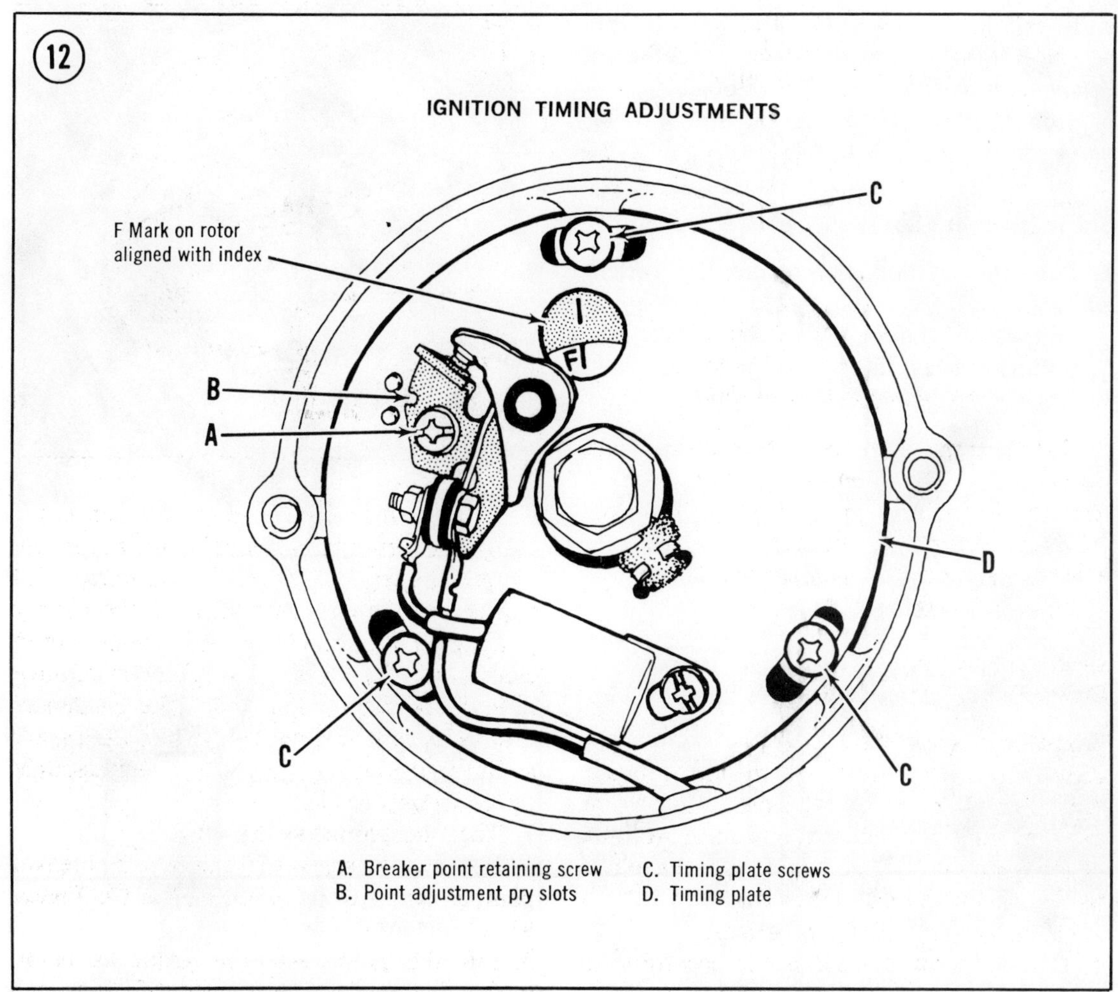

turn may cause poor performance, overheating, knocking, or engine damage.

Clean the contact points and adjust their gap before inspecting ignition timing.

There are 2 ways to inspect ignition timing: *Static* (engine not running) and *Dynamic* (engine running). Dynamic timing inspection is preferable if a strobe timing light is available, because it checks timing under actual operating conditions and allows inspection of the ignition advance function.

Dynamic Ignition Timing

1. Hook up a tachometer and a stroboscopic timing light according to the manufacturer's instructions.
2. Start the engine and allow it to idle. If idle speed is not within the specifications listed in **Table 3**, adjust it as described in this chapter.
3. Shine the light at the timing inspection hole. The "F" mark should align with the index mark at idle (**Figure 12**). If the "F" mark does not align at idle, loosen the timing plate screws (C, **Figure 12**) and rotate the timing plate as required to align the marks. Tighten the timing plate screws.

NOTE
*On some 1977 models, unstable idle may result if the timing marks are aligned as shown in **Figure 12**. A more stable idle is possible if the left edge of the "F" mark is aligned with the index mark. This sets timing at 15°BTDC at idle and 45°BTDC at full advance. Premium fuel may be required to prevent gas knock.*

4. Increase the engine speed to 3,500 rpm and check that the double line advance mark aligns

with the index mark (**Figure 13**). If the advance does not work correctly, refer to *Ignition Advance Unit* in Chapter Four.

5. Stop the engine and install the timing cover and gasket.

Static Ignition Timing

1. Turn the ignition switch and kill switch OFF.
2. Connect a timing tester, buzz box, or ohmmeter between the contact point terminal and the engine case for a good ground.

NOTE

If you don't have a timing tester, you can tell approximately when the points open by inserting a piece of cellophane (a cigarette package wrapper works) between the points and pulling lightly on it while you turn the crankshaft.

*A simple test light **(Figure 14)** also will work with the ignition switch ON.*

3. Using the 17 mm bolt on the end of the crankshaft, slowly turn the crankshaft to the left (counterclockwise) until the "F" mark aligns with the index mark (**Figure 12**). The timing tester should indicate the breaker points are just beginning to open when the marks align (the tone will change, the bulb will light, or the ohmmeter needle will flicker).

CAUTION

Do not use the small inner bolt to turn the engine or you will damage the ignition advance mechanism.

4. If the ignition timing is incorrect, continue turning the crankshaft until the "F" mark aligns with the index mark again. Loosen the timing plate screws (C, **Figure 12**) and rotate the timing plate as required so the points are just beginning to open.
5. Tighten the timing plate screws and recheck timing as described in Step 3.

NOTE

*On 1977 models, unstable idle may result if the timing marks are aligned as shown in **Figure 12**. A more stable idle is possible if the left edge of the "F" mark is aligned with the index mark. This sets timing at 15°BTDC at idle and 45°BTDC at full advance. Premium fuel may be required to prevent gas knock.*

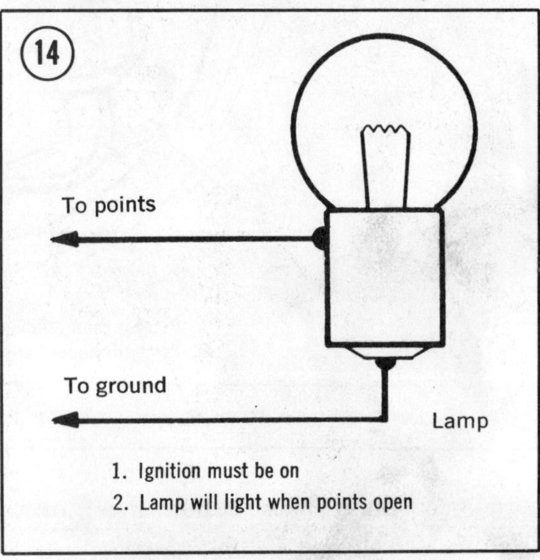

6. Install the timing cover and gasket.

CARBURETOR

The carburetor should be adjusted only when the engine is fully warmed up and all other tune-up operations are done.

Throttle Cable Play

Always check the throttle cables before you make any carburetor adjustments. Too much

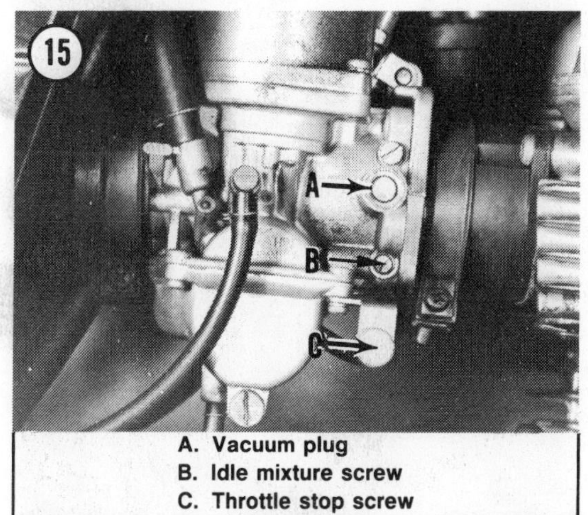

A. Vacuum plug
B. Idle mixture screw
C. Throttle stop screw

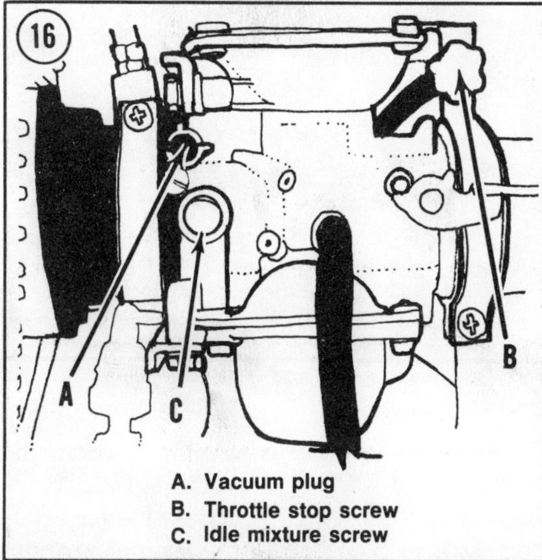

A. Vacuum plug
B. Throttle stop screw
C. Idle mixture screw

free play causes delayed throttle response; too little free play will cause unstable idling.

Check free play at the throttle grip flange. Kawasaki specifies about 1/8 in. (2-3 mm). If adjustment is required, proceed as follows.

1. Loosen both throttle grip cable adjuster locknuts and shorten both adjusters fully for maximum cable play.
2. Lengthen the return cable (rear cable) by backing the adjuster out 3 full turns.
3. Lengthen the open cable (front cable) adjuster until all play is removed. Tighten its locknut.
4. Go back to the return cable adjuster and shorten it to get your desired free play. Tighten its locknut.

NOTE

If all the adjustment range is used up at the throttle grip, use the adjusters at the carburetor end of the throttle cables.

Idle Speed

Proper idle speed setting is necessary to prevent stalling and to provide adequate engine compression braking, but you can't set it perfectly with the bike's tachometer—it's just not accurate at the low end. You'll need a portable tachometer, or you're about as well off setting idle by ear and feel: if it stalls, set idle higher; if you want more engine braking, set idle lower.

1. Attach a portable tachometer, following the manufacturer's instructions.
2. Start the engine and warm it up fully (about 10 minutes).
3. Turn the throttle stop screw (**Figure 15** or **Figure 16**) to set idle speed as specified in **Table 3** at the end of the chapter. If you have no tachometer, set the idle at the lowest speed at which the engine will idle smoothly.
4. Rev the engine a couple of times to see if it settles down to the set speed. Readjust, if necessary.

Idle Mixture

The idle fuel/air mixture affects low-speed emissions, as well as idling stability and response off idle. The range of adjustment is limited by a limiter cap on 1978 and later models (**Figure 15**). Do not remove the limiter caps from the mixture screws; no standard specification of idle mixture screw initial setting is available for 1979 U.S. models.

Idle mixture adjustment (1974-1978)

1. Adjust the idle speed to specification.
2. Turn each idle mixture screw (**Figure 15** or **Figure 16**) in or out to the setting that gives the highest stable idle speed.
3. Readjust idle speed to specification, if necessary.
4. Turn each mixture screw slightly again and see if the idle speed increases. Readjust idle speed, if necessary.

Idle mixture adjustment (1979)

1. Adjust the idle speed to specification.
2. Turn each idle mixture screw (**Figure 16**) to the right (clockwise) against its stop.
3. Turn each idle mixture screw to the left (counterclockwise) against its stop, observing idle speed.
4. If idle speed rose as the screw was turned to the left, turn it back in to the point just before idle speed increased.
5. If idle speed did not rise as the screw was turned to the left, turn it back all the way to the right against its stop.

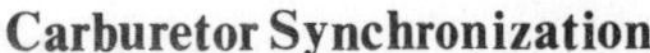

Carburetor Synchronization

Synchronizing the carburetors makes sure that one cylinder doesn't try to run faster than the other, cutting power and gas mileage. You can check for a rough balance by listening to the exhaust noise at idle and feeling pressure at the mufflers, but the only accurate way to synchronize the carburetors is to use a set of vacuum gauges (a manometer) that measure the intake vacuum of both cylinders at the same time.

NOTE

Before you try to synchronize the carburetors, make sure all of the following are checked or adjusted first. If not, you won't get a good synch.

a. Air filter
b. Spark plugs
c. Valve clearance
d. Point gap and ignition timing
e. Throttle cable play
f. Carburetor holders and clamps air-tight

1. Start the engine, warm it up fully, set the idle speed, then stop the engine.
2. Remove the vacuum port plug screws (see **Figure 15** for 1974-1977 or **Figure 16** for 1978-1979), and attach a set of vacuum gauges, following the manufacturer's instructions.
3. Start the engine and check that the difference between the cylinders is less than 1.2 in. (3 cm) Hg. Identical readings are desirable.

4. If the difference is greater, loosen the locknut and turn the synchronizing screw located between the carburetors (**Figure 17**) as required to equalize the vacuum in both cylinders. Tighten the locknut. You may have to remove the fuel tank to get at the synchronizing screw. If you can synchronize the carburetors before the float bowls run dry, fine; if not, you'll have to supply fuel from a temporary hookup.

WARNING

When supplying fuel by temporary means, make sure the fuel tank is secure and that all fuel lines are tight—no leaks.

5. Reset the idle speed, stop the engine, and install the vacuum plug screws, checking that their sealing gaskets are in good condition.

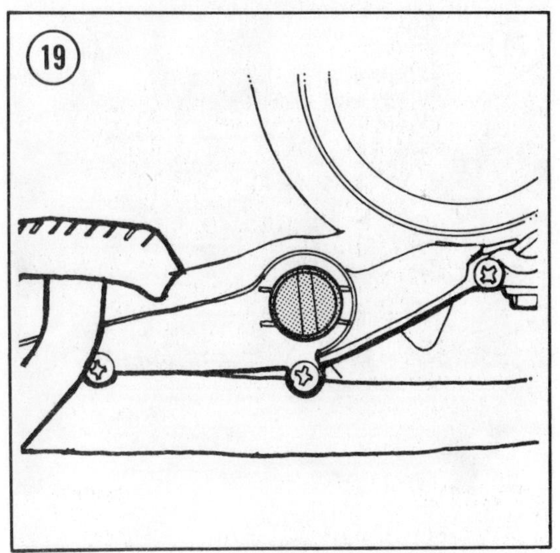

CYLINDER COMPRESSION

A cylinder cranking compression check is not *required maintenance*, but it is the quickest way to check the internal condition of the engine: rings, valves, head gasket, etc. It's a good idea to check compression at each tune-up, write it down, and compare it with the reading you get at the next tune-up. This will help you spot any developing problems before they cost too much repair money.

1. Warm the engine to normal operating temperature. Make sure the choke is OFF.
2. Remove the spark plugs.
3. Insert the tip of the gauge into the hole, making sure it's seated correctly (**Figure 18**).
4. Turn the kill switch off, hold the throttle wide open, and crank the engine several revolutions until the gauge gives its highest reading. Record the figure and repeat for the other cylinder.

When interpreting the results, the actual reading is not as important as the difference from the last check and the difference between cylinders. Individual gauge calibrations vary widely. A significant drop (more than 15 psi) since the last check (made with the same gauge) may indicate engine top end problems.

If the compression is 125 psi or more and there is less than a 15 psi difference between cylinders, compression is normal. If either cylinder reads less than about 110 psi, check your readings with a recently calibrated gauge. It may be time to rebuild the top end (rings and valves).

To tell the source of the problem, pour about a teaspoon of motor oil into the spark plug hole. Turn the engine over once to distribute the oil, then take another compression reading. If the compression returns to normal, the valves are good, but the rings on that cylinder are worn. If compression does not increase, the valves may be damaged.

ENGINE OIL AND FILTER

Engine Oil Level Inspection

1. Wait several minutes after shutting off the engine before making the check, to give the oil enough time to run down into the crankcase.

2. Put the bike on its centerstand (or hold it level).

3. Look at the oil inspection window near the bottom of the clutch cover (lower right side of the engine) to see that the oil level visible through the window lies between the upper and lower lines on the clutch cover (**Figure 19**).

4. If the oil level lies beneath the lower line, add oil slowly, in small quantities, through the filler. Add enough to raise the oil level up to (but not above) the top line. Use SAE 10W40, 10W50, 20W40, or 20W50 motor oil designated "For Service SE."

Engine Oil and Filter Change

The factory-recommended oil change interval is 3,000 miles. The filter should be changed every other oil change. If you ride hard or in dusty areas or if you take a lot of short trips, change the oil more frequently.

Try to stay with one brand of oil. The use of oil additives is not recommended: anything you add to the engine oil also gets on the clutch plates and could cause clutch slippage or damage.

1. Start the engine and warm it up fully, then turn it off.
2. Put the bike on its centerstand.

3. Put a drain pan under the crankcase and remove the drain plug. See **Figure 20** for 1974-1977 models or **Figure 21** for 1978 and later models.
4. The oil filter should be replaced every other engine oil change. If the oil filter is not to be changed, skip to Step 9. After the oil has drained, install the drain plug and torque it as specified:
   a. 1978 and later: 22 ft.-lb. (3.0 mkg).
   b. 1974-1977: 16 ft.-lb. (2.25 mkg).
5. To remove the oil filter, unscrew the filter cover bolt (**Figure 20** or **Figure 21**).
6. Remove the cover and filter, discard the filter, and clean the cover and the bolt.
7. Inspect the O-rings on the cover and on the filter bolt. Replace them if damaged.

NOTE
Before installing the cover, clean off the mating surface of the crankcase—do not allow any road dirt to enter the oil system.

8. Insert the bolt into the cover and install the spring and washer. Insert the filter and reinstall into the crankcase. Torque the filter bolt to 14.5 ft.-lb. (3.0 mkg).
9. Remove the oil filler cap and add the specified oil until it just reaches the upper line at the inspection window. Be sure to give the oil enough time to run down into the crankcase before checking the level in the inspection window.
10. Screw in the filler cap and start the engine, let it idle and check for leaks.
11. Turn off the engine and recheck for correct oil level.

GENERAL LUBRICATION

The following items should be lubricated according to the maintenance schedule and after cleaning the motorcycle. Special lubricants are available for control cables and other applications, but regular lubrication is more important than the type of lubricant you use: oil, grease, WD40, LPS3, etc.

Control Cables

The most positive method of control cable lubrication involves the use of a lubricator like the one shown in **Figure 22**. Disconnect the

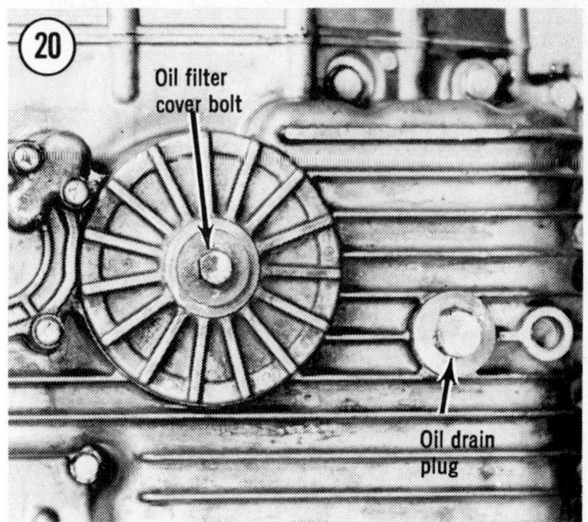

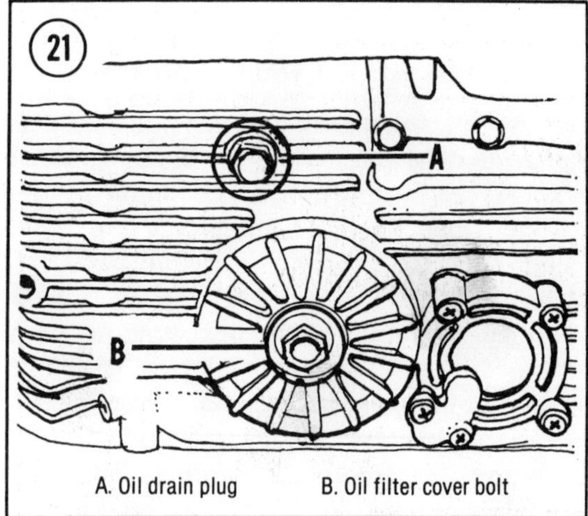

A. Oil drain plug B. Oil filter cover bolt

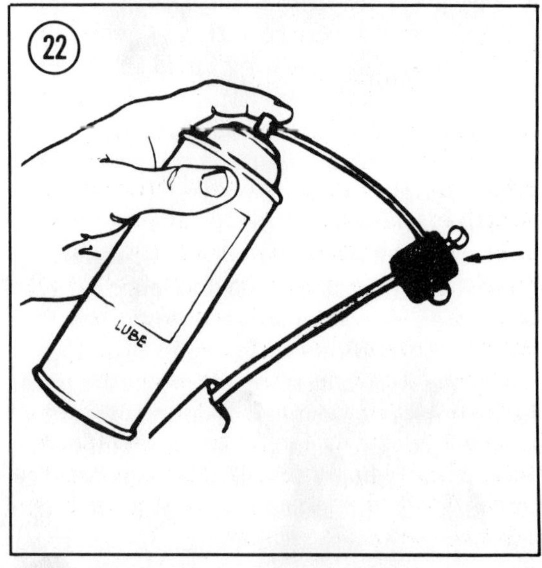

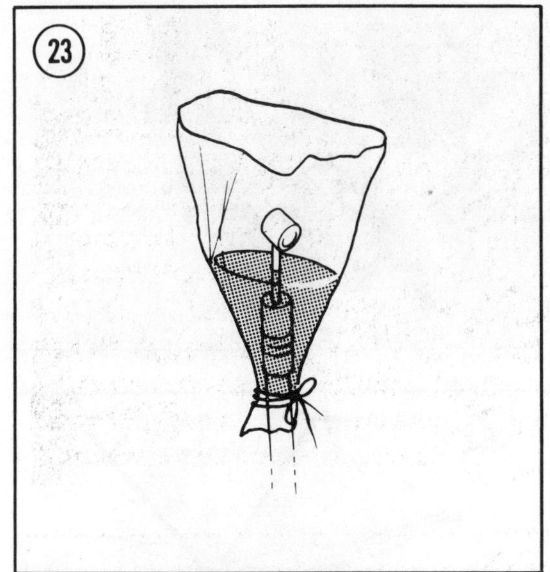

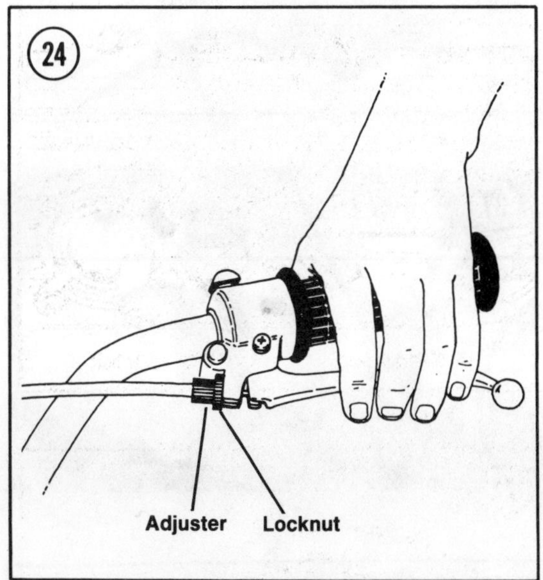

cable at the control, attach the lubricator, and inject lubricant into the cable sheath until it runs out of the other end. When lubricating a throttle cable with this type of device, the other end of the cable should first be disconnected from the carburetor.

If you do not have a lubricator, make a funnel from stiff paper or a plastic bag and tape it securely to one end of the cable (**Figure 23**). Hold the cable upright and add lubricant to the funnel. Work the cable in and out to help the lubricant work down the cable.

Control Pivots

Lubricate the brake pedal, footpeg, kickstarter, control lever pivots, and the control cable ends.

Throttle Grip Lubrication

1. Remove the screws that assemble the twist grip housing. Remove the top half of the housing.
2. Grease the throttle cables and the handlebar where the grip rotates.
3. Reassemble the twist grip housing. If the upper housing has a peg, it must fit into the hole in the handlebar.

Speedometer/Tachometer Cables

Disconnect the cables at the lower end. Pull the inner cable out, apply a light coat of grease and reinstall the cables. You may have to rotate the wheel to allow the speedometer cable to seat. If the tachometer cable won't seat, rotate the engine with the starter. Tighten the cable fasteners securely.

Ignition Advance Lubrication

To lubricate the ignition advance mechanism, refer to *Advancer Removal/ Installation* in Chapter Four.

CLUTCH

Clutch Lever Play

The clutch cable should have about 1/8 in. (2-3 mm) play at the lever before the clutch starts to disengage (**Figure 24**). Minor adjustments can be made at the hand lever. Loosen the locknut, turn the adjuster as required, and tighten the locknut.

At regular service intervals and when the hand lever adjustment range is used up, adjust the clutch release as described here.

Clutch Release Adjustment

As the clutch cable stretches, cable play will exceed the range of the cable adjusters. As the clutch plates and discs inside the engine wear, the clutch release must be adjusted even when the cable play is within tolerance or the clutch can slip and cause rapid wear. Adjust the clutch as follows.

1. In front of the engine, loosen the clutch midcable adjuster locknut and shorten the adjuster all the way (**Figure 25**).
2. At the clutch lever, loosen the locknut and turn the adjuster until 3/16-1/4 in. (5-6 mm) of threads are showing between the locknut and the adjuster body (**Figure 26**).
3. Remove the 2 clutch adjuster cover screws and the cover.
4. Loosen the locknut (A, **Figure 27**).
5. *1974-1977*: turn the screw (B, **Figure 27**) out until it turns freely. Then turn the adjuster in until the point is reached where it becomes hard to turn. Then turn the screw out 1/2 turn.
6. *1978 and later*: turn the screw (B, **Figure 27**) in until it turns freely. Then turn the screw out until the point is reached where it becomes hard to turn. Then turn the screw in 1/4 turn.
7. Hold the screw in position and tighten the locknut.
8. In front of the engine, lengthen the mid-cable adjuster until it has just taken all the slack out of the cable and the clutch lever has no free play. Tighten the locknut.
9. Check that the lower end of the clutch cable (below the engine) is fully seated in its socket.
10. At the clutch lever, turn the adjuster as required to get about 1/8 in. (2-3 mm) of cable play at the clutch lever.
11. Install the clutch adjuster cover.

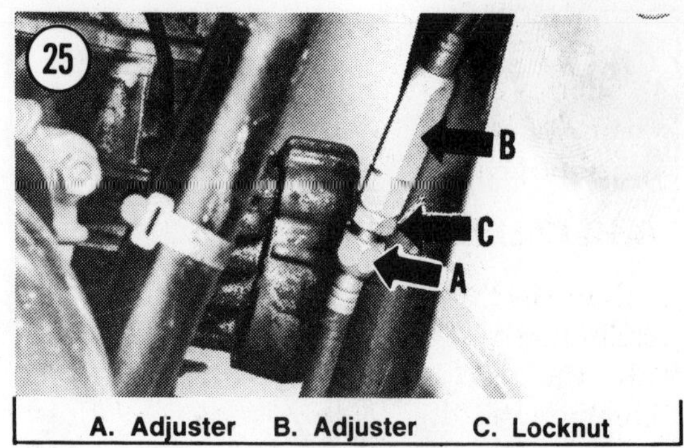

A. Adjuster B. Adjuster C. Locknut

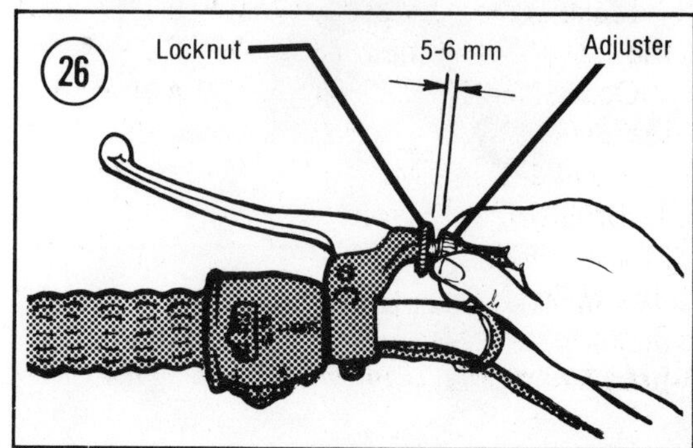

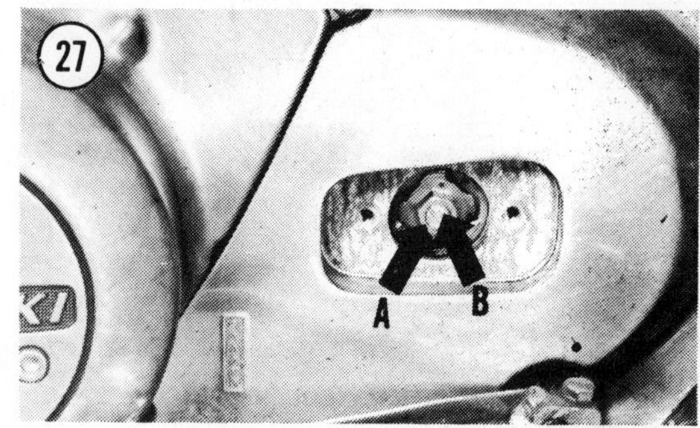

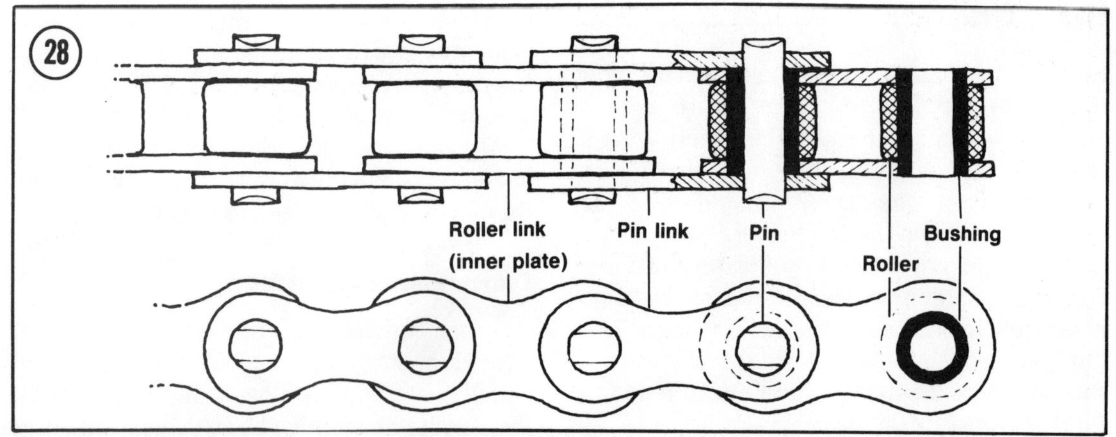

DRIVE CHAIN

Lubricate, clean, adjust, and check the drive chain for wear according to the maintenance schedule given in **Table 1**.

Drive Chain Lubrication

Kawasaki recommends SAE 90 gear oil for chain lubrication; it is less likely to be thrown off the chain than lighter oils. Many commercial drive chain lubricants are also available that do an excellent job.

Make sure the lubricant penetrates between the side plates of the drive chain (**Figure 28**).

Occasionally, the drive chain should be removed from the bike for a thorough cleaning and soak lubrication.

1. Brush off excess dirt and grit.
2. Remove the master link clip and the master link (**Figure 29**).
3. Soak the chain in solvent for about half an hour and clean it thoroughly.

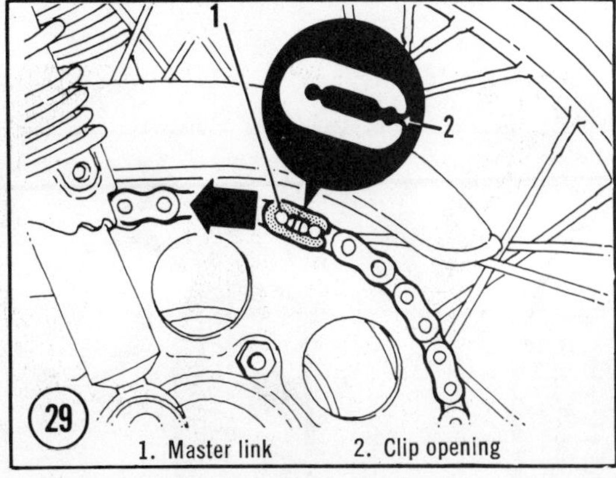

1. Master link 2. Clip opening

4. Soak the chain in heavy oil or hot grease and shake the chain around in the oil/grease to ensure thorough penetration of the lubricant.
5. Install the chain on the motorcycle, with the master link clip the closed end facing the direction of chain travel (**Figure 29**).

Chain Play Inspection

The drive chain must have adequate play so that the chain is not strung tight when the swing arm is horizontal (when the rider is seated). On the other hand, too much play may cause the chain to jump off the sprockets with potentially disastrous results.

1. Put the motorcycle on its centerstand, if it has one; use the side stand if there is no centerstand.
2. Turn the rear wheel slowly until you locate the part of chain that stretches tightest between the 2 sprockets on the bottom chain run (the chain wears unevenly).
3. With thumb and forefinger, lift up and press down the chain at that point, measuring the distance the chain moves vertically.
4. *On the centerstand:* the chain should have about 1-1/4 in. (30 mm) of vertical travel at midpoint (**Figure 30**). If it has less than 1 in. (25 mm) or more than 1-3/8 in. (35 mm) of travel, adjust the chain play.
5. *On the side stand:* the chain should have about 1 in. (25 mm) of vertical travel at midpoint (**Figure 30**). If it has less than 3/4 in. (20 mm) or more than 1-1/4 in. (30 mm) of travel, adjust the chain play.

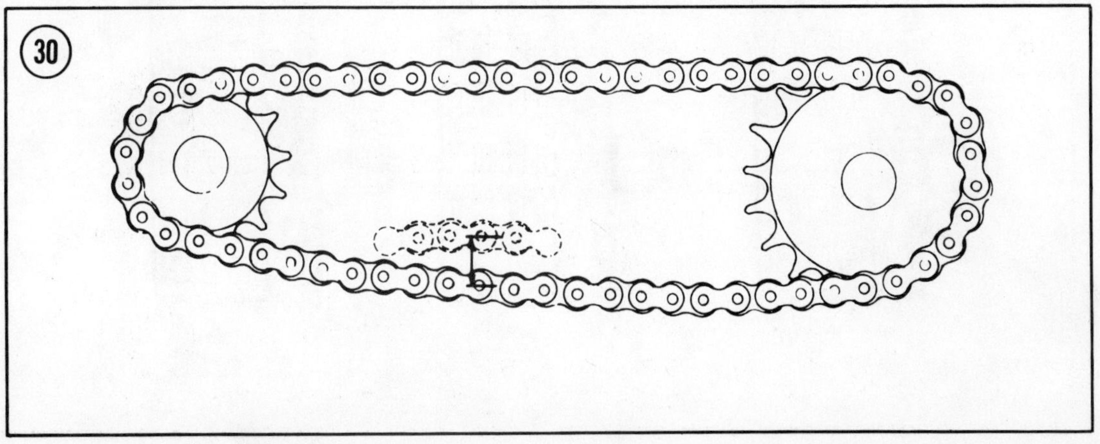

3

Drive Chain Adjustment

When adjusting the drive chain, you must also maintain rear wheel alignment. A misaligned rear wheel can cause poor handling and pulling to one side or the other, as well as increased chain, sprocket, and tire wear. All models have wheel alignment marks on the swing arm and chain adjusters. If both adjusters are moved an equal amount (equal turns of the bolts or equal mark movement), the rear wheel should be aligned correctly.

1. Loosen the rear torque link nut and the axle nut (**Figure 31**).
2. Loosen the locknuts on both chain adjusters (**Figure 31**).
3. *If the chain was too tight,* back out both adjuster bolts an equal amount and kick the rear wheel forward until the chain is too loose.
4. Turn both adjuster bolts in an equal amount until the chain play is within specification. The notch in each chain adjuster should be positioned the same distance along the swing arm alignment marks (**Figure 31**).
5. When chain play is correct, check wheel alignment by sighting along the chain from the rear sprocket. It should leave the sprocket in a

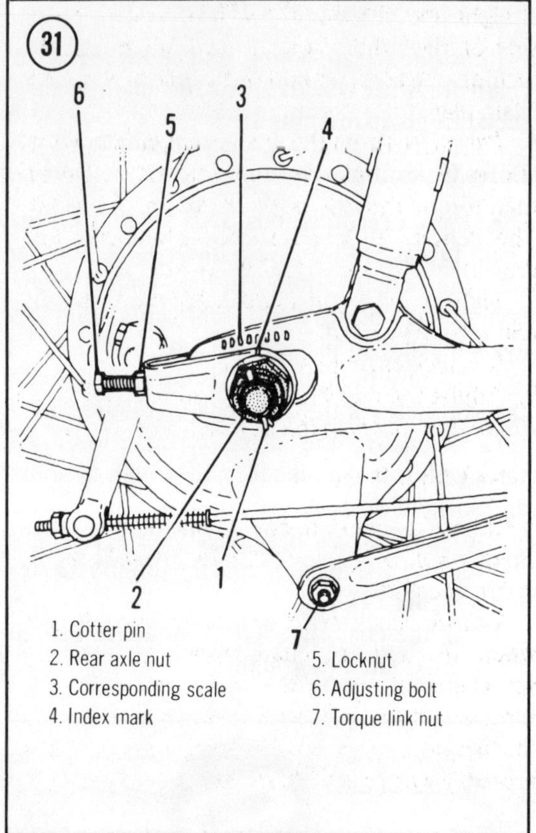

1. Cotter pin
2. Rear axle nut
3. Corresponding scale
4. Index mark
5. Locknut
6. Adjusting bolt
7. Torque link nut

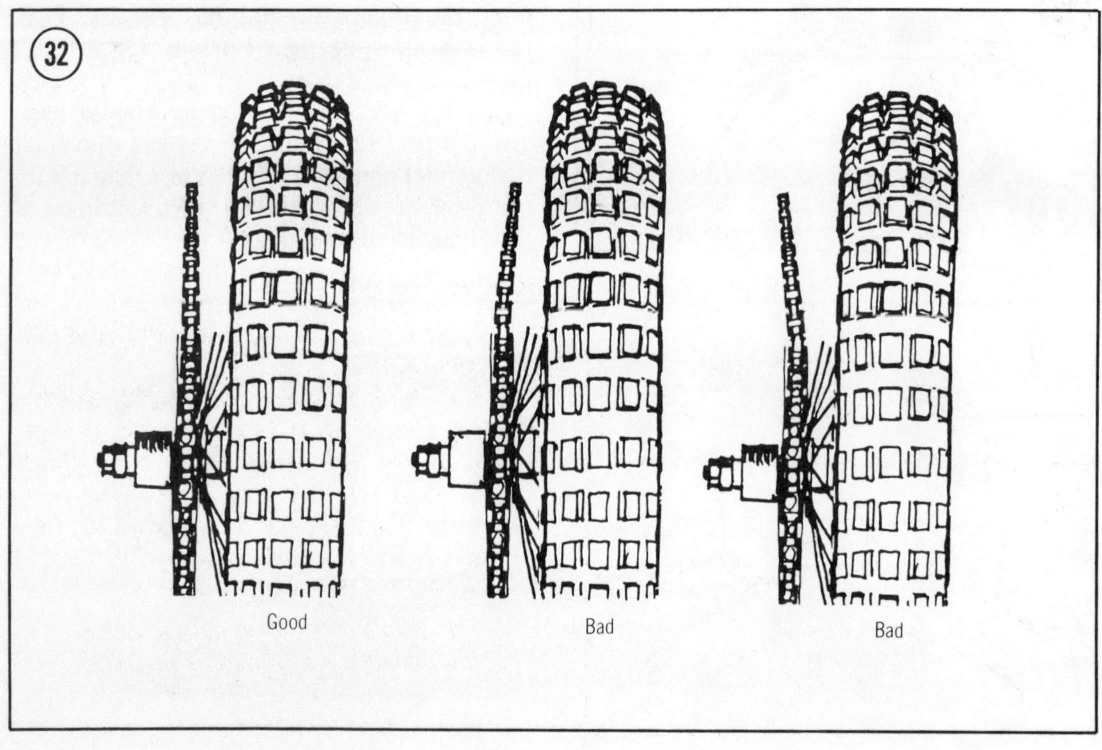

straight line (**Figure 32**). If it is cocked to one side or the other, adjust wheel alignment by turning one adjuster bolt or the other. Recheck chain play.

6. *Partially* tighten the axle nut, spin the wheel and stop it forcefully with the brake pedal, then torque the axle nut to 85 ft.-lb. (12 mkg). This centers the brake shoes in the drum and prevents a "spongy" feeling brake.
7. Tighten the chain adjuster locknuts and the rear torque link nut.
8. Recheck chain play.
9. Adjust the rear brake, if required. See *Rear Brake Adjustment* in this chapter.

Drive Chain Wear

Kawasaki recommends replacing the drive chain when it has worn longer than 2% of its original length.

A quick check will give you an indication of when to measure chain wear: at the rear sprocket pull one of the links away from the sprocket. If the link pulls away more than 1/2 the height of a sprocket tooth, the chain has probably worn out (**Figure 33**).

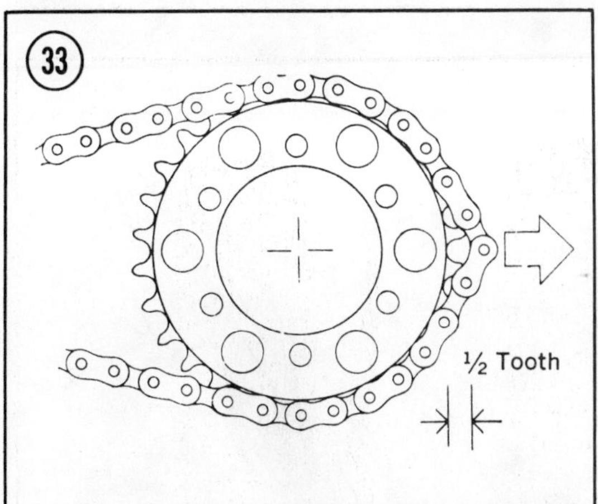

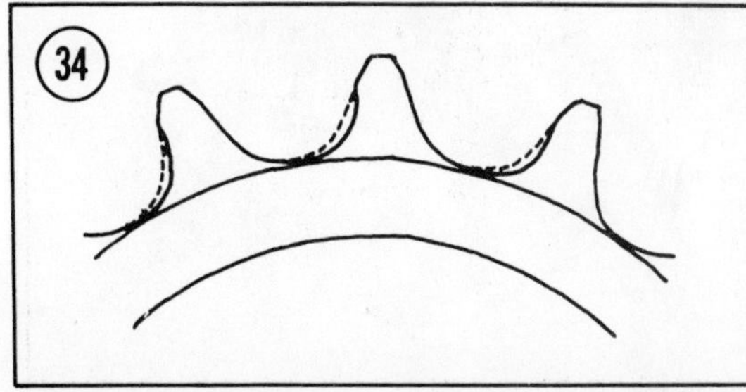

To measure chain wear perform the following:

1. Remove the drive chain and stretch it out tight on a tabletop.
2. Lay a scale along the top chain run and measure the length of any 20 links in the chain, from the center of the first pin you select to the 21st pin. If the 20 link length is more than 12.7 in. (323 mm), install a new drive chain.
3. If the drive chain is worn, inspect the rear wheel and engine drive sprockets for undercutting or sharp teeth (**Figure 34**). If wear is evident, replace the sprockets too or you'll soon wear out your new drive chain.

3

SWING ARM

Swing Arm Lubrication

1. Use a grease gun to force grease into the fitting on the swing arm crossmember, until the grease runs out both ends.
2. If grease will not run out of the ends of the swing arm, unscrew the grease fitting from the swing arm. Clean the fitting and make certain that the ball check valve is free. Reinstall the fitting.
3. Apply the grease gun again. If grease does not run out both ends of the swing arm, remove the swing arm, clean out the old grease, lubricate the bearings and install the swing arm.

STEERING

Steering Play Inspection

1. Prop up the motorcycle so that the front tire clears the ground.
2. Center the front wheel. Push lightly against the left handlebar grip to start the wheel turning to the right, then let go. The wheel should continue turning under its own momentum until the forks hit their stop. Try the same in the other direction.

NOTE

On some bikes, the wiring and control cables tend to stop the wheel movement. If the steering drags, make sure it's not because of wiring stiffness.

3. If the front wheel will not turn all the way to either stop, with a light push in either direction, the steering adjustment is too tight.
4. Center the front wheel and kneel in front of it. Grasp the bottoms of the fork legs. Try to pull the forks toward you and then try to push them toward the engine. If play is felt, the steering adjustment is too loose.
5. If the steering is too tight or too loose, adjust it as described under *Steering Stem Installation* in Chapter Seven.

Steering Head Lubrication

The steering head should be disassembled and the bearings cleaned, inspected for wear, and lubricated with a waterproof grease according to the maintenance schedule given in **Table 1**. Refer to Chapter Seven, *Steering Stem.*

FRONT FORKS

Fork Inspection

Apply the front brake and pump the forks up and down forcefully. You should hear the fork oil as it flows through its passages. There should be no binding. Inspect for fork oil leakage around the fork seals. If there is evidence of leakage, check the fork oil level; see *Fork Oil Change*. Check the upper and lower triple clamp mounting bolts for tightness.

Fork Oil Change

This procedure tells how to change the fork oil without removing the forks from the motorcycle. If the forks are removed and disassembled (Chapter Seven), more of the old oil will be drained.
1. Place a drain pan under the fork and remove the drain bolt (**Figure 35**). Let the fork drain for a few minutes, then pump the fork (keeping your hand on the brake lever) to help expel the oil. Install the drain screw and repeat for the other fork leg.

WARNING
Do not allow the fork oil to contact the brake disc or pads. Stopping power would be greatly reduced.

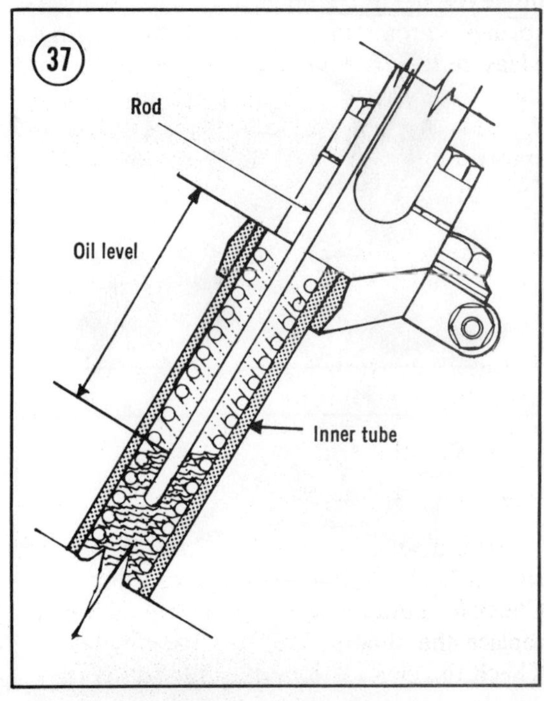

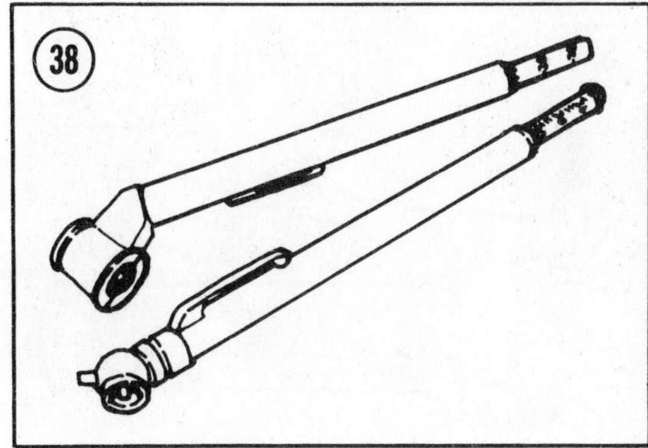

2. Support the bike under the engine so the front wheel clears the ground.
3. Loosen the upper triple clamp bolts, then remove the fork cap bolts (**Figure 36**).
4. Fill the fork tubes with slightly less than the specified quantity of oil. See **Table 4** at the end of the chapter.

NOTE
The amount of oil poured in is not as accurate a measurement as the actual level of the oil. You may have to add more oil later in this procedure.

5. After filling both tubes, slowly pump the forks up and down by hand several times to distribute the oil throughout the fork damper.
6. Refer to **Table 4** and, if your model's fork oil level must be measured with the fork springs removed, remove the springs. Measure the distance from the top of the fork tube to the surface of the oil (**Figure 37**).
7. Add oil, if required, to bring the level up to specification. See **Table 4**. Do not overfill the fork legs.

CAUTION
An excessive amount of oil can cause a hydraulic locking of the forks during compression, destroying the oil seals.

8. Install the fork top caps and tighten the upper triple clamp bolts.

REAR SHOCK ABSORBERS

Rear Shock Inspection

Force the rear of the bike up and down. You should hear the fluid working in the shocks. Check for fluid leakage. If there is fluid leakage replace the shocks; they are not rebuildable. Check the shock mounting bolts for tightness and their rubber bushings for wear. Make sure both shock absorbers are set at the same spring preload.

WHEELS AND TIRES

Tire Pressure

Tire pressure must be checked with the tires cold. Correct tire pressure depends a lot on the load you are carrying and how fast you are going. A simple, accurate gauge (**Figure 38**) can be purchased for a few dollars and should be carried in your motorcycle tool kit. See **Table 5** at the end of the chapter for inflation specifications.

Tire Wear

Check the tread for excessive wear, deep cuts, and imbedded objects such as stones, nails, etc. If you find a nail in a tire, mark its location with a light crayon before pulling it out. This will help locate the hole in the inner tube. Refer to *Tire Changing* in Chapter Seven.

Check local traffic regulations concerning minimum tread depth. Measure with a small ruler. Kawasaki recommends replacement when the front tread depth is 0.04 in. (1 mm) or less. For the rear tire, the recommended limits are 0.08 in. (2 mm) for speeds below 70 mph and 0.12 in. (3 mm) for higher speeds.

Wheel Spokes

Check wire spokes for tightness according to the maintenance schedule given in **Table 1**. The "tuning fork" method for checking spoke tightness is simple and works well. Tap each spoke with a spoke wrench or the shank of a screwdriver and listen to the tone. A tight spoke will emit a clear, ringing tone and a loose spoke will sound flat. All of the spokes in a correctly tightened wheel will sound approximately the same pitch. Tighten any loose spokes with a spoke wrench or a small, adjustable wrench.

Bent or damaged spokes should be replaced as soon as they are detected. Refer to *Spokes*, Chapter Seven.

Wheel Runout

Wheel rim runout is the amount of "wobble" a wheel shows as it rotates. You can check runout with the wheels on the bike by simply supporting the wheel off the ground and turning the wheel slowly while you hold a pointer solidly against a fork leg or the swing arm. Just be sure any wobble you observe isn't caused by your own hand.

The maximum allowable side-to-side runout is about 1/8 in. (3 mm). The up-and-down maximum is about 1/16 in. (2 mm).

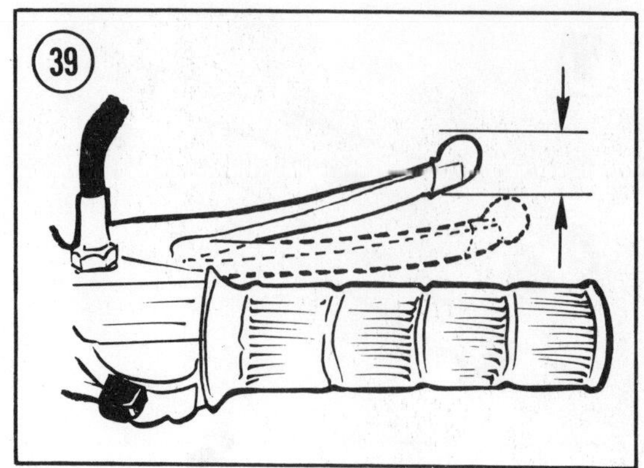

Wheel Bearing Lubrication

The ball bearings in the wheel hubs should be lubricated with high temperature grease according to the maintenance schedule given in **Table 1**. See *Front Hub and Rear Hub*, Chapter Seven.

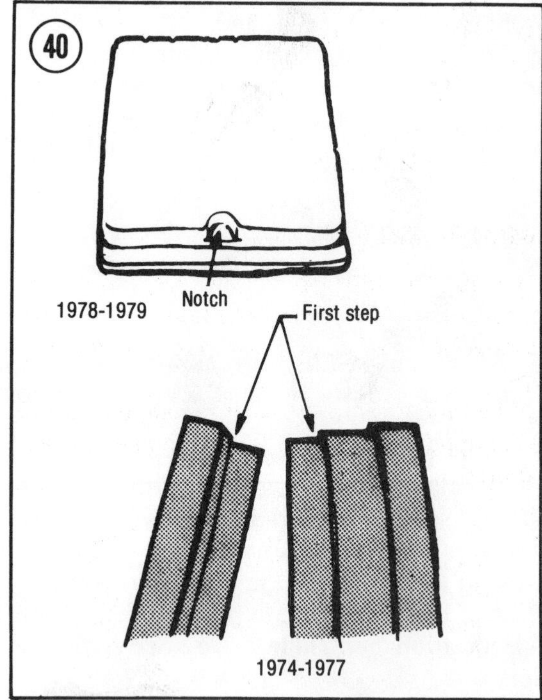

Speedometer Gear Housing Lubrication

The speedometer gears at the front wheel should be lubricated with high temperature grease according to the maintenance schedule given in **Table 1**.

1. Remove the speedometer gear housing; see *Front Hub Disassembly*, Chapter Seven.
2. Pull the grease seal out of the speedometer gear housing and remove the speedometer drive gear.
3. Clean all old grease from the housing and gear and apply high temperature grease.
4. Install a new grease seal and assemble the front wheel; see *Front Hub Assembly*, Chapter Seven.

FRONT DISC BRAKE

Brake Function

Check for a solid feel at the lever. If the hydraulic brake feels spongy, perform *Bleeding Front Brake*, Chapter Seven.

Brake Fluid Level Inspection

On models with translucent reservoirs or transparent windows, check that the fluid level is between the upper and lower level lines or above the lower line. Remove the reservoir cap if you cannot see the fluid level.

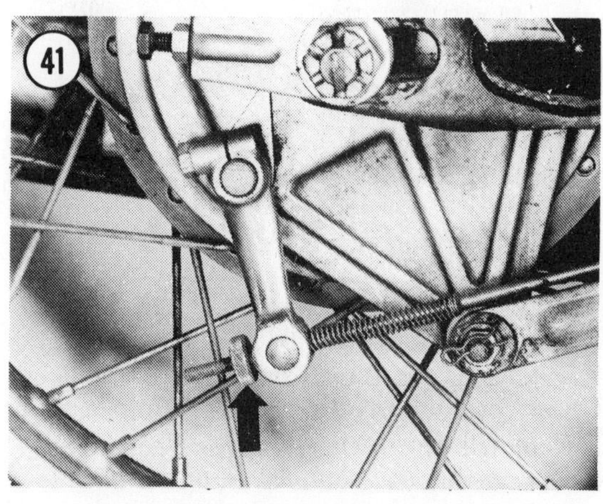

NOTE
Hold the handlebar as close to horizontal as possible when checking fluid level.

Adding Brake Fluid

1. Clean the outside of the reservoir cap thoroughly with a dry rag and remove the cap. Remove the washer and diaphragm under the cap.
2. The fluid level in the reservoir should be up to the upper level line. Add fresh brake fluid as required.

WARNING
Kawasaki recommends DOT 3 brake fluid only. Lower grades may vaporize and cause brake failure. Never use old brake fluid or fluid from a container that has been left unsealed for a long time. Do not leave the reservoir cap off too long or the fluid will absorb moisture from the air and will vaporize more easily.

WARNING
Brake fluid is an irritant. Keep it away from your skin and eyes.

CAUTION
Be careful not to spill brake fluid on painted or plastic surfaces as it will destroy the finish. Wash spills immediately with soapy water and thoroughly rinse.

3. Reinstall the washer, diaphragm, and cap. Make sure that the cap is tightly secured.

Disc Brake Lever Play (1974-1977)

The free play at the lever must be maintained to avoid brake drag. It should be 1/8-3/16 in. (3-5 mm) at the ball end of the lever (**Figure 39**).

Straighten the locking tab on the lockwasher and loosen the locknut under the lever pivot. Turn the adjusting bolt in or out until the proper amount of free play is achieved. After adjustment is completed, tighten the locknut and bend the locking tab up against the locknut.

Pad Wear Inspection

Inspect the disc brake pads for wear according to the maintenance schedule.

1. Apply the front brake.
2. Shine a light between the caliper and the disc (from in front of the fork leg) and inspect the brake pads.
3. If either pad has worn to the bottom of the first step (1974-1977) or to the bottom of the notch (1978-1979), replace both pads as a set. See **Figure 40**. Refer to *Brake Pad Replacement*, Chapter Seven.

REAR DRUM BRAKE

Brake Pedal Travel

Turn the adjustment nut on the end of the brake rod (**Figure 41**) until the brake pedal has 3/4-1 to 1/4 in. (20-30 mm) travel from the rest position to the applied position when the pedal is depressed lightly by hand.

Rotate the rear wheel and check for brake drag. Also operate the pedal several times to make sure it returns to the rest position immediately after release.

Adjust the rear brake light switch.

Brake Light Switch Adjustment

1. Turn the ignition switch ON.
2. Depress the brake pedal. The light should come on just as the brake begins to work.
3. To make the light come on earlier, hold the switch body (**Figure 42**) and turn the adjusting locknuts to move the switch body *up*. Move the switch body *down* to delay the light. Tighten the locknuts.

NOTE
Some riders prefer having the light come on a little early. This way, they can tap the pedal without braking to warn drivers who follow too closely.

Brake Pedal Height

Brake pedal *height adjustment* should not be routinely required once you have set it to your preference, but it does affect pedal travel. Normal brake pedal height is about 1 in. (20-30 mm) below the top of the footpeg.

1. Loosen the locknut (B, **Figure 43**) and turn the adjustment bolt (A) to achieve the correct pedal height.
2. Tighten the locknut.
3. Adjust brake pedal play.

Lining Wear Inspection

Inspect the brake linings for wear according to the maintenance schedule given in **Table 1**.

1. Apply the brake fully.
2. Check the brake lining wear indicator on the backing plate (**Figure 44**). When the wear indicator pointer moves out of the USABLE RANGE, disassemble the brake and inspect the linings. See *Drum Brake Inspection*, Chapter Seven.
3. The brake cam lever should form an angle of 80-90° with the brake rod (**Figure 45**). If the angle exceeds 100°, disassemble the brake and inspect the linings. See *Drum Brake Inspection*, Chapter Seven.

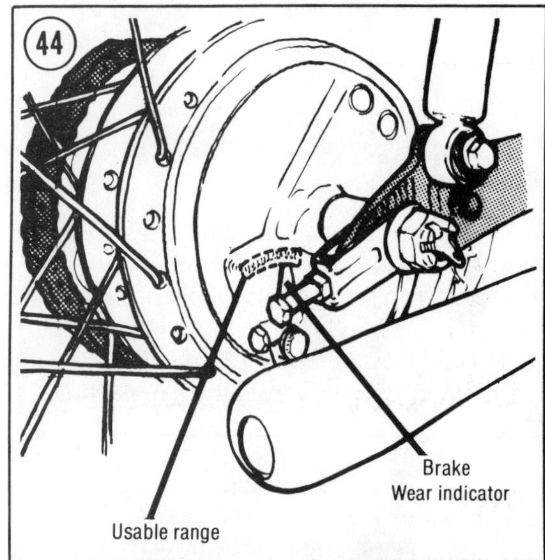

Brake Lubrication

The brake cam and pivot (**Figure 46**) should be lubricated according to the maintenance schedule given in **Table 1**. Refer to Chapter Seven, *Drum Brake Assembly*.

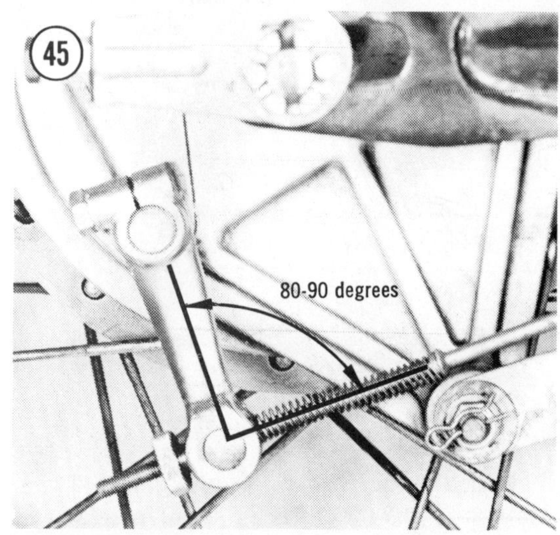

FRONT DRUM BRAKE

Brake Lever Play

Normal free play is about 3/16 in. (4-5 mm) at the cable end of the lever (**Figure 47**).

To adjust lever play, loosen the large knurled locknut on the brake lever and turn the adjuster until the desired brake cable free play is achieved. If, due to brake wear, the adjustment at the hand lever is used up, turn

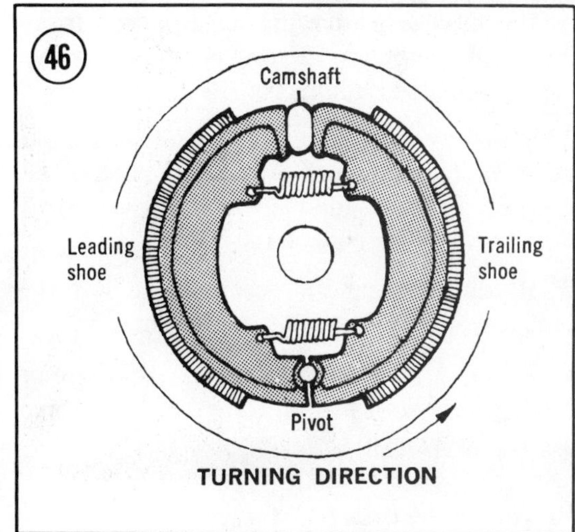

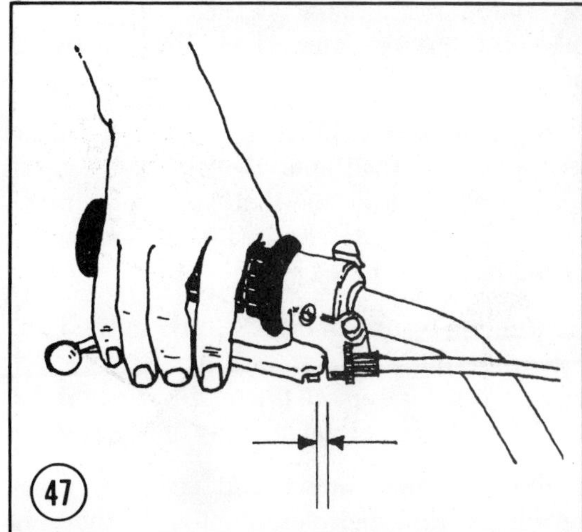

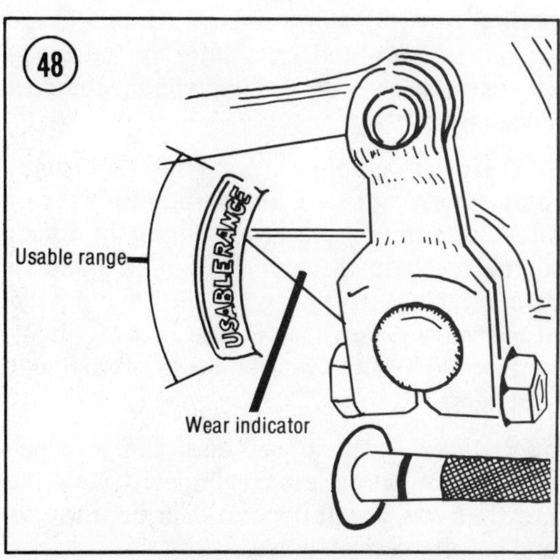

the adjuster at the lower end of the cable until brake lever free play is as desired.

Lining Wear Inspection

Inspect the brake linings for wear according to the maintenance schedule in **Table 1**.

1. Apply the brake fully.
2. Check the brake lining wear indicator on the backing plate (**Figure 48**). When the wear indicator pointer moves out of the USABLE RANGE, disassemble the brake and inspect the linings. See *Drum Brake Inspection*, Chapter Seven.

Brake Shoe Synchronization

The front brake's double leading shoes must be synchronized for effective braking. Normally, synchronization will not be required unless the front wheel is removed or the brake is disassembled.

1. Apply the front brake fully.
2. Both brake cam levers should form an angle of 80-90° with the brake rod (**Figure 45**). If either lever's angle exceeds 100°, disassemble the brake and inspect the linings. See *Drum Brake Inspection*, Chapter Seven.
3. Loosen the locknut on the brake lever connecting link (B, **Figure 49**) and lengthen the connecting link (back it out) one turn to loosen the rear shoe.
4. Support the front wheel off the ground and spin it. Turn the adjuster (A, **Figure 49**) until the wheel just begins to drag.

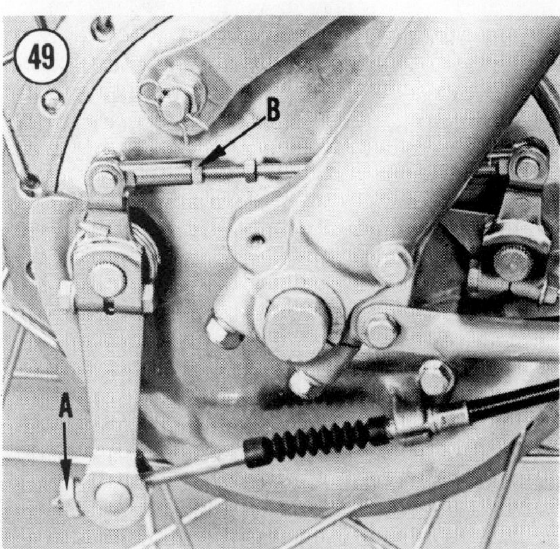

5. Spin the wheel again and shorten the connecting link (turn it in) until the drag from the rear shoe just becomes noticeable. Tighten the locknut (B, **Figure 49**).
6. Adjust free play at the lower cable adjuster (A, **Figure 49**).

Brake Lubrication

The brake cam and pivot (**Figure 46**) should be lubricated according to the maintenance schedule (**Table 1**). Refer to Chapter Seven, *Drum Brake Assembly*.

NUTS, BOLTS, FASTENERS

Check all exposed nuts, bolts, cotter pins, safety clips and circlips. Pay particular attention to:

a. Control lever, pedal, and linkage pivots
b. Engine mount bolts
c. Handlebar clamp bolts
d. Top triple clamp bolts
e. Bottom triple clamp bolts
f. Front axle clamp nuts
g. Shock absorber mounts
h. Swing arm pivot
i. Rear brake torque link
j. Rear axle nut

This check is *especially* important on high mileage machines.

STORAGE

Several months of inactivity can cause problems and a general deterioration of bike condition if proper care is neglected. This is especially true in areas of weather extremes. During the winter months you should prepare your bike carefully for "hibernation."

Selecting a Storage Area

Most cyclists store their bikes in their home garages. If you do not have a garage, facilities suitable for long-term motorcycle storage are available for rent or lease in most areas. In selecting a building, consider the following points.

1. The storage area must be dry, free from excessive dampness. Heating is not necessary, but an insulated building is preferable.

2. Buildings with large window areas should be avoided, or such windows should be masked (also a good security measure) if direct sunlight can fall on the bike.

3. If you live near the ocean, make sure the area is sealed against salt spray and mist.

4. Select an area with minimum risk of fire or theft. Check your insurance to see if your bike is covered while in storage.

Preparing the Bike for Storage

Careful preparation will minimize deterioration and make it easier to restore the bike to service later. Use the following procedure.

1. Wash the bike completely. Make certain to remove any road salt which may have accumulated during the first weeks of winter. Wax all painted and polished surfaces, including any chromed areas.

2. Run the engine until it is fully warmed up. Drain the oil, regardless of mileage since the last oil change. Replace the oil filter and fill the engine with the normal quantity of fresh oil.

3. Remove the battery and coat the cable terminals with petroleum jelly. If there is evidence of acid spillage in the battery box, neutralize with baking soda, wash clean, and repaint the damaged area. Store the battery in an area where it will not freeze and recharge it once a month.

4. Drain all gasoline from the fuel tank, interconnecting hoses, and carburetors. As an alternative, a fuel preservative may be added to the fuel and the tank should be filled to minimize water condensation. These preservatives are available from many motorcycle shops and marine equipment suppliers.

5. Remove spark plugs and add a small quantity of oil to each cylinder. Crank the engine a few revolutions to distribute the oil and install the spark plugs.

6. Check the tire pressures. Move the machine to the storage area and store it on the centerstand.
7. Cover the bike with material that will allow air circulation. Don't use plastic.

Inspection During Storage

Try to inspect bike weekly while in storage. Any deterioration should be corrected as soon as possible. For example, if corrosion of bright metal parts is observed, cover them with a light film of grease or silicone spray.

Restoring to Service

A bike that has been properly prepared and stored in a suitable area, requires only light maintenance to restore it to service. It is advisable, however, to perform a spring tune-up.

1. Before removing the bike from the storage area, re-inflate tires to the correct pressures. Air loss during storage period may have nearly flattened the tires, and moving the bike can cause damage to the tires, tubes, or rims.
2. When the bike is brought to the work area, immediately install the battery. If fuel preservative was used, drain the system, then fill the fuel tank. The fuel shutoff valve is in the RESERVE position; do not move yet.
the carburetor float bowl and allow several cups of fuel to pass through the system.
4. Remove the cylinder protector and install a fresh spark plug.

NOTE
Prior to installation of the spark plug, squirt a small amount of fuel into the cylinder to help remove the oil coating.

5. *Do not* attach the spark plug wire. Kick the engine over a couple of times, then connect the spark plug wire and start up the engine.

6. Perform the normal tune-up as described earlier in this chapter.

7. Check safety items such as lights, horn, etc., as oxidation of switch contacts and/or sockets during storage may make one of these critical devices inoperative.

8. Test ride and clean the motorcycle.

Table 1 MAINTENANCE SCHEDULE

Weekly / Gas Stop Maintenance	
Tire pressure	Check cold and adjust to suit load and speed
Brake function	Check for a solid feel
Brake lever play (1974-1977)	Check and adjust if necessary
Brake pedal play	Check and adjust if necessary
Throttle grip return	Check for smooth opening and return
Clutch lever play	Check and adjust if necessary
Steering	Smooth but not loose
Drive chain	Lubricate every 200 miles (300 km) Check and adjust play if necessary
Drive belt tension	Inspect with tension gauge
Nuts, bolts, fasteners	Check axles, suspension, controls and linkage
Engine oil	Check level
Lights and horn	Check operation, especially brake light
Engine noise and leaks	Check
Kill switch	Check operation
Monthly / 3,000 Mile (5,000 km) Maintenance	
Battery electrolyte level	Check and add water (check more frequently in hot weather)
Disc brake fluid level	Check and add if necessary
(continued)	

Table 1 MAINTENANCE SCHEDULE (continued)

6 Month/3,000 Mile (5,000 km) Maintenance	
All items above, plus:	
Air filter	Clean or replace
Fuel system	Clean fuel tap and float bowls
Spark plugs	Clean, set gap and replace if necessary
Cam chain (1974-1979)	Adjust tension
Valve clearance	Check and adjust
Contact points	Clean, adjust gap and lube cam
Ignition timing	Check and adjust
Throttle cables	Check and adjust free play
Carburetors	Adjust idle and synchronize
Engine oil and filter	Change (filter every other time)
General lubrication	Lube cables, levers, pedals, pivots, throttle grip
Clutch	Adjust clutch release
Tires	Check wear
Wire spokes and rim runout	Check
Drive chain wear	Check
Brake pad/lining wear	Check
Steering play	Check and adjust if necessary
Suspension	Check
Yearly/6,000 Mile (10,000 km) Maintenance	
All items above, plus:	
Fork oil	Change
Brake fluid	Change
Air filter	Replace
Ignition advance	Lubricate
Nuts, bolts, fasteners	Check/tighten all
Swing arm	Lubricate pivot
2 Year/12,000 Mile (20,000 km) Maintenance	
All items above, plus:	
Speedometer gear housing	Grease
Wheel bearings	Grease
Steering bearings	Grease
Drum brake cam and pivot post	Grease

Table 2 MODEL YEAR/SUFFIX EQUIVALENTS

1974	1975	1976	1977
KZ400	KZ400S	KZ400-S2	KZ400-S3
—	KZ400D	KZ400-D3	KZ400-D4
—	—	—	KZ400-A1 (Deluxe)
—	—	—	—
—	—	—	—

1978	1979	1980
KZ400-C1	—	KZ440-A1 (LTD chain)
KZ400-B1	KZ400-B2	Z440-A1 (European)
KZ400-A2 (Deluxe)	KZ400-H1 (LTD)	KZ440-B1
—	—	Z440-C1 (European)
—	—	KZ440-D1 (LTD belt)

Table 3 TUNE-UP SPECIFICATIONS

Spark Plugs	
Type	
1978 and later	B7ES (NGK) or W22ES-U (ND)
1974-1977	B8ES (NGK) or W24ES (ND)
Gap	0.028-0.032 in. (0.7-0.8 mm)
Breaker Points	
Gap	0.014 in. (0.35 mm)
Dwell	53% (193 degrees)
Valve Clearance (Cold, Intake and Exhaust)	
1978 and later	0.007-0.009 in. (0.17-0.22 mm)
1977	0.005-0.006 in. (0.13-0.15 mm)
1974-1976	0.004-0.006 in. (0.10-0.15 mm)
Idle Speed	
All models	1,100-1,300 rpm
Idle Mixture (Turns Out From Seated)	
1979 H	2 1/4
1979 B	1 1/4
1978	1 1/4
1977	1 1/2
1976	1 5/8
1975	1 1/2
1974	7/8

Table 4 STANDARD FORK OIL

Year/Model	Dry Capacity		Oil Level*		Oil Grade
	U.S. fl. oz.	cc	Inch	mm	SAE
1979-on A, D, H	5.1	150	R 18.7	R 475	5W20
1979-on B, C	5.1	150	R 17.1	R 435	5W20
1978	5.1	150	R 17.1	R 435	5W20
1977	5.4	160	I 13.5	I 343	5W20
1974-1976	5.4	160	I 13.8	I 350	5W20

* Fork oil level is checked with forks fully extended; R: fork springs removed, I: fork springs installed.

Table 5 TIRES AND TIRE PRESSURE

Model/Tire Size	Pressure @ Load (psi @ lb.)		
1979 H			
Front - 3.25S-19 4PR	25 @ 0-215		25 @ over 215
Rear - 130/90-16 67S	21 @ 0-215		25 @ over 215
1979 B			
Front - 3.00S-18 4PR	25 @ 215		25 @ over 215
Rear - 3.50S-18 4PR	28 @ 0-215		36 @ over 215
1977-1978 A			
Front - 3.25S-18 4PR	32 @ 0-280	32 @ 280-330	32 @ over 330
Rear - 3.50S-18 6PR	32 @ 0-280	36 @ 280-330	40 @ over 330
1974-1977 D, S			
Front - 3.25S-18 4PR	25 @ 0-215		25 @ over 215
Rear - 3.50S-18 4PR	28 @ 0-215		36 @ over 215

NOTE: If you own a 1980 or later model, first check the Supplement at the back of the book for any new service information.

CHAPTER FOUR

ENGINE, TRANSMISSION, AND CLUTCH

The Kawasaki KZ400 is equipped with a vertical twin engine. Valves are operated by a chain-driven overhead camshaft. The crankshaft and pistons are so arranged that cylinders fire alternately; while either piston is at firing position on its compression stroke, the other piston is on its exhaust stroke.

Many engine components may be serviced without removing the engine from the frame. The cylinder head, cylinders, and pistons are all accessible, as are the primary sprockets, clutch, oil pump, and external shift linkage. On the left side of the engine are the clutch release mechanism, engine sprocket, alternator, starter, and starter drive mechanism. All of these items may be serviced with the engine in place.

Models B and C Component Variation

The engine in the KZ400 Models B and C is basically the same as that in Models D and S with the exception of the cylinder head components and the balancer assembly.

The clutch is modified to eliminate the steel rings and the shifter mechanism has the addition of an overshift limiter.

The transmission in the Model B has a 6-speed unit and the Model C has a 5-speed one that is different from Models D and S.

The majority of engine disassembly, inspection, and assembly procedures are the same. Where differences occur throughout this chapter, they are identified.

PREPARATION FOR ENGINE DISASSEMBLY

1. If the engine runs, warm it to operating temperature, then drain as much oil as possible. Otherwise drain oil with the engine cold.
2. Thoroughly clean engine of dirt, grease, and foreign material, using one of the preparation formulated for the purpose.
3. Be sure that you have the proper tools for the job. Snap ring pliers are required for some operations and a rotor puller is necessary if the alternator rotor is to be removed. A rubber mallet will be a big help.
4. Clean all parts thoroughly upon removal, then place them in trays, together with their associated mounting hardware, in the order of disassembly.
5. Pay particular attention to the way that all small parts, such as spacers and thrust washers, are installed. It is very easy to forget the way they came apart. Make rough sketches of parts layout if necessary.

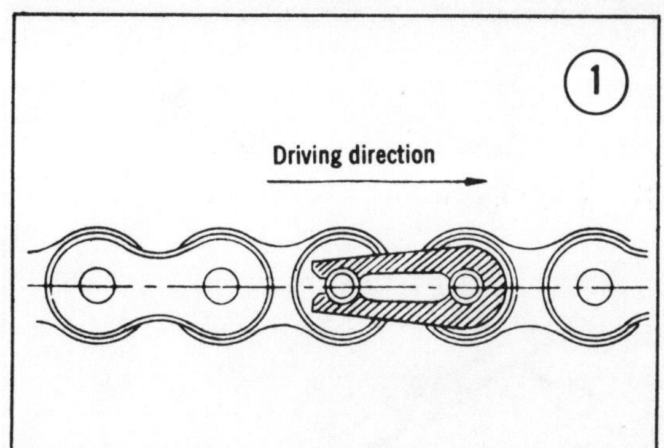

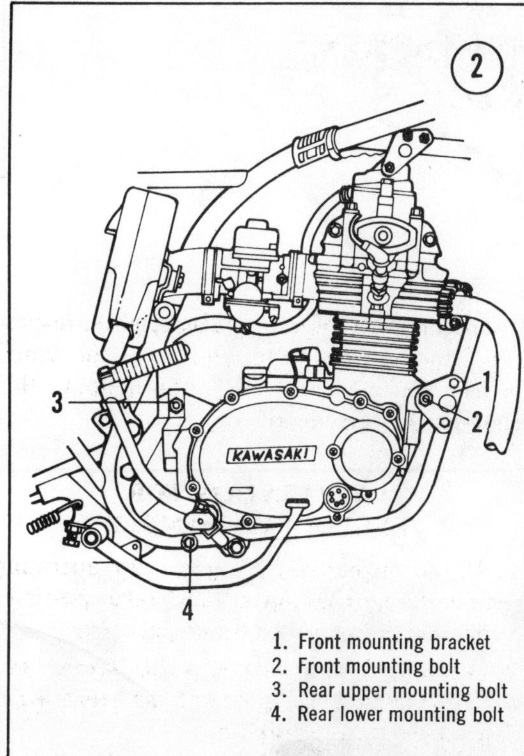

1. Front mounting bracket
2. Front mounting bolt
3. Rear upper mounting bolt
4. Rear lower mounting bolt

6. There are numerous O-rings in KZ400 engines. Note where they are and be sure to replace them all upon reassembly.

7. Many engine components are retained by Phillips screws. Don't try to loosen these with a screwdriver; use an impact driver.

8. In general, all parts should come apart easily, without undue force. If some part seems difficult to remove or install, stop and check to see what might be the problem. Frequently a retaining screw is missed, or perhaps a snap ring. Don't force anything.

ENGINE REMOVAL

1. Place motorcycle on its centerstand.
2. Turn fuel petcock to STOP; disconnect fuel lines at each carburetor. Open seat. Unhook rubber fuel tank retaining band; lift fuel tank upward and to rear to remove it.
3. Disconnect cables from each spark plug.
4. Disconnect plug from blue breaker point wire where it joins blue wire in harness. Remove breaker point wire clips from frame tube.
5. Remove tachometer cable at cylinder head.
6. Remove both side covers.
7. Disconnect both white plugs from under voltage regulator. Note that there is a lock tab on each plug.
8. Remove starter cable from starter relay.
9. Disconnect breather hose at breather cover on top of engine.
10. Loosen rubber ducts at each carburetor.
11. Work carburetors out from ducts, then pull carburetors free.
12. Remove each muffler and exhaust pipe as a unit.
13. Place transmission in NEUTRAL. Remove shift pedal pinch bolt. Remove shift pedal.
14. Remove left footpeg and kickstand spring.
15. Remove engine sprocket cover. If engine sprocket is to be removed, bend its lock tab, then apply rear brake and loosen sprocket retaining nut.
16. Turn rear wheel until master link is in position for removal. Remove master link. Remove drain chain. Assemble master link to chain to prevent it from becoming lost. Upon installation, position master link as shown in **Figure 1**.
17. Remove breather cover-to-frame brace.
18. Remove breather cover.
19. Remove rear stoplight switch.
20. Remove engine mount bolts. See **Figure 2**. Take note of spacer locations.
21. Remove left front engine mount bracket.
22. Remove straps which secure clutch cable to frame tube, then move engine sprocket cover well forward, away from engine area.
23. Straddle frame. Tilt engine upward at front, then remove it from left side of frame.

4

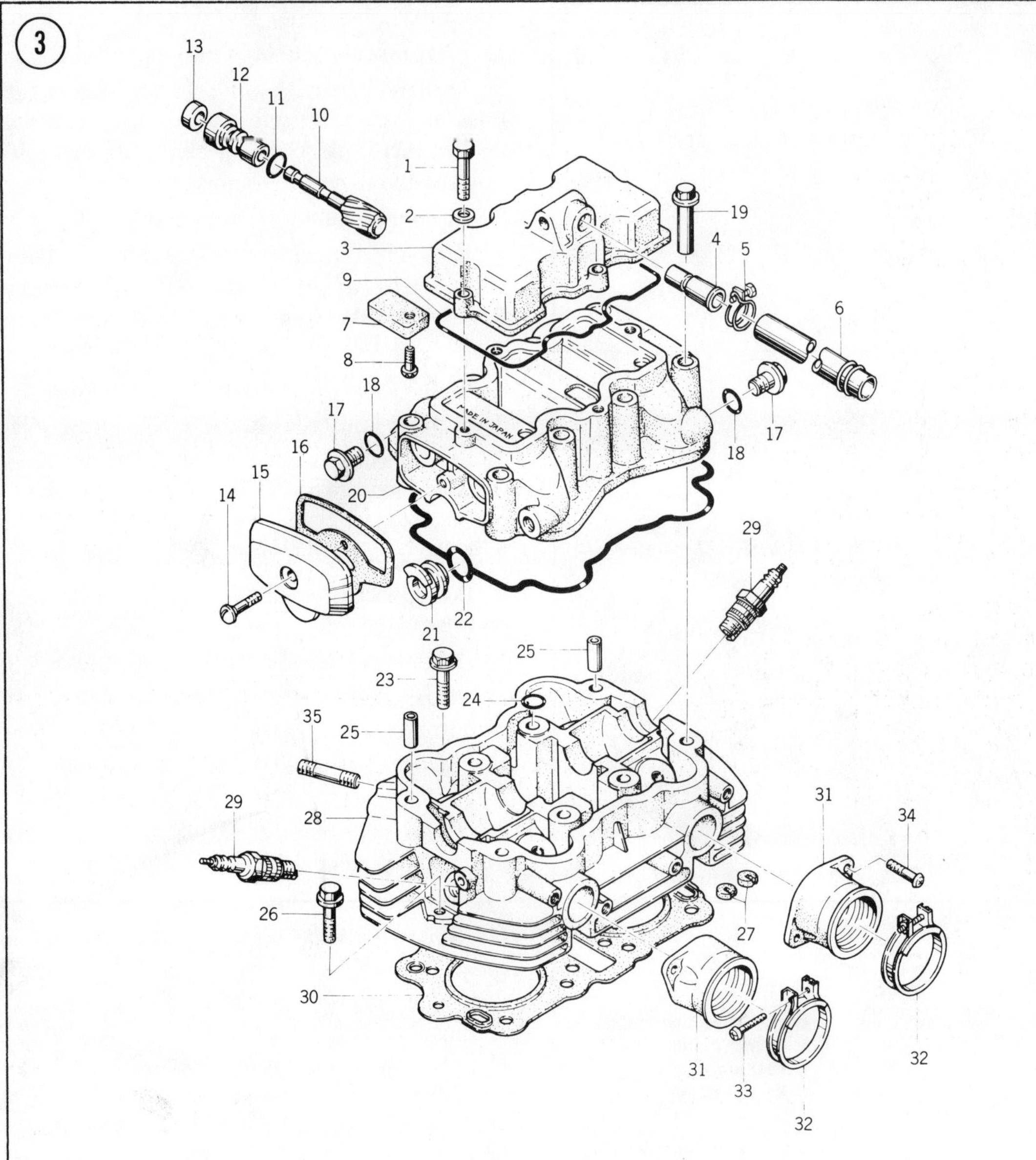

CYLINDER HEAD AND CYLINDER HEAD COVER — MODELS D AND S

1. Bolt
2. Washer
3. Breather cover
4. Connector
5. Clamp
6. Hose
7. Plate
8. Screw
9. O-ring
10. Tachometer gear
11. O-ring
12. Guide
13. Oil seal
14. Screw
15. Cap
16. Gasket
17. Plug
18. O-ring
19. Nut
20. Cylinder head cover
21. Plug
22. O-ring
23. Bolt
24. O-ring
25. Dowel
26. Bolt
27. Damper
28. Cylinder head
29. Spark plug
30. Gasket
31. Duct
32. Clamp
33. Screw
34. Screw
35. Stud

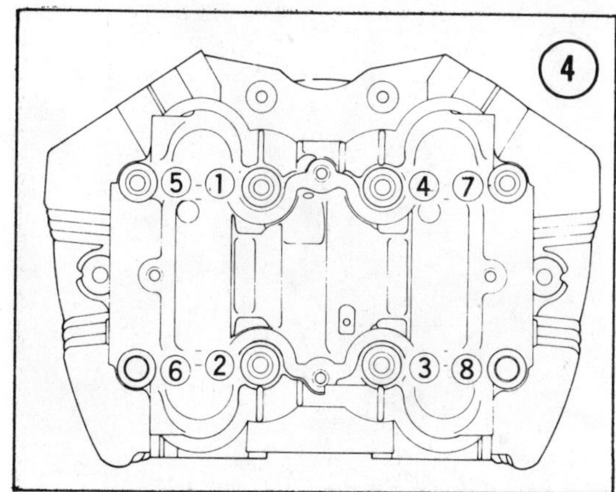

4

5

6

24. Reverse the removal procedure to install the engine. Before starting it, check the following items:

a. Oil supply
b. Valve adjustment
c. Drive chain adjustment
d. Clutch adjustment
e. Throttle cable adjustment
f. Engine mounting bolt tightness (see **Table 1** at end of chapter)
g. Fuel line connections
h. Ignition timing

CYLINDER HEAD AND CYLINDER HEAD COVER (MODEL D AND S)

Figure 3 is an exploded view of the cylinder head and cylinder head cover. Refer to that illustration during service on those components.

The cylinder head cover contains the rocker arms and their shafts. It also forms the upper surfaces of the camshaft bearings.

Cylinder Head Cover Removal

Refer to **Figure 4**. Remove each retaining nut in the order shown. Tap the cover lightly with a rubber mallet, if necessary, then lift it from the cylinder head (**Figure 5**).

Rocker Arm Removal/Installation

If it is necessary to remove the rocker arms, proceed as follows:

1. Remove side cover (**Figure 6**).
2. Remove valve adjuster locknuts, then pull off plates (**Figure 7**).
3. Carefully tape the jaws of a pair of pliers, then pull out rocker shafts.
4. Lift rocker arm as rocker shaft comes out (**Figure 8**).

Inspect both contact surfaces of each rocker arm for damage or uneven wear. Replace any rocker arm that exhibits such defects. Measure inside diameter of each rocker arm. Standard diameter is 0.512 in. (13.0mm). Replace any arm that is worn to 0.514 in. (13.05mm).

Measure diameter of each rocker shaft where it passes through the rocker arm. Replace any shaft worn to 0.509 in. (12.94mm). Standard diameter is 0.511 in. (12.97mm).

Upon assembly, apply engine oil to the O-ring and all bearing surfaces. Be sure that rocker arms are installed so that their large ends

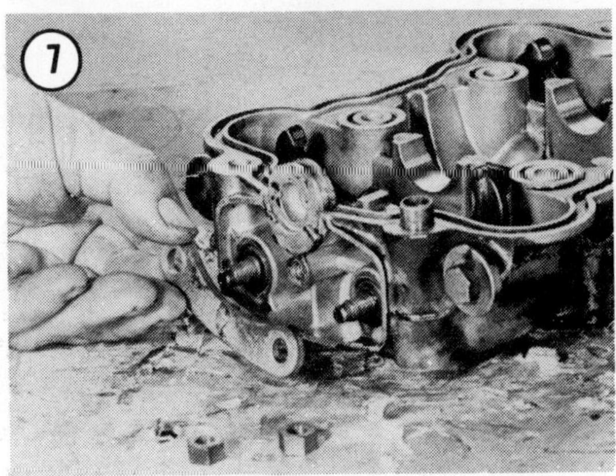

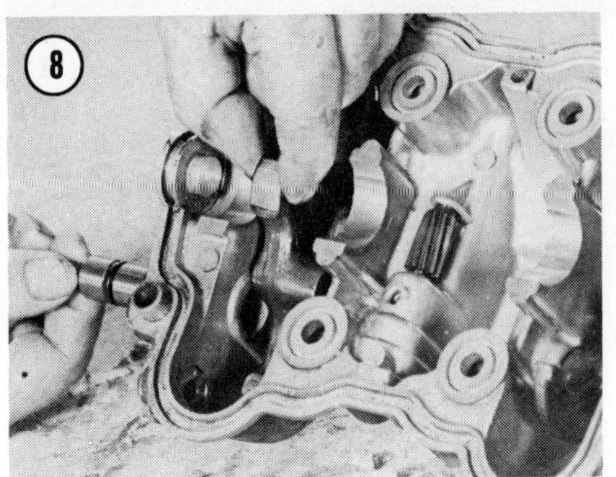

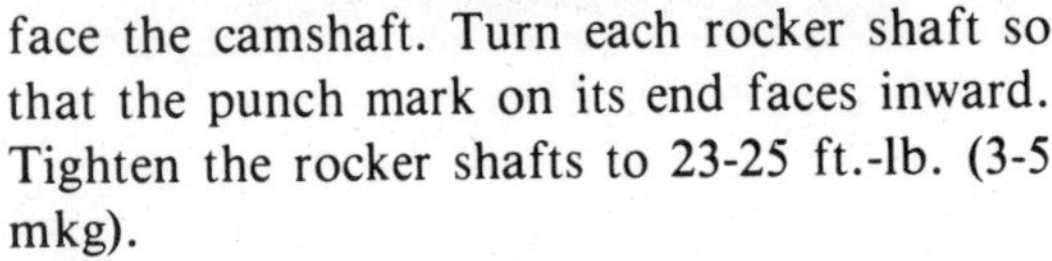

face the camshaft. Turn each rocker shaft so that the punch mark on its end faces inward. Tighten the rocker shafts to 23-25 ft.-lb. (3-5 mkg).

Cylinder Head Cover Installation

1. Remove both spark plugs.
2. Remove breaker cover, then turn engine counterclockwise until "T" mark on advance mechanism aligns with pointer.
3. Be sure that all small O-rings are in place. Apply gasket sealer to large O-ring.
4. Carefully position cylinder head cover, then tighten retaining nuts to 13.0-16.5 ft.-lb. (1.8-2.3 mkg) in the order shown in **Figure 4**.

Camshaft and Cylinder Head Removal

1. Remove cam chain tensioner cover, then cam chain tensioner mechanism **(Figure 9)**.
2. Remove cam sprocket bolts **(Figure 10)**. Turn engine as necessary with a wrench on the larger bolt under the breaker cover.
3. Slide cam sprocket along camshaft until chain can be removed from sprocket.
4. Remove camshaft and sprocket together **(Figure 11)**.

> NOTE: *Prevent the cam chain from dropping into the engine by inserting a screwdriver or similar tool through it.*

Measure height of each cam lobe **(Figure 12)**. Standard height is 0.884 in. (22.45mm). Replace the camshaft if any lobe is worn to 0.878 in. (22.30mm) or is badly scuffed or otherwise damaged.

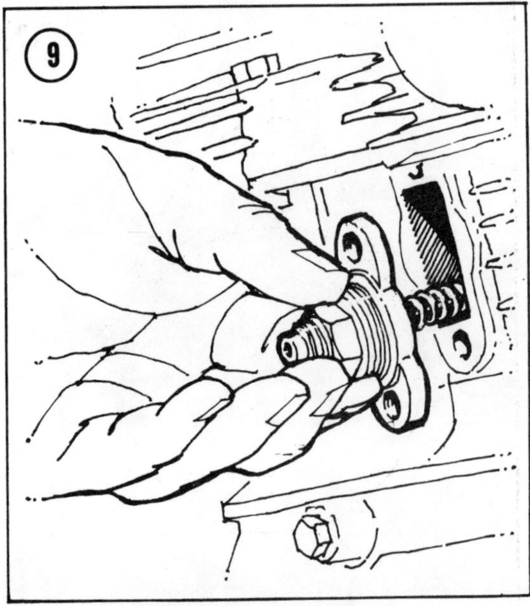

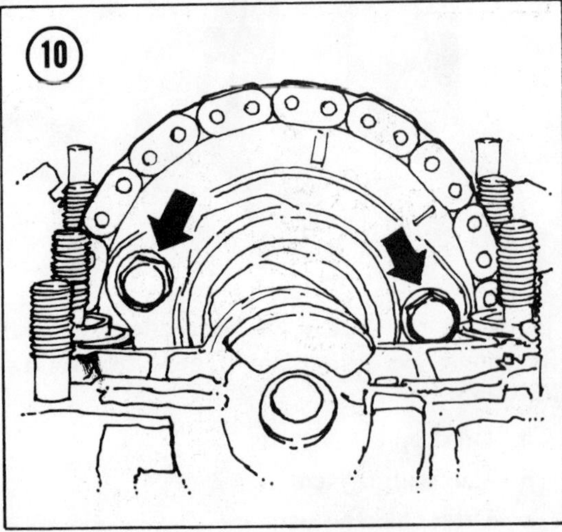

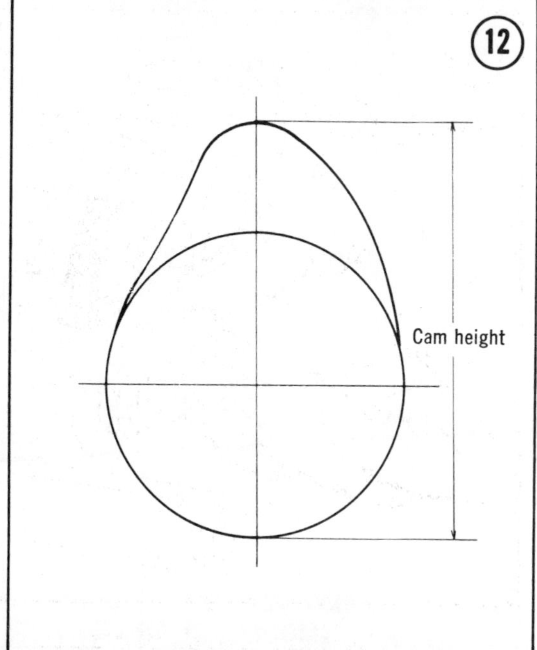

Measure diameter of each camshaft journal. Standard diameter is 1.100 in. (27.955mm). Replace the camshaft if any journal is worn to 1.099 in. (27.91mm) or is otherwise defective.

Measure clearance between each camshaft journal and its bearing. Standard clearance is 0.0013 in. (0.033mm). Replace the camshaft and/or the cylinder head and cylinder head cover if clearance exceeds 0.008 in. (0.18mm).

Camshaft bearing clearance is most easily measured with Plastigage, which is available at auto parts stores. Be sure to specify the approximate measurement range desired. Follow the instructions on the envelope exactly.

Place the camshaft outer bearings in V-blocks or some other suitable centering device, then measure runout at its center. Runout on a new camshaft is less than 0.0008 in. (0.02mm). Replace the camshaft if runout exceeds 0.004 in. (0.10mm).

Remove the remaining cylinder head bolts, then lift it from the engine (**Figure 13**). Tap it lightly with a rubber mallet to free it, if necessary.

Cylinder Head Disassembly

Cylinder head service is generally a job for a shop with facilities for such work. The following material is set forth for those with the necessary skills and equipment. Refer to **Figure 14**.

1. Using a valve spring compressor designed for small engines, compress each valve spring until both keepers (**Figure 15**) may be removed.

4

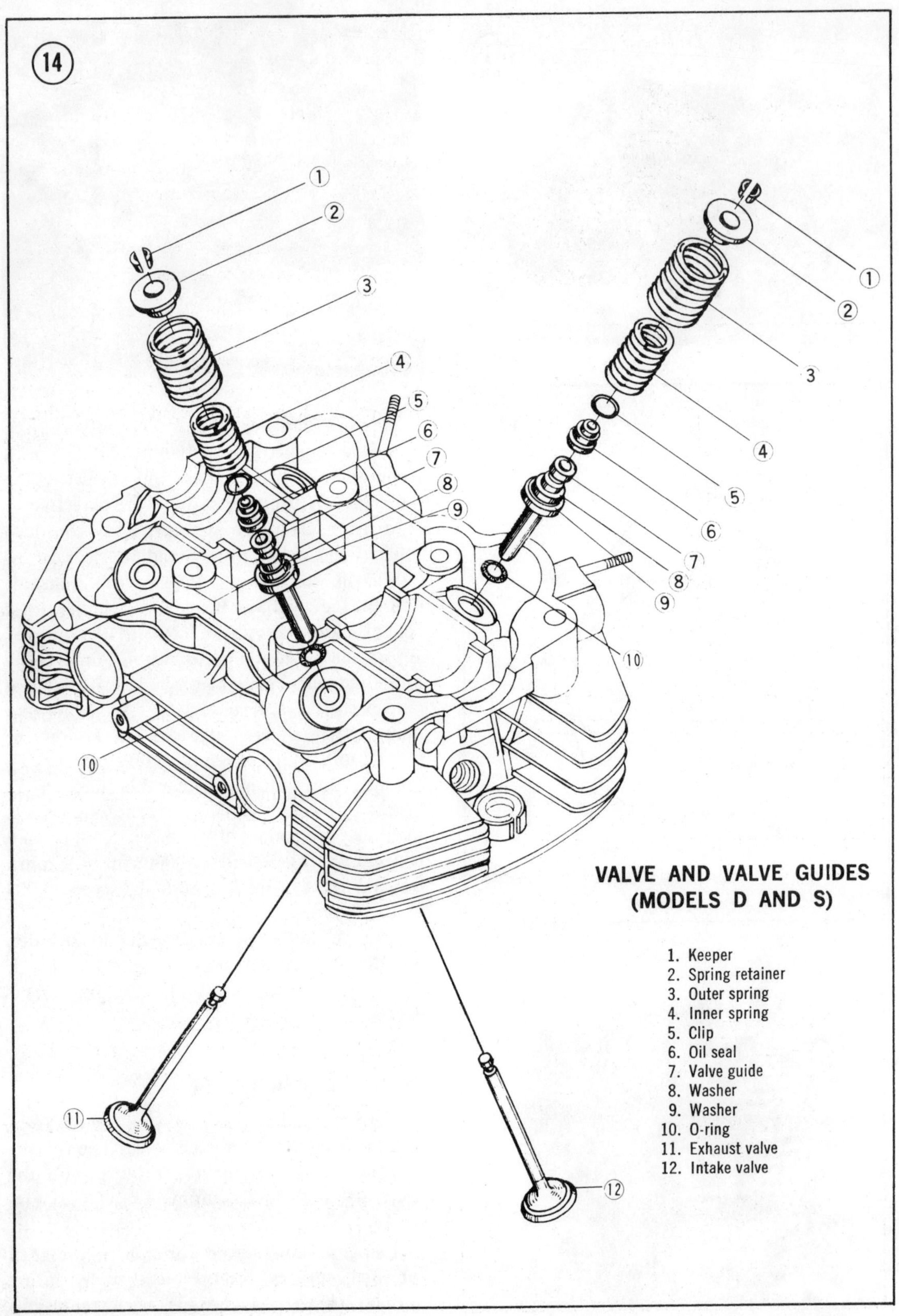
14
1
2
3
4
5
6
7
8
9
10
11
12
VALVE AND VALVE GUIDES
(MODELS D AND S)
1. Keeper
2. Spring retainer
3. Outer spring
4. Inner spring
5. Clip
6. Oil seal
7. Valve guide
8. Washer
9. Washer
10. O-ring
11. Exhaust valve
12. Intake valve

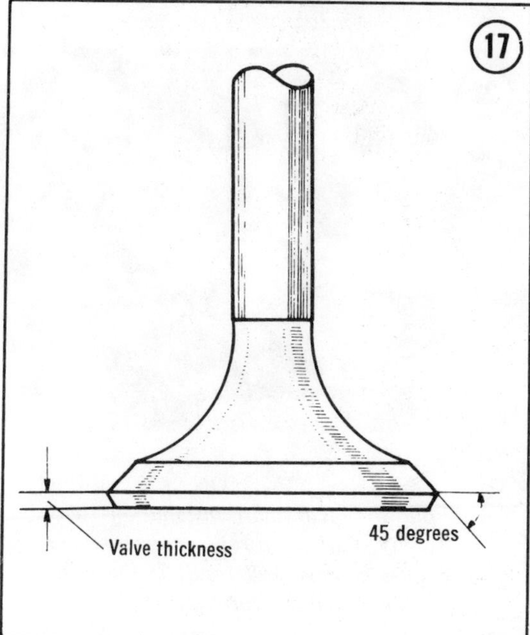

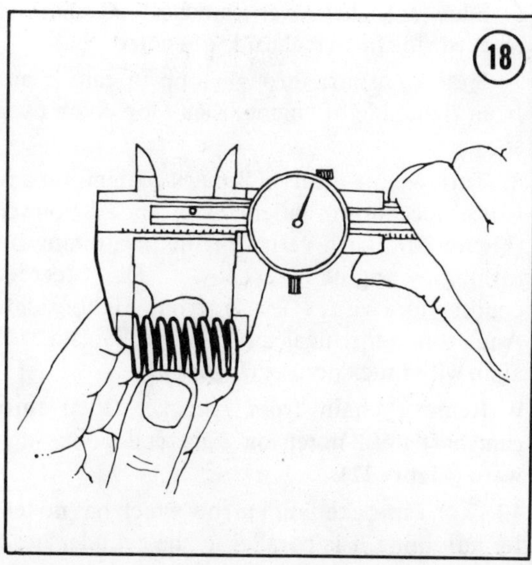

2. Release all pressure from the valve spring compressor.

3. Remove the spring retainer and both valve springs (**Figure 16**). Note that each spring should be installed so that the end with the closer coils goes downward.

4. Pull valve out from combustion chamber.

Cylinder Head and Valve Inspection

Refer to **Figure 17**. Measure thickness of each valve. Standard thickness is 0.05 in. (1.25mm). Replace any valve worn to 0.02 in. (0.50mm). Mount each valve in a suitable test fixture and check that the stem is not bent more than 0.002 (0.05mm). Replace any valve if bend exceeds that amount.

Measure valve stem diameter at several places. Replace intake valves if any measurement is 0.2701 in. (6.86mm) or less. Replace exhaust valve if any measurement is 0.2696 in. (6.85mm) or less.

Measure clearance between valve stems and valve guides. Standard clearance for intake valves is 0.0008 in. (0.02mm), and 0.0012 in. (0.03mm) for exhaust valves. Replace any valve and/or its guide if clearance exceeds 0.004 in. (0.10mm).

Angles on valves and valve seals should both be refaced to an angle of 45 degrees. After refacing, valve seats should be 0.019-0.04 in. (0.5-1.0mm) wide.

Measure free length of each valve spring (**Figure 18**). Standard length for inner springs is 1.28 in. (32.4mm). Replace any inner spring if its free length is 1.22 in. (31.0mm) or less. Standard length for outer springs is 1.47 in. (37.3mm). Replace any outer spring if it measures 1.42 in. (36.0mm) or less.

Refer to **Figure 19**. Replace any spring that is bent by 0.06 in. (1.5mm) or more.

It is good practice to replace the oil seals around each valve stem whenever the cylinder head is removed.

After cleaning the cylinder head thoroughly, place a straightedge across it at several points. Measure warp by inserting a feeler gauge between the straightedge and cylinder head at each location. If cylinder head warp exceeds 0.010 in. (0.25mm), replace the cylinder head.

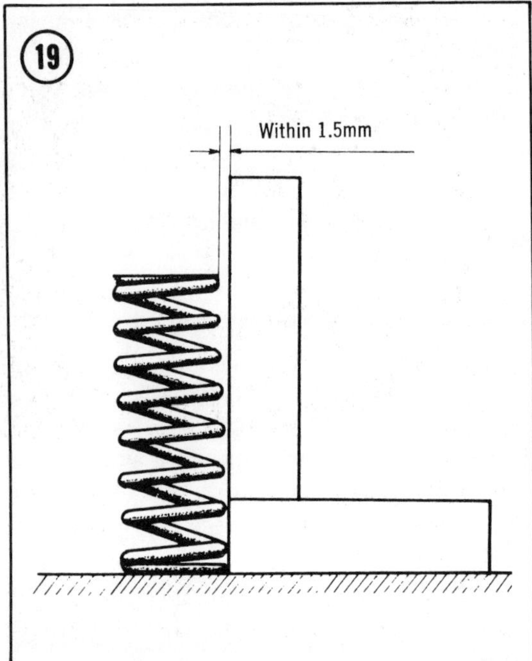

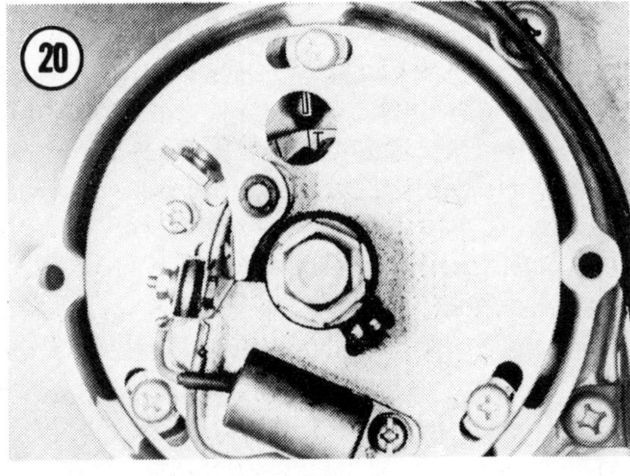

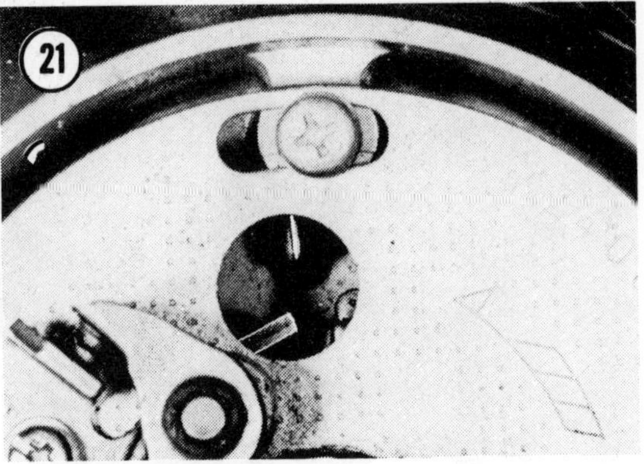

Cylinder Head Reassembly and Installation

Reverse the removal and disassembly procedure to install the cylinder head. Observe the following notes:

1. Always replace gaskets and O-rings.
2. Hold cam chain in position with any convenient tool until camshaft is installed.
3. Hold cylinder head in place with cylinder head cover nuts and several washers of suitable thickness until camshaft is installed.
4. Lubricate all moving parts liberally with engine oil upon assembly.
5. With the cylinder head in position, install the camshaft and its sprocket.

CAUTION

Follow all camshaft installation steps exactly. Failure to run, or even severe engine damage will result if the camshaft is installed incorrectly.

6. Slide sprocket over camshaft so that its marked side faces right side of engine.
7. Slide camshaft through loop in cam chain from right side of engine, then loop chain over sprocket.
8. Turn engine until "T" mark on ignition advance mechanism aligns with index pointer (**Figure 20**). Then verify engine positioning by turning engine exactly 90 degrees counterclockwise (viewed from right side). Angle on centrifugal advance mechanism will align with index pointer (**Figure 21**).
9. Remove chain from sprocket, then turn camshaft until notch on right end points upward (**Figure 22**).
10. Turn sprocket until arrow which has no letter adjoining it is parallel to the cylinder head

23

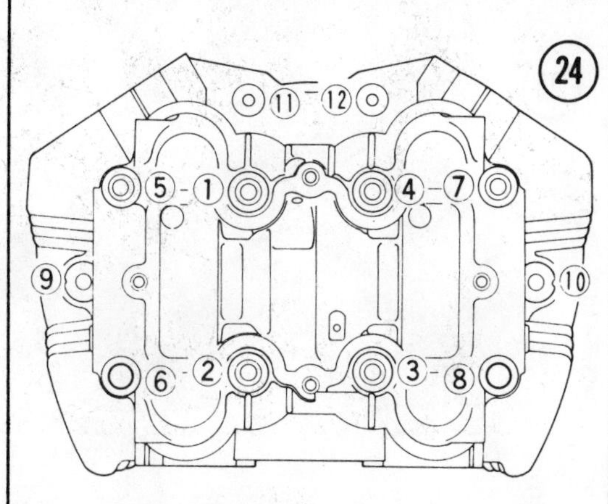

24

surface and pointing toward front of engine (**Figure 23**).

11. Fit cam chain over sprocket, then slide sprocket into position on camshaft. It is normal that bolt holes are not aligned at this time.

12. Hold camshaft in position, then turn engine until camshaft sprocket holes align with corresponding holes in camshaft. Note that sprocket will fit only one way.

13. Apply thread sealer to sprocket bolts, then tighten them to 10.0-11.5 ft.-lb. (1.4-1.6 mkg).

14. Turn engine counterclockwise until "T" mark on advance mechanism aligns with index pointer. Check that arrow next to "T" mark points to front of engine and is parallel to cylinder head surface. Notch on right end of cam must face up.

15. Remove cylinder head cover bolts and temporary spacer washers.

16. Remove tachometer gear and caps from cylinder head cover.

25

17. Turn engine counterclockwise until "T" mark on ignition advance unit aligns with its index pointer.

18. Be sure that all O-rings are in place. Apply gasket sealer to large O-ring to hold it in position.

19. Place cylinder head cover into position.

20. Tighten cylinder head cover nuts in the order shown in **Figure 24** to 11 ft.-lb. (1.5 mkg), then after all are tightened, retighten them in the same order to 18 ft.-lb. (2.5 mkg).

21. Tighten 8mm cylinder head bolts to 18-22 ft.-lb. (2.5-3.0 mkg), then tighten 6mm bolts to 8-9 ft.-lb. (1.1-1.3 mkg). See **Figure 24**.

22. Apply a small quantity of grease to tachometer gear, then install gear.

23. Install cam chain tensioner, then adjust it. Refer to Chapter Three for adjustment details.

24. Adjust valves. Refer to Chapter Three for adjustment details.

CYLINDER HEAD AND CYLINDER HEAD COVER (MODELS B AND C)

The cylinder head cover contains the rocker arms and their related shafts.

Cylinder Head Cover Removal

1. Remove the 2 screws securing the contact breaker cover and remove it.

2. Rotate the engine using a 17mm wrench on the bolt on the end of crankshaft (A, **Figure 25**). Rotate the crankshaft until the "T" mark

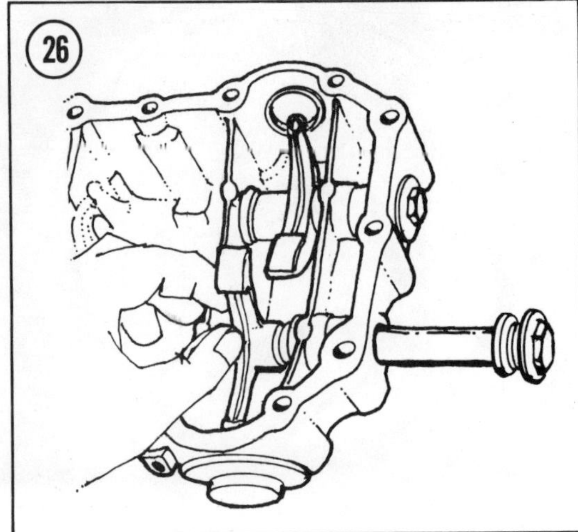

on the ignition advance mechanism aligns with the index pointer (B, **Figure 25**). This indicates that one of the cylinders is at top dead center (TDC).

3. Remove the screw securing the tachometer pinion holder and remove the pinion and holder from the cylinder head.

4. Remove the eight 8mm bolts and eight 6mm bolts securing the cylinder head cover.

5. Tap around the perimeter of the cover with a plastic or rubber mallet, if necessary, and lift it off the cylinder head.

Rocker Arm Removal/Inspection/Installation

1. Unscrew the rocker arm shaft and withdraw it and the flat washer (**Figure 26**).

> NOTE: *Prior to removal, mark each rocker arm and shaft with an R or L (right- or left-hand cylinder) and I or E (intake or exhaust). This will avoid any mixup of parts upon installation.*

2. Lift up on the rocker arms as the shaft is withdrawn and remove them.

3. Wash all parts in cleaning solvent and thoroughly dry with compressed air.

4. Inspect both contact surfaces of each rocker arm for damage or uneven wear. Replace any rocker arm that exhibits such defects. Measure inside diameter of each rocker arm. Standard diameter is 0.512 in. (13.0mm). Replace any arm that is worn to 0.514 in. (13.05mm).

5. Measure diameter of each rocker shaft where it passes through the rocker arm. Replace any shaft worn to 0.509 in. (12.94mm). Standard dimension is 0.510-0.511 in. (12.966-12.984mm).

6. Apply assembly oil to all bearing surfaces. Correctly position the rocker arm (refer to marks made in *Removal*, Step 1), and slide the rocker arm shaft into it. Screw the rocker arm shaft in and tighten to 18 ft.-lb. (2.5 mkg). Repeat for all 4 shafts.

> NOTE: *Don't forget the flat washer under the head of the rocker arm shaft.*

Cylinder Head Cover Installation

1. Clean the mating surfaces of the cylinder head and cover.

2. Make sure that the tachometer pinion is still removed from the cylinder head and that the 2 locating dowels are in position.

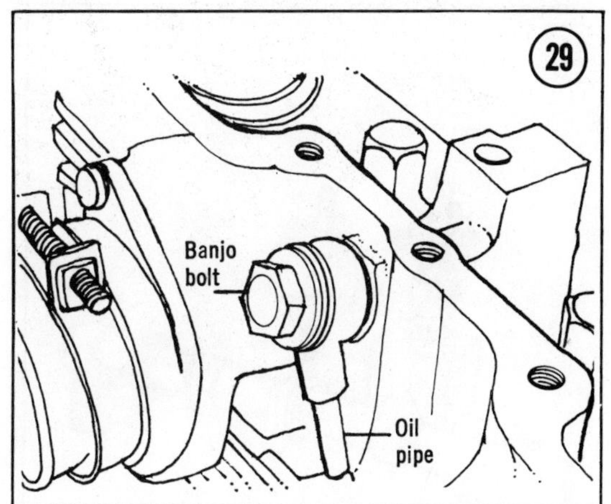

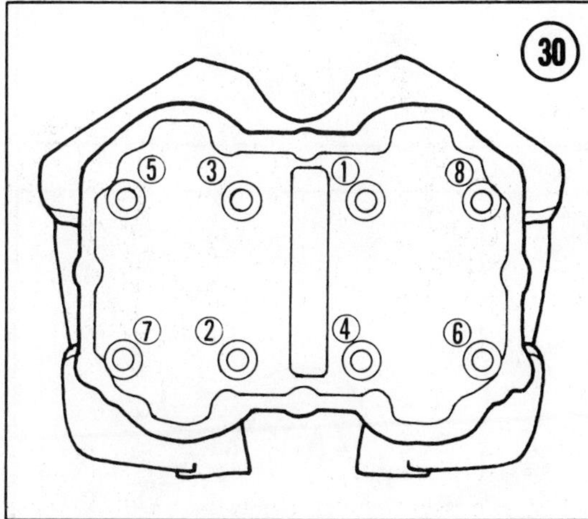

3. Check that the crankshaft is still positioned at TDC. Refer to *Removal*, Step 2.

4. Apply a non-hardening gasket cement like Gasgacinch Gasket Sealer, or equivalent, to both mating surfaces and install the cylinder head cover and its bolts.

5. Finger-tighten all bolts at first, then tighten the eight 8mm bolts to 18 ft.-lb. (2.5 mkg). Tighten the eight 6mm bolts to 7¼ ft.-lb. (1.0 mkg).

6. Apply a small amount of high temperature grease to the tachometer pinion shaft and install it and the holder into the cylinder head. Install the holder stop screw.

7. Install the contact breaker cover.

Camshaft and Cylinder Head Removal

1. Remove the cylinder head cover.

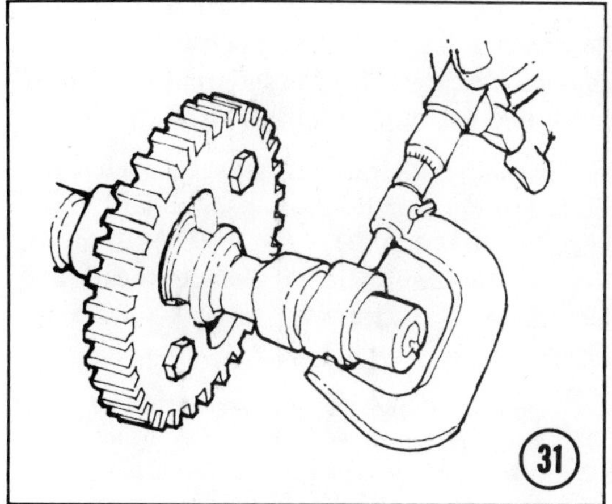

2. Remove the cam chain tensioner cover, then the cam chain tensioner mechanism (**Figure 27**).

3. Remove cam sprocket bolts (**Figure 28**). Turn the engine as necessary to expose bolts, with a 17mm wrench on the bolt on the end of the crankshaft under the contact breaker cover.

4. Slide the cam sprocket along the camshaft until the chain can be removed from the sprocket.

5. Remove the bolts securing the 3 cam bearing caps and remove them.

6. Remove the cam and sprocket together.

> NOTE: *Prevent the cam chain from dropping into the engine by inserting a screwdriver or similar tool through it.*

7. Remove the banjo bolt securing the oil pipe upper end to the cylinder head (**Figure 29**). Hold the upper end of the pipe stationary with a wrench while removing the bolt.

8. Loosen the 8 cylinder head nuts a little at a time in the sequence shown in **Figure 30**. Remove all nuts and washers.

9. Tap around the cylinder head perimeter with a plastic or rubber mallet to free the head. Pull the head straight up and off the cylinder and crankcase studs.

Camshaft and Cylinder Head Inspection

1. Measure height of each cam lobe (**Figure 31**). Standard height is 1.509-1.515 in. (38.339-38.479mm). Replace the camshaft if any lobe is worn to 1.506 in. (38.25mm) or is badly scuffed or otherwise damaged.

4

2. Measure each camshaft journal. Standard dimension is 0.982-0.983 in. (24.950-24.970mm). Replace the camshaft if any journal is worn to 0.981 in (24.93mm) or is otherwise defective.

3. Measure the clearance between each camshaft journal and its bearing. Standard clearance is 0.0012-0.0055 in. (0.03-0.14mm). Replace the camshaft or cylinder head and bearing caps if clearance exceeds 0.0075 in. (0.19mm).

NOTE: *Camshaft clearance is most easily measured with Plastigage, which is available at most motorcycle and auto parts stores. Be sure to specify the approximate measurement range desired. Follow the instructions on the envelope exactly.*

4. Place the camshaft outer bearings in V-blocks **(Figure 32)** or some other suitable centering device, then measure runout at its center. Runout on a new camshaft is less than 0.0004 in. (0.01mm). Replace the camshaft if runout exceeds 0.004 in. (0.1mm).

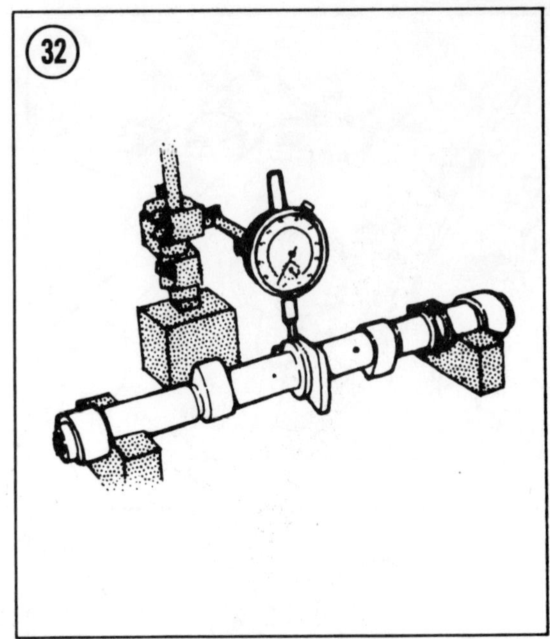

Cylinder Head Disassembly/Assembly

Cylinder head service is generally a job for a shop with facilities for such work. The following material is set forth for those with the necessary skills and equipment. Refer to **Figure 33** for this procedure.

1. Using a valve spring compressor designed for small engines, compress each valve spring until both keepers may be removed **(Figure 34)**.
2. Release all pressure from the valve spring compressor.
3. Remove the spring retainer and both valve springs **(Figure 35)**. Note that each spring should be installed so that the end with the closer coils goes downward.
4. Pull valve out from combustion chamber.
5. Coat the valve stems with molybdenum disulfide paste and insert them into the cylinder head.
6. Install bottom spring retainers and new seals.
7. Install valve springs with the narrow pitch end (end with coils closest together) facing the head, and install upper valve spring retainers.

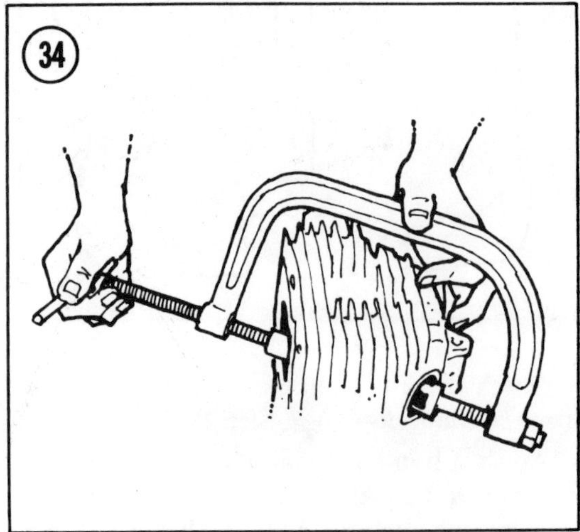

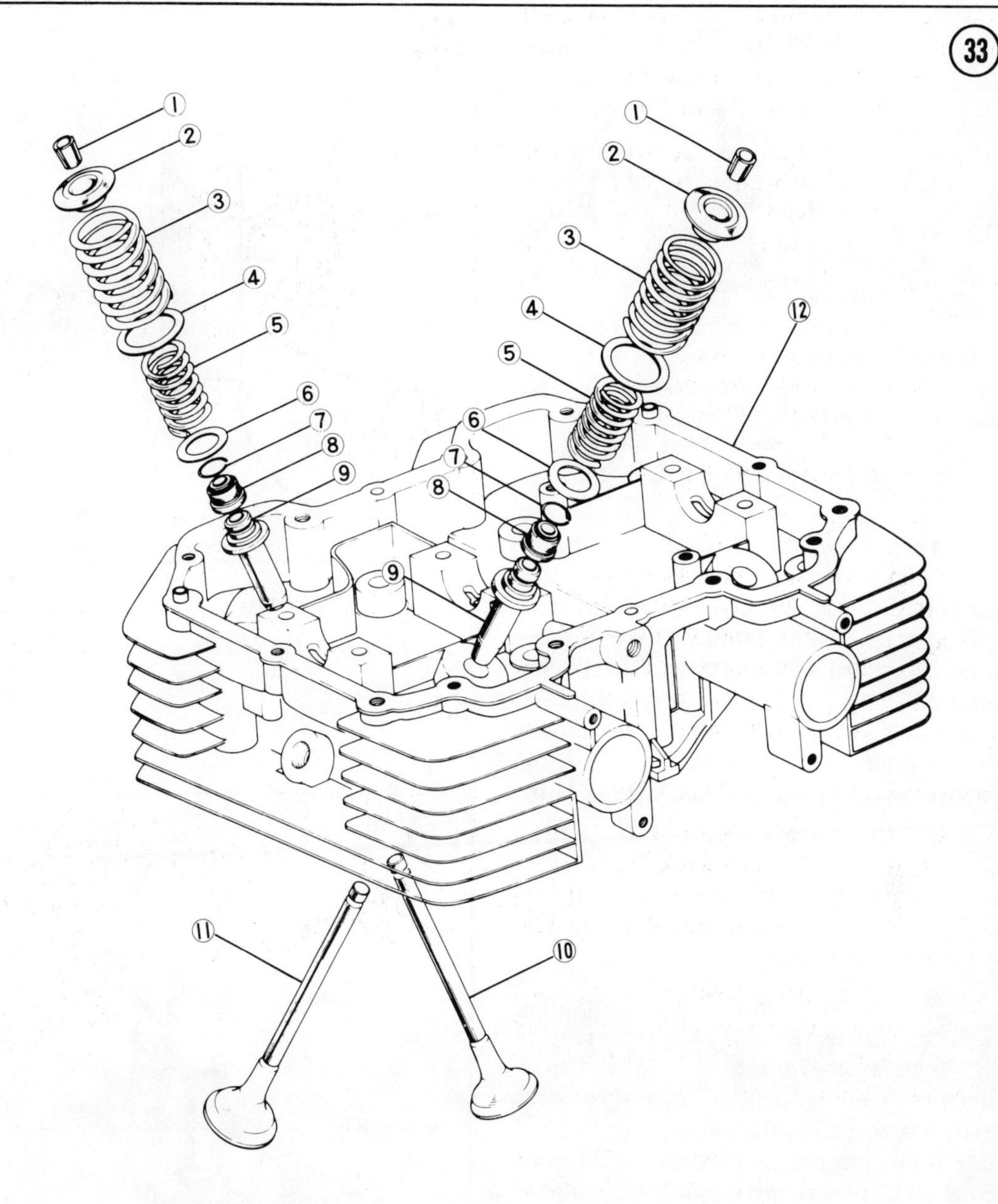

VALVE AND VALVE GUIDES — MODELS B AND C

1. Split keeper
2. Spring retainer
3. Outer spring
4. Outer spring seat
5. Inner spring
6. Inner spring seat
7. Clip
8. Oil seal
9. Valve guide
10. Exhaust valve
11. Intake valve
12. Cylinder head

8. Push down on upper valve spring retainers with the valve spring compressor and install valve keepers.

Cylinder Head and Valve Inspection

Refer to **Figure 36**. Measure thickness of each valve. Standard thickness is 0.05 in. (1.25mm). Replace any valve worn to 0.02 in. (0.50mm). Mount each valve in a suitable test fixture and check that the stem is not bent more than 0.002 in. (0.05mm). Replace any valve if bend exceeds that amount.

Measure valve stem diameter at several places. Replace either intake or exhaust valve if any measurement is 0.272 in. (6.90mm) or less.

Measure clearance between valve stems and valve guides. Standard clearance for intake is 0.0021-0.0055 in. (0.053-0.139mm). Replace if clearance exceeds 0.0102 in. (0.26mm). Exhaust valve standard clearance is 0.0029-0.0067 in. (0.075-0.169mm). Replace if clearance exceeds 0.0098 in. (0.25mm).

Angles on valves and valve seats should both be refaced to an angle of 45°. After refacing, valve seats should be 0.019-0.04 in. (0.5-1.0 mm).

Measure the tension of each inner and outer valve spring. This test requires the use of a special valve spring tester (**Figure 37**). Compress the inner spring to the length of 0.874 in. (22.2mm); replace any if the tension is 60.185 lb. (27.3kg) or less. Compress the outer spring to 1.012 in. (25.7mm); replace any if the tension is 113.32 lb. (51.4kg) or less.

Refer to **Figure 38**. Replace any spring that is bent by 0.06 in. (1.5mm) or more.

It is good practice to replace the oil seals around each valve stem whenever the cylinder head is removed.

After cleaning the cylinder head thoroughly, place a straightedge across it at several points. Measure warp by inserting a feeler gauge between the straightedge and cylinder head at each location. If cylinder head warp exceeds 0.0019. in. (0.05mm), replace the cylinder head.

Cylinder Head and Camshaft Installation

1. Install both locating dowels and new head gasket.

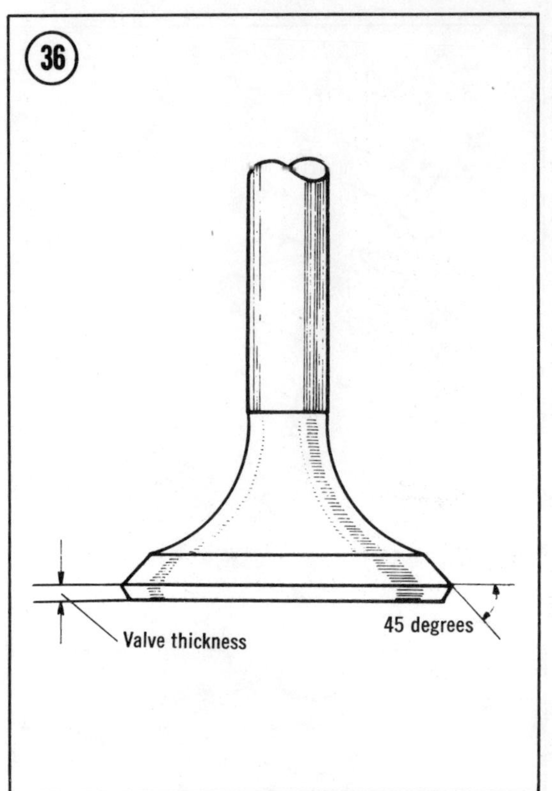

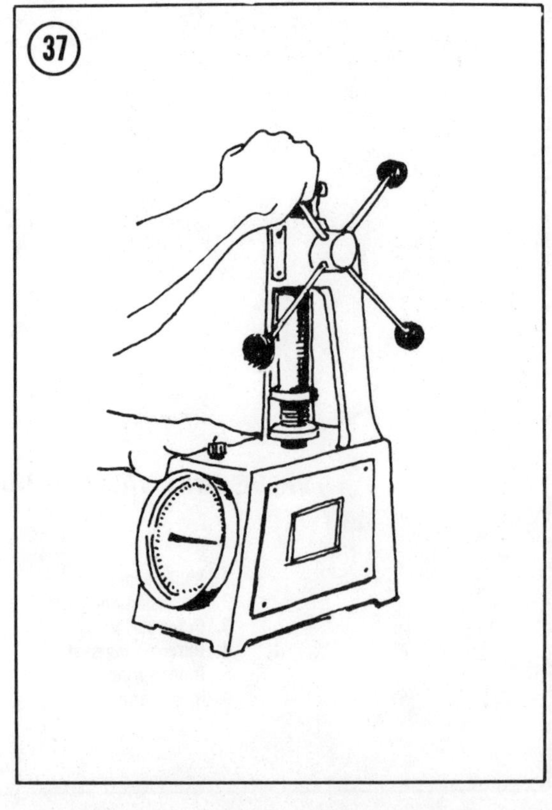

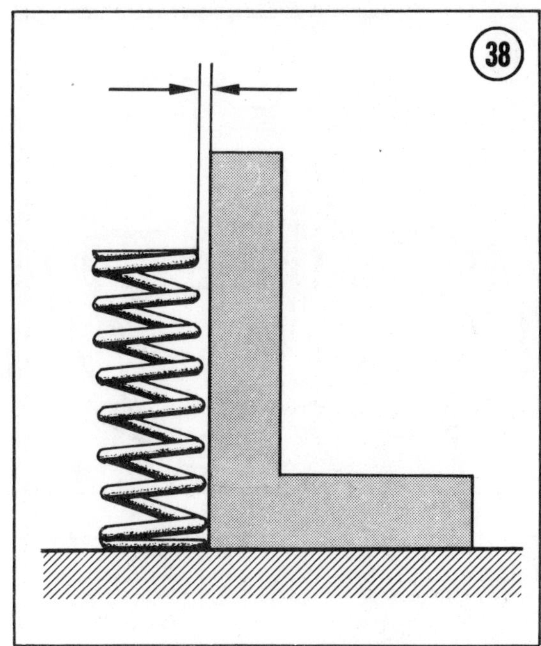

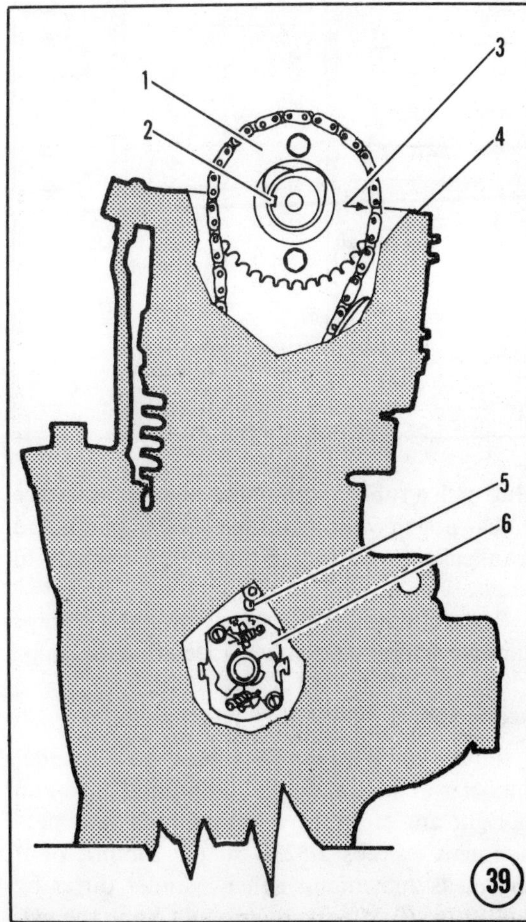

NOTE: *Install the head gasket with the projection, in the area of the cam chain opening, located at the rear left-hand side.*

2. Install the cylinder head. Be careful not to bend the oil pipe. Pull the cam chain up through the opening in the head and insert a screwdriver through it to prevent it from falling into the crankcase.
3. Install the 8 copper washers and 8 cylinder head nuts. Tighten the nuts in 2 steps using the torque sequence shown in **Figure 30**. Tighten in the first step to about 14 ft.-lb. (2.0 mkg) then to 29 ft.-lb. (4.0 mkg).
4. Install the banjo bolt into the upper end of the oil pipe using new washers on each end of the pipe. Hold the upper end of the pipe with a wrench and tighten the banjo bolt to 14.5 ft.-lb. (2.0 mkg).
5. If the oil receiver was removed, reinstall it with the arrow facing toward the front of the bike. Apply Loctite Lock N' Seal to the screw threads prior to installation.
6. Apply assembly oil to all bearing surfaces of the cam, cam bearing caps, and bearing surfaces on the head.
7. Install the cam through the cam chain from the right-hand side. The end of the cam with the notch must be on the right-hand side of the engine.
8. Install the cam sprocket (1, **Figure 39**) from the right-hand side so that the side with the arrow faces the right-hand side of the engine. Do not slide the sprocket into its final position at this time.
9. Ensure that the engine is still at TDC. Refer to **Figure 39**, items 5 and 6, and readjust if necessary.

CAUTION

Be sure to pull the cam chain taut when rotating the crankshaft to avoid damage to the chain and timing sprocket on the crankshaft.

10. Position the cam sprocket so that its arrow (3, **Figure 39**) is pointing to the front of the bike and is aligned with the cylinder head surface (4, **Figure 39**). Install the cam chain onto the sprocket.

4

11. Slide the sprocket and chain up into its correct position. Turn the cam so that the notch on the right-hand end is facing toward the rear (2, **Figure 39**). Hold the sprocket stationary.

12. Apply Loctite Lock N' Seal to the sprocket bolts and tighten to 11 ft.-lb. (1.5 mkg).

13. Install all 6 cam bearing cap locating dowels and install the 3 cam bearing caps. The arrow on cap must face forward **(Figure 40)**. Tighten the cap bolts to 8.5 ft.-lb. (1.2 mkg) in the sequence shown in **Figure 40**.

14. Install the cam chain tensioner assembly.

15. Rotate the crankshaft *counterclockwise* until the cam sprocket arrow is again facing to the front of the engine. Check that all the timing marks (5, 6, **Figure 39)** again align. If they do, cam timing is correct; if not, *correct immediately* by repeating Steps 9-14 until the timing is correct.

CAUTION
Follow all camshaft installation steps exactly. If the camshaft is installed incorrectly, it could cause engine failure or severe engine damage.

16. Install the cylinder head cover.

17. Adjust the valves as described under *Valve Adjustment* in this chapter.

CAUTION
Before proceeding, rotate the crankshaft several revolutions ***by hand****. If there is any binding,* ***STOP****. Retrace your steps and determine the cause.*

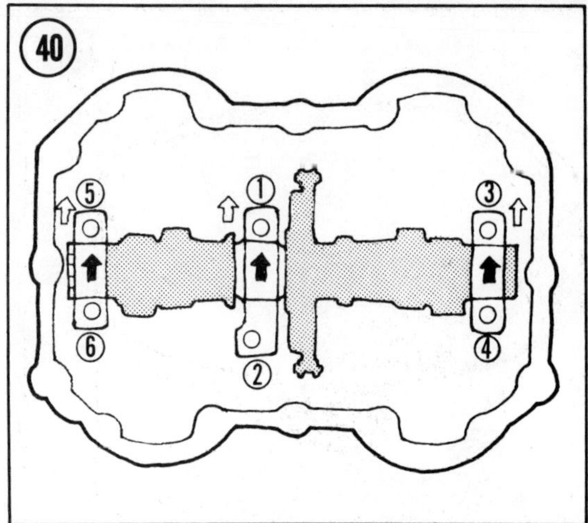

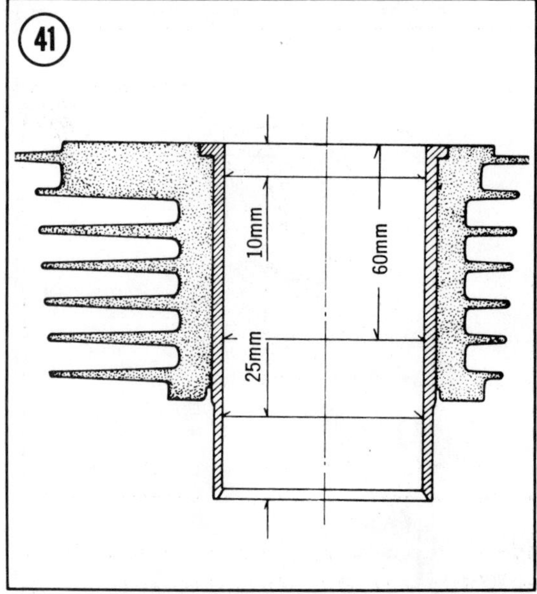

CYLINDERS

Cylinders are cast together of aluminum alloy for good heat dissipation. Each cylinder contains an iron sleeve for durability. These sleeves are of sufficient thickness to permit boring and honing after long service or a piston seizure.

Removal

After removing the cylinder head, it is only necessary to lift the cylinder block from its studs to remove it. Since the cylinder may adhere stubbornly to the crankcase, some tapping with a rubber mallet may be helpful to free it. Do not pry between the cylinder block and crankcase to loosen it; leaks are certain to result.

Be careful not to bend or damage the oil pipe during cylinder removal on Models B and C only.

Inspection

Refer to **Figure 41**. Measure cylinder diameter at several depths both parallel to and at right angles to the crankshaft. If any measurement exceeds 2.5236 in. (64.10mm), or if any measurements in either cylinder differ by 0.0019 in. (0.05mm), rebore and hone the cyl-

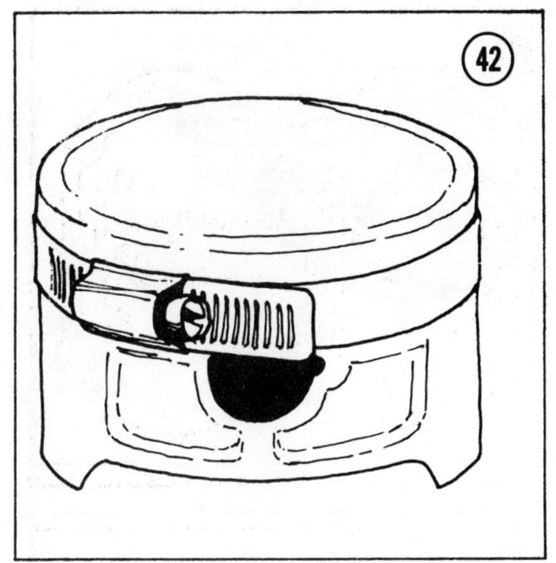

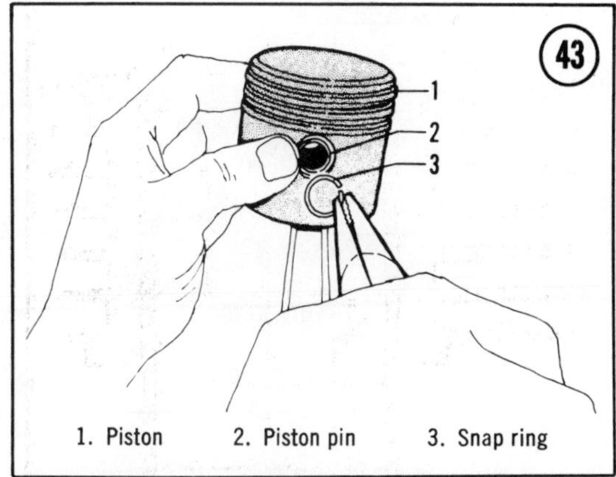

1. Piston 2. Piston pin 3. Snap ring

inder to the next oversize (refer to *Piston Clearance*). However, if boring would increase cylinder diameter to more than 2.5587 in. (64.99mm), replace the cylinder block.

In the case of oversize cylinders, the service limit is the diameter the cylinder was bored to, plus 0.004 in. (0.20mm).

Boring and Honing

If boring and honing are to be performed, observe the following notes.

1. First measure each replacement oversize piston (refer to *Piston Clearance*), then bore and hone each cylinder to provide a piston clearance of 0.0013-0.0021 in. (0.034-0.054mm) on Models D and S. On Models B and C, the clearance is 0.0012-0.0019 in. (0.031-0.048mm).

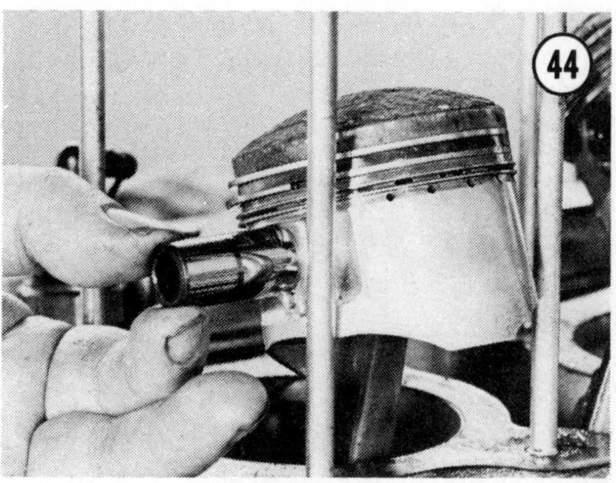

2. Cylinder taper and out-of-round must not exceed 0.0004 in. (0.01mm) after boring and honing.

3. Make all measurements with cylinders and pistons cold. Allow cylinders to cool after maching before measuring them.

4

Installation

Reverse the removal procedure to install the cylinder block. Always install a new cylinder base gasket and make sure that the 2 locating dowels are in place. Lubricate cylinder bores and pistons liberally with engine oil upon installation. It will be necessary to compress the piston rings as they enter the cylinder bores; aircraft-type hose clamps (**Figure 42**) of appropriate diameter make suitable piston ring compressors.

PISTONS, PISTON RINGS, AND PISTON PINS

Pistons are made from aluminum alloy. Each is equipped with 2 compression rings and one oil control ring. They are so manufactured that they are not round when cold, but as they warm up, they become round to match the cylinders. Piston pins are full floating and retained by snap ring clips at each end.

Piston Removal/Installation

Using a small screwdriver, pry out the clip at the outer end of each piston pin (**Figure 43**). Then press out the piston pin (**Figure 44**). It

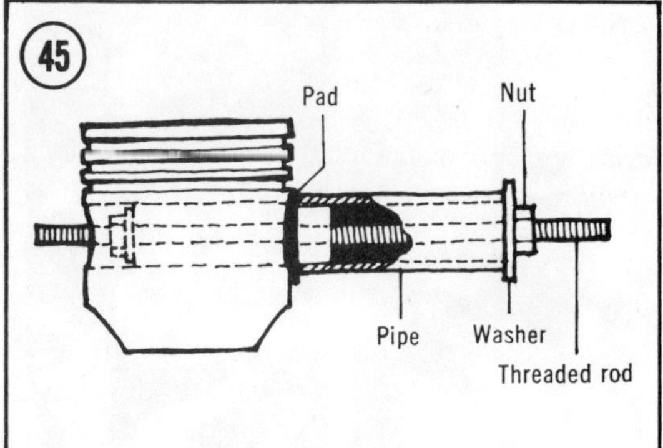

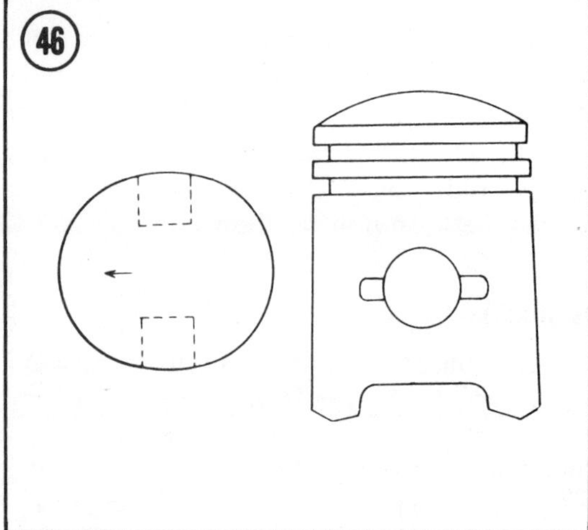

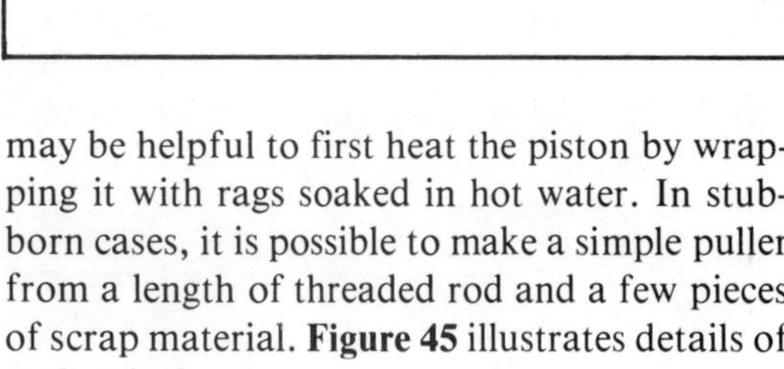

may be helpful to first heat the piston by wrapping it with rags soaked in hot water. In stubborn cases, it is possible to make a simple puller from a length of threaded rod and a few pieces of scrap material. **Figure 45** illustrates details of such a device.

After long service, a ridge may build up around the piston pin clip grooves, which makes piston pin removal difficult. In such cases, do not drive the piston pin out by hammering it. Protect the crankcase openings with rags, then carefully chamfer the raised outer groove edge with a knife to remove the ridge. The piston pin should then slide out with little difficulty.

Be sure to tag each piston in some manner so that it may be returned to its proper cylinder.

Reverse the removal procedure to install the piston. Be sure that the arrow on top of the piston faces the front of the engine **(Figure 46)**. Always install new piston pin retaining clips.

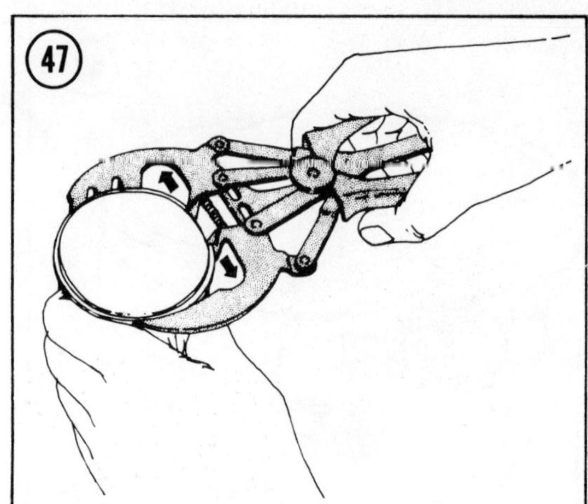

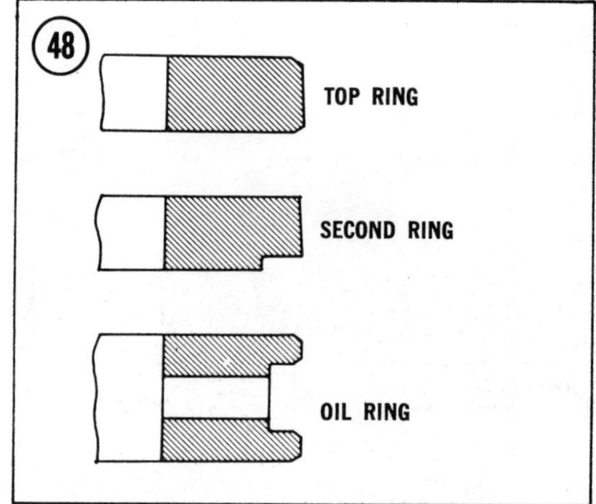

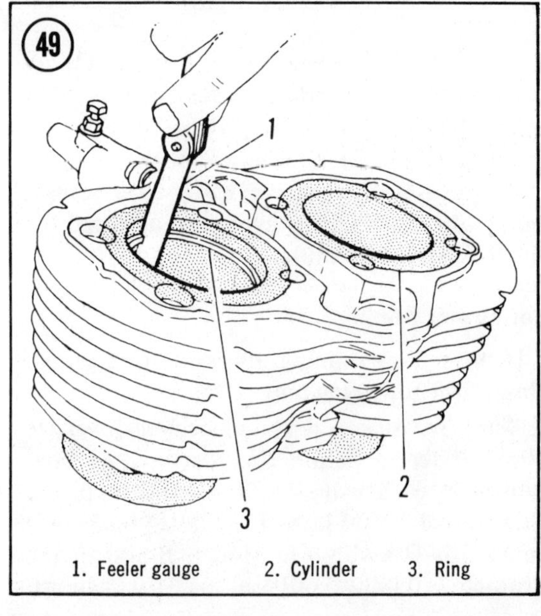

1. Feeler gauge 2. Cylinder 3. Ring

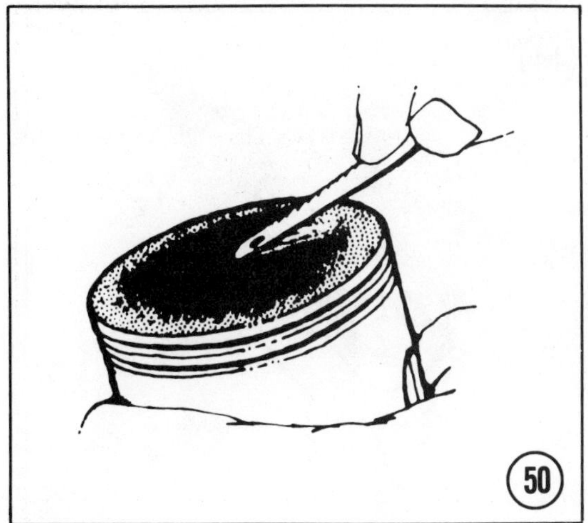
50

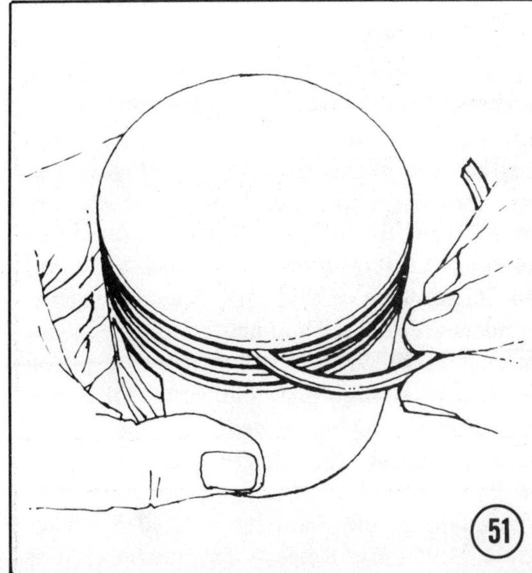
51

Piston Ring Removal/Installation

Remove the piston rings by carefully spreading the top one with your thumbs, just enough to slip it over the head of the piston or as shown in **Figure 47**. Repeat this procedure for each remaining ring.

Reverse the removal procedure to install the rings. Be sure that each ring goes into its proper groove **(Figure 48)**. Also be sure that the markings on the rings go toward the top of the piston. Align end gaps on the top and oil rings so that they face the front of the engine; the end gap on the lower compression ring goes toward the rear of the engine.

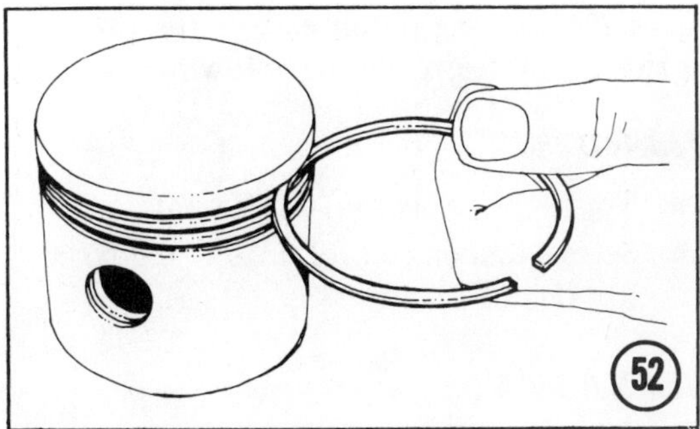
52

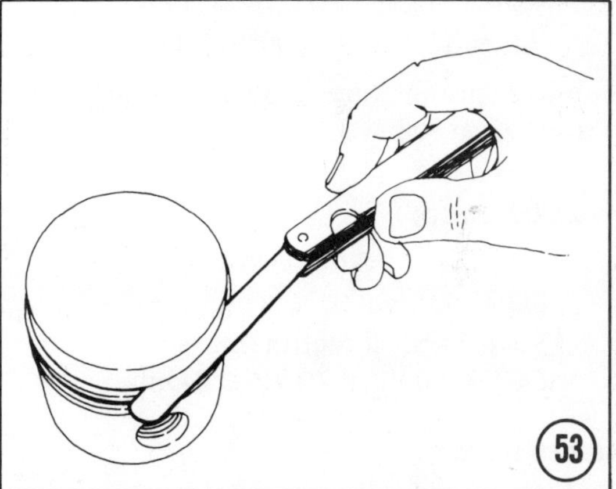
53

Checking Piston Rings

Measure each ring for wear as shown in **Figure 49**. Insert the piston ring into the cylinder near the bottom, where wear is least, then measure piston ring gap with a feeler gauge. To ensure that the piston ring is square in the cylinder, push it into position with the head of the piston on unworn piston rings. Gap will be 0.008-0.016 in. (0.2-0.4mm). Replace all rings if gap on any one exceeds 0.028 in. (0.7mm).

Scrape carbon deposits from the piston head **(Figure 50)**. Clean all carbon and gum from the piston ring grooves, using a broken piston ring **(Figure 51)**. Any deposits left in the grooves will cause the rings to stick, leading to gas blow-by and loss of power.

To check fit of the piston ring in its groove, slip the outer surface of the ring into the groove, then roll the ring completely around the piston **(Figure 52)**. If any binding occurs, determine and correct the cause before proceeding. Then after the rings are installed, measure ring groove side clearance **(Figure 53)** in several places. Replace the piston and/or the rings if the side clearance exceeds the following:

Models D and S

a. Top ring — 0.0063 in. (0.160mm)
b. Second and oil control rings — 0.0057 in. (0.145mm)

Models B and C

a. Top ring — 0.0071 in. (0.18mm)
b. Second ring — 0.0055 in. (0.14mm)
c. Oil control ring — 0.0059 in. (0.15mm)

Standard piston ring groove to ring side clearance is as follows:

Models D and S

a. Top ring — 0.0010-0.0024 in. (0.025-0.060mm)
b. Second and oil control ring — 0.0004-0.0018 in. (0.010-0.045mm)

Models B and C

a. Top ring — 0.0016-0.0031 in. (0.040-0.080mm)
b. Second ring — 0.0004-0.0018 in. (0.010-0.045mm)
c. Oil control ring — 0.0008-0.0022 in. (0.020-0.055mm)

Piston Reconditioning

A piston exhibiting signs of seizure will result in noise, loss of power, and cylinder wall damage. If such a piston is reused without correction, another seizure will develop. To correct this condition, try lightly smoothing the affected area with No. 400 emery paper or a fine oilstone. Replace the piston if the seizure marks cannot be removed with absolutely minimal polishing. If any doubt exists, replace the piston.

Carefully examine the entire piston surface. Check for cracks, partially melted piston crown, score marks, broken or deformed ring grooves, or any other defect which might interfere with correct piston performance. Replace the piston if any of these defects exist. Also see *Piston Pin*.

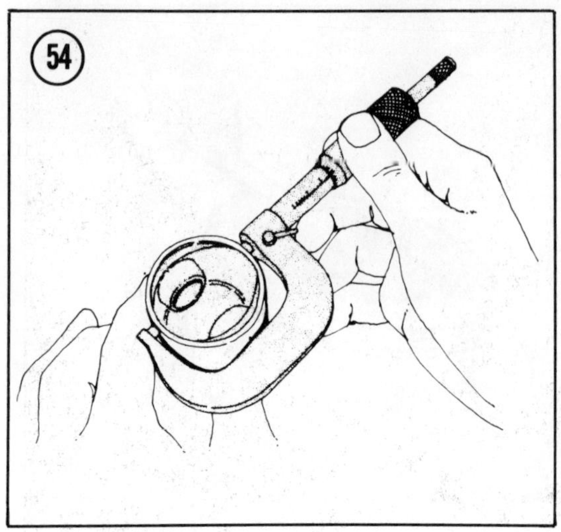

Piston Clearance

Piston clearance is the difference between maximum piston diameter and minimum cylinder diameter. Measure diameter of the piston skirt at right angles to piston pin (**Figure 54**). This measurement should be made 0.2 in. (5mm) from the bottom of the piston. Ideal clearance is 0.0013-0.0021 in. (0.034-0.054mm) and it must be within this range whenever cylinders are rebored and new pistons installed. On engines which have been in service, piston clearance will be greater; individual tolerances for piston and cylinder wear will then be the deciding factor for determining need for service.

Standard piston diameter is 2.517-2.518 in. (63.94-63.96mm). Replace any piston if it is worn to less than 2.512 in. (63.8mm). The service limit for oversize pistons is the original diameter minus 0.006 in. (0.15mm).

Piston Pin

Measure piston pin diameter. Also measure inside diameter of both piston holes and the piston pin hole in the connecting rod. Piston pin standard diameter is 0.5903-0.5905 in. (14.994-15.000mm). Replace the piston pin if it measures less than 0.5889 in. (14.96mm). Piston hole standard clearance is 0.5907-0.5910 in. (15.004-15.010mm). Replace the piston if the piston holes measure 0.5937 in. (15.08mm) or more. Connecting rod upper end standard diameter is 0.5907-0.5911 in. (15.004-

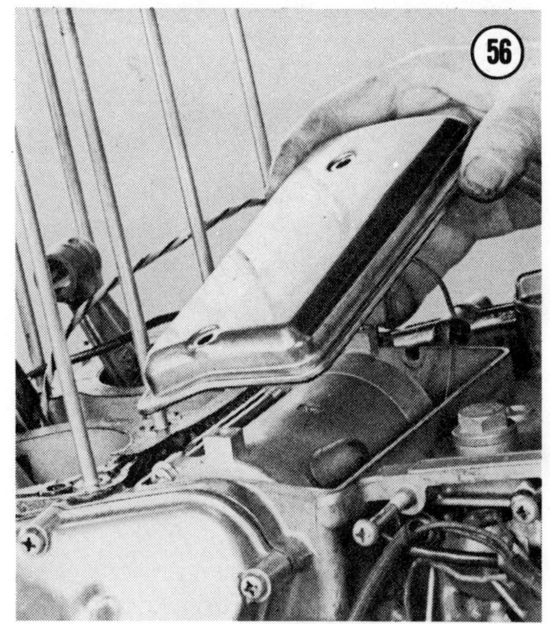

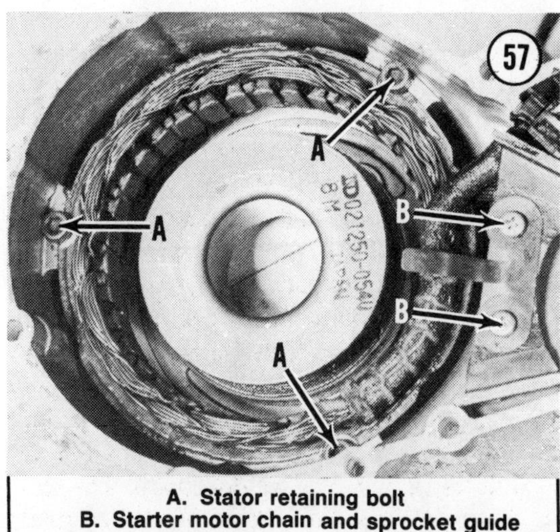

A. Stator retaining bolt
B. Starter motor chain and sprocket guide

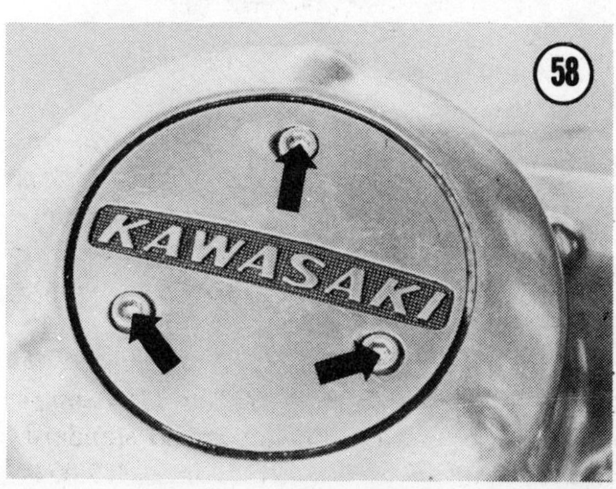

15.014mm). Replace the connecting rod if the piston pin hole is worn to 0.5925 in. (15.05mm).

Whenever a new piston or piston pin is installed, clearance between the piston pin and piston should be 0.0002-0.0005 in. (0.0055-0.0135mm). Also check that clearance between the piston pin and connecting rod is 0.0001-0.0008 in. (0.003-0.020mm).

ALTERNATOR AND STARTER

The alternator and starter are discussed together, because complete removal of one entails removal of the other. Removal and installation only of these items are covered in this chapter. Refer to Chapter Six for details of alternator and starter service.

Alternator Removal (Models D and S)

Refer to **Figure 55** for this procedure.

If the engine is installed in the motorcycle, perform Steps 1 through 14; begin with Step 5 if the engine has been removed.

1. Remove field coil plug from connector under voltage regulator.
2. Remove shift pedal.
3. Remove left footpeg and kickstand spring.
4. Remove engine sprocket cover.
5. Remove wiring harness clip from above engine sprocket.
6. Remove starter cover (**Figure 56**).
7. Disconnect oil pressure switch at inline connector.
8. Disconnect wire at neutral indicator switch.
9. Remove alternator cover. Do not remove Allen bolts from center of cover.
10. Remove starter motor chain guide and sprocket guide (B, **Figure 57**).
11. Remove stator retaining bolts (A, **Figure 57**); pull out stator.
12. Remove field coil retaining bolts (**Figure 58**), then pull out field coil.
13. Remove rotor retaining bolt. Note that this bolt has a left-hand thread.

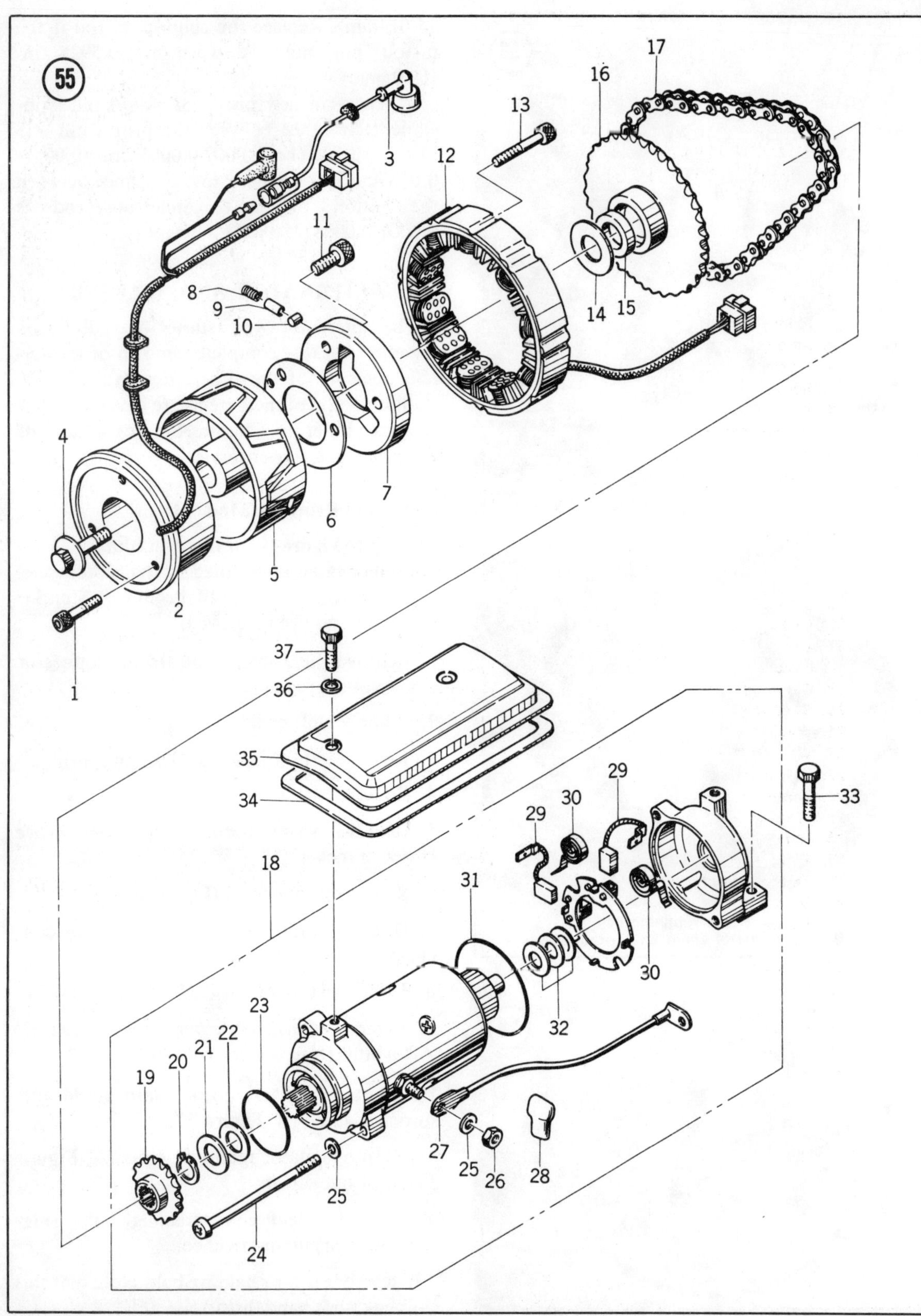
55
1
2
3
4
5
6
7
8
9
10
11
12
13
14
15
16
17
18
19
20
21
22
23
24
25
25
26
27
28
29
29
30
30
31
32
33
34
35
36
37

ALTERNATOR/STARTER
(MODELS D AND S)

1. Bolt
2. Field coil
3. Wire
4. Bolt
5. Rotor
6. Plate
7. Starter clutch
8. Spring
9. Plug
10. Roller
11. Bolt
12. Stator
13. Bolt
14. Washer
15. Oil seal
16. Gear
17. Chain
18. Motor
19. Sprocket
20. Snap ring
21. Washer
22. Washer
23. O-ring
24. Screw
25. Washer
26. Nut
27. Wire
28. Terminal cap
29. Brush
30. Spring
31. O-ring
32. Washer
33. Bolt
34. Gasket
35. Cover
36. Washer
37. Bolt

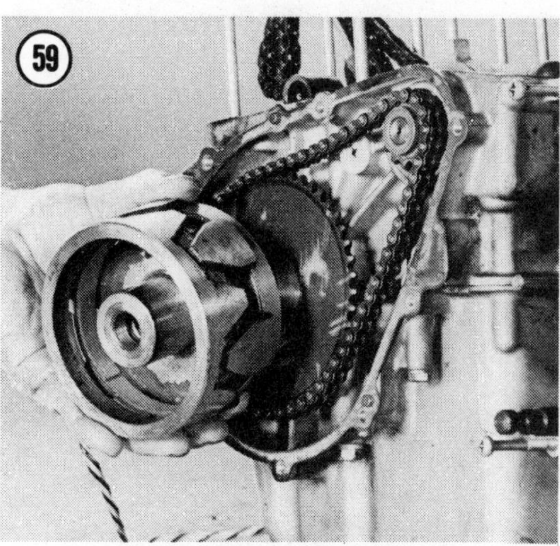

14. Using a rotor puller, remove alternator rotor and starter clutch (**Figure 59**). Remove thrust washer if necessary.

4

Alternator Installation (Models D and S)

Reverse the removal procedure to install the alternator. Observe the following notes.

1. Apply thread cement to field coil and stator bolts, then tighten them to 5-6 ft.-lb. (0.7-0.8 mkg).
2. Be sure that there is no foreign material on tapered portion of the crankshaft when installing the rotor.
3. Tighten rotor retaining bolt (left-hand thread) to 47-51 ft.lb. (6.5-7.0 mkg).
4. Install shift pedal so that its end is level with lower alternator cover screw.

Alternator Removal/Installation (Models B and C)

Refer to **Figure 60** for this procedure.

1. Remove the engine sprocket cover as described in this chapter.
2. Disconnect the 2 yellow electrical leads coming from the alternator.
3. Place a drip pan under the alternator cover as some oil will drain out when the cover is removed.
4. Remove the 9 screws securing the cover and remove it and the gasket.
5. Remove the bolt securing the rotor.

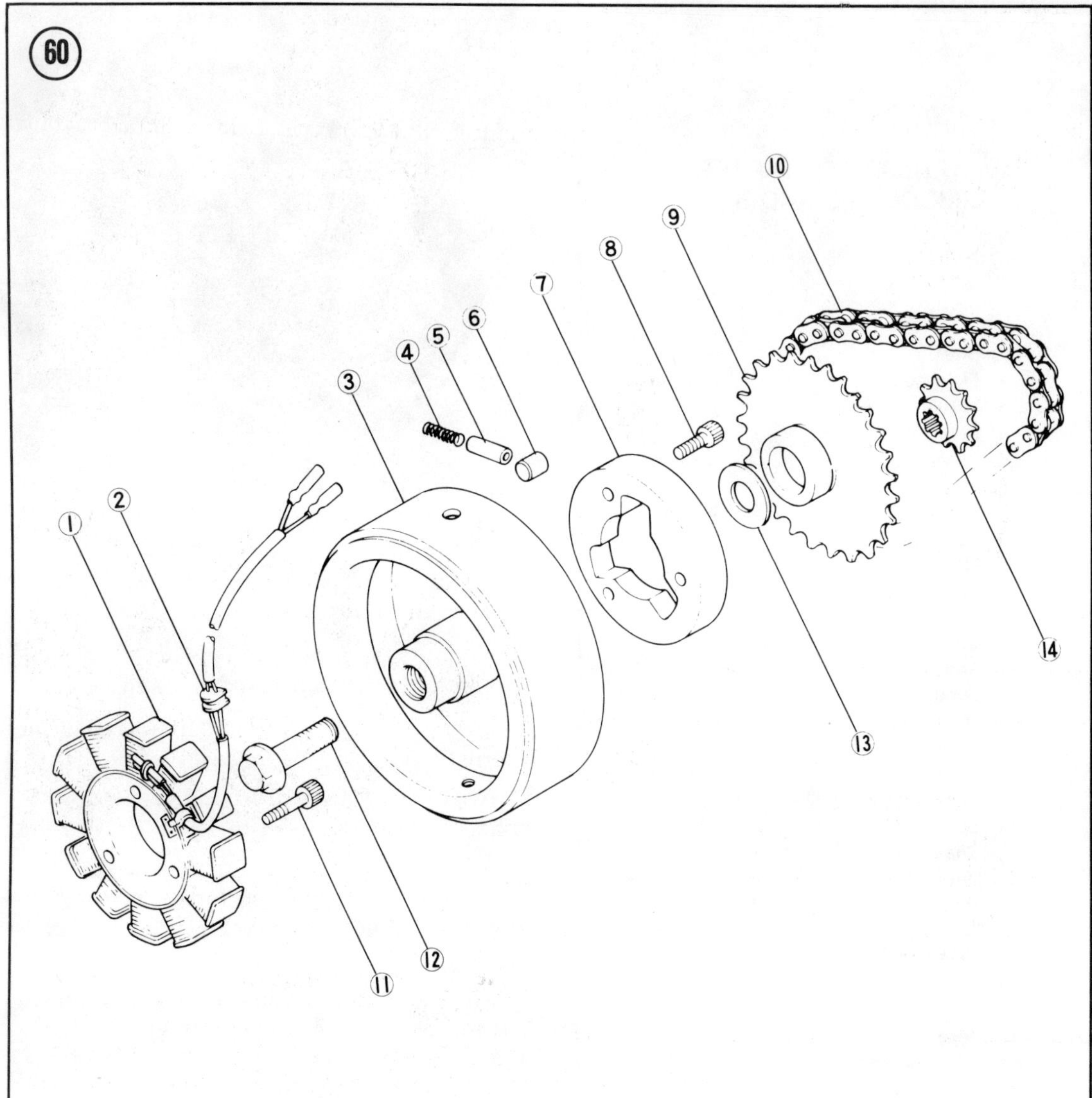

ALTERNATOR — MODELS B AND C

1. Alternator field coil
2. Grommet
3. Alternator rotor
4. Spring
5. Spring cap
6. Roller
7. Starter motor clutch
8. Allen bolt
9. Starter motor sprocket
10. Starter chain
11. Allen bolt
12. Flywheel bolt
13. Washer or collar
14. Starter motor sprocket

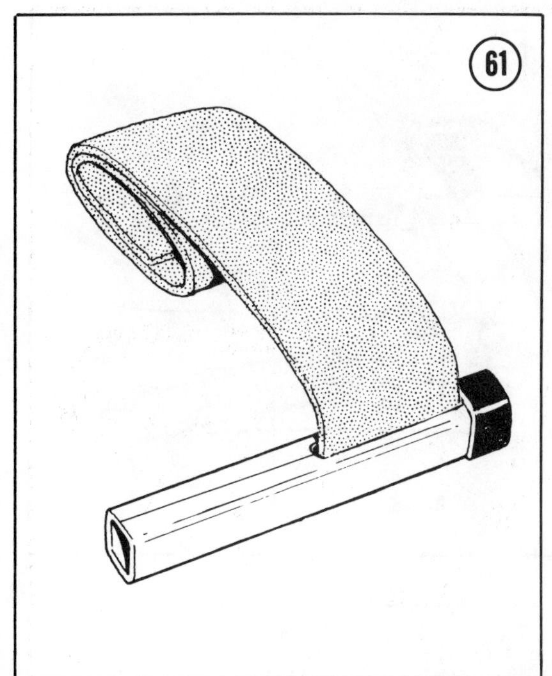

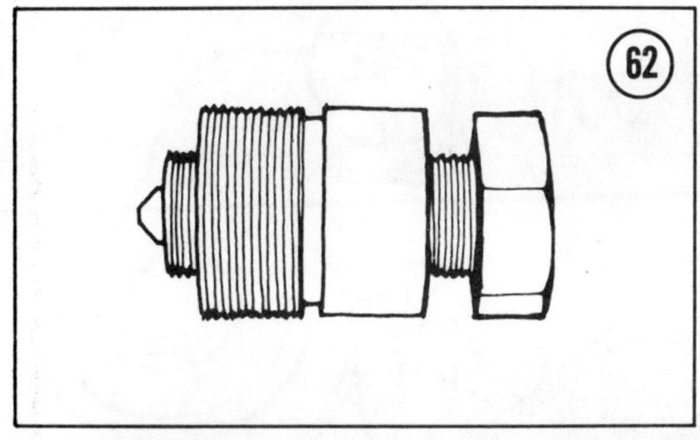

> NOTE: *If necessary, use a strap wrench **(Figure 61)** to secure the rotor from turning while removing the bolt.*

6. Screw in the flywheel puller **(Figure 62)** until it stops. Use a wrench on the puller and turn it until the rotor disengages. Remove the puller and the rotor/starter clutch assembly.

> NOTE: *On Model B, there is a thrust washer and on Model C a collar behind the rotor/starter clutch assembly.*

7. Install by reversing these removal steps. Thoroughly clean the crankshaft taper of any dirt or oil prior to installing the rotor.
8. Be sure to install either the thrust washer (Model B) or collar (Model C) onto the crankshaft, then install the rotor. Tighten the rotor bolt to 51 ft.-lb. (7.0 mkg).

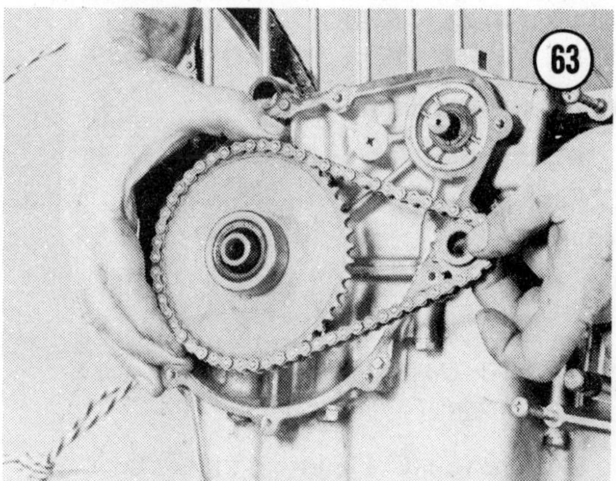

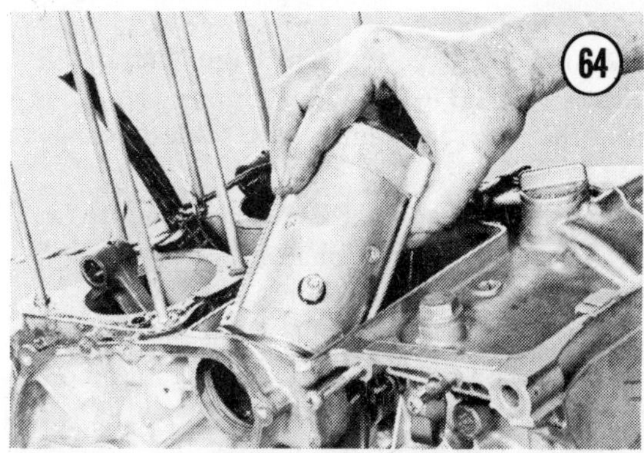

Starter Chain and Sprockets (All Models)

Once the rotor and starter clutch have been removed, it is only necessary to pull off both starter sprockets and drive chain as an assembly **(Figure 63)**. Installation is the reverse of removal.

Starter Motor (All Models)

1. Disconnect cable from terminal on starter motor.
2. Remove starter motor retaining bolts.
3. Tap starter motor with a plastic mallet to free it, then lift it from engine **(Figure 64)**. Do not tap starter shaft; doing so may result in damage.
4. Reverse the removal procedure to install the starter. Apply a little oil to its O-ring before installation.

4

ENGINE SPROCKET COVER (MODELS B AND C)

Removal/Installation

1. Remove the left-hand footpeg.
2. Remove the bolt securing the shift lever and remove it.
3. Remove the side stand drive lever pivot bolt (A, **Figure 65**) and lever (B, **Figure 65**).

> NOTE: *Don't lose the lockwasher, flat washer, and collar on the bolt.*

4. Slide the rod (C, **Figure 65**) to the rear.
5. Remove the 4 screws securing the sprocket cover and remove it.
6. Remove the cotter pin from the clutch release lever (**Figure 66**). Remove the cable from the lever and remove the cable from the cover.
7. Install by reversing these removal steps. Be sure to use a new cotter pin on the clutch cable — never reuse an old cotter pin.
8. Be sure to install the collar, flat washer, and lockwasher on the pivot bolt. Hook the rod onto the lever.

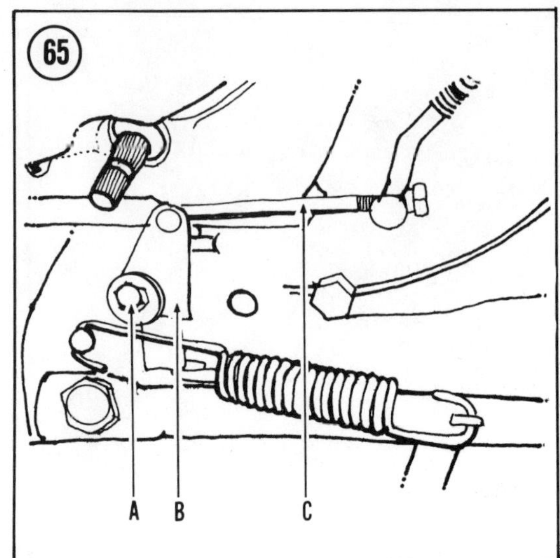

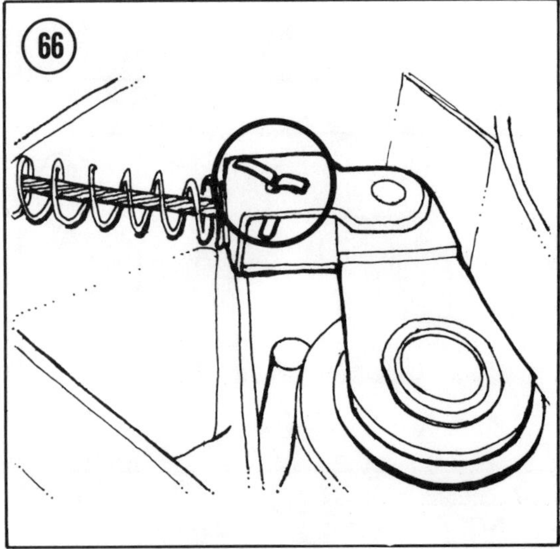

ENGINE SPROCKET

The engine sprocket is subject to heavy loads, wear, and abrasion from road dirt. It is made from abrasion-resistant steel to minimize the effects of its operating condition.

Removal/Installation (Models D and S)

1. Remove engine sprocket cover.
2. Using a blunted chisel, flatten tab on sprocket lockwasher.
3. If engine is in motorcycle, apply rear brake firmly, then remove sprocket nut. If engine has been removed, a suitable sprocket holder can be fabricated from the drive chain and a wooden board. Secure the chain to the board in such a manner that the assembly can be used much as a strap wrench.
4. Pull off sprocket (**Figure 67**).
5. Inspect sprocket teeth for wear. Excessive wear results in shortened chain life. Replace the sprocket if it is worn. **Figure 68** compares worn and serviceable sprockets.

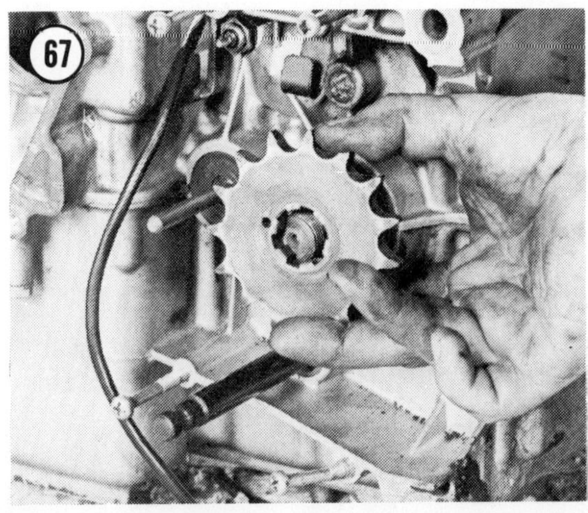

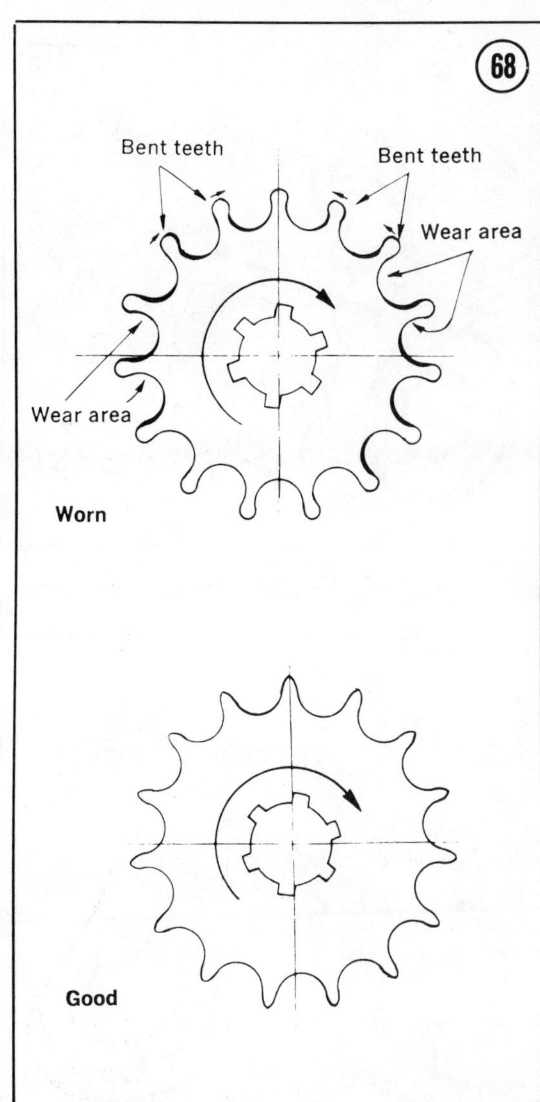

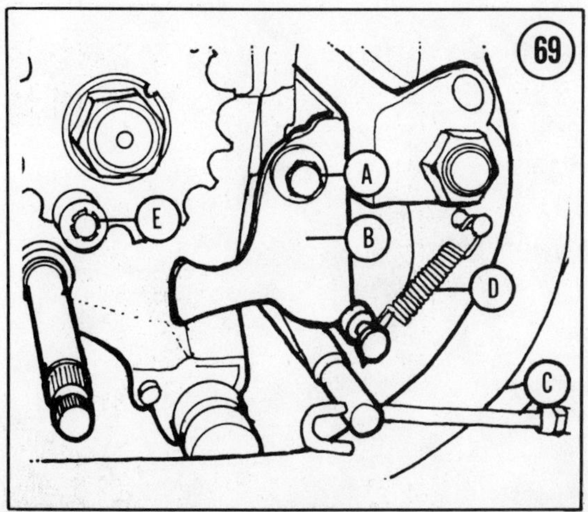

6. Reverse the removal procedure to install the sprocket. Tighten its retaining nut to 87-108 ft.-lb. (12-15 mkg). Be sure to bend up a tab on the lockwasher.

> NOTE: *Use a shifter shaft oil seal guide to protect the oil seal when the sprocket cover is installed.*

Removal/Installation (Models B and C)

1. Remove the engine sprocket cover as described in this chapter.
2. Remove the pivot bolt (A, **Figure 69**), lever (B, **Figure 69**), rod (C, **Figure 69**) and return spring (D, **Figure 69**).

> NOTE: *Don't lose the nut, collar, and flat washer on the pivot bolt.*

3. Remove the E-clip (or cotter pin), flat washer, and collar from the pin on the engine sprocket.
4. Straighten out the tab on the lockwasher and remove the nut and toothed washer securing the engine sprocket.

> NOTE: *To keep the sprocket from turning, have an assistant hold the rear brake on to keep the chain from moving.*

5. Loosen rear axle nut and slide rear wheel forward to provide chain slack.
6. Remove the engine sprocket and drive chain.
7. Install by reversing these removal steps. Always install a new lockwasher and be sure to install the tooth into the hole in the sprocket (**Figure 70**).
8. Install the engine sprocket nut and tighten to 58 ft.-lb. (8.0 mkg).
9. Bend up one side of the toothed lockwasher against a side of the nut.

IGNITION ADVANCE UNIT

Figure 71 is an exploded view of the ignition advance mechanism. Refer to it during disassembly and service.

1. Remove breaker point cover.

4

2. Remove breaker plate, breaker points, and condenser as an assembly (**Figure 72**).

3. Remove the smaller bolt from end of crankshaft.

4. Pull advance mechanism from crankshaft (**Figure 73**).

5. Check all parts for wear or binding. Be sure that neither spring is broken.

6. When installing the cam, be sure to align the mark on the cam with the notch on the advance unit. Tighten the retaining bolt to 16.5-19.5 ft.-lb. (2.3-2.7 mkg).

7. Install the timing advancer onto the crankshaft — be sure to align the notch on back of the advancer with the pin on the end of the crankshaft.

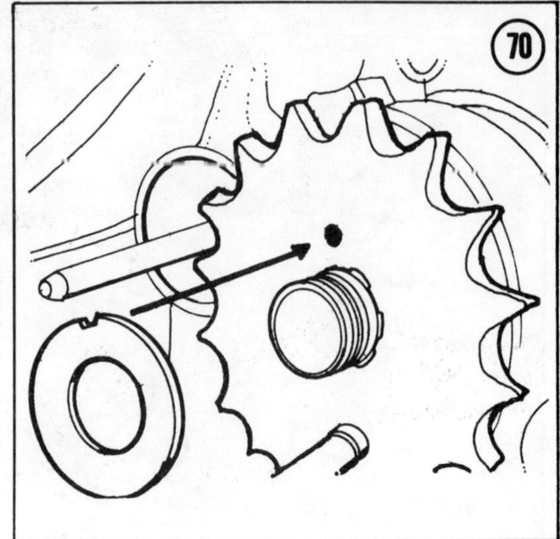

70

71

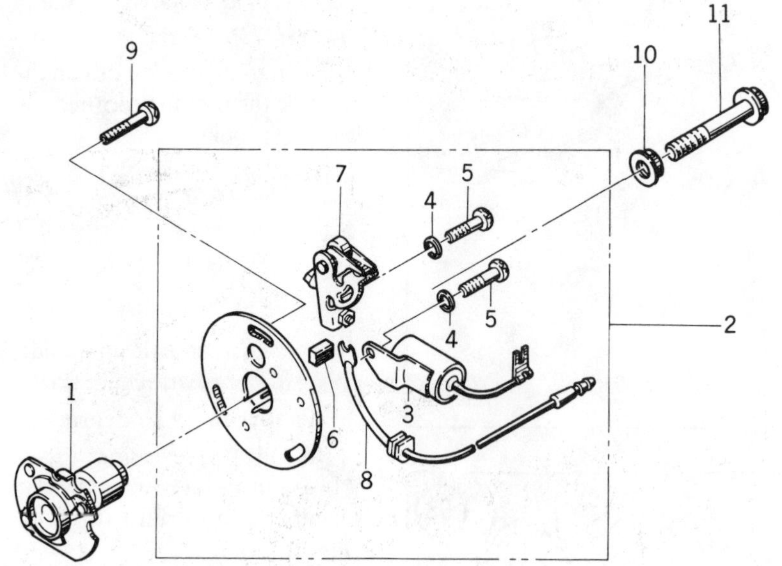

IGNITION ADVANCE MECHANISM

1. Advancer
2. Breaker assembly
3. Condenser
4. Washer
5. Screw
6. Lubricator
7. Contact breaker
8. Harness
9. Screw
10. Washer
11. Bolt

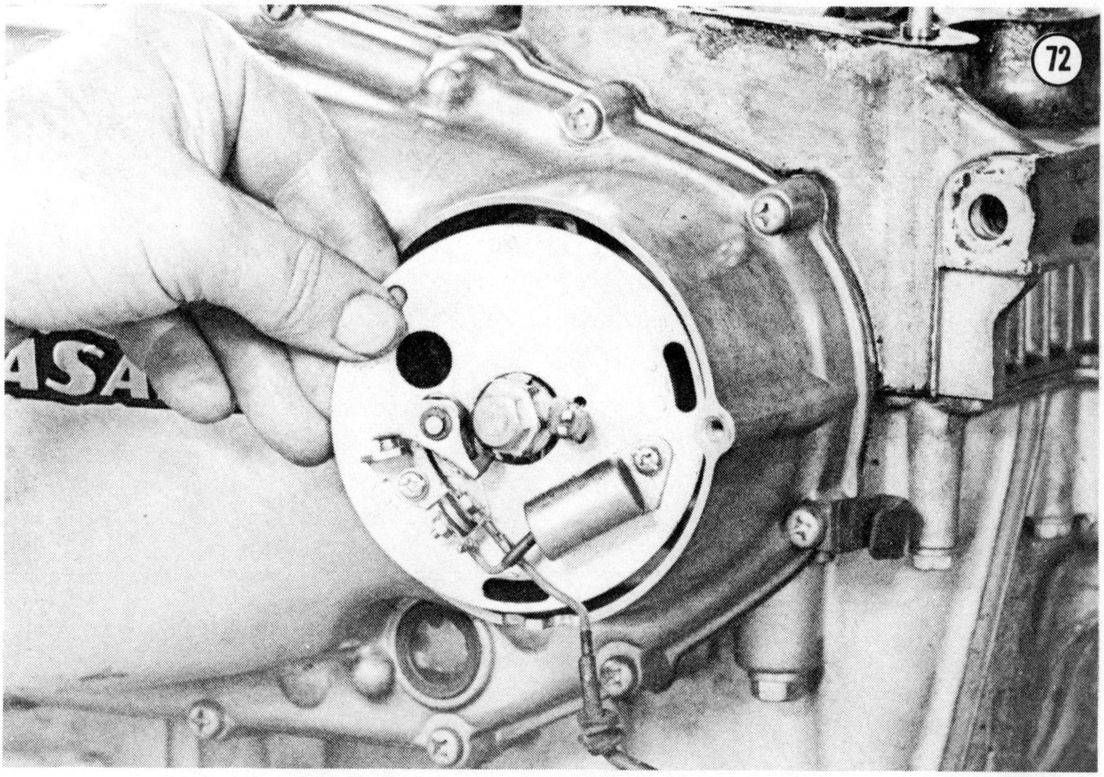

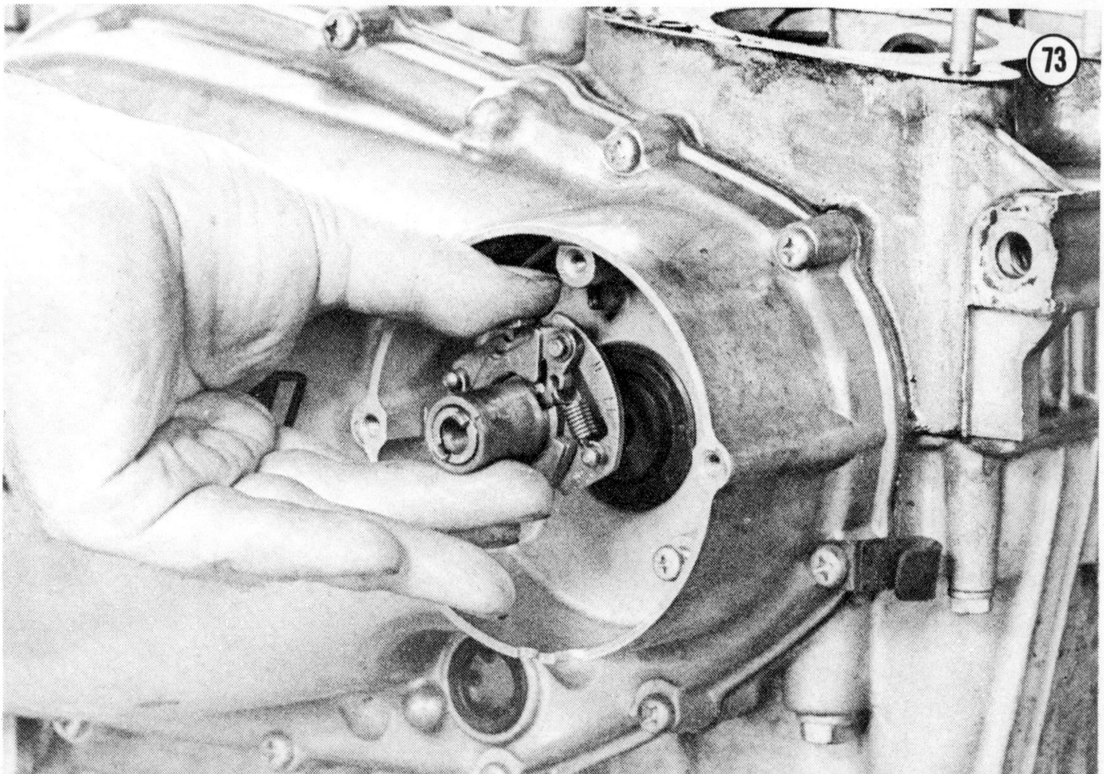

72

73

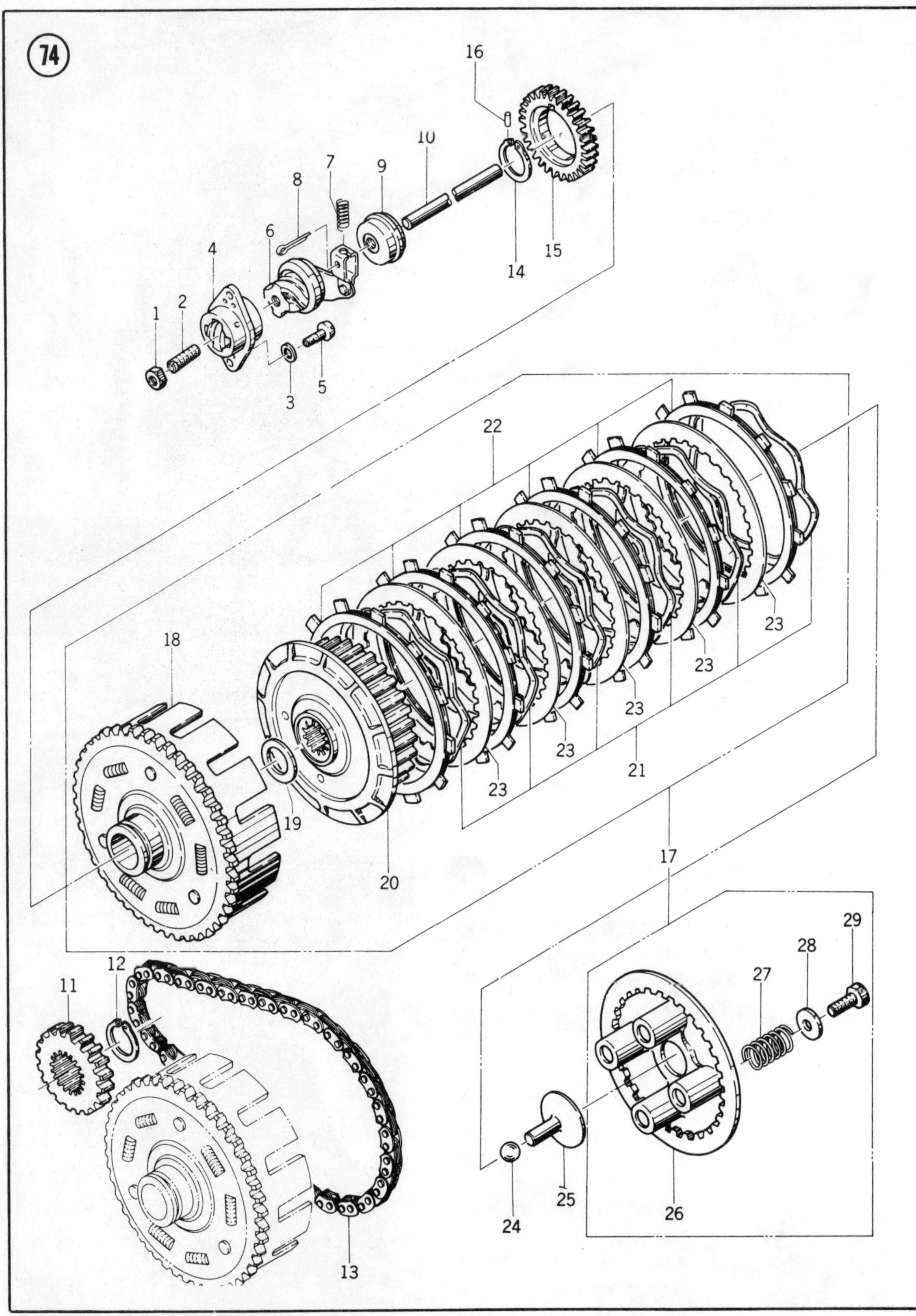
74
1
2
3
4
5
6
7
8
9
10
11
12
13
14
15
16
17
18
19
20
21
22
23
24
25
26
27
28
29

CLUTCH AND PRIMARY DRIVE CHAIN (MODELS D AND S)

1. Nut
2. Screw
3. Washer
4. Outer clutch release
5. Screw
6. Inner clutch release
7. Clutch release spring
8. Cotter pin
9. Oil seal
10. Clutch pushrod
11. Primary sprocket
12. Circlip
13. Primary drive chain
14. Circlip
15. Oil pump gear
16. Dowel pin
17. Clutch assembly
18. Clutch housing
19. Clutch thrust washer
20. Clutch hub
21. Steel ring
22. Friction plate
23. Steel plate
24. Steel ball
25. Pressure plate lifter
26. Spring plate
27. Clutch spring
28. Clutch spring holder
29. Hex bolt

8. After installing the advance mechanism, it is necessary to apply a small quantity of distributor cam lubricant to the breaker cam. Be sure to adjust ignition timing. Refer to Chapter Three for details.

RIGHT CRANKCASE COVER

It is necessary to remove the right crankcase cover to gain access to the primary reduction sprockets, clutch, oil pump, and shifter linkage.

> NOTE: *A small quantity of oil remains under the cover, even though the engine was drained previously. Place a suitable drain pan underneath before removing the cover.*

4

Removal/Installation

1. Remove ignition advance unit and right-hand footpeg.
2. Remove pinch bolt from kickstarter pedal, then pull pedal from shaft.
3. Remove all cover retaining screws.
4. Tap cover with a rubber mallet to free it, then remove it from engine.

> NOTE: *Do not pry the cover from the engine. If any damage occurs to either sealing surface, an oil leak will result.*

5. Reverse the removal procedure to install the cover. Replace the kickstarter oil seal if it leaks or if there is any doubt about its condition. Always install a new gasket.

CLUTCH AND PRIMARY DRIVE (MODELS D AND S)

Figure 74 is an exploded view of the clutch and primary drive chain. Refer to it during service on these items. Be sure to take note of how all small parts, such as thrust washers and springs, are installed.

Clutch Removal

1. Remove bolts, washers, and springs. See **Figure 75**.

2. Remove pressure plate (**Figure 76**).

3. Remove pressure plate lifter (**Figure 77**).

4. Tilt engine to the right, then catch small ball (24, **Figure 74**) as it comes from the hole or use a small magnet to extract it.

5. Pull out steel rings, steel discs, and friction discs (**Figure 78**). Note how these parts are installed.

6. Remove snap ring and any shims from transmission shaft.

7. Remove clutch hub (**Figure 79**) and thrust washer.

8. Remove snap ring from primary drive sprocket.

9. Pull off clutch housing, primary chain, and primary sprocket as an assembly (**Figure 80**).

10. Pull out clutch pushrod from left side of engine (**Figure 81**).

Clutch Inspection

1. Measure free length of each clutch spring (**Figure 82**). If free length of any spring is less than 1.27 in. (32.3mm), replace them all.

2. Measure thickness of each friction disc at several places (**Figure 83**). Replace any disc that is worn unevenly or if it is worn at any point to 0.098 in. (2.5mm). Standard friction disc thickness is 0.122 in. (3.90mm).

3. Check each metal disc for warpage by placing it on a surface plate. Then try to insert a 0.016 in. (0.40mm) feeler gauge between the surface plate and metal disc. Replace any metal disc that is warped by that amount.

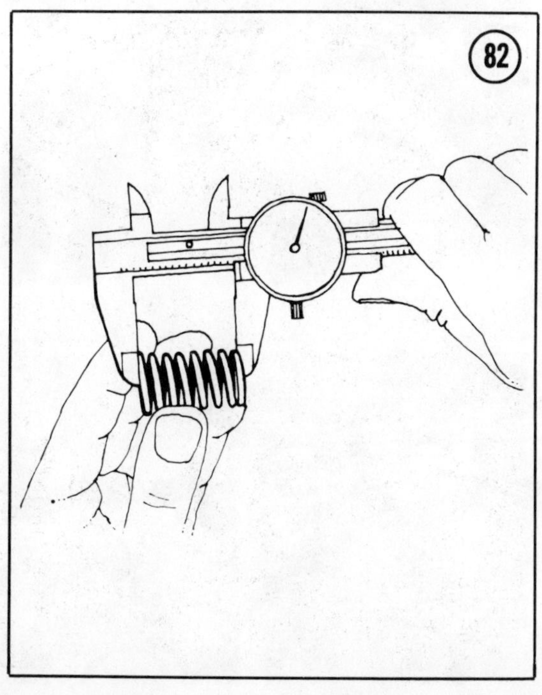

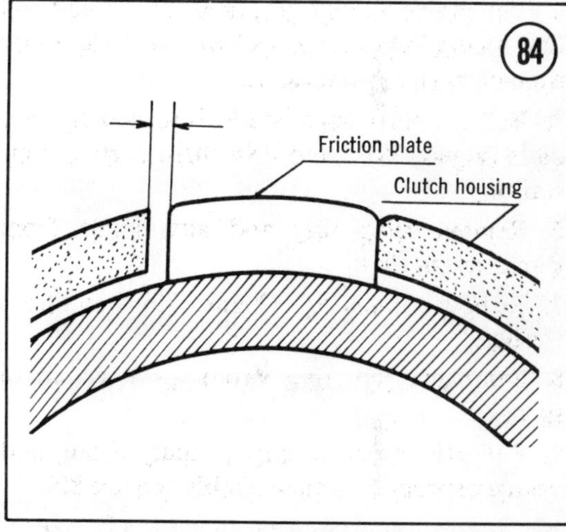

4. Check each friction disc as specified in Step 3. Replace any friction disc that is warped by 0.012 in. (0.30mm).

5. Check for broken or bent steel rings. Replace any defective ones.

6. Measure clearance between the fingers on the clutch housing and the tangs on the friction plates (**Figure 84**). Standard clearance is 0.006 in. (0.15mm). Replace any friction disc with clearance greater than 0.024 in. (0.60mm).

7. Refer to **Figure 85**. Replace the clutch housing if deep notches exist.

8. Measure clearance between the clutch hub and transmission shaft. Replace the clutch housing if clearance exceeds 0.0064 in. (0.162mm). Standard clearance is 0.0008 in. (0.02mm).

4

9. Roll the clutch release pushrod on a flat surface. Straighten or replace it if it is bent.

10. Inspect clutch sprocket teeth. Minor roughness may be smoothed with an oilstone. If damage cannot be corrected, replace the sprocket, and examine the primary chain for damage also.

Clutch Installation

Reverse the disassembly procedure to install the clutch. Take care to install all spacers correctly. Be sure that the punch mark on the clutch hub aligns with the raised dot on the pressure plate (**Figure 86**).

Primary Chain

Measure primary chain wear as shown in **Figure 87**. Measure vertical play in the center of the upper chain run. Replace the chain if vertical play exceeds 0.78 in. (20mm).

Also measure thickness of both chain guides. Replace them if they are worn to 0.14 in. (3.5mm). Standard thickness is 0.29 in. (7.5mm). Apply thread cement to the chain guide retaining screws when installing them.

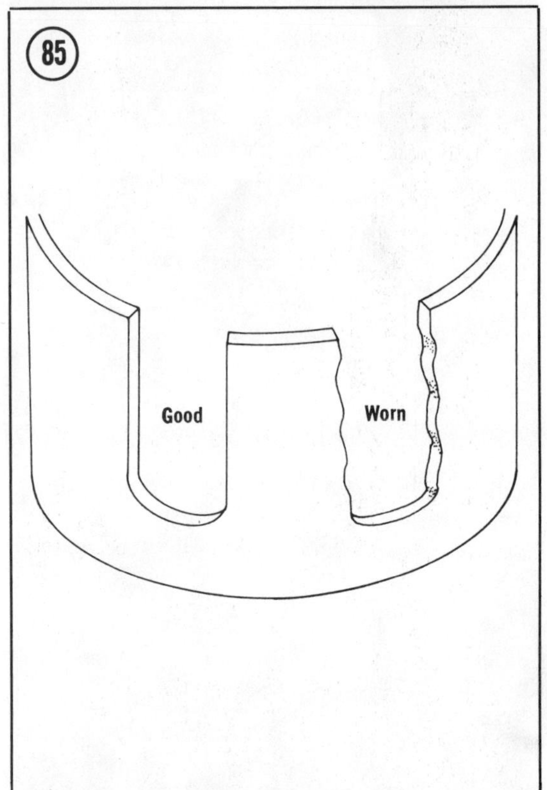

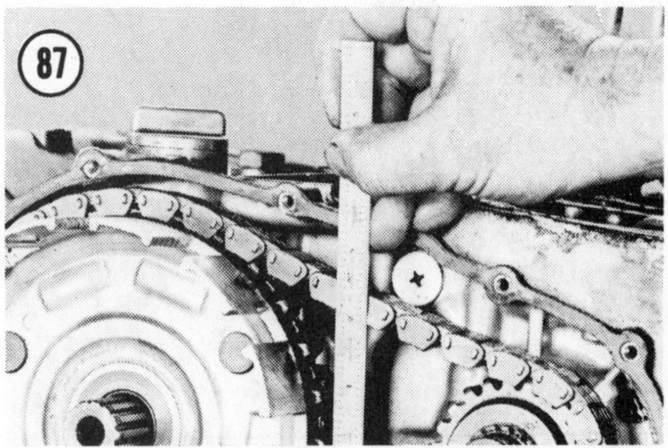

CLUTCH AND PRIMARY DRIVE (MODELS B AND C)

Figure 88 is an exploded view of the clutch and primary drive chain. Refer to it during service on these items. Be sure to take note of how all small parts, such as thrust washers and springs, are installed.

Clutch Removal

1. Remove bolts, washers, and springs. See **Figure 89**.
2. Remove pressure plate (**Figure 90**).
3. Remove pressure plate lifter (15, **Figure 88**).
4. Tilt engine to the right, then catch small ball (14, **Figure 88**) as it comes from the hole or use a small magnet to extract it.
5. Remove the 6 friction plates and 5 steel plates. Note how these parts are installed.
6. Remove the circlip and shim(s) securing the clutch hub.
7. Remove the clutch hub (**Figure 91**) and thrust washer.

88

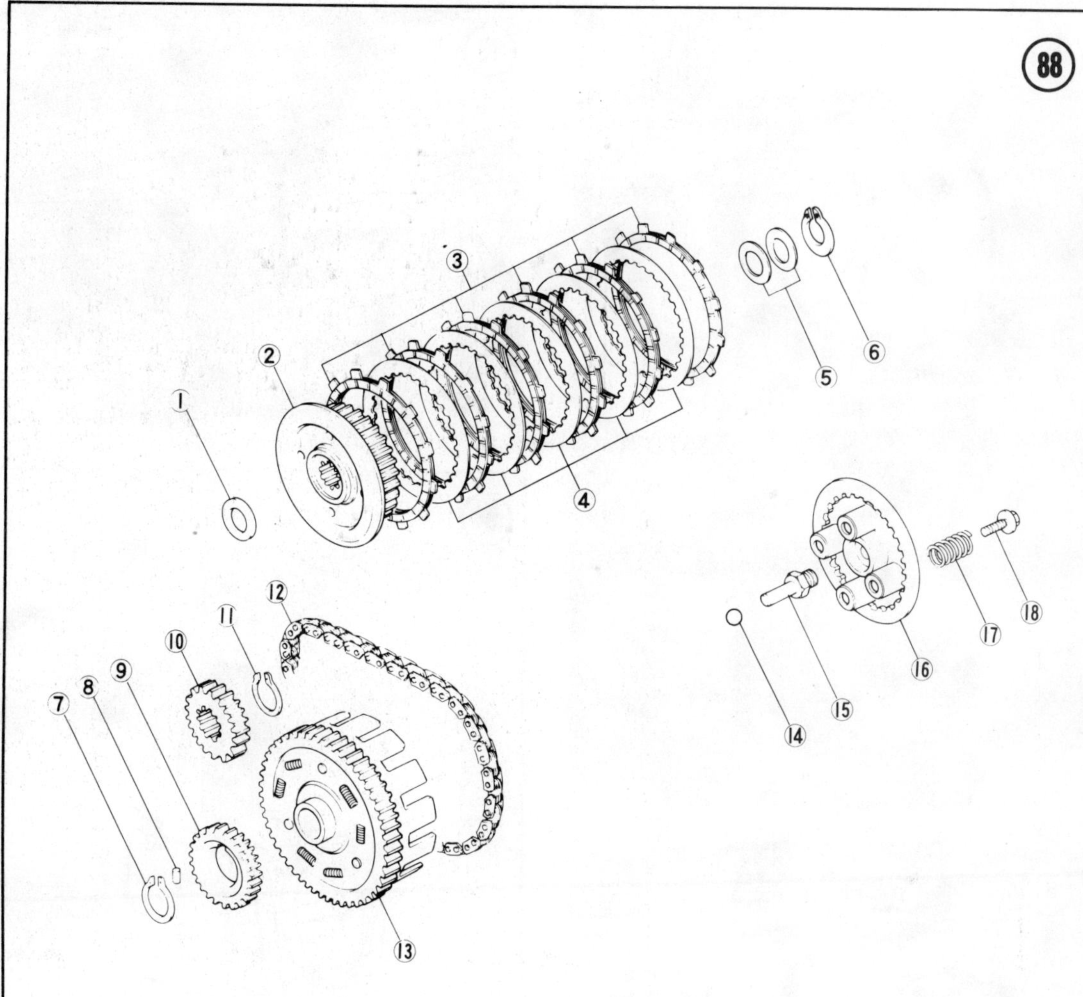

CLUTCH AND PRIMARY DRIVE CHAIN — MODELS B AND C

1. Thrust washer
2. Clutch hub
3. Friction plate
4. Steel plate
5. Shim(s)
6. Circlip
7. Circlip
8. Pin
9. Oil pump drive gear
10. Primary sprocket
11. Circlip
12. Primary chain
13. Clutch housing
14. Steel ball
15. Pressure plate lifter
16. Pressure plate
17. Spring
18. Bolt

89

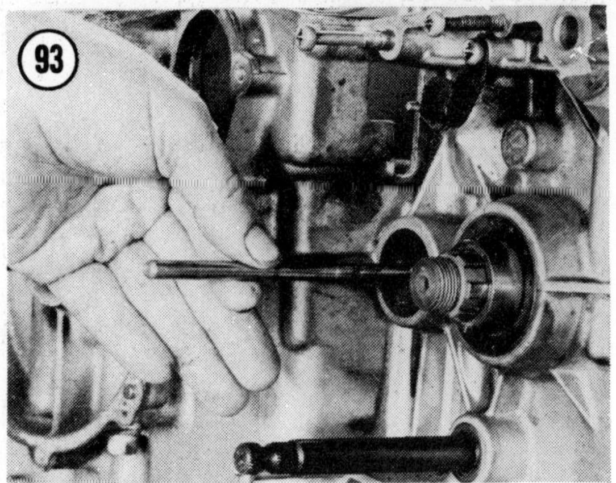
93

90

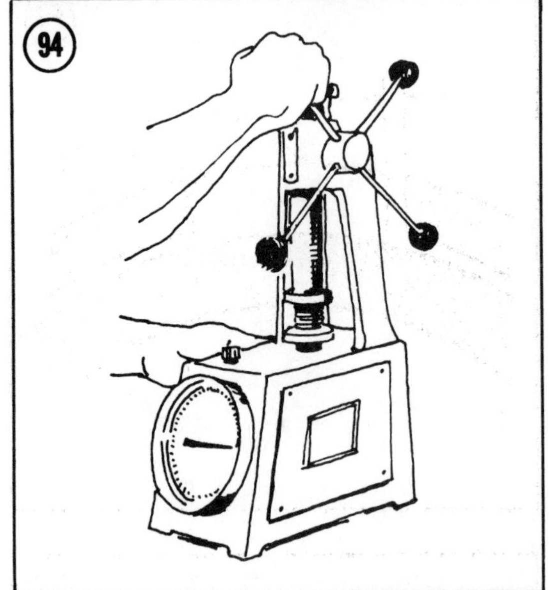
94

91

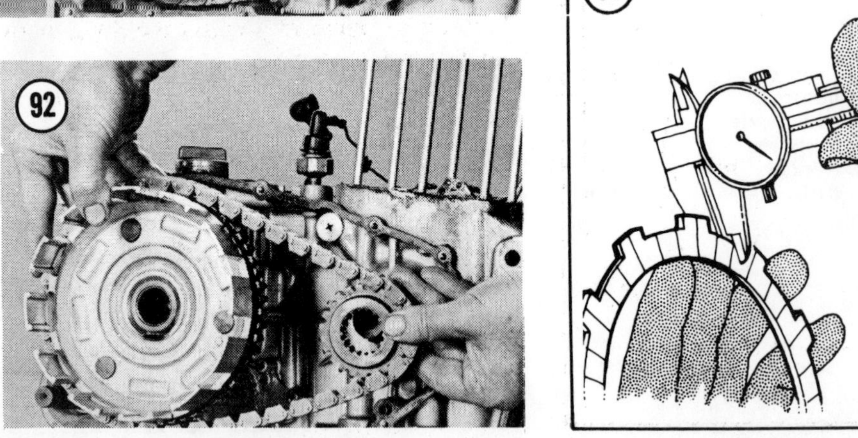
92
95

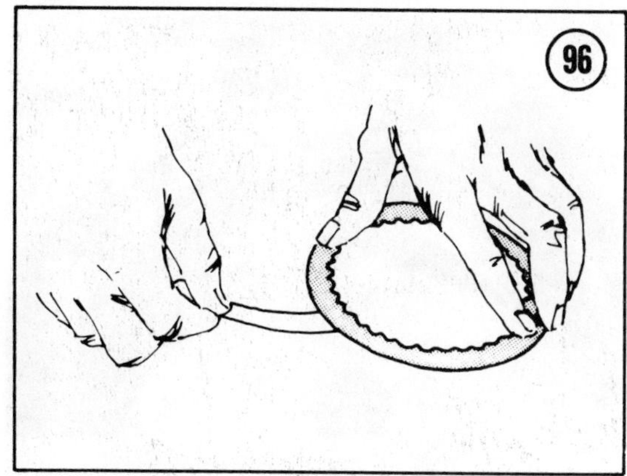

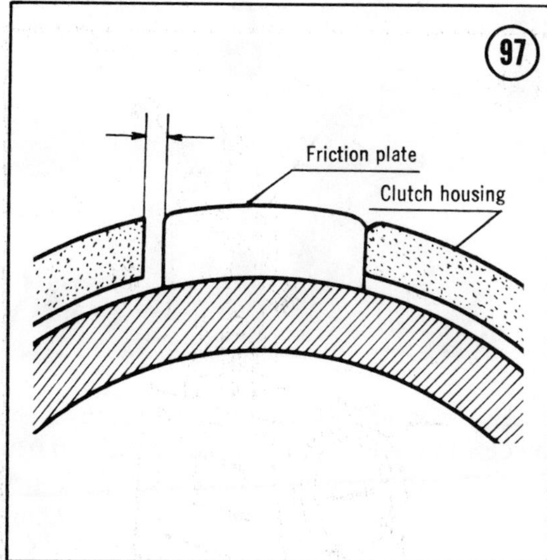

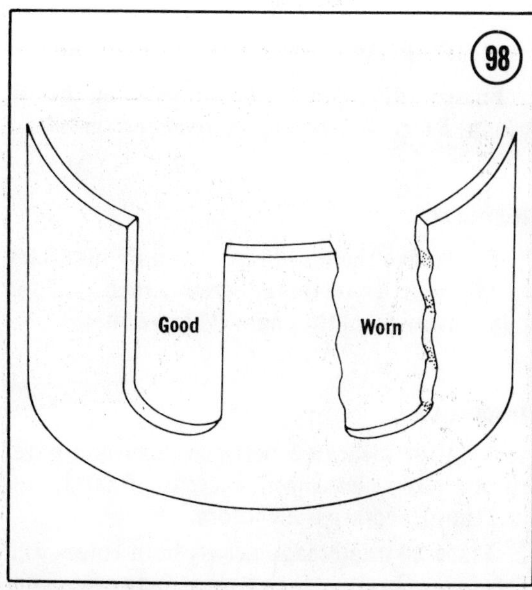

8. Remove the circlip from the primary drive sprocket.

9. Pull off clutch housing, primary chain, and primary sprocket as an assembly (**Figure 92**).

10. Pull the clutch pushrod from the left-hand side of the engine (**Figure 93**).

Inspection

1. Measure the tension of the clutch springs. This test requires the use of a special spring testing tool (**Figure 94**). Compress each spring to the length of 0.925 in. (23.5mm); replace all springs if one has a tension of 47.398 lb. (21.5kg) or less.
2. Measure the thickness of each friction disc at several places (**Figure 95**). Replace any disc that is worn unevenly or if it is worn at any point to 0.106 in. (2.7mm). Standard friction disc thickness is 0.114-0.122 in. (2.9-3.1mm).
3. Check each metal disc for warpage by placing it on a surface plate. Then try to insert a 0.016 in. (0.40mm) feeler gauge (**Figure 96**) between the surface plate and metal disc. Replace any metal disc that is warped by that amount.
4. Check each friction disc as specified in Step 3. Replace any friction disc that is warped by 0.012 in. (0.30mm).
5. Check for broken or bent steel rings. Replace any defective ones.
6. Measure clearance between the fingers on the clutch housing and the tangs on the friction plates (**Figure 97**). Standard clearance is 0.008 in. (0.2mm). Replace any friction disc with clearance greater than 0.0157 in. (0.4mm).
7. Refer to **Figure 98**. Replace the clutch housing if deep notches exist.
8. Measure the inside diameter of the clutch housing with an inside micrometer or cylinder gauge. Standard dimension is 0.9842-0.9851 in. (25.0-25.021mm). Replace it if the dimension is 0.9854 in. (25.03mm) or greater.
9. Measure the outside diameter of the drive shaft, in the area where the clutch housing operates, with a micrometer. Standard dimension is 0.9825-0.9835 in. (24.959-24.980mm). Replace the shaft if the dimension is 0.9819 in. (24.94mm) or less.

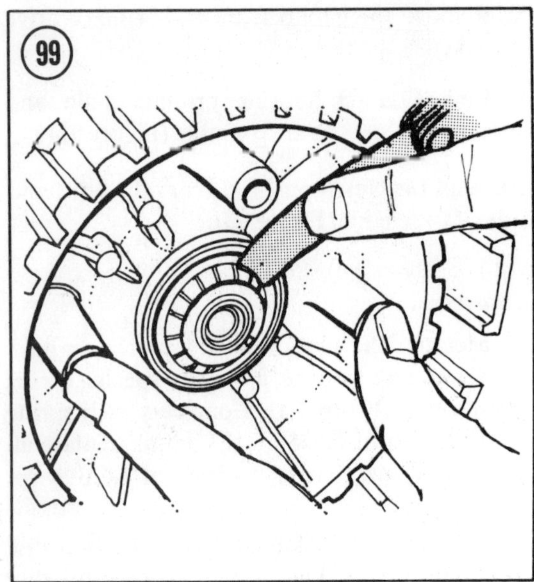

99

10. Roll the clutch release pushrod on a flat surface. Straighten or replace it if it is bent.

11. Inspect clutch sprocket teeth. Minor roughness may be smoothed with an oilstone. If damage cannot be corrected, replace the sprocket, and examine the primary chain for damage also.

Installation

1. Installation is the reverse of the removal steps, noting the following.

2. After the clutch hub, shim, and circlip have been installed, measure the clearance between the clutch hub and shim (**Figure 99**). Standard clearance is 0.3mm and shims are available in thicknesses of 0.3 and 0.5mm. Add to or replace the existing shim to achieve the correct clearance.

3. If new friction and/or steel plates are installed, coat all surfaces with engine oil prior to installation to avoid clutch seizure.

4. Install the pressure plate. Make sure to align the punch mark on the clutch hub with raised dot on the pressure plate (**Figure 100**).

Primary Chain

Measure primary chain wear as shown in **Figure 101**. Measure vertical play in the center of the upper chain run. Replace the chain if vertical play exceeds 0.78 in. (20mm).

100

101

Also measure the thickness of both chain guides. Replace them if they are worn to 0.079 in. (2.0mm). Standard thickness for the upper one is 0.177 in. (4.5mm) and 0.236 in. (6.0mm) for the lower one.

OIL PUMP (MODELS D AND S)

Figure 102 is an exploded view of the oil pump. Refer to it during removal and service.

Removal

To remove the oil pump, it is only necessary to take out its retaining screws, then pull the pump away from the engine (**Figure 103**).

Inspection

1. Measure clearance between inner and outer rotors. If clearance exceeds 0.0083 in. (0.21mm), replace both rotors.

2. Place a straightedge across both rotors and the pump body. If clearance between either

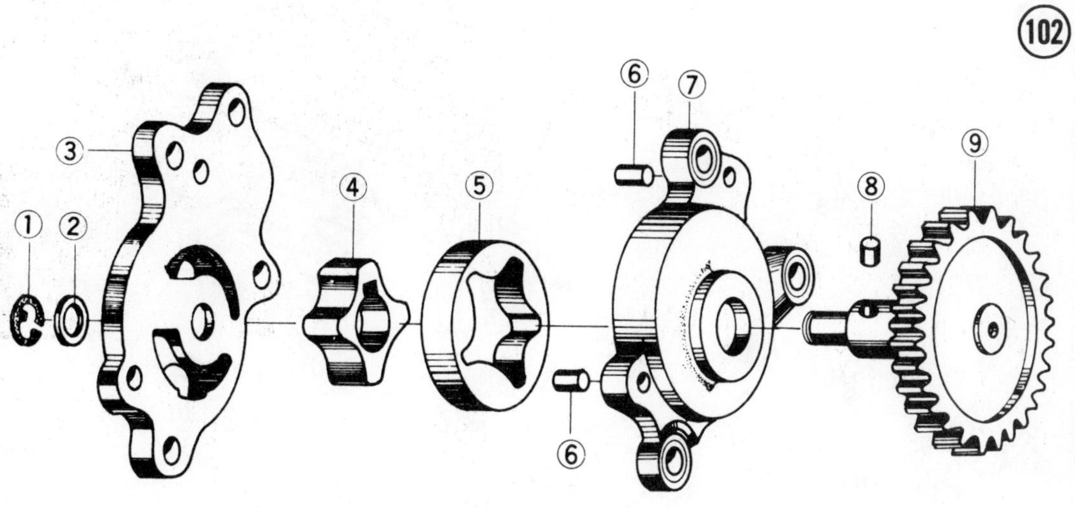

(102)

OIL PUMP — MODELS D AND S

1. Clip
2. Washer
3. Outer body
4. Inner rotor
5. Outer rotor
6. Dowel
7. Inner body
8. Pin
9. Oil pump gear

(103)

rotor and the straightedge exceeds 0.006 in. (0.15mm), replace both rotors.

3. Measure clearance between the outer rotor and pump body. Replace the outer rotor or the pump body if clearance exceeds 0.01 in. (0.25mm).

Installation

Be sure to install the pump rotors so that the punched marks face outward, away from the drive gear.

Reverse the removal procedure to install the oil pump. It is a good idea to replace all O-rings upon installation.

OIL PUMP (MODELS B AND C)

Figure 104 is an exploded view of the oil pump. Refer to it during removal and service.

Removal

To remove the oil pump, it is only necessary to take out its retaining screws, then pull the pump away from the engine **(Figure 105)**.

Disassembly

Remove the bolt and lockwasher **(Figure 106)** and remove the cover plate.

Inspection

1. Measure clearance between inner and outer rotors. If clearance exceeds 0.0083 in. (0.21mm), replace both rotors.

2. Place a straightedge across both rotors and the pump body. If clearance between either

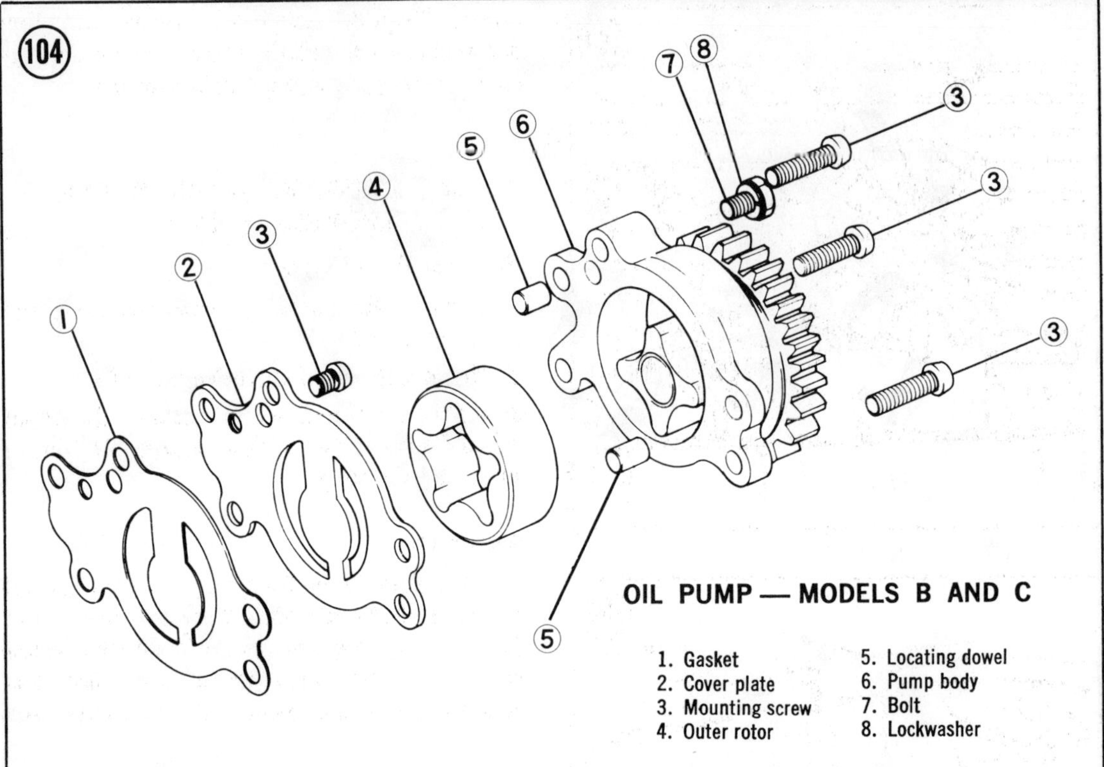

rotor and the straightedge exceeds 0.006 in. (0.15mm), replace both rotors.

3. Measure clearance between the outer rotor and pump body. Replace the outer rotor or the pump body if clearance exceeds 0.01 in. (0.25mm).

Assembly

Make sure the locating dowels (5, **Figure 104**) are in place. After assembly, rotate the gear and make sure all parts turn smoothly.

Installation

Install the pump onto the engine and install the three screws. Always install a new gasket.

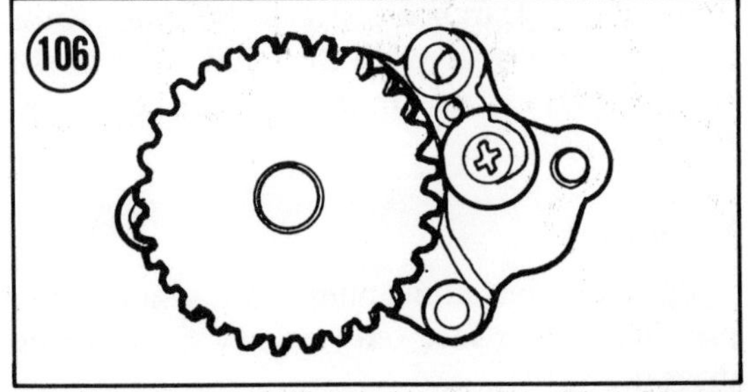

Oil Pump Screen

To protect the oil pump, a screen is installed in the lower crankcase. It removes any small metal particles and other foreign matter that may otherwise damage the pump.

Remove the 5 screws (**Figure 107**) securing the oil screen cover and remove it and the

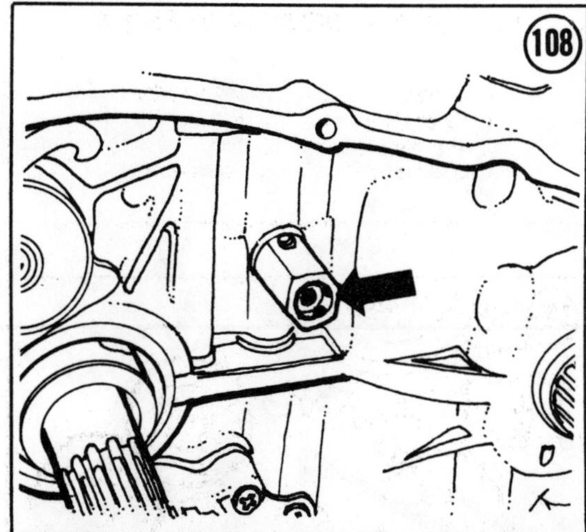

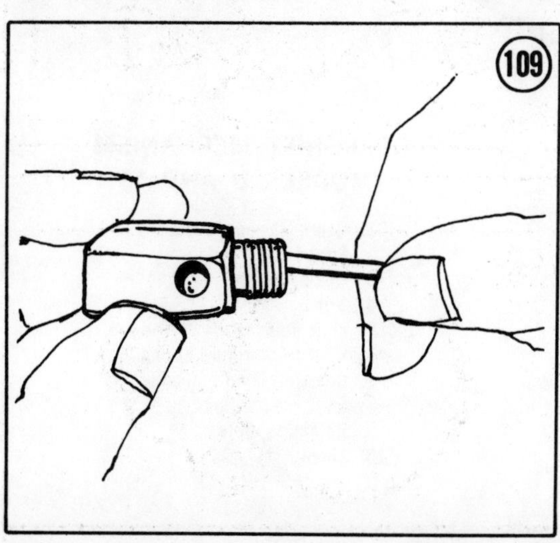

screen. Clean the screen with solvent and blow dry with compressed air. If the screen is damaged in any way, replace it with a new one.

OIL PRESSURE RELIEF VALVE (MODELS B AND C)

Removal/Installation

1. Remove the clutch, primary sprocket, and primary chain.
2. Remove the relief valve (**Figure 108**).
3. Apply Loctite Lock N' Seal to the relief valve threads prior to installation. Tighten to 11 ft.-lb (1.5 mkg).

Inspection

Push in on the ball with a small wood dowel or soft rod (**Figure 109**). Check to make sure the spring pushes the ball back into its seated position. If not, clean the valve assembly (intact) in solvent and blow dry with compressed air.

NOTE: *Do not disassemble the valve as this may affect or change valve operation.*

If the ball will not seat correctly, replace the entire unit. Replacement parts are not available.

SHIFTER LINKAGE

Refer to **Figure 110** (Models D and S) or **Figure 111** (Models B and C) for this procedure.

Removal

1. Remove the 2 screws (**Figure 112**) securing the shifter shaft retaining plate (8) and remove it.
2. Move the shift mechanism arm(s) from the shift drum.
3. Slide the shifter linkage and shaft out from the engine. See **Figure 113** (Models D and S) and **Figure 111**, items 1, 4, and 7 (Models B and C).

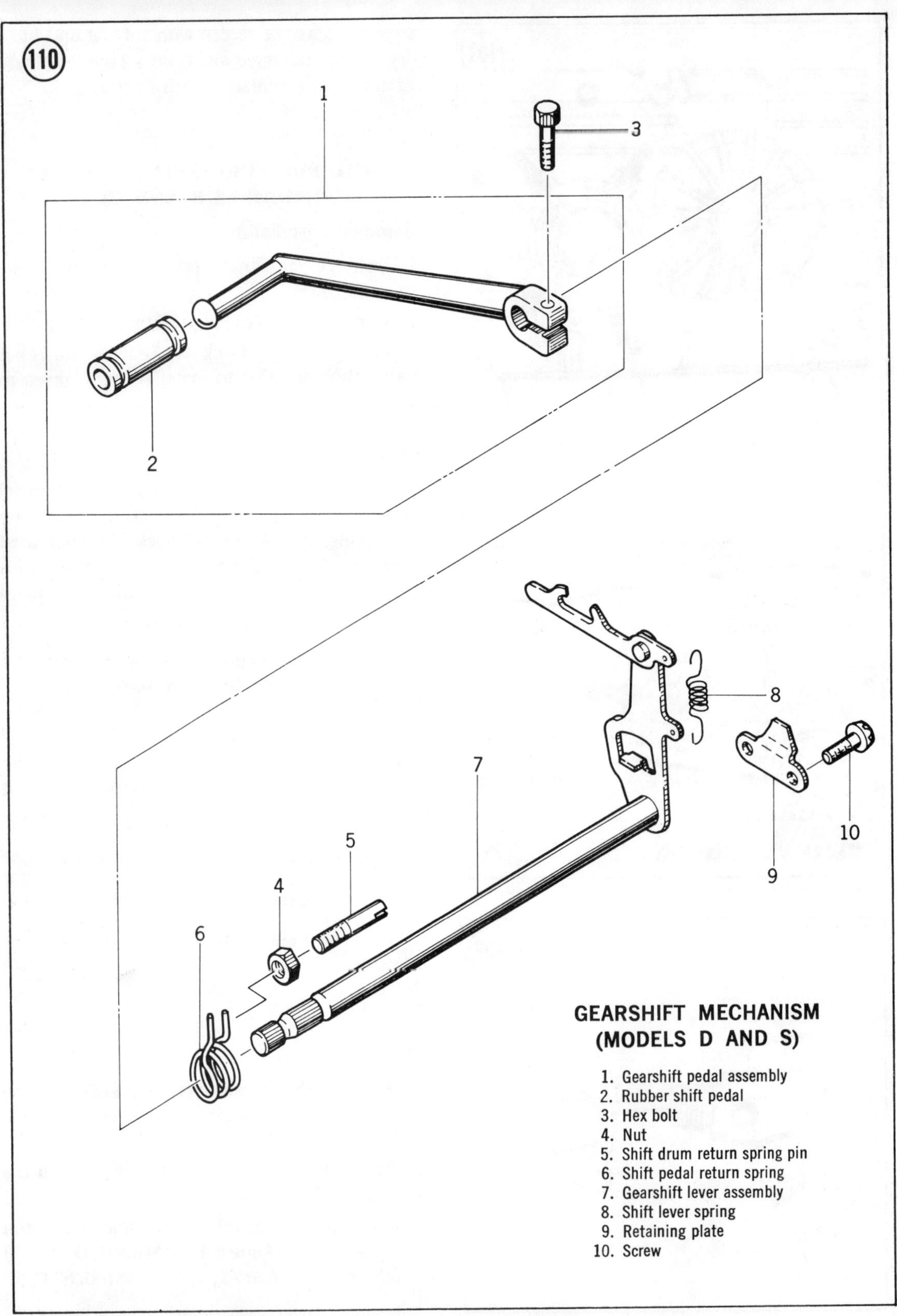
110
1
2
3
4
5
6
7
8
9
10
GEARSHIFT MECHANISM
(MODELS D AND S)
1. Gearshift pedal assembly
2. Rubber shift pedal
3. Hex bolt
4. Nut
5. Shift drum return spring pin
6. Shift pedal return spring
7. Gearshift lever assembly
8. Shift lever spring
9. Retaining plate
10. Screw

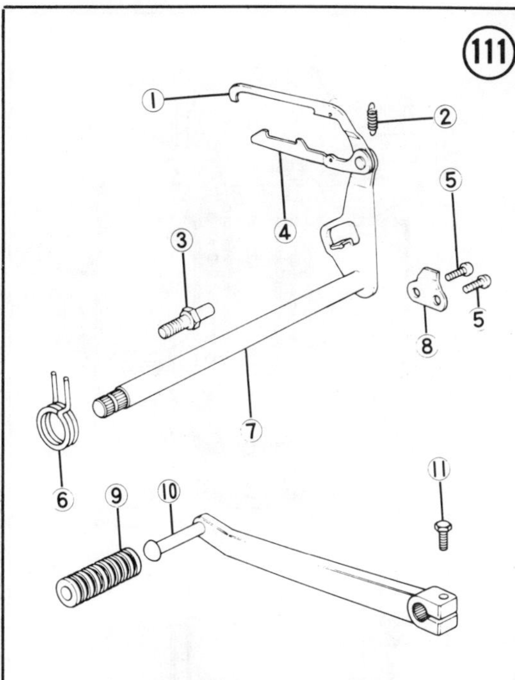

GEARSHIFT MECHANISM
(MODELS B AND C)

1. Overshift limiter
2. Pawl spring
3. Return spring pin
4. Shift mechanism arm
5. Screw
6. Return spring
7. Shift shaft
8. Shift mechanism stop
9. Pedal rubber
10. Shift pedal
11. Bolt

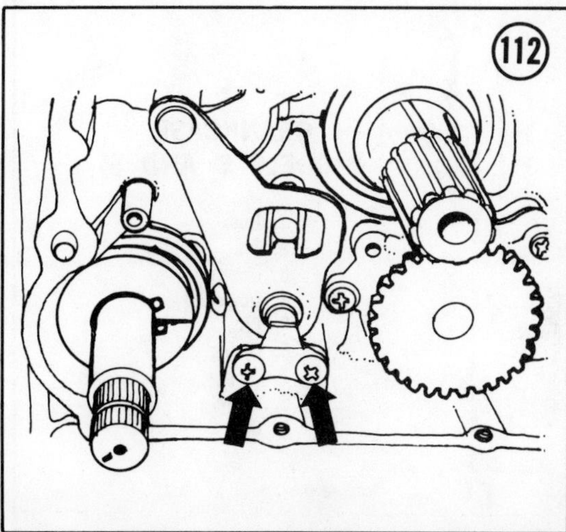

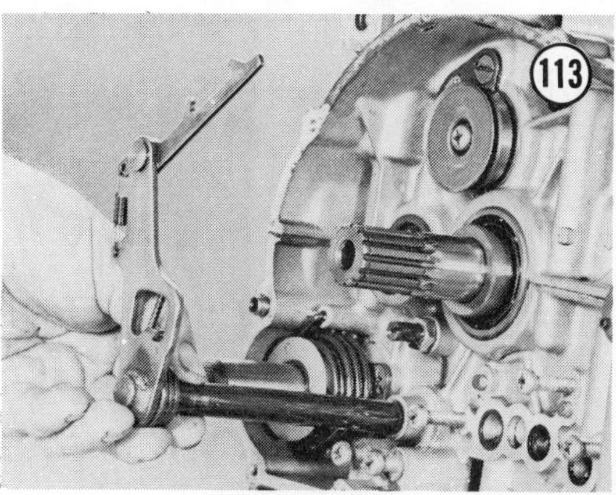

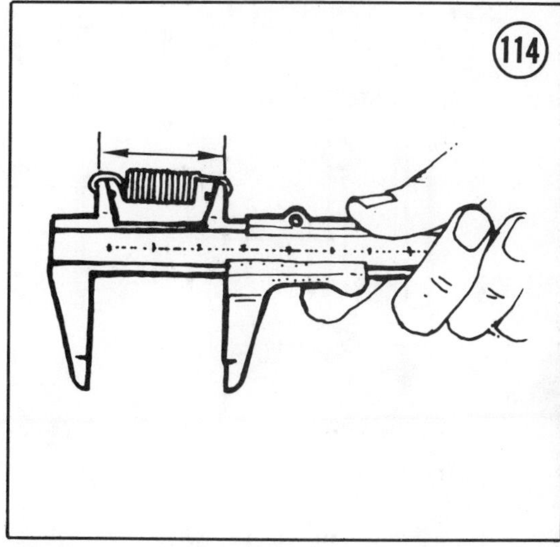

Inspection

1. Measure the length of the shift pawl spring as shown in **Figure 114**. Replace the spring if its length exceeds 1.22 in. (31 mm) for Models D and S and 0.75 in. (19 mm) for Models B and C.
2. Check all other parts for obvious wear or damage. Replace any which are doubtful.
3. Be sure that the return spring pin is not loose. If it is, remove it, clean it and its threaded hole, and reinstall it, using a suitable thread locking compound.

Installation

Shifter installation is the reverse of removal. Be sure to protect the oil seal with a suitable guide when inserting the shaft through it.

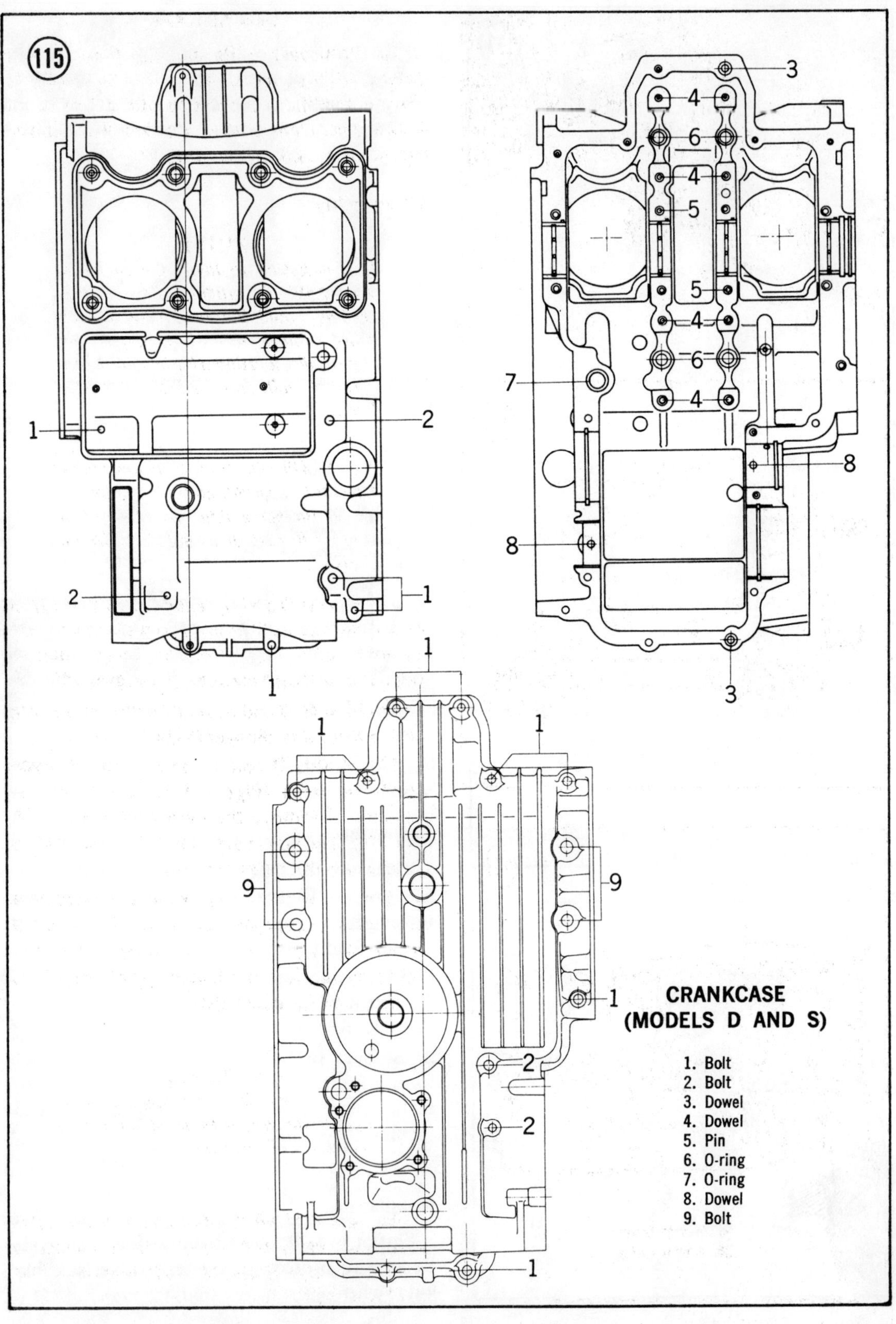
115
1
2
3
4
5
6
7
8
9
CRANKCASE
(MODELS D AND S)
1. Bolt
2. Bolt
3. Dowel
4. Dowel
5. Pin
6. O-ring
7. O-ring
8. Dowel
9. Bolt

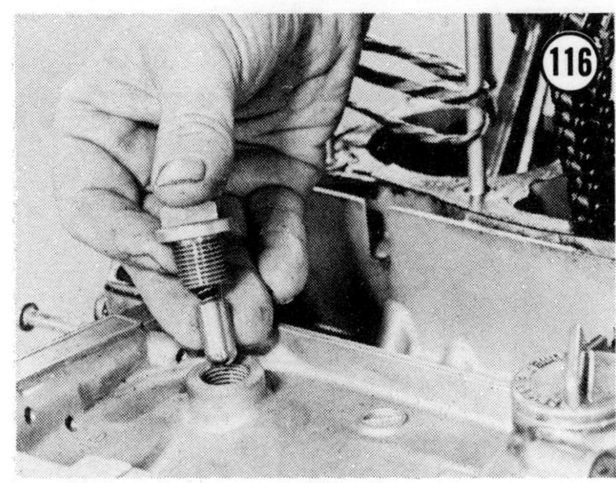

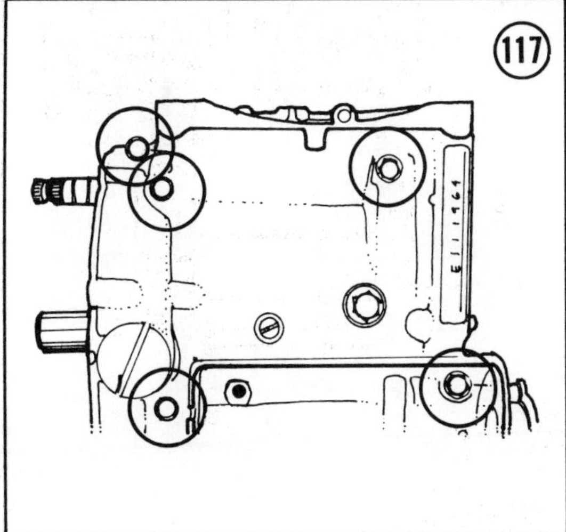

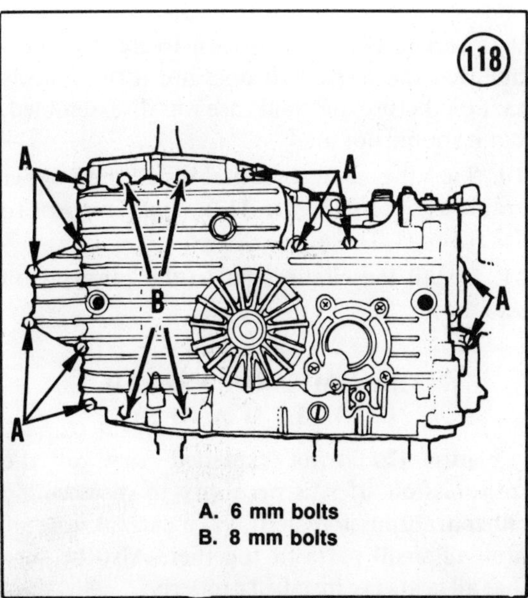

A. 6 mm bolts
B. 8 mm bolts

CRANKCASE

The crankcase splits into upper and lower halves, without special tools. It is necessary to disassemble the crankcase to gain access to the kickstarter, transmission, crankshaft, balancer mechanism, and engine bearings.

Disassembly

CAUTION
It is necessary to invert the engine to disassemble the crankcase. Before proceeding, obtain blocks of wood or some other suitable means to support the engine. Do not support the engine by the cylinder hold-down studs; they may bend.

NOTE: *Oil will drain from the engine when it is inverted, and will continue to do so for some time. Be prepared to catch it in rags or a suitable collection vessel.*

1. On Models D and S, remove the 6 bolts from upper crankcase, then invert engine and remove 14 lower bolts. A few bolts are longer than the others; note their locations. See **Figure 115**.
2. On Models D and S, remove the neutral stop bolt, spring, and plunger (**Figure 116**).
3. On Models B and C, remove the 5 upper crankcase bolts (**Figure 117**) and invert the engine and remove the eleven 6mm bolts (A, **ure 118**). The bolts vary in length; make note of their locations during removal.
4. Gently lift the lower crankcase away from the upper crankcase. There are 3 pry points where the crankcase halves mate. Use these points carefully with a broad tipped screwdriver to help split the case halves.

CAUTION
Do not pry the cases apart between mating surfaces with any metal tool or an oil leak will develop.

5. Be sure that all shafts remain in the upper crankcase half; tap them with a rubber or plastic mallet, if necessary, to loosen them from the lower half.

4

Inspection

Clean both halves thoroughly in solvent and blow dry with compressed air. Inspect them for cracks or other damage. Pay close attention to mating surfaces. Nicks and gouges will result in oil leaks.

Assembly

1. Be sure that all internal components are installed properly, fasteners are tight, oil seals and O-rings properly installed, and crankcase locating dowels are in position.
2. Place transmission in NEUTRAL.
3. Make sure case half sealing surfaces are perfectly clean and dry.
4. Apply a light coat of gasket sealer to the sealing surfaces of both halves. Cover only flat surfaces, not curved bearing surfaces. Make the coating as thin as possible or the case can shift and hammer out bearings. Join both halves and tap them together lightly with a plastic mallet — do not use a metal hammer as it will damage the cases.

> NOTE: *Use Gasgacinch Gasket Sealer, or equivalent. When selecting an equivalent, avoid thick and hard setting materials.*

5. Make sure the oil seals don't slip out of place.
6. On Models D and S, set lower crankcase into position, then tighten 8mm crankshaft bearing bolts in the order shown in **Figure 119** (disregard bolts 1, 2, 3, and 4). Tightening torque for these bolts is 18-22 ft.-lb. (2.5-3.0 mkg). Then tighten all remaining lower bolts lightly, and finally tighten them to 5.8-7.2 ft.-lb. (0.8-1.0 mkg).
7. Turn engine upright, then tighten upper crankcase bolts to 5.8-7.2 ft.-lb. (0.8-1.0 mkg).
8. On Models B and C, install and finger-tighten only the 4 lower crankcase 8mm bolts (B, **Figure 118**) and eleven 6mm bolts (A, **Figure 118**). Then tighten all 8mm bolts first to 11 ft.-lb. (1.5 mkg) and then to 18 ft.-lb. (2.5 mkg). Use the torque sequence indicated by the bolt number adjacent to the bolt hole. Tighten the 6mm bolts to 7.2 ft.-lb. (1.0 mkg).

119

CRANKCASE (MODELS D AND S)

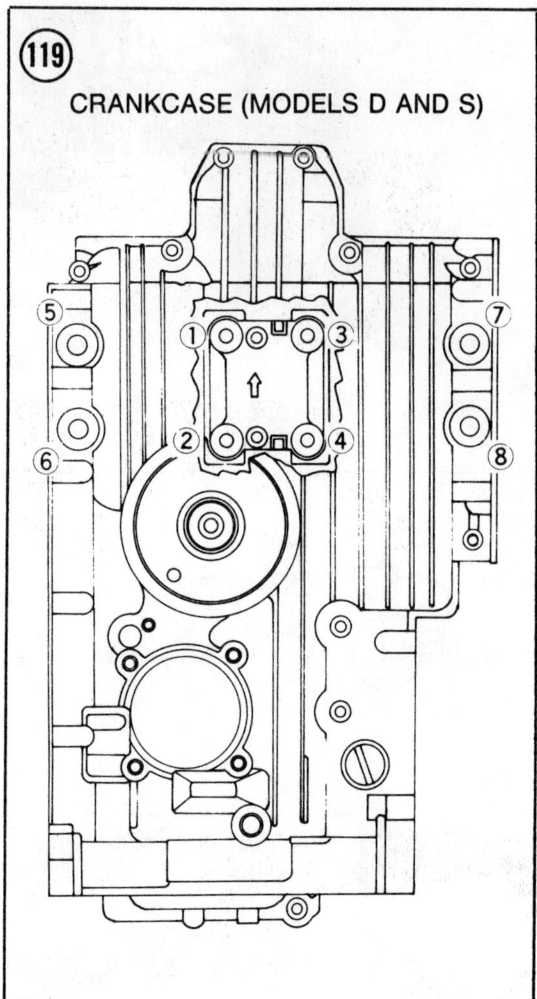

9. Check that the shafts turn freely. It is normal that the crankshaft does not turn as easily as it did before the crankcase was disassembled, but it should not bind.
10. Turn the engine over and install the 5 upper crankcase bolts (**Figure 117**). Tighten them to 7.2 ft.-lb. (1.0 mkg).
11. Install the circlip next to the pushrod oil seal.

TRANSMISSION/5-SPEED (MODELS D AND S)

Figure 120 is an exploded view of the transmission. If it is necessary to disassemble either transmission shaft, take careful note of how all small parts fit together. Also be sure that all gears are installed properly.

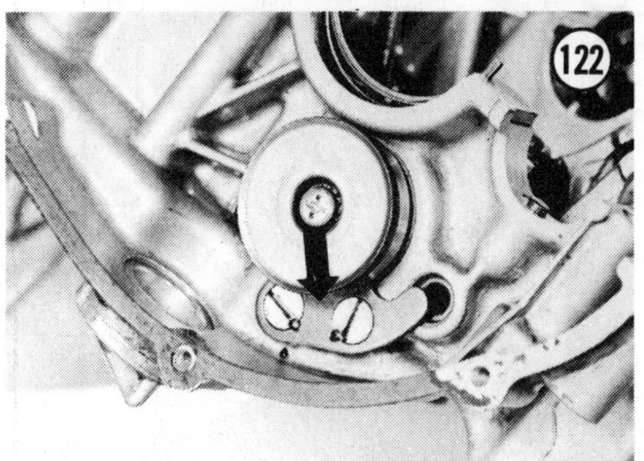

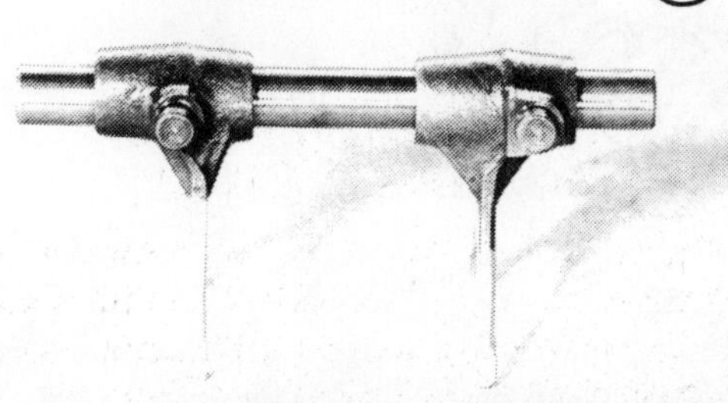

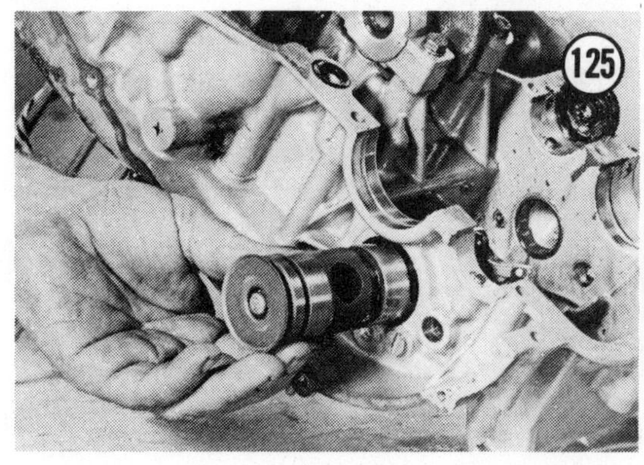

Removal

1. Lift main shaft and countershaft from upper crankcase **(Figure 121)**.

2. Remove shift cam retainer plate **(Figure 122)** then pull out shift fork guide rail and its associated shift forks **(Figure 123)**.

> NOTE: *These forks are slightly different.* ***Figure 124*** *shows proper assembly. Keep these parts assembled to prevent the forks from becoming interchanged.*

3. Remove cotter pin and guide pin from remaining shift fork.

4. Pull out shift cam as far as it will go. See **Figure 125**.

5. Remove snap ring which retains shift cam operating plate.

6. Remove shift cam from engine.

Shaft Disassembly

Transmission shaft disassembly requires special tools, not available to the average home mechanic. It is recommended that transmission shafts be disassembled by a competent shop.

Inspection

1. Slide each splined gear along the shaft. If only minor roughness exists, it may be possible to smooth it with an oilstone. Replace the gear and/or shaft in the event of severe damage.

2. Check each gear for chipped or cracked teeth or cracked wall sections. Replace any damaged gear.

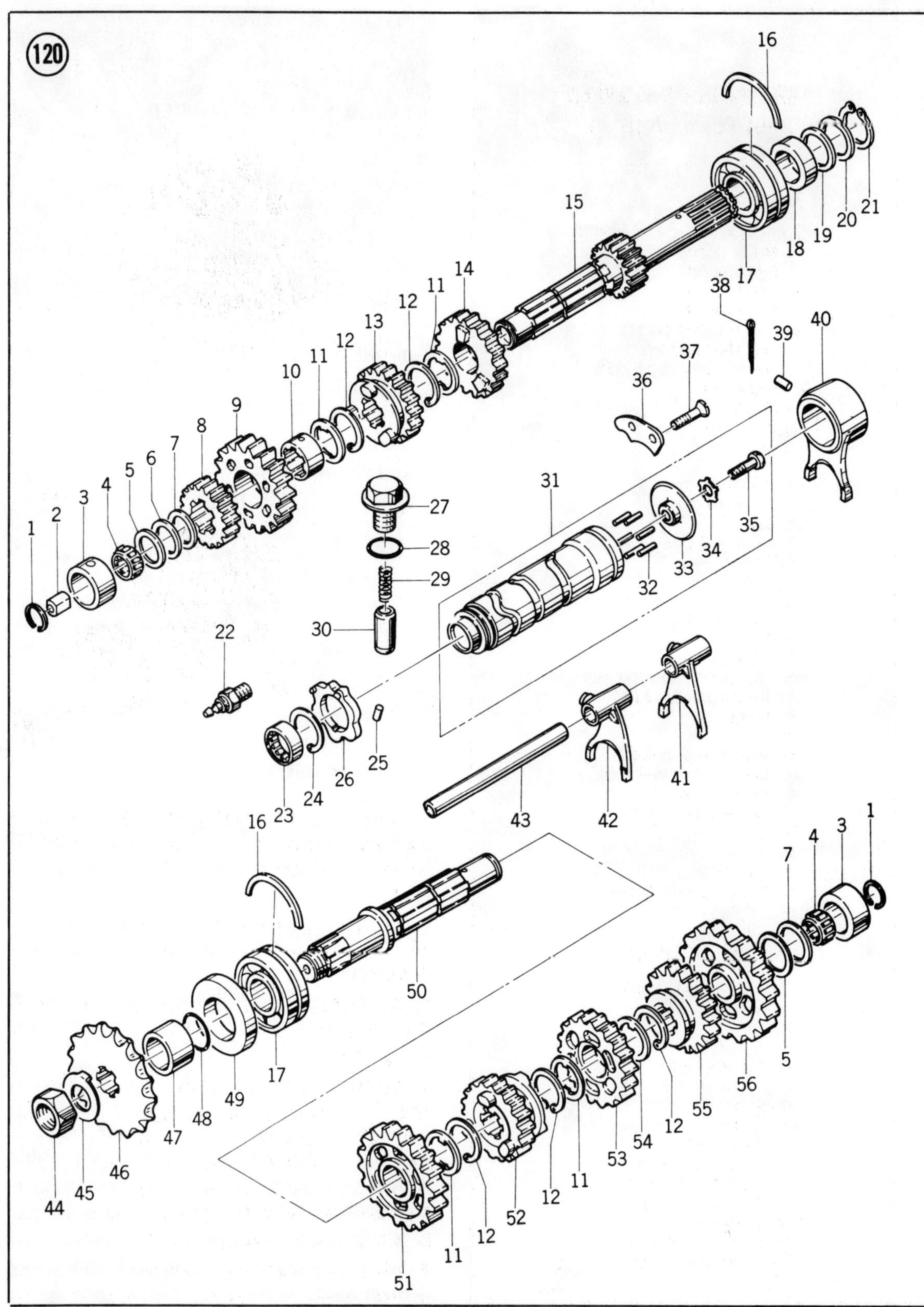
120

TRANSMISSION/5-SPEED (MODELS D AND S)

1. Circlip
2. Drive shaft bushing
3. Output and drive shaft bushing
4. Needle bearing
5. Thrust washer
6. Thrust washer
7. Thrust washer
8. Drive shaft 2nd gear
9. Drive shaft top gear
10. Drive shaft top gear bushing
11. Lockwasher
12. Circlip
13. Drive shaft 3rd gear
14. Drive shaft 4th gear
15. Drive shaft
16. Positioning ring
17. Ball bearing
18. Collar
19. Thrust washer
20. Thrust washer
21. Circlip
22. Neutral indicator switch
23. Needle bearing
24. Circlip
25. Dowel pin
26. Change drum operating disc
27. Neutral positioning bolt
28. O-ring
29. Spring
30. Neutral positioning pin
31. Gearshift drum assembly
32. Gearshift drum pin
33. Gearshift drum pin plate
34. Lockwasher
35. Pan head screw
36. Shift drum positioning plate
37. Countersunk head screw
38. Cotter pin
39. Dowel pin
40. 4th and top shift fork
41. Low shift fork
42. 2nd and 3rd shift fork
43. Shift rod
44. Nut
45. Lockwasher
46. Engine sprocket
47. Engine sprocket collar
48. O-ring
49. Oil seal
50. Output shaft
51. 2nd gear output shaft
52. Top gear output shaft
53. 3rd gear output shaft
54. Lockwasher
55. Output shaft 4th gear
56. Output shaft low gear

4

3. Check dog clutches (**Figure 126**) for rounded teeth and also check that they engage properly. Replace any gear with severely rounded clutch teeth.

4. Be sure that shift forks are not bent or burned. Replace any shift fork if its condition is doubtful.

5. Replace the shift fork guide rail if it is bent. Roll it across a flat surface to check for straightness.

6. Measure clearance between each shift fork and the groove on its associated gear (**Figure 127**). Replace the fork and/or gear if clearance exceeds 0.0022 in. (0.55mm).

7. Measure width of each shift fork groove. Replace any gear if its groove is worn to greater than 0.206 in. (5.25mm).

8. Measure thickness of each shift fork at the points where it engages the groove in its

128

129

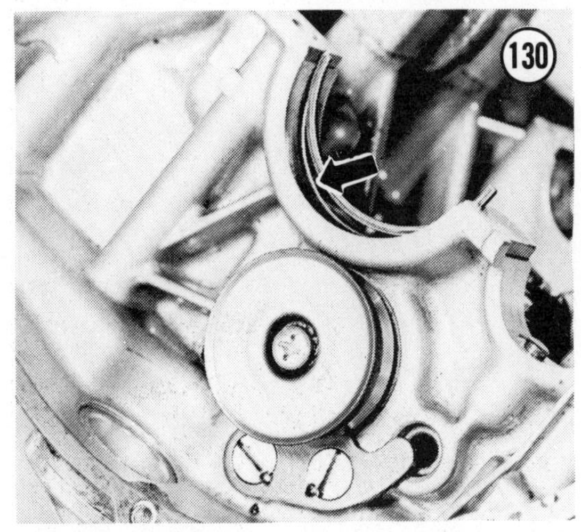

associated gear. Replace the shift fork if it is worn to less than 0.185 in. (4.7mm).

9. Measure width of each groove in the shifter cam. Replace the cam if any groove is worn to wider than 0.325 in. (8.25mm).

10. Measure thickness of each shift fork guide pin. Fourth and fifth gear guide pins must be replaced if they are worn to 0.309 in. (7.85mm). Remaining shift forks must be replaced if their guide pins are worn to 0.312 in. (7.93mm) or less.

11. Measure backlash between each pair of gears as shown in **Figure 128**. Hold one gear stationary, then move the gear under measurement. Replace both gears if backlash exceeds 0.012 in. (0.3mm).

12. Measure clearance between each free-spinning gear and its shaft. Replace any gear if clearance exceeds 0.0063 in. (0.16mm).

13. Check transmission bearings by cleaning them thoroughly, oiling them lightly, and spinning them by hand. Replace any bearing that is rough, noisy, or does not turn smoothly.

Installation

Reverse the removal procedure to install the transmission. **Figure 129** illustrates all gears and bearings assembled correctly. Refer to it as necessary. Be sure that the countershaft oil seal is installed so that its spring is inward. Also be sure that both bearings engage their locating pins and that both bearing positioning rings are in position (**Figure 130**).

TRANSMISSION/5- AND 6-SPEED (MODELS B AND C)

The KZ400 Model B is equipped with a 6-speed constant mesh transmission **(Figure 131)** and the Model C comes with a 5-speed constant mesh unit **(Figure 132)**.

Removal and installation of the transmission components and shift drum are identical on both Models B and C. Disassembly and assembly of the transmission shafts differ and are covered separately in the following procedures.

Removal

1. Lift the main shaft and countershaft assemblies from the crankcase (**Figure 133**).

2. Remove the shift drum positioning bolt (20), washer, spring, and pin (23).

3. Remove the 2 screws **(Figure 134)** securing the shift drum guide plate (38).

4. Withdraw the shift rod (37) while removing both shift forks (35 and 36).

5. Remove the circlip (32) securing the operating plate (33) and remove it.

6. Remove the operating plate pin (34).

7. Remove the cotter pin (24) securing the large shift fork (26), and remove the guide pin (25).

8. Hold onto the large shift fork and withdraw the shift fork drum.

Installation

1. Coat all surfaces of the shift drum, shift forks, and shift shafts with engine oil.

2. Partially install the shift drum into the crankcase. Position the large shift drum with the guide pin housing facing toward the crankshaft and slide the shift drum in the remaining way until it seats.

3. Install the operating plate pin into the shift drum and install the operating plate with the projection facing toward the neutral switch. Install the circlip.

4. Install the large shift fork so that the guide pin will fit into the middle of the three grooves in the shift drum.

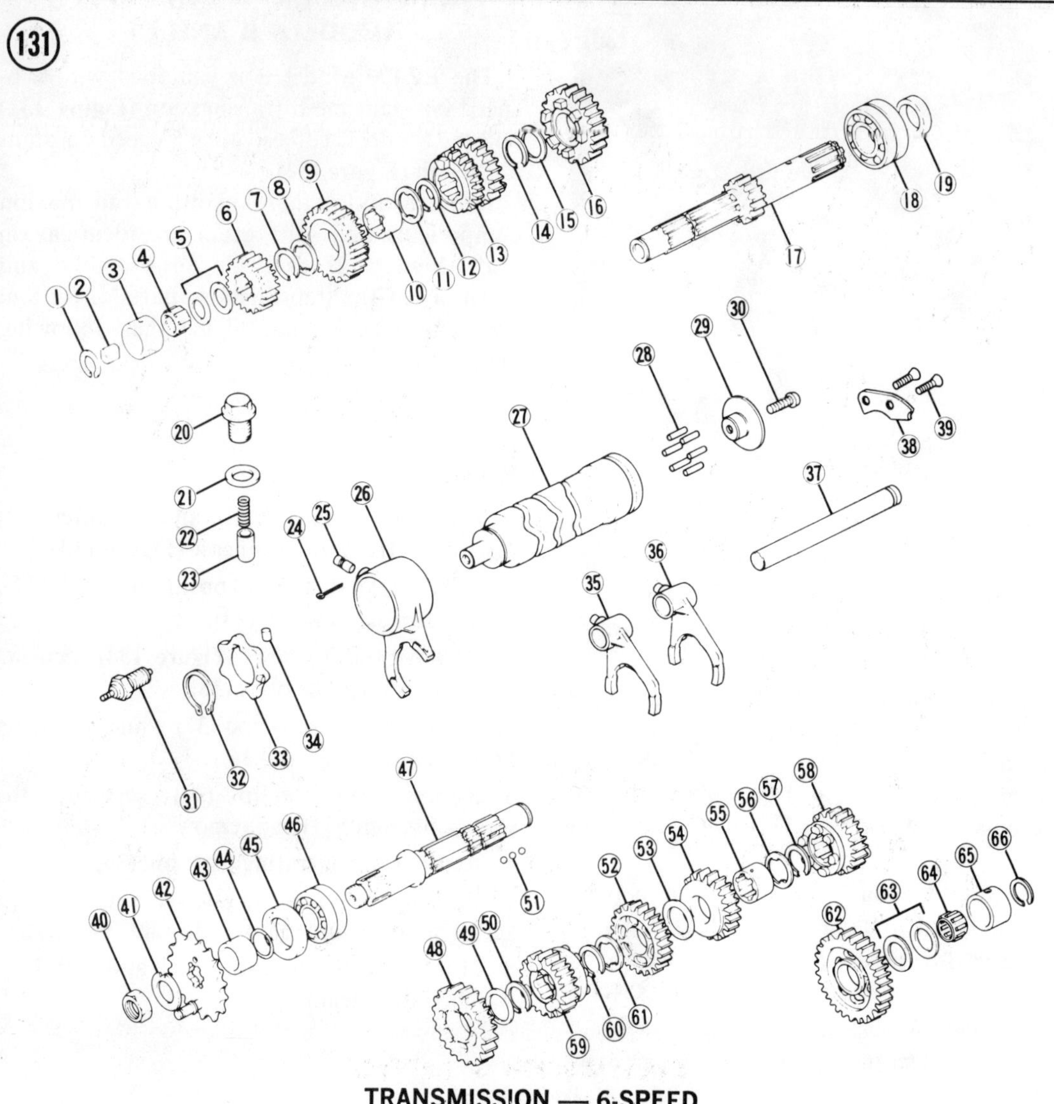

TRANSMISSION — 6-SPEED (MODEL B)

1. Circlip
2. Bushing
3. Bearing outer race
4. Needle bearing
5. Washers
6. Countershaft 2nd gear
7. Circlip
8. Splined washer
9. Countershaft 6th gear
10. Bushing
11. Splined washer
12. Circlip
13. Countershaft 3rd/4th gear
14. Circlip
15. Washer
16. Countershaft 5th gear
17. Countershaft
18. Ball bearing
19. Collar
20. Positioning bolt
21. Aluminum washer
22. Spring
23. Pin
24. Cotter pin
25. Shift fork guide pin
26. 3rd/4th gear shift fork (large)
27. Shift drum
28. Shift drum pin
29. Shift drum pin plate
30. Screw
31. Neutral indicator switch
32. Circlip
33. Operating plate
34. Pin
35. Shift fork (6th)
36. Shift fork (5th)
37. Shift rod
38. Shift drum guide plate
39. Screw
40. Nut
41. Toothed washer
42. Engine sprocket
43. Collar
44. O-ring
45. Oil seal
46. Ball bearing
47. Main shaft
48. Main shaft 2nd gear
49. Washer
50. Circlip
51. Steel balls
52. Main shaft 3rd gear
53. Washer
54. Main shaft 4th gear
55. Bushing
56. Splined washer
57. Circlip
58. Main shaft 5th gear
59. Main shaft 6th gear
60. Circlip
61. Splined washer
62. Main shaft 1st gear
63. Washer(s)
64. Needle bearing
65. Bearing outer race
66. Circlip

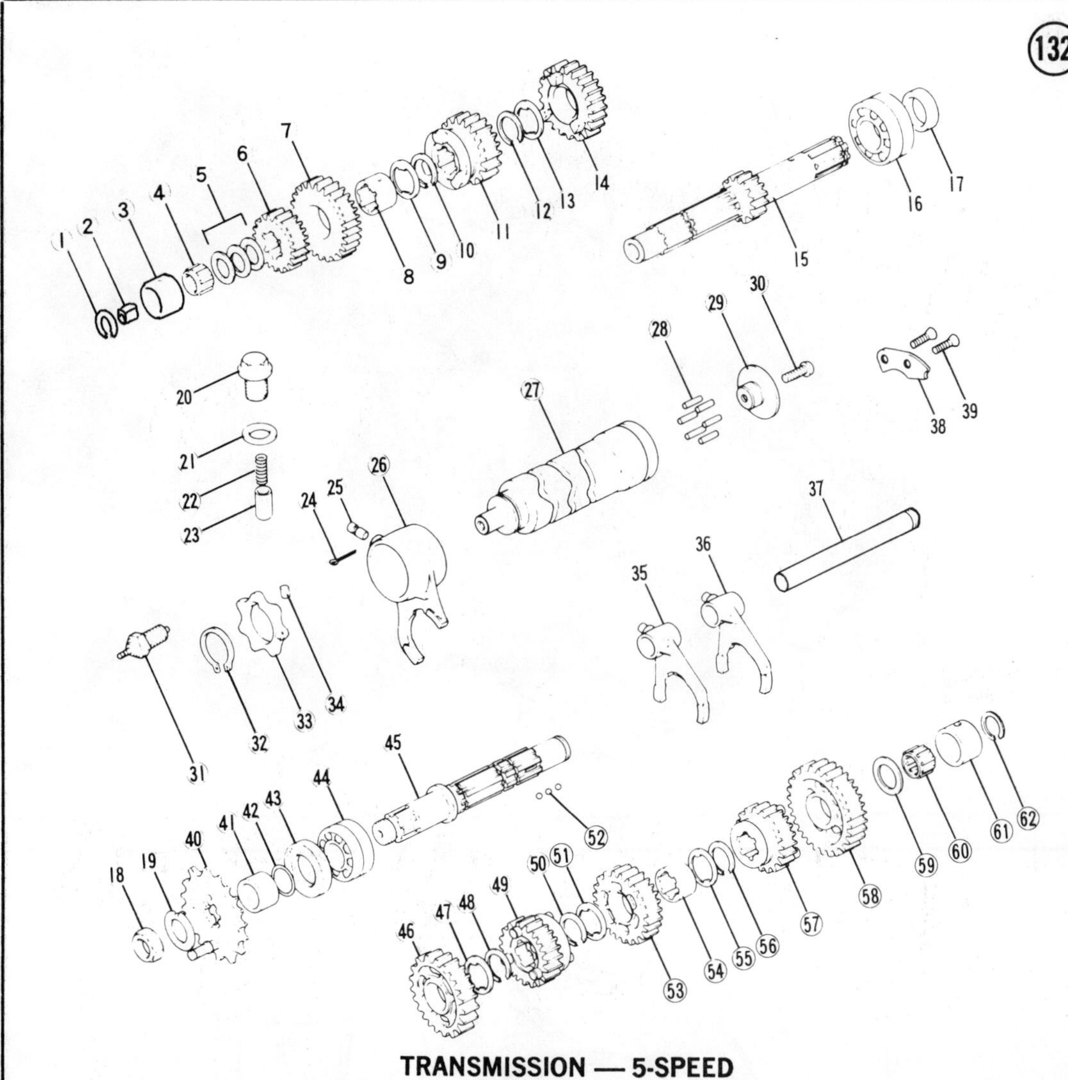

TRANSMISSION — 5-SPEED (MODEL C)

1. Circlip
2. Bushing
3. Bearing outer race
4. Needle bearing
5. Washer(s)
6. Countershaft 2nd gear
7. Countershaft 5th gear
8. Bushing
9. Splined washer
10. Circlip
11. Countershaft 3rd gear
12. Circlip
13. Splined washer
14. Countershaft 4th gear
15. Countershaft
16. Ball bearing
17. Collar
18. Nut
19. Toothed washer
20. Positioning bolt
21. Aluminum washer
22. Spring
23. Pin
24. Cotter pin
25. Shift fork guide pin
26. 3rd gear shift fork (large)
27. Shift drum
28. Shift drum pin
29. Shift drum pin plate
30. Screw
31. Neutral indicator switch
32. Circlip
33. Operating plate
34. Pin
35. 5th gear shift fork
36. 4th gear shift fork
37. Shift rod
38. Shift drum guide plate
39. Screw
40. Engine sprocket
41. Collar
42. O-ring
43. Oil seal
44. Ball bearing
45. Main shaft
46. Main shaft 2nd gear
47. Splined washer
48. Circlip
49. Main shaft 5th gear
50. Circlip
51. Splined washer
52. Steel ball
53. Main shaft 3rd gear
54. Bushing
55. Splined washer
56. Circlip
57. Main shaft 5th gear
58. Main shaft 1st gear
59. Washer
60. Needle bearing
61. Bearing outer race
62. Circlip

133

134

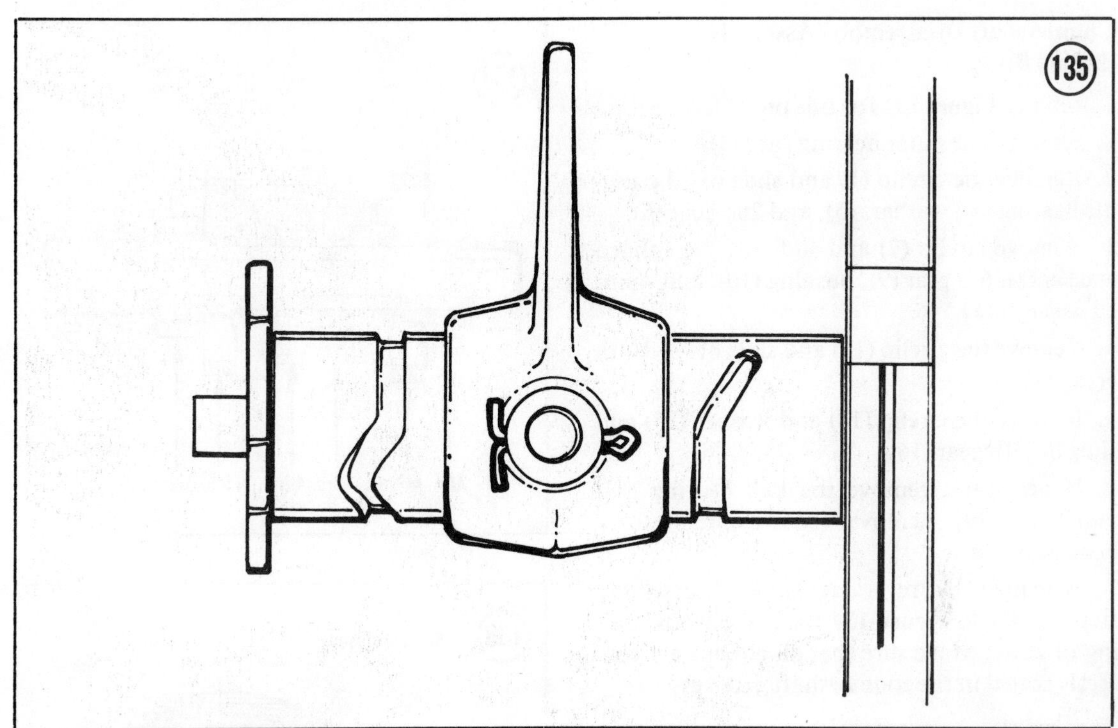

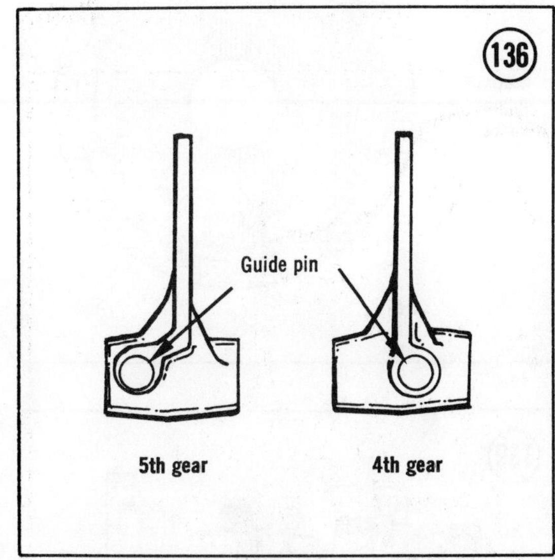

5. Install the guide pin (25) into the large shift fork and install a new cotter pin (**Figure 135**).

> NOTE: *Always install a new cotter pin; never install a used one.*

6. On Model B, insert the shift rod (37) partially into the crankcase. Correctly position the 5th and 6th gear shift forks with their guide pins located in the shift drum. Slide the shift rod through both forks until it completely seats.

> NOTE: *These 2 shift forks are identical so there is no problem of intermixing their positions.*

7. On Model C, insert the shift rod (37) partially into the crankcase. Correctly position the 4th gear shift fork (guide pin on the right-hand side of the fork hub) and through the 5th gear shift fork (guide pin on the left-hand side of the fork hub). Refer to **Figure 136** *for Model C only*. Be sure to correctly position their guide pins into the shift drum.

> NOTE: *These 2 shift forks are slightly different and must be installed in the correct position; refer to* ***Figure 136****.*

8. Install the shift fork guide plate and stake both screws with a centerpunch to prevent them from working loose.

9. Install the shift drum positioning pin, spring, *new* washer and bolt. Tighten the bolt to 25 ft.-lb. (3.5 mkg).

10. Install the main shaft and countershaft assemblies into the crankcase.

4

Countershaft Disassembly/Assembly (Model B)

Refer to **Figure 131** for this procedure.

1. Slide off the outer bearing race (3).
2. Remove the circlip (1) and slide off the needle bearing (4), washers (5), and 2nd gear (6).
3. Remove circlip (7) and slide off the splined washer (8), 6th gear (9), bushing (10), and splined washer (11).
4. Remove the circlip (12) and slide off 3rd/4th gear (13).
5. Remove the circlip (14) and washer (15) and slide off 5th gear (16).
6. If necessary, remove the ball bearing (18) and collar (19). Removal requires the use of a bearing puller.
7. Assemble by reversing these disassembly steps. Refer to **Figure 137** for correct positioning of gears. Make sure that all circlips are correctly seated in the countershaft grooves.

> NOTE: *Install splined washers and circlips as indicated in* ***Figure 138.***

Main Shaft Disassembly/Assembly (Model B)

Refer to **Figure 131** for this procedure.

1. Slide off the outer bearing race (65).
2. Remove the circlip (66) and slide off the needle bearing (64), washers (63), and 1st gear (62).
3. Remove 5th gear (58). The 5th gear has 3 steel balls located between the gear and the shaft. This is used for neutral location when shifting from 1st gear. To remove the gear, spin the shaft in a vertical position, holding onto 3rd gear. Pull the 5th gear up and off the shaft.

> NOTE: *Perform this procedure over and close down to a workbench with some shop cloths spread over it. This lessens the chance of losing the balls when the gear comes off.*

4. Remove the circlip (57) and slide off the splined washer (56), 4th gear (54), washer (53), 3rd gear (52), bushing (55), and the splined washer (61).
5. Remove the circlip (60) and slide off 6th gear (59).

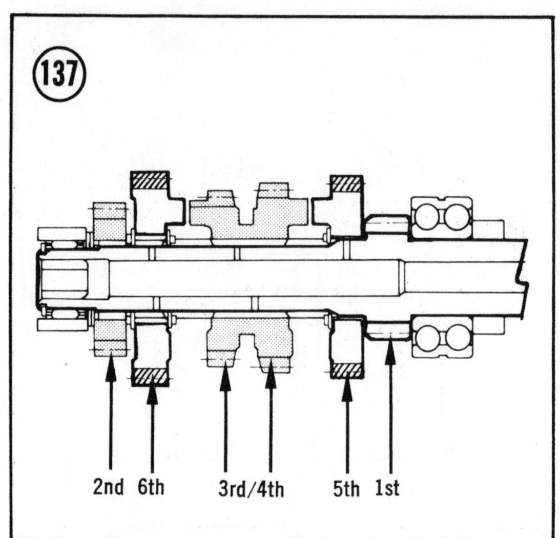

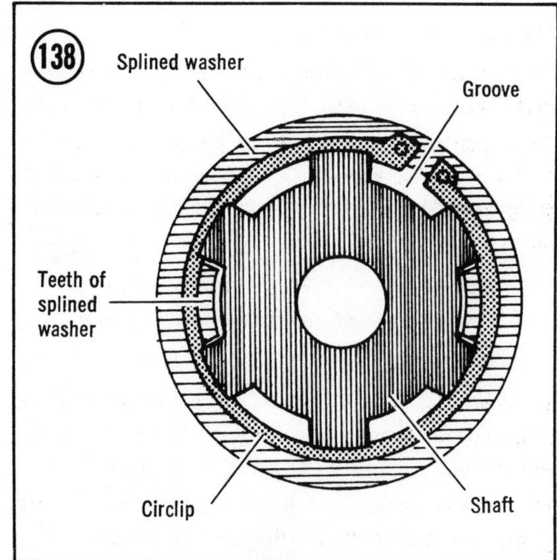

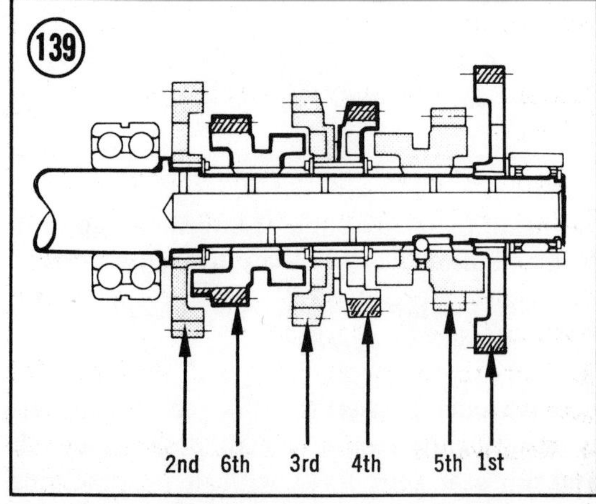

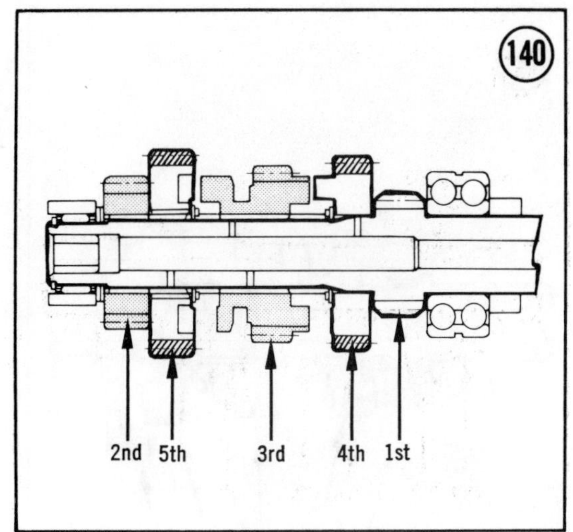

6. Remove the circlip (50) and washer (40) and slide off 2nd gear (48).

7. If necessary, remove the ball bearing (46). Removal requires the use of a bearing puller.

8. Assemble by reversing these disassembly steps. Refer to **Figure 139** for correct placement of gears. Make sure that all circlips are seated correctly in the main shaft grooves.

> NOTE: *Refer to **Figure 138** for correct installation of splined washers and circlips.*

9. When installing 3rd/4th gear bushing (55), align the bushing oil holes with the holes in the main shaft.

10. When installing the 3 balls into the 5th gear, *do not use lightweight grease* (or any grease) to hold them in place. They must be able to move freely during normal operation of the transmission.

Countershaft Disassembly/Assembly (Model C)

Refer to **Figure 132** for this procedure.

1. Slide off the outer bearing race (3).
2. Remove the circlip (1) and slide off the needle bearing (4), washer (5), 2nd gear (6), bushing (8), and the splined washer (9).
3. Remove the circlip (10) and slide off 3rd gear (11).
4. Remove the circlip (12) and splined washer (13).
5. Slide off 4th gear (14).
6. If necessary, remove the ball bearing (16) and collar (17). Removal requires the use of a bearing puller.
7. Assemble by reversing these disassembly steps. Refer to **Figure 140** for correct positioning of gears. Make sure that all circlips are correctly seated in the countershaft grooves.

> NOTE: *Install splined washers and circlips as indicated in **Figure 138**.*

Main Shaft Disassembly/Assembly (Model C)

Refer to **Figure 132** for this procedure.

1. Slide off the outer bearing race (61).
2. Remove the circlip (62) and slide off the needle bearing (60), washer (59), and 1st gear (58).
3. Remove 4th gear (57). The 4th gear has 3 steel balls located between the gear and the shaft. This is used for neutral location when shifting from 1st gear. To remove the gear, spin the shaft in a vertical position, holding onto 3rd gear. Pull the 4th gear up and off the shaft.

> NOTE: *Perform this procedure over and close down to a workbench with some shop cloths spread over it. This will lessen the chance of losing the balls when the gear comes off.*

4. Remove the circlip (56), splined washer (55), 3rd gear (53), bushing (54), and splined washer (51).
5. Remove the circlip (50) and slide off 5th gear (49).
6. Remove the circlip (48), splined washer (47), and 2nd gear (46).
7. Remove the ball bearing if necessary. Removal requires the use of a bearing puller.
8. Assemble by reversing these disassembly steps. Refer to **Figure 141** for correct placement of gears. Make sure all circlips are seated correctly in the main shaft grooves.

> NOTE: *Refer to **Figure 138** for correct installation of splined washers and circlips.*

4

9. When installing the 3rd gear bushing (54), align the bushing oil holes with the holes in the main shaft.

10. When installing the 3 steel balls into the 4th gear, *do not use lightweight grease* (or any grease) to hold them in place. They must be able to move freely during normal operation of the transmission.

Transmission Inspection

1. Clean all parts in cleaning solvent and thoroughly dry.

2. Check each gear for excessive wear, burrs, pitting, chipped or missing teeth. Make sure the lugs on ends of the gears are in good condition.

> NOTE: *Defective gears should be replaced, and it is a good idea to replace the mating gear on the opposite shaft even though it may not show as much wear or damage.*

3. Make sure that all gears slide smoothly on their respective shaft splines.

4. Check the condition of the bearing. Make sure it rotates smoothly (**Figure 142**) with no signs of wear or damage. Replace if necessary.

Shift Drum and Fork Inspection

1. Inspect each shift fork for signs of wear or cracking. Make sure the forks slide smoothly on their respective shaft or drum. Make sure the shaft is not bent.

> NOTE: *Check for any arc shaped wear or burned marks on the shift forks. If this is apparent, the shift fork has come in contact with the gear, indicating the fingers are worn beyond use and the fork must be replaced.*

2. Check the grooves in the shift drum for wear or roughness.

3. Check the shift drum bearing. Make sure it operates smoothly with no signs of wear or damage.

4. Check the cam pin followers in each shift fork. They should fit snug but not too tight. Check the end that rides in the shift drum for wear or burrs. Replace as necessary.

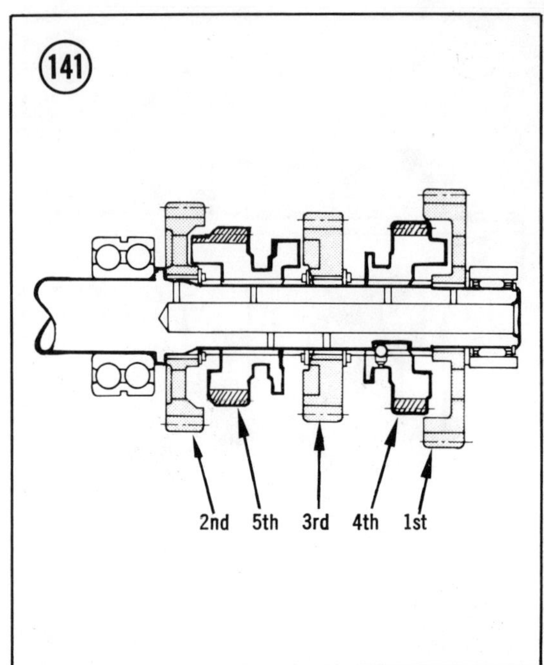

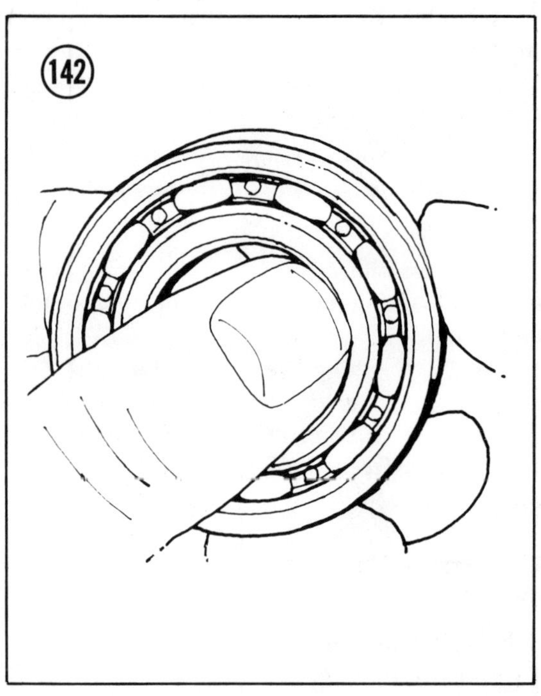

KICKSTARTER

The kickstarter is a simple, rugged mechanism which should give no trouble. The cause of any malfunction will be obvious upon disassembly. **Figure 143** is an exploded view of the kickstarter.

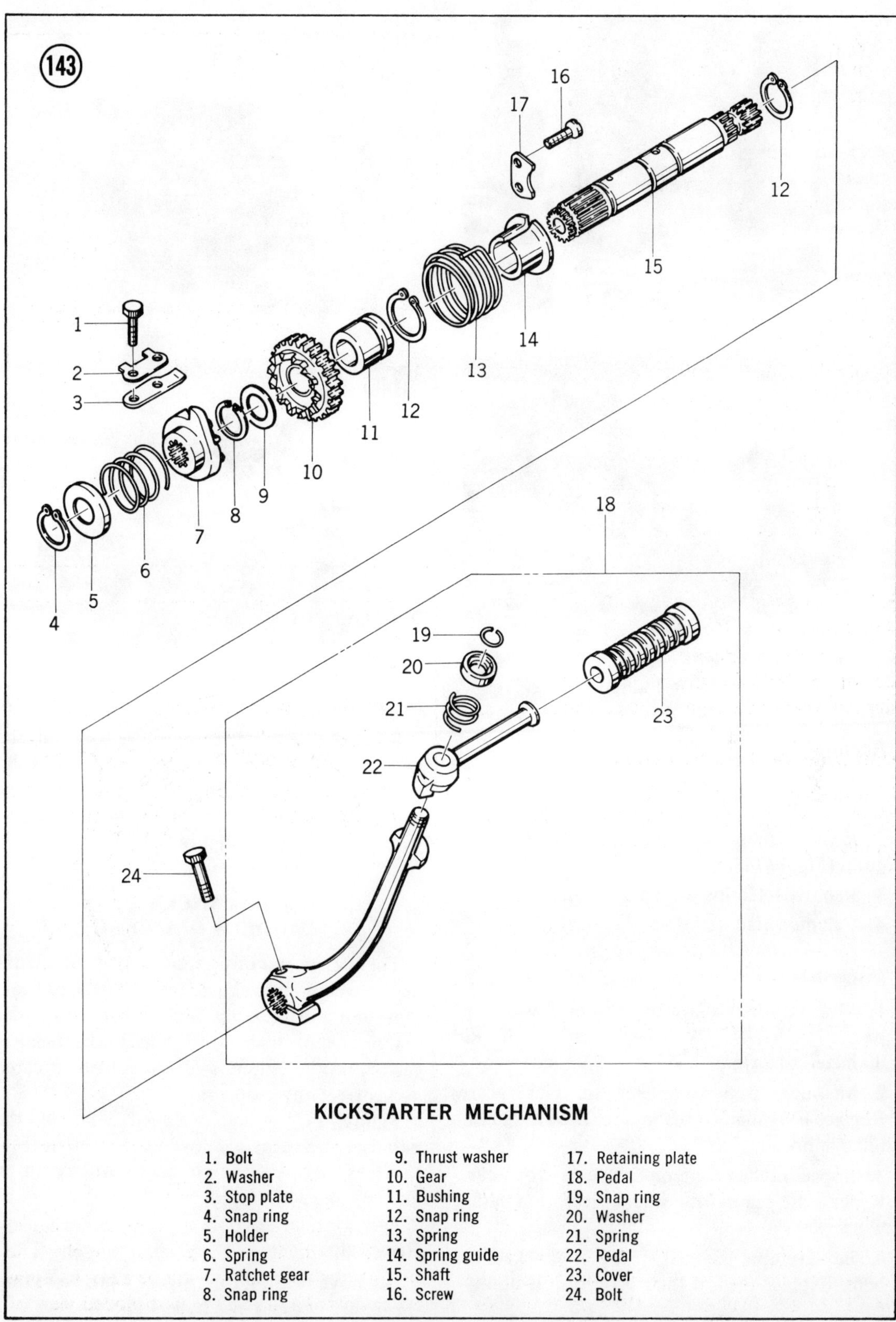

KICKSTARTER MECHANISM

1. Bolt
2. Washer
3. Stop plate
4. Snap ring
5. Holder
6. Spring
7. Ratchet gear
8. Snap ring
9. Thrust washer
10. Gear
11. Bushing
12. Snap ring
13. Spring
14. Spring guide
15. Shaft
16. Screw
17. Retaining plate
18. Pedal
19. Snap ring
20. Washer
21. Spring
22. Pedal
23. Cover
24. Bolt

Removal

1. Bend down locking tabs, then remove retaining bolts and stop plate **(Figure 144)**.
2. Remove snap ring, then spring and spring guide **(Figure 145)**.
3. Remove retaining plate and collar.
4. Pull out shaft.

Inspection

1. Measure shaft diameter at point where it passes through kick gear. Replace if its diameter is less than 0.785 in. (19.93mm).
2. Measure inside diameter of kick gear. Replace if its diameter is greater than 0.790 in. (20.07mm).
3. Inspect ratchet teeth on both gears for wear. Replace the gears if the ratchet teeth are badly worn.
4. Be sure that neither spring is cracked or bent. Replace them if their condition is doubtful.

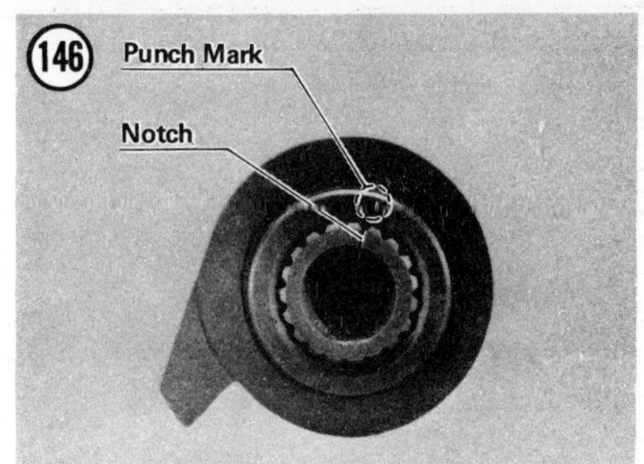

Installation

Reverse the removal procedure to install the kickstarter mechanism. Turn the shaft fully clockwise before inserting the end of the return spring. Be sure that mark on ratchet gear aligns with notch on shaft **(Figure 146)**.

BALANCER (MODELS D AND S)

The balancer consists of a pair of chain-driven weight assemblies, their associated bearings, and a drive chain. Since it operates under conditions of high stress, check the balance each time the engine is disassembled to catch and correct any problems.

Figure 147 is an exploded view of the balancer. Be sure to follow installation instructions exactly. Failure to do so will result in engine vibration.

Removal

1. Remove bearing cap **(Figure 148)**. Note that the longer bolts go into holes 1 and 4.

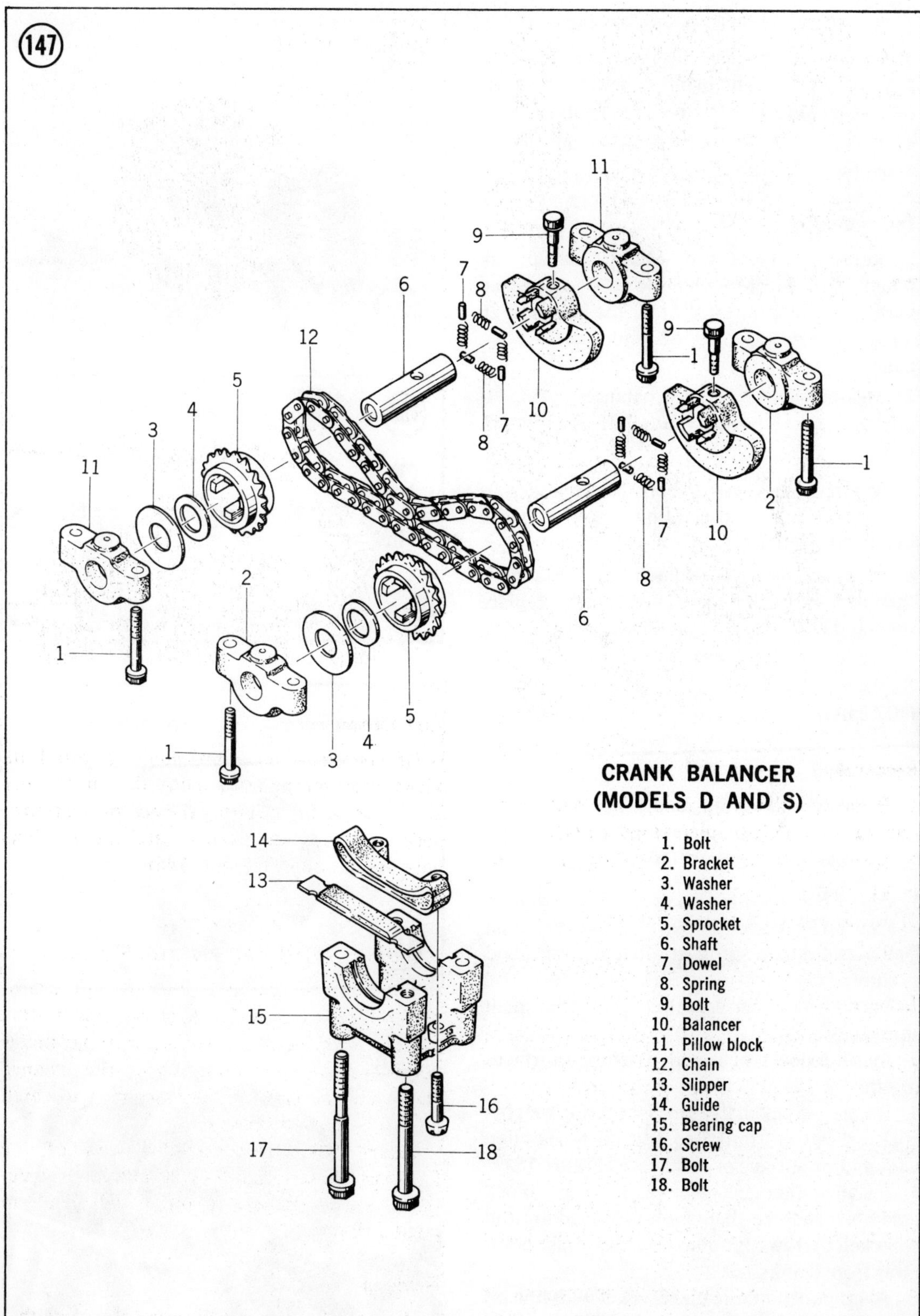

CRANK BALANCER (MODELS D AND S)

1. Bolt
2. Bracket
3. Washer
4. Washer
5. Sprocket
6. Shaft
7. Dowel
8. Spring
9. Bolt
10. Balancer
11. Pillow block
12. Chain
13. Slipper
14. Guide
15. Bearing cap
16. Screw
17. Bolt
18. Bolt

2. Remove balancer guide (**Figure 149**).
3. Remove all balance weight retaining bolts, then lift off each balance weight and its associated pillow blocks as an assembly.
4. Remove the balancer from engine as an assembly.

Inspection

1. Refer to **Figure 150**. Measure a 20 link length of the balancer chain when it is stretched with an 11 lb. (5 kg) weight. If the length of 20 links exceeds 6.39 in. (162.4mm), replace the chain.
2. Measure length of each balancer spring. If any spring is shorter than 0.35 in. (9mm), replace it.
3. Measure thickness of both chain guides. If either is worn to 0.16 in. (4mm), or is damaged in any way, replace it.
4. Measure thickness of each shaft. Standard thickness is 0.7861 in. (19.907mm). Replace them if they are worn to 0.785 in. (19.93mm).
5. Measure pillow block inside diameter. Replace them if they are worn to 0.790 in. (20.08mm).

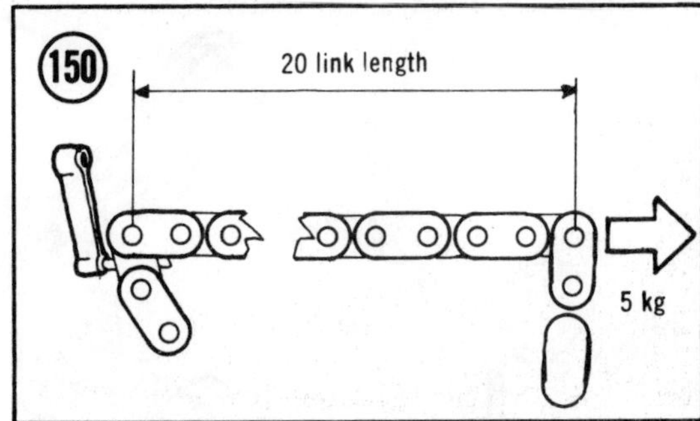

Installation

> NOTE: *Follow installation instructions exactly. Engine vibration will result if the balance is installed incorrectly.*

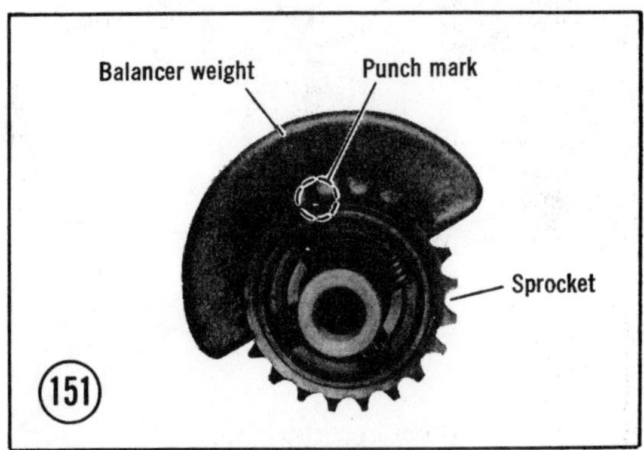

1. Assemble weights and sprockets as shown in **Figure 151**. Punch marks on sprockets must face outward, and sprocket must be positioned as shown.
2. Install shims on sprocket side. The small shim goes on first.
3. Install pillow blocks with machined surfaces inward.
4. Rotate crankshaft until counterweights stick up out of crankcase and oil holes align with mating surface of crankcase (**Figure 152**).
5. Install either balancer and pillow block assembly. Be sure that chain is looped around sprocket. Arrows on pillow blocks must point away from crankshaft.
6. Align punch marks on sprocket with line on pillow block. See **Figure 153**. Do not allow crankshaft to turn.

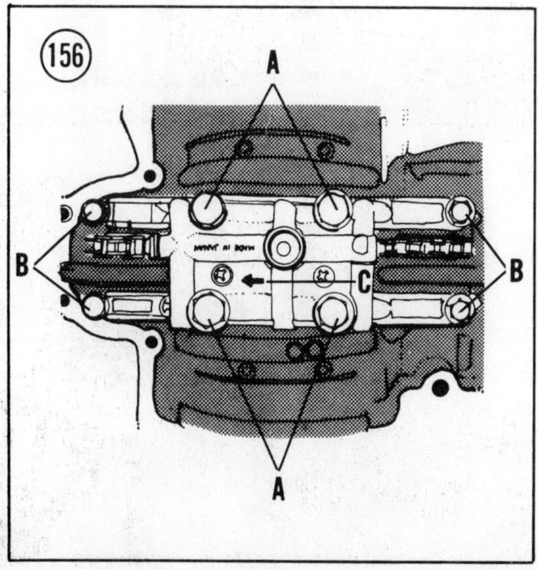

7. Loop chain on sprocket so that chrome-plated link aligns with line on pillow block (**Figure 154**).

8. Check that remaining chrome-plated link is reasonably close to installed position of other sprocket. If not, repeat Step 7, but align the other chrome-plated link with the line.

9. Install remaining balance weight assembly. Punch mark, stamped line, and chrome-plated links must all align.

10. Tighten balance bolts to 8.0-9.4 ft.-lb. (1.1-1.3 mkg). Use thread locking cement on these bolts.

11. Install chain guide and bearing cap. Be sure that bearings are clean, then lubricate them with engine oil. Tighten bearing cap bolts, in the order marked on the cap, to 18-22 ft.-lb. (2.5-3.0 mkg). Note that the longer bolts go into locations 1 and 4. Use thread locking cement on these bolts.

4

BALANCER (MODELS B AND C)

The balancer consists of a pair of chain-driven weight assemblies, their associated bearings, and a drive chain. Since it operates under conditions of high stress, check the balance each time the engine is disassembled to catch and correct any problems.

Figure 155 is an exploded view of the balancer.

Removal

Split the crankcase as described under *Crankcase Disassembly* in this chapter.

Remove the four 10mm bolts (A, **Figure 156**) and four 8mm bolts (B, **Figure 156**) securing the main bearing cap/balancer assembly and remove it.

Installation

1. Install the 4 assembly locating dowels into the upper crankcase.

2. Make sure that the 2 main bearing inserts are in place in the assembly.

3. Rotate the crankshaft until the oil holes in the crankshaft are centered on the mating sur-

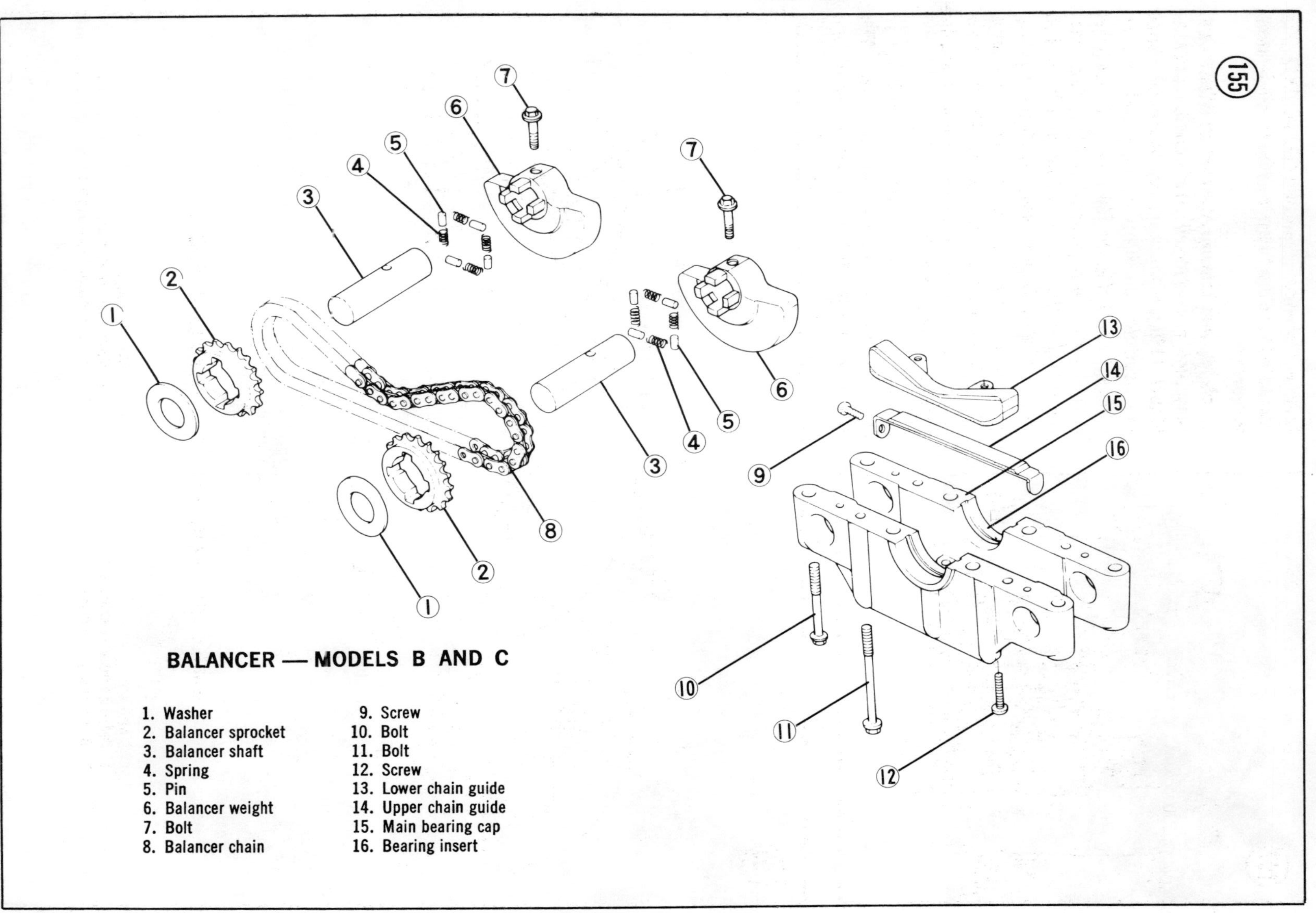

155

BALANCER — MODELS B AND C

1. Washer
2. Balancer sprocket
3. Balancer shaft
4. Spring
5. Pin
6. Balancer weight
7. Bolt
8. Balancer chain
9. Screw
10. Bolt
11. Bolt
12. Screw
13. Lower chain guide
14. Upper chain guide
15. Main bearing cap
16. Bearing insert

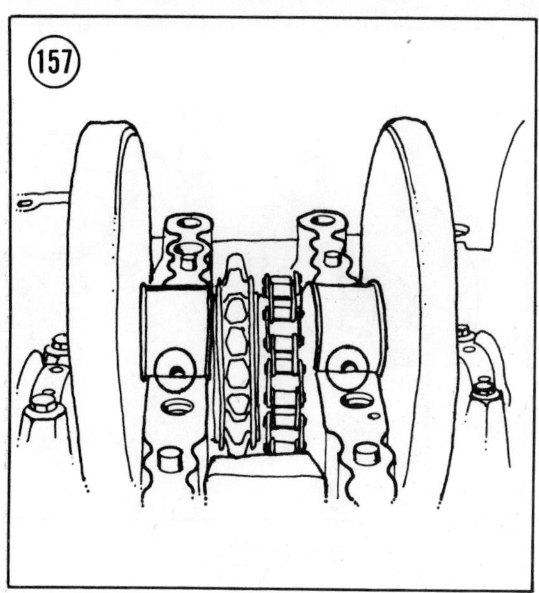

face of the upper crankcase (**Figure 157**). The crankshaft counterbalance weights will be positioned up.

4. Make sure that the balancer chain and sprockets are correctly positioned. Refer to **Figure 158**. On the front sprocket the plated link must be positioned on the punch marked sprocket tooth **(Figure 159)**. The rear sprocket must have the 4th plated link (counting from the front of the chain) on the punch marked sprocket tooth **(Figure 159)**. With the 2 plated links in the correct position, the 2 remaining plated links must be centered within the main bearing cap surface area as viewed from the bottom of the assembly.

5. Install the main bearing cap/balancer assembly onto the upper crankcase half. The arrow (C, **Figure 156**) must point toward the

158

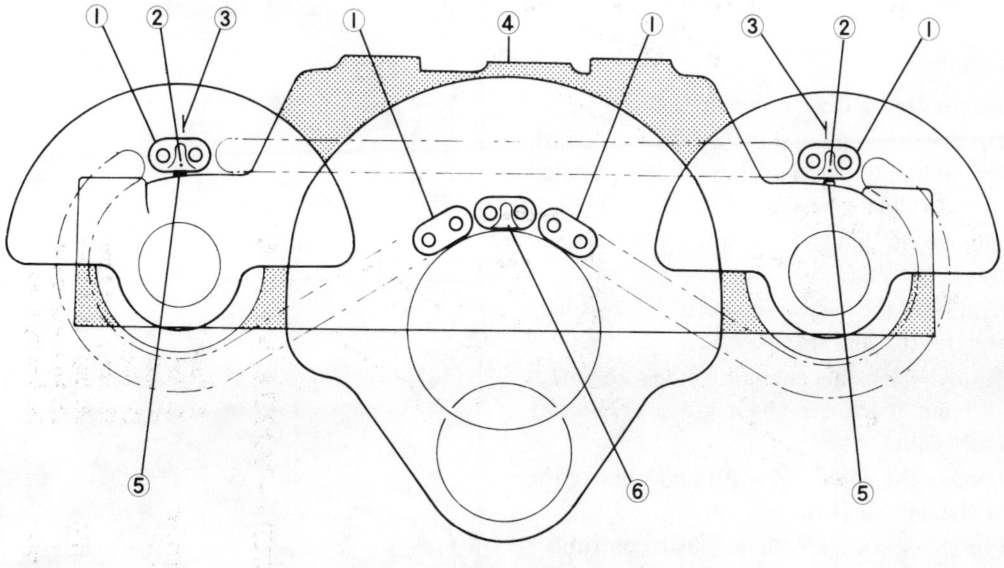

BALANCER CHAIN TIMING — MODELS B AND C

1. Plated link
2. Balancer sprocket punch mark
3. Balancer weight line mark
4. Main bearing cap
5. Main bearing cap mark
6. Crankshaft sprocket top tooth

front of the engine. Engage the link between the 2nd and 3rd plated link onto the top tooth of the crankshaft sprocket (**Figure 158**).

6. Make sure that the painted line on each balancer weight aligns with the raised bar on the main bearing cap assembly (**Figure 160**). Also the plated link must be positioned on the punch marked sprocket tooth (**Figure 159**).

CAUTION

If any of the 4 alignment points is incorrect, remove the main bearing cap/ balancer assembly and correct it. This alignment is absolutely necessary for proper engine operation.

7. Install, and finger-tighten only, the four 10mm and four 8mm bolts. Tighten the bolts in two stages using the torque sequence shown in **Figure 161**. First tighten the 8mm bolts to 11 ft.-lb. (1.5 mkg) and the 10mm bolts to 18 ft.-lb. (2.5 mkg). Finally tighten the 8mm bolts to 18 ft.-lb. (2.5 mkg) and the 10mm bolts to 29 ft.-lb. (4.0 mkg).

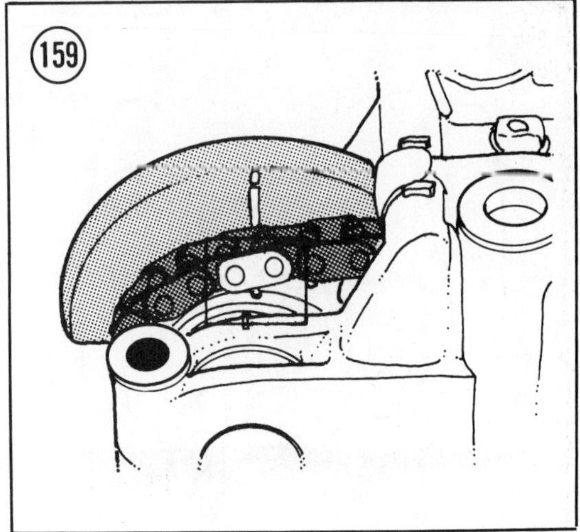

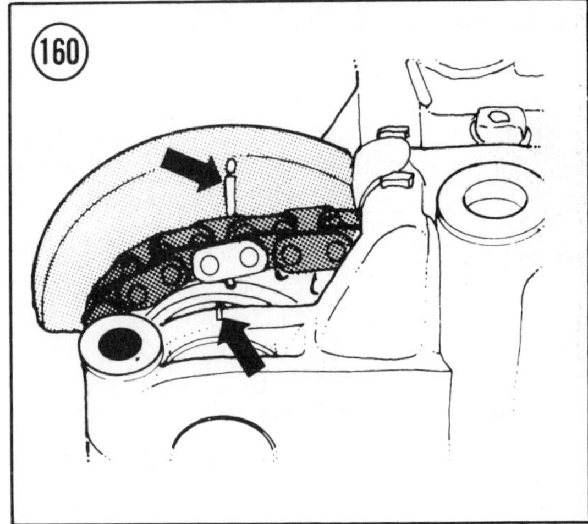

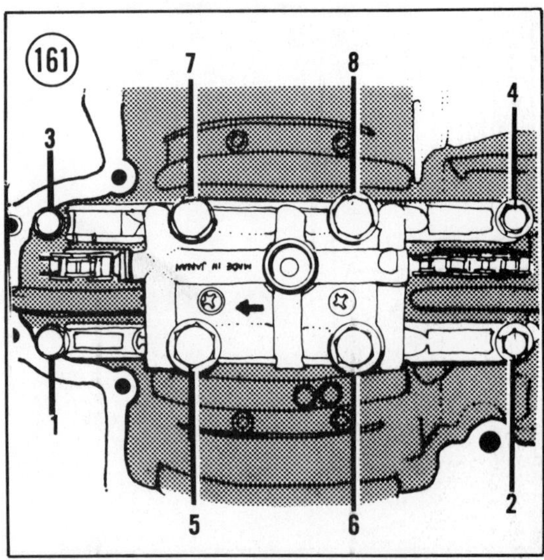

Disassembly

Refer to **Figure 155** for this procedure.

1. Remove both main bearing inserts. Mark them right and left so that they will be installed into their original position.
2. Remove the bolts (7) securing the balancer weights to the shaft.
3. Withdraw the balancer shafts (3), washers (1), weights (6), and sprockets (2).
4. Remove the balancer chain guide screws (12) and lift out the lower chain guide (13) along with the chain.
5. Remove the guide screw (9) and remove the upper chain guide (14).
6. Tap the sprocket with a plastic or rubber mallet to separate it from the balancer weight. The springs (4) and pins (5) will come off at the same time.

Inspection

1. Measure the outer diameter of the balancer shaft (3) at each end where it rotates in the main bearing cap. The standard dimension is 0.7864-0.7866 in. (19.967-19.980mm). Replace

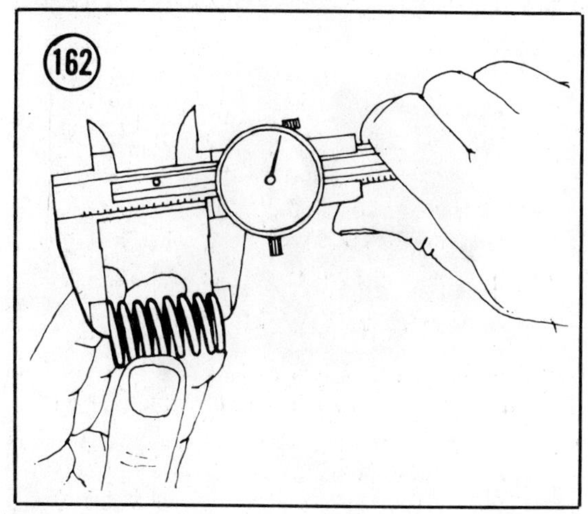

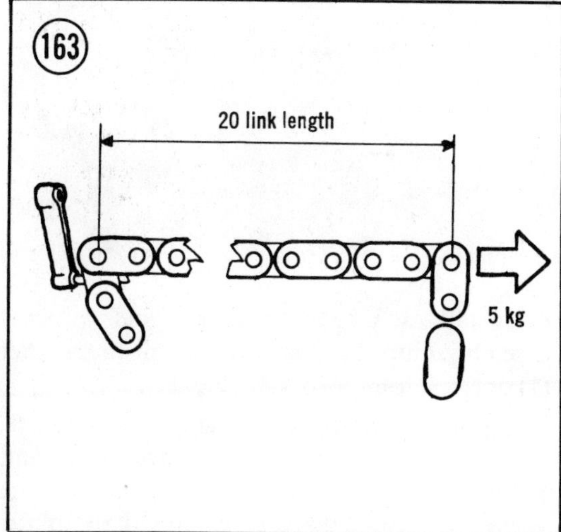

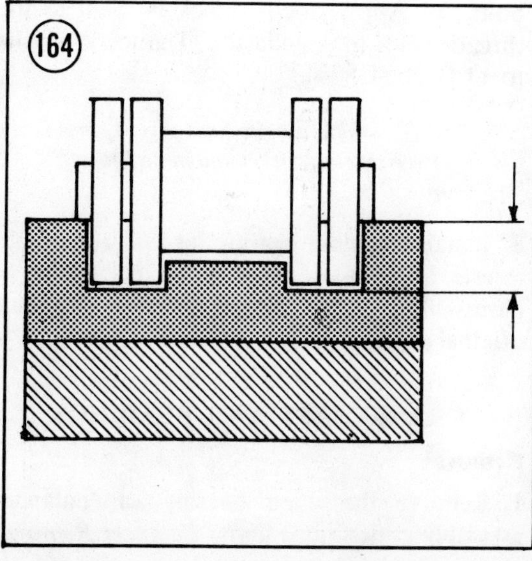

the shaft if the dimension is 0.7846 in. (19.93mm) or less.

2. Measure the inside diameter of each balancer shaft hole in the main bearing cap. The standard dimension is 0.7874-0.7885 in. (20.000-20.030mm). *If any balancer hole exceeds* 0.7905 in. (20.08mm), replace both the main bearing cap and upper crankcase half as a set.

3. Measure the free length of each spring (4) as shown in **Figure 162**. Replace any spring that is shorter than 0.366 in. (9.3mm).

4. Hold the chain taut and measure a 20 link length **(Figure 163)**. The standard dimension is 6.299-6.311 in. (160.0-160.3mm). Replace the chain if it is longer than 6.394 in. (162.4mm).

NOTE: *If the chain has to be replaced, carefully inspect all sprockets (both balancers and crankshaft) for wear. If the sprockets are damaged or worn, they must be replaced. If the crankshaft sprocket is worn, the entire crankshaft must be replaced.*

5. Inspect the chain guides for wear and deterioration. Measure the depth of the grooves where the chain links travel (**Figure 164**). The minimum thickness on the upper guide (14) is 0.0394 in. (1.0mm) and 0.0591 in. (1.5mm) for the lower guide (13). Replace either or both guides if the dimension is less than specified.

Assembly

1. Install the upper chain guide (14). Install the screw (9); apply Loctite Lock N' Seal to the screw threads prior to installation.

NOTE

When installing a new guide, tighten the screw and bend the opposite end up and over the main bearing cap.

2. Install the lower chain guide (13) and chain. Install the 2 screws (12); apply Loctite Lock N' Seal to the threads prior to installation.

NOTE

Install the chain with the 4 plated links facing toward the left-hand side of the engine when installed.

4

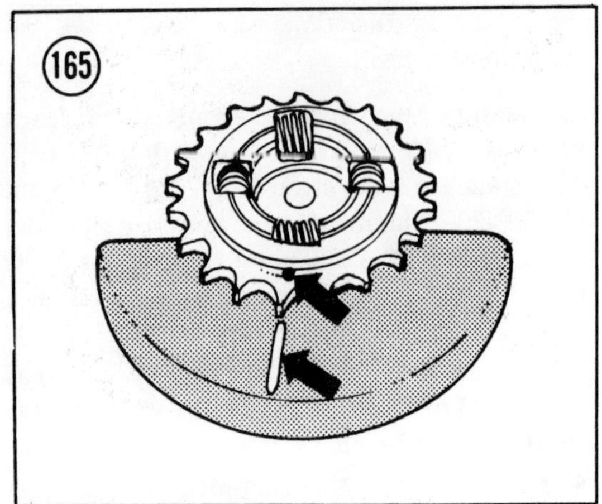

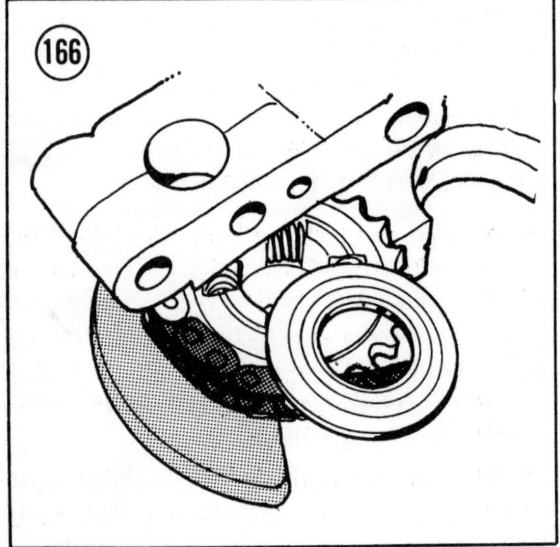

3. Install the 4 springs (4) and pins (5) into position in the inner circumference of the balancer weight (6). Install the sprocket (2) with the punch mark facing away from the balancer weight.

CAUTION

*Align the punch mark on the sprocket with the painted line on the balancer weight (**Figure 165**).*

4. After the sprocket is correctly positioned, move each spring and pin outward within its groove so that it will not interfere with the balancer shaft when it is inserted through the balancer weight.

5. Repeat Steps 3 and 4 for the other balancer weight assembly.

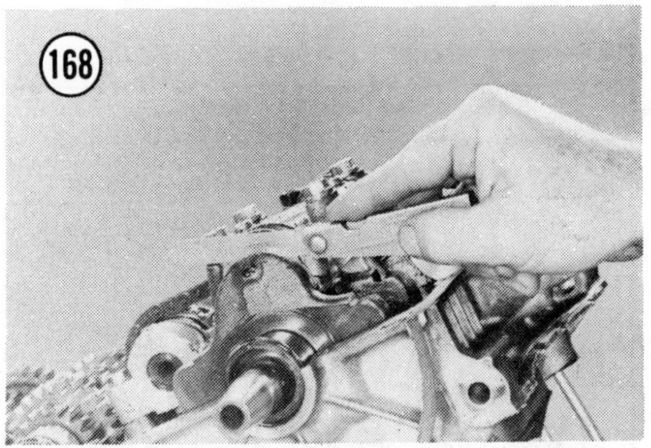

6. Install each balancer weight and sprocket assembly onto the chain and install the washer (1) onto each sprocket side (**Figure 166**).

7. Apply assembly oil to the balancer shafts; install them into the main bearing cap and balancer weight (keep the chain on the sprocket). Align the hole in the shaft to the hole in the balancer weight and install the bolts (7). Apply Loctite Lock N' Seal to the threads prior to installation. Tighten the bolts to 11 ft.-lb (1.5 mkg).

NOTE: *Make sure the washer is in place between each sprocket and main bearing cap.*

8. Install the main bearing inserts (16). If old inserts are reused, refer to marks made in *Disassembly*, Step 1, and install them into their original position.

CRANKSHAFT AND BEARINGS

Removal

1. Remove the main bearing cap/balancer assembly as described under *Balancer Removal*

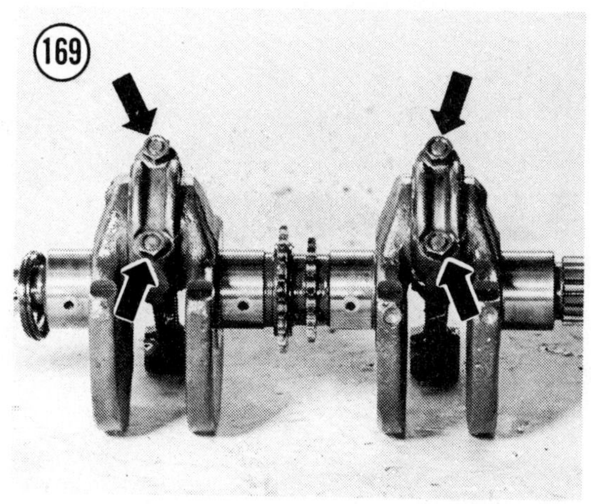

Table 1 ENGINE BOLT TIGHTENING TORQUE CHART

Bolt	Length (mm)	Torque (Ft.-lb)
Front bracket bolts		
Lower	60	17.5
Upper	253	17.5
Rear right upper bracket bolts		
Rear	40	17.5
Front	25	17.5
Upper bracket bolts	55	13.0
Engine mounting bolts		
Rear upper	220	29
Rear lower	292	29
Front	50	29

— *Models D and S* or *Models B and C* in this chapter.

2. Lift the crankshaft and camshaft chain from the engine **(Figure 167)**.

Inspection

1. Measure connecting rod side clearance **(Figure 168)**. Replace the crankshaft if side clearance of either connecting rod exceeds 0.018 in. (0.45mm).

2. Using Plastigage, measure clearance between each crankshaft journal and its associated bearing. Replace all bearings if any clearance exceeds 0.0043 in. (0.11mm). Standard clearance is 0.0014 in. (0.036mm). Plastigage is available at auto parts stores. Be sure to follow instructions on the envelope exactly.

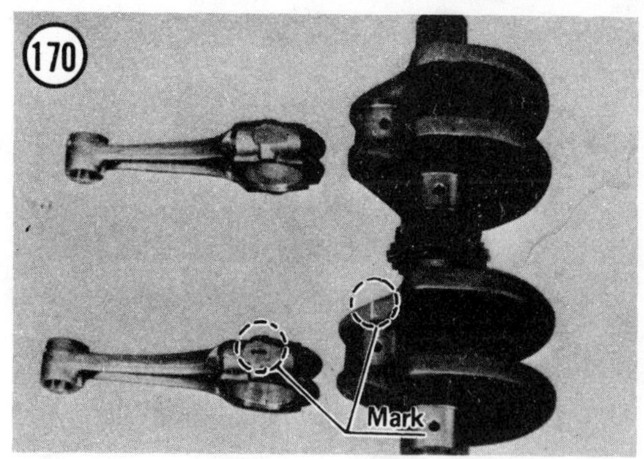

3. Remove cap nuts and caps from connecting rods **(Figure 169)**, then measure clearance between the connecting rod bearings and their journals. Replace both bearings if clearance of either exceeds 0.004 in. (0.1mm). Standard clearance is 0.0016 in. (0.041mm).

4. Support both ends of the crankshaft in a lathe, V-blocks, or crankshaft alignment jig. Rotate it through several revolutions, and measure runout at either center journal. If runout exceeds 0.002 in. (0.05mm), replace the crankshaft. Runout on a new unit will not exceed 0.008 in. (0.02mm).

5. Measure connecting rod journal diameter. Replace the crankshaft if either is worn to less than 1.415 in. (35.94mm). Standard journal diameter is 1.417 in. (36.00mm).

6. Measure diameter of each main bearing journal. Replace the crankshaft if any is worn to less than 1.415 in. (35.94mm). Standard diameter is 1.417 in. (36.00mm).

Installation

Reverse the removal procedure to install the crankshaft. Be sure to lubricate all bearings with engine oil. Tighten connecting rod bearing nuts to 18-22 ft.-lb. (2.5-3.0 mkg) on Models D and S, and to 17.5 ft.-lb. (2.4 mkg) on Models B and C. Be sure the marks align **(Figure 170)**. Install the bearing cap and balancer assembly as described under *Balancer Installation, Models D and S,* or *Models B and C,* in this chapter.

NOTE: If you own a 1980 or later model, first check the Supplement at the back of the book for any new service information.

CHAPTER FIVE

FUEL SYSTEM

This chapter discusses carburetor service, adjustment, and troubleshooting.

For proper operation, a gasoline engine must be supplied with fuel and air mixed in proper proportions by weight. A mixture in which there is an excess of fuel is said to be rich. A lean mixture is one which contains insufficient fuel. It is the function of the carburetors to supply the proper mixture to the engine under all operating conditions.

CARBURETOR SERVICE

Removal/Installation

1. Remove both side covers from motorcycle.
2. Turn fuel petcock to STOP, then remove both fuel lines at petcock.
3. Loosen all clamps which secure rubber ducts to carburetors.
4. Remove both ducts which go from carburetors to air filters.
5. Slide carburetors downward and to right side to disconnect them from intake ducts.
6. Disconnect throttle cables from their brackets and pulleys to complete carburetor removal.
7. Reverse the removal procedure to install the carburetors.

Disassembly/Assembly (Models D and S)

There is no set rule regarding frequency of carburetor overhaul. Carburetors on a machine used for street riding may go more than 5,000 miles without attention. If the machine is used under extremely dusty conditions, the carburetors might need an overhaul in less than 1,000 miles. Poor engine performance, hesitation, and little or no response to mixture adjustment are all symptoms of possible carburetor malfunctions.

Refer to **Figure 1** for this procedure.

1. Remove cap (**Figure 2**).
2. Remove piston (**Figure 3**) and its gasket.
3. Remove jet cover plate and its gasket (**Figure 4**).
4. Remove both air jets (**Figure 5**).
5. Remove float bowl (**Figure 6**).
6. Remove jet keeper (**Figure 7**).
7. Note carefully how float is installed, then pull out pivot pin and gently remove float (**Figure 8**).
8. Shake the float to check for gasoline inside.

> NOTE: *If fuel leaks into the float, the float chamber fuel level will rise, resulting in an overrich mixture. Replace the float if it is deformed or leaking.*

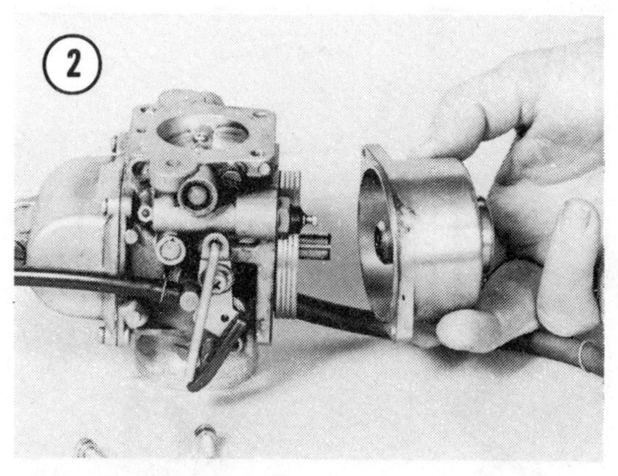
2

5

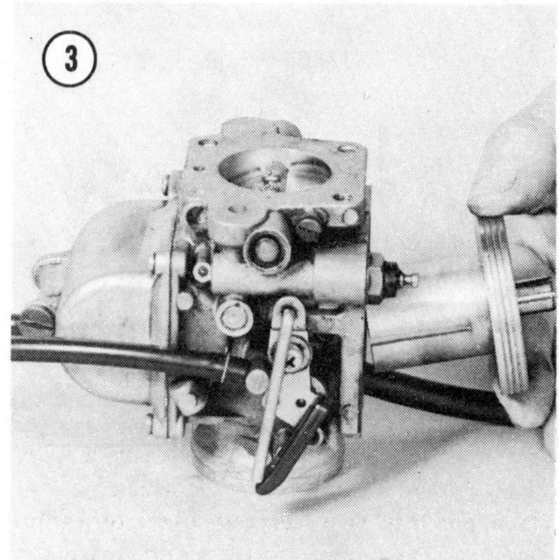
3

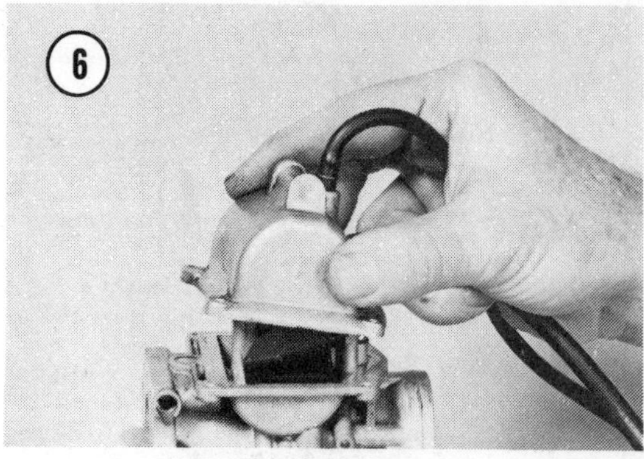
6

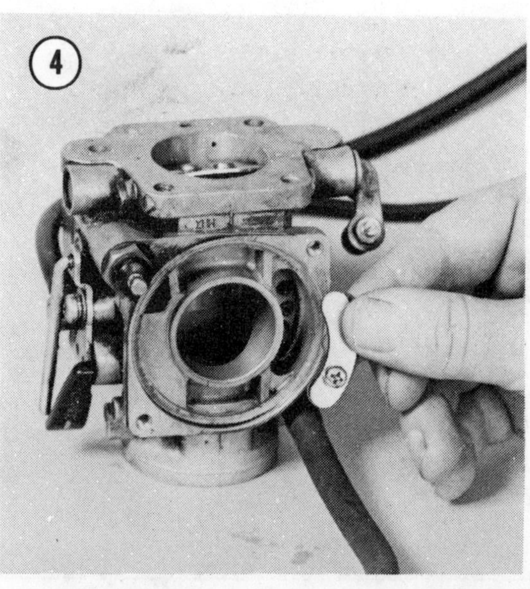
4

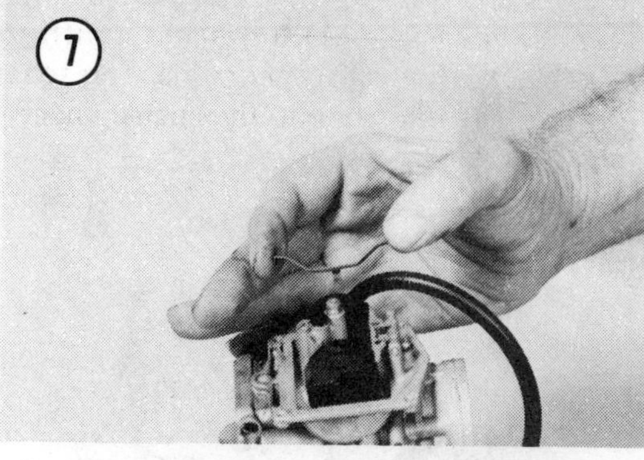
7

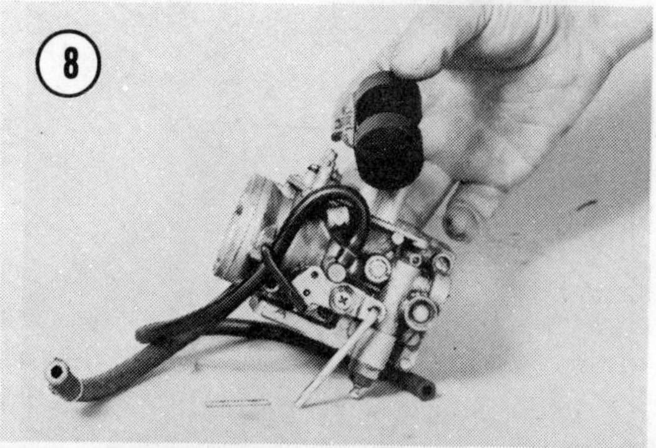
8

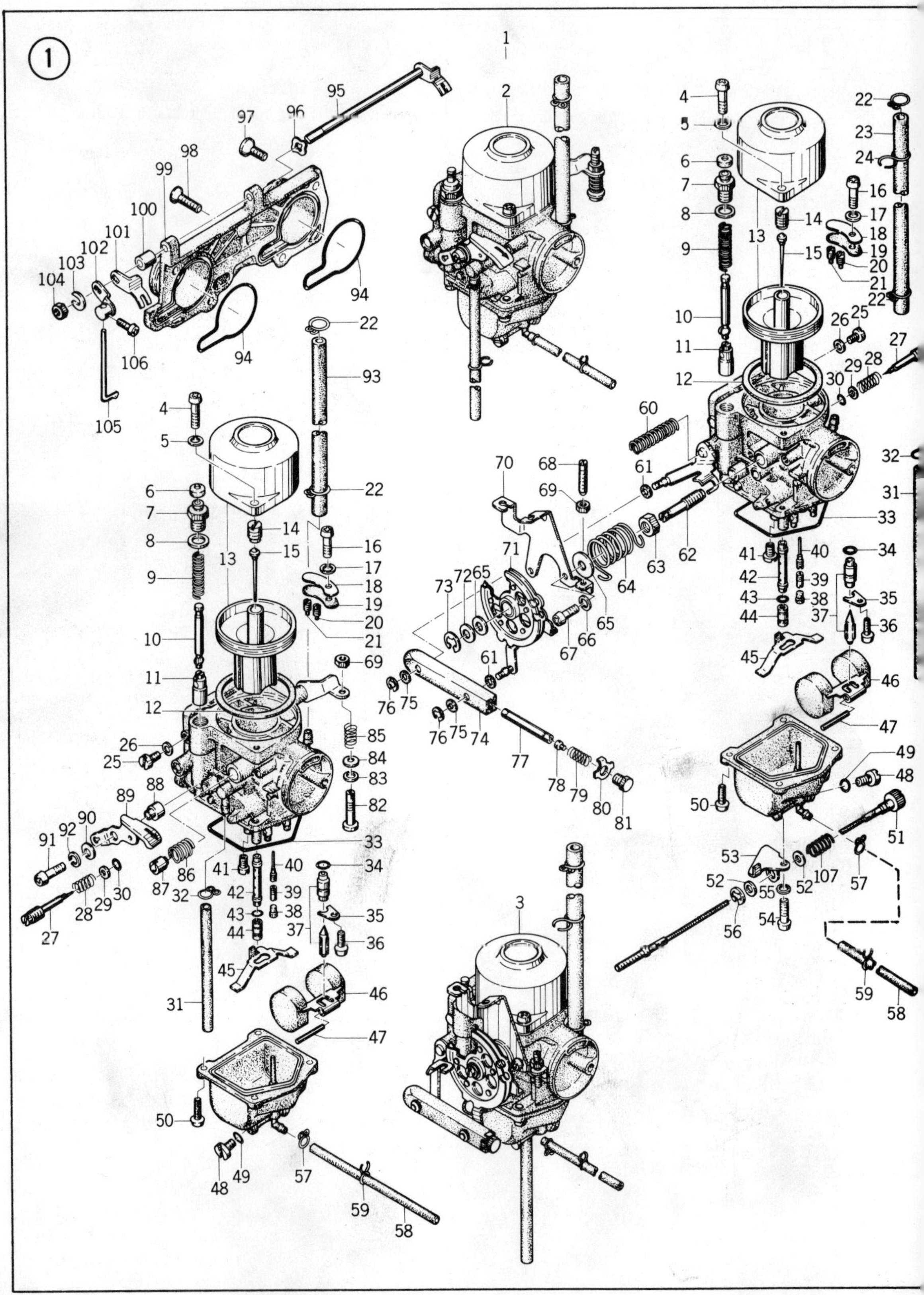
1

CARBURETOR (MODELS D AND S)

1. Carburetor assembly
2. Carburetor
3. Carburetor
4. Screw
5. Washer
6. Cap
7. Cap
8. Washer
9. Spring
10. Shaft
11. Plunger
12. Gasket
13. Piston and carburetor cap
14. Holder
15. Jet needle
16. Screw
17. Washer
18. Plate
19. Gasket
20. Air jet
21. Air jet
22. Clamp
23. Tube
24. Clamp
25. Screw
26. Washer
27. Pilot screw
28. Spring
29. Washer
30. Pilot screw O-ring
31. Tube
32. Clamp
33. O-ring
34. O-ring
35. Plate
36. Screw
37. Float valve
38. Cap
39. Pilot jet
40. Slow jet
41. Starter jet
42. Needle jet
43. O-ring
44. Main jet
45. Plate
46. Float
47. Float pin
48. Screw
49. O-ring
50. Screw
51. Throttle stop screw
52. Washer
53. Plate
54. Screw
55. Washer
56. Snap ring
57. Clamp
58. Tube
59. Clamp
60. Spring
61. Washer
62. Balance screw
63. Nut
64. Spring
65. Washer
66. Washer
67. Screw
68. Screw
69. Nut
70. Holder
71. Pulley
72. Washer
73. Snap ring
74. Link
75. Washer
76. Snap ring
77. Rod
78. Plug
79. Spring
80. Washer
81. Bolt
82. Screw
83. Washer
84. Washer
85. Spring
86. Spring
87. Contact
88. Collar
89. Lever
90. Washer
91. Screw
92. Washer
93. Tube
94. O-ring
95. Shaft
96. Washer
97. Screw
98. Screw
99. Plate
100. Collar
101. Lever
102. Lever
103. Washer
104. Nut
105. Rod
106. Screw
107. Spring

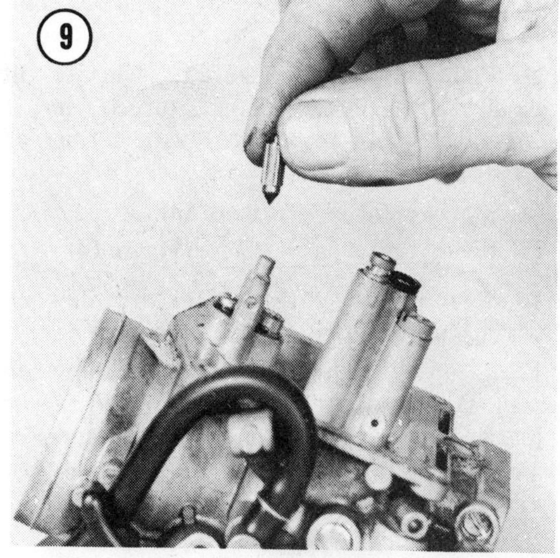
9

10

9. Remove float needle (**Figure 9**).

10. Remove float needle seat retainer, then use pliers with taped jaws to pull out float valve seat (**Figure 10**).

11. Replace the float valve and seat if seating end is scratched or worn. Press the float valve gently with your finger and make sure that the valve seats properly.

CAUTION

If the float valve does not seat properly, fuel will overflow, causing an overrich mixture and flooding the float chamber whenever the fuel petcock is open.

5

12. Using pliers with taped jaws, pull out main jet (**Figure 11**).

13. Pull out needle jet (**Figure 12**). This jet will usually fall out if carburetor is turned over; if not, push it out from above with a fiber or plastic tool.

14. Remove starter jet (**Figure 13**).

15. Remove pilot passage plug (**Figure 14**).

16. Remove pilot jet (**Figure 15**), then slow jet, which is visible after pilot jet is removed.

17. Clean all parts in carburetor cleaning solvent. Dry the parts with compressed air. Clean jets and other delicate parts with compressed air after the float bowl has been removed. Use new gaskets upon reassembly.

CAUTION
Never blow compressed air into any assembled carburetor; doing so may result in damage to the float needle valve.

18. If it is necessary to remove the jet needle, take out the retaining screw that is inside the piston bore (**Figure 16**).

19. Further disassembly should not normally be required, but it should present no difficulty.

20. Reverse the disassembly procedure to assemble the carburetor. Always install new gaskets. Check fuel level after overhauling the carburetor. Refer to *Fuel Level*.

Disassembly/Assembly (Models B and C)

Refer to **Figure 17** for this procedure.

1. Remove the 4 screws securing the upper chamber (39) and remove it.

2. Remove the idle adjust screw bracket (6) and return spring (17).

3. Remove the vacuum piston (45) along with the diaphragm (44).

4. Remove the circlip (41), jet needle holder (42), and jet needle (43).

5. Remove the limiter (54). Refer to A, **Figure 18**.

6. Remove the pilot screw (53), spring (52), washer (51), and O-ring (50). See B, **Figure 18**.

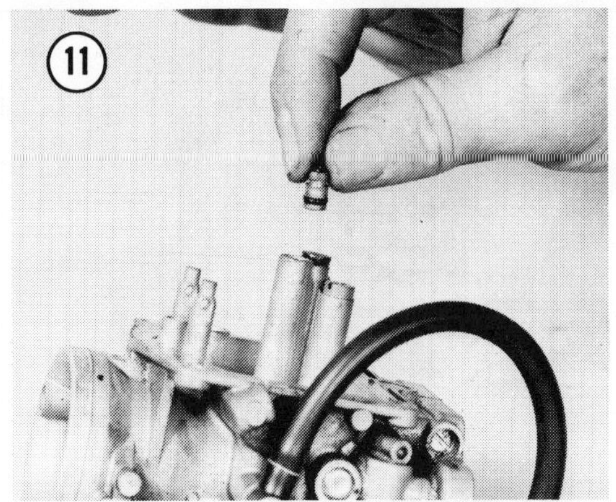

11

12

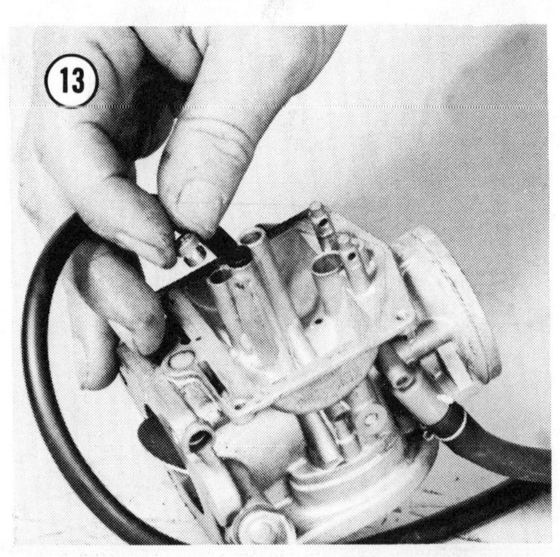

13

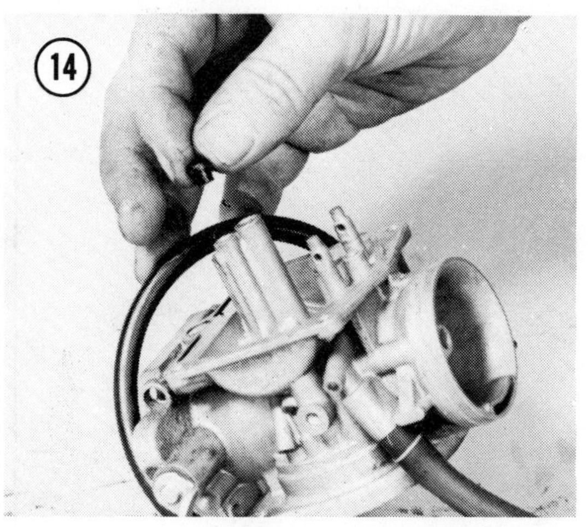

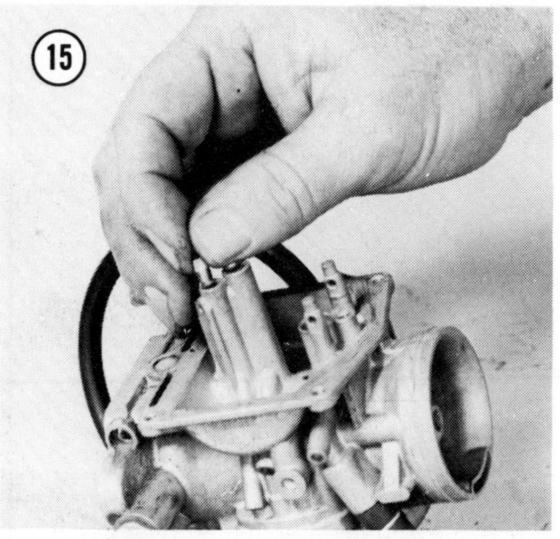

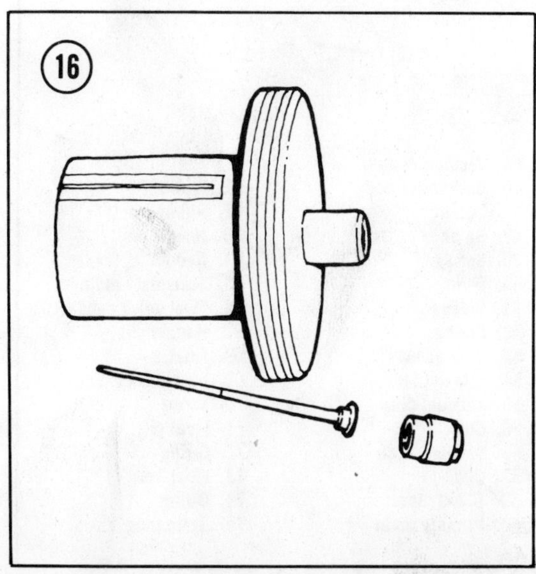

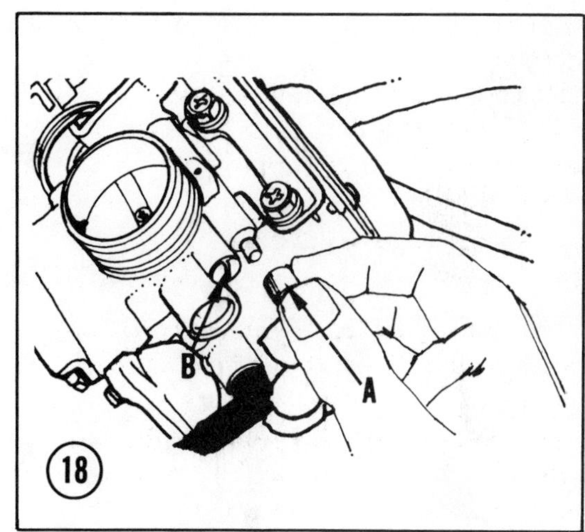

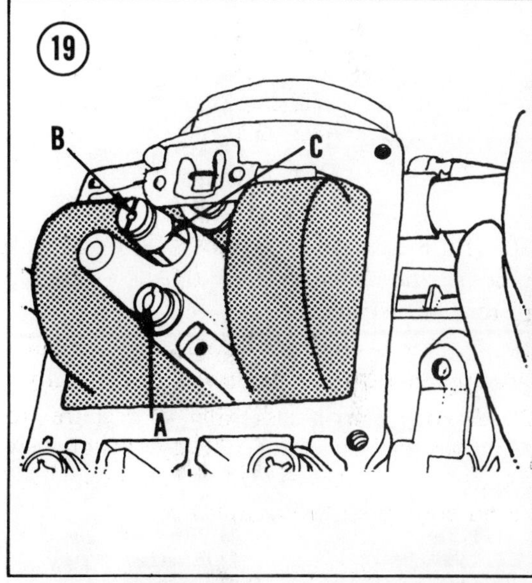

7. Remove the 4 screws and lockwashers and remove the float bowl (73) and O-ring gasket (72).

8. Remove the primary main jet (60); see A, **Figure 19**.

9. Remove the main jet bleed pipe (59), and secondary main jet (65); see B, **Figure 19**.

10. Remove the needle jet holder (64); see C, **Figure 19**.

11. Push out the float pin (71) and remove the float (68).

> NOTE: *Be sure to catch the float valve needle (66) and its hanger clip (67). See* ***Figure 20****.*

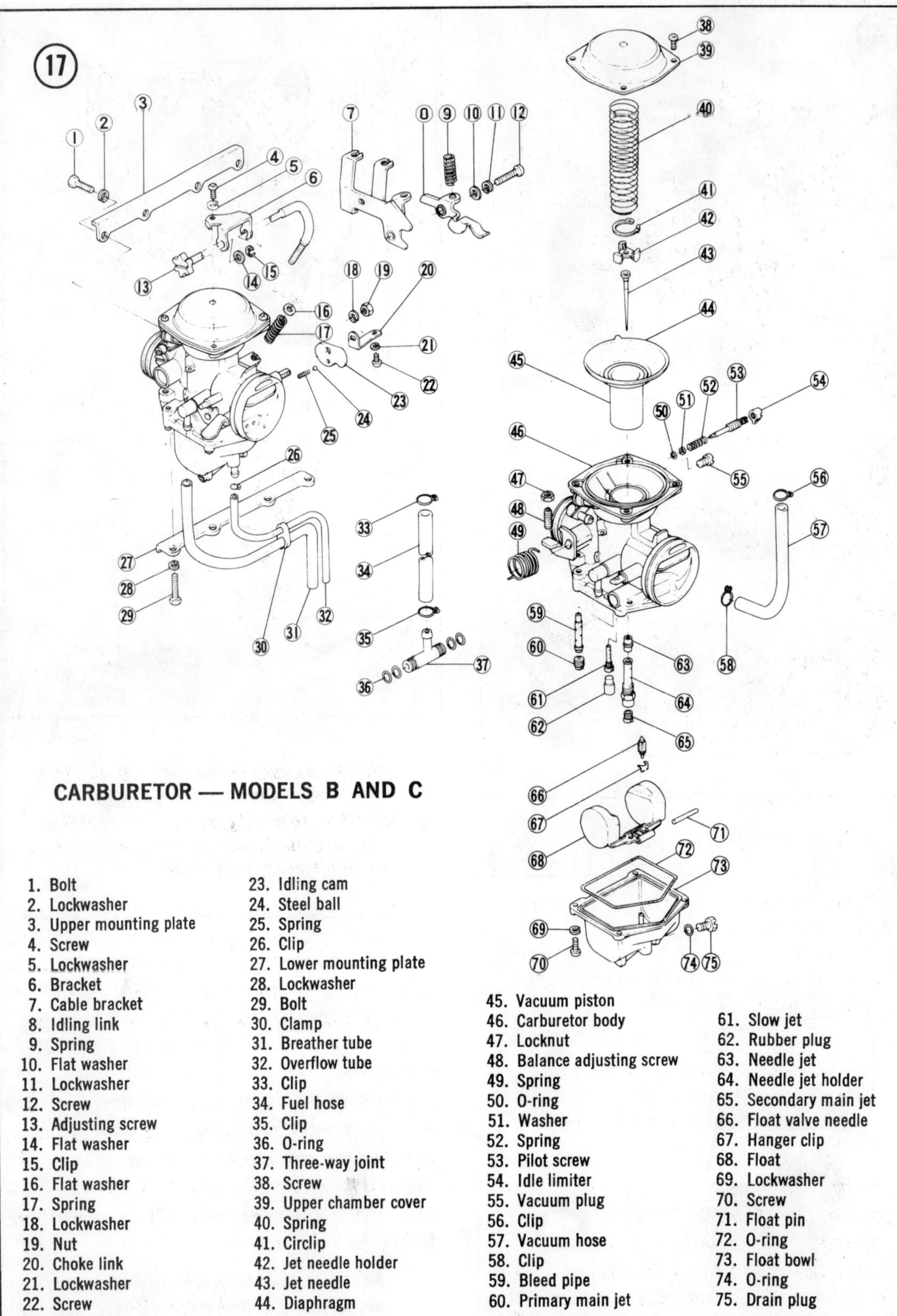

CARBURETOR — MODELS B AND C

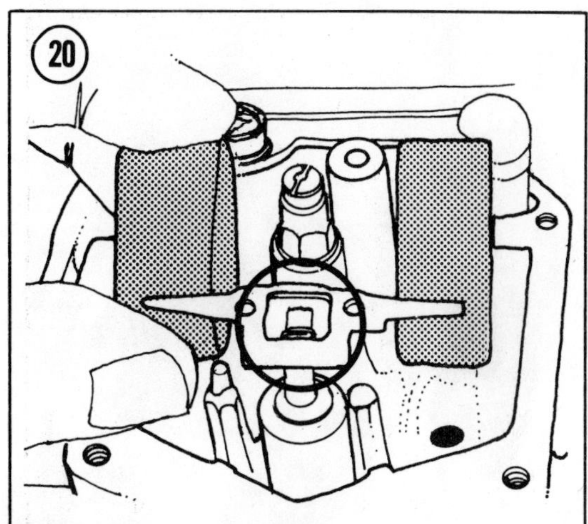

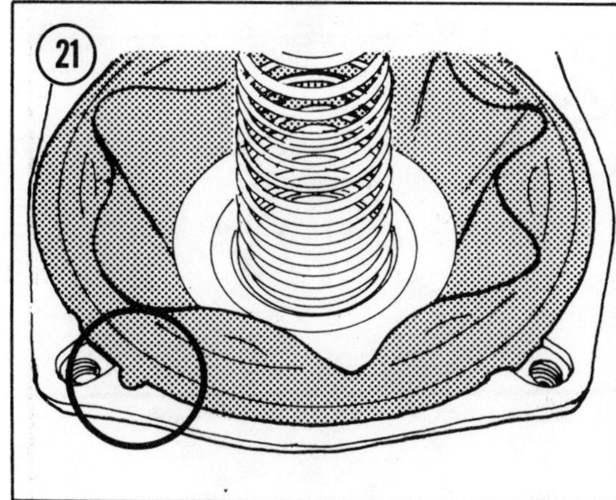

12. Remove the rubber plug (62) and slow jet (61).

13. Clean all parts in carburetor cleaning solvent. Dry the parts with compressed air. Clean jets and other delicate parts with compressed air after the float bowl has been removed. Use new gaskets upon reassembly.

CAUTION

Never blow compressed air into any assembled carburetor; doing so may result in damage to the float needle valve.

14. Further disassembly should not normally be required; but it should present no difficulty.

15. Reverse the disassembly procedure to assemble the carburetor. Always install new gaskets. Check fuel level after overhauling the carburetor. Refer to *Fuel Level*.

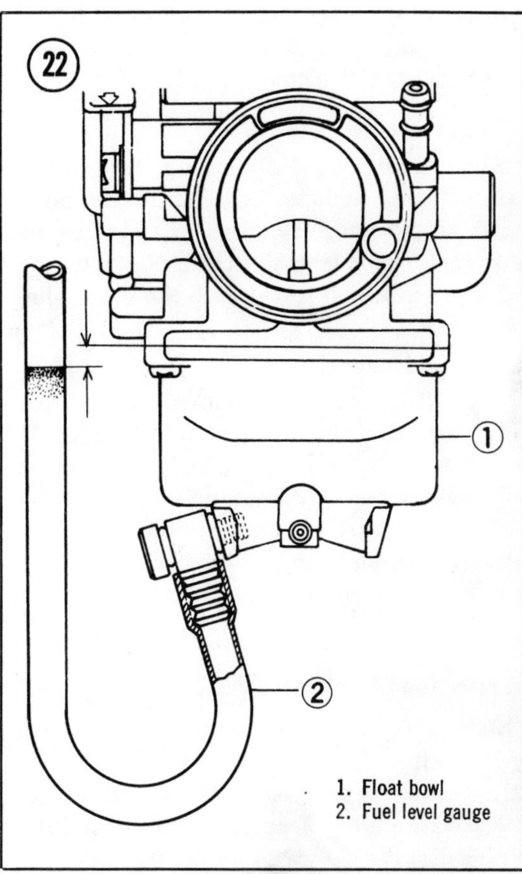

1. Float bowl
2. Fuel level gauge

NOTE: *Be sure to align the tab on the diaphragm with the notch on the upper chamber cover (**Figure 21**). Fit the sealing lip of the diaphragm into the groove in the upper chamber cover.*

16. When installing the upper chamber cover, push up on the piston just enough so that there is no crease on the diaphragm lip. Install the upper chamber cover and 3 screws. Attach the idle adjust screw bracket and remaining screw.

Fuel Level

KZ400 carburetors leave the factory with float levels properly adjusted. Rough riding, a worn needle valve, or a bent float arm can cause the float level to change. To adjust float level on these carburetors, refer to **Figure 22** then proceed as follows.

WARNING

Some gasoline will drain from carburetor during this procedure. Work in

5

a well-ventilated area, at least 50 feet from any open flame. Do not smoke. Wipe up spills immediately.

1. Turn fuel petcock to OFF.
2. Remove float bowl drain plug, then install fuel level gauge midway between side float bowl screws. If no gauge is available, one can be fabricated from a length of clean plastic tubing and a fitting which screws into the drain plug hole.
3. Turn fuel petcock to ON.
4. Hold fuel level gauge against carburetor body. Fuel level should be 2-4mm (Models D and S) or 1.5-3.5mm (Models B and C) below bottom surface of carburetor body.

If adjustment is required, remove the carburetor float, and bend its tang (**Figure 23**) as required to raise or lower fuel level.

23

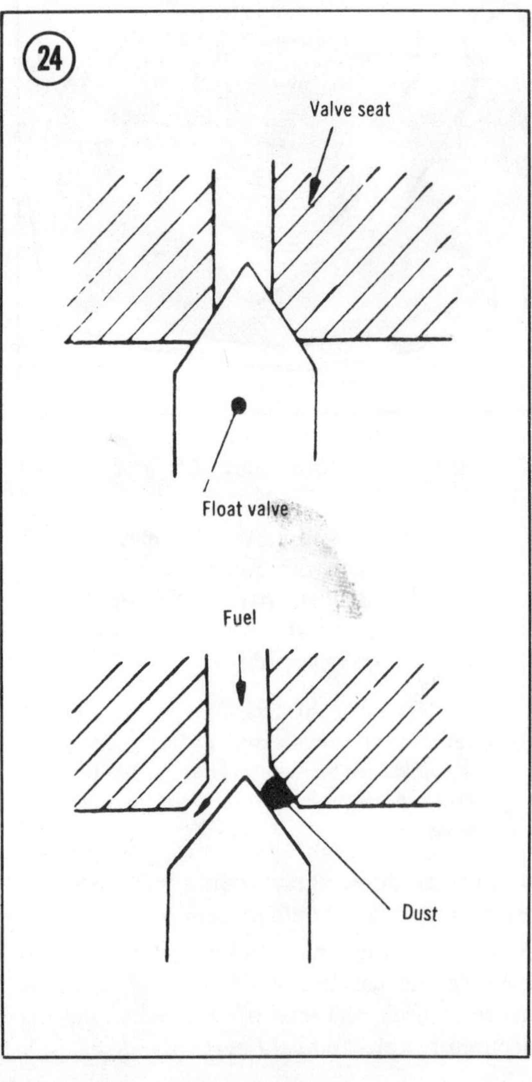

Jet Selection (All Models)

Make a road test at full throttle for final determination of main jet size. To make such a test, operate the motorcycle at full throttle for at least 2 minutes, then shut the engine off, release the clutch, and bring the machine to a stop.

If at full throttle the engine runs "heavily," the main jet is too large. If the engine runs better by closing the throttle slightly, the main jet is too small. The engine will run at full throttle evenly and regularly if the main jet is of correct size.

After each such test, remove and examine the spark plugs. The insulators should have a light tan color. If the insulators have black sooty deposits, the mixture is too rich. If there are signs of intense heat, such as a blistered white appearance, the mixture is too lean.

As a general rule, main jet size should be reduced approximately 5 percent for each 3,000 feet (1,000 meters) above sea level.

Table 1 lists symptoms caused by rich and lean mixtures.

Routine Adjustments (All Models)

Refer to Chapter Three for details of idle speed, idle mixture, and balance adjustments.

Table 1 MIXTURE TROUBLESHOOTING

Condition	Symptom
Rich mixture	Rough idle Black exhaust smoke Hard starting, especially when hot Gas-fouled spark plugs Black deposits in exhaust pipe Poor gas mileage Engine performs worse as it warms up
Lean mixture	Backfiring Rough idle Overheating Hesitation upon acceleration Engine speed varies at fixed throttle Loss of power White color on spark plug insulator Poor acceleration

MISCELLANEOUS CARBURETOR PROBLEMS

Water in carburetor float bowls and sticking carburetor slide valves can result from careless washing of the motorcycle. To remedy the problem, remove and clean the carburetor bowl, main jet, and any other affected parts. Be sure to cover the air intake when washing the machine.

If gasoline leaks past the float bowl gasket, high speed fuel starvation may occur. Varnish deposits on the outside of the float bowl are evidence of this condition.

Dirt in the fuel may lodge in the float valve and cause an overrich mixture (**Figure 24**). As a temporary measure, tap the carburetor lightly with a tool to dislodge dirt. Clean the fuel tank, petcock, fuel line, and carburetor at the first opportunity, should this situation occur.

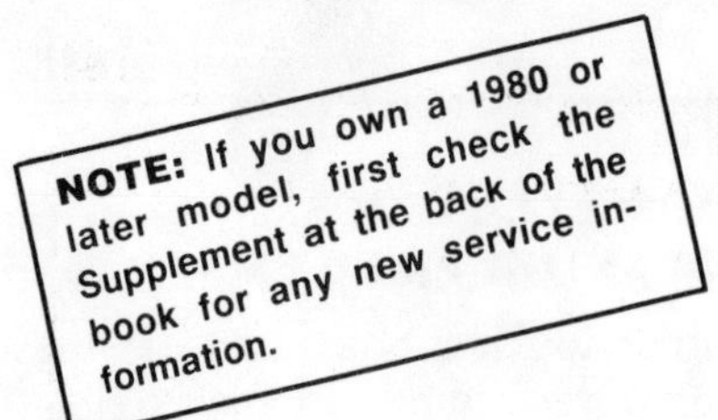

CHAPTER SIX

ELECTRICAL SYSTEM

Kawasaki KZ400 models are equipped with battery ignition systems and regulator-controlled alternators. Some models are equipped with electric starters.

This chapter discusses operation, maintenance, and troubleshooting of the ignition, charging, and signal systems on these bikes. Refer to Chapter Three for routine ignition system maintenance.

The alternator on Models B and C is slightly different from that on Models D and S. The voltage regulator on Models B and C is of solid state construction. Full color wiring diagrams will be found at the end of the manual.

Table 1 IGNITION TROUBLESHOOTING

Symptom	Probable Cause	Remedy
No spark or weak spark, both cylinders	Discharged battery	Charge battery
	Defective fuse	Replace fuse
	Defective points	Clean or replace
	Defective coil	Replace coil
	Defective condenser	Replace condenser
	Broken wire	Repair wire
	Loose or corroded connection	Clean and tighten
Misfires	Fouled spark plug	Clean or replace
	Spark plugs too hot	Put in colder plugs
	Spark plugs too cold	Put in hotter plugs
	Defective points	Service or replace
	Defective coil	Replace
	Defective condenser	Replace
	Incorrect timing	Adjust timing

IGNITION SYSTEM

Figure 1 is a functional diagram of the KZ400 ignition system. A single set of points and a coil with a double-ended secondary winding fire both spark plugs simultaneously. This system is possible because as either cylinder fires on its compression stroke, the other cylinder is on its exhaust stroke.

Troubleshooting

Ignition system problems can be classified as no spark, weak spark, or improperly timed spark. **Table 1** lists common causes and remedies for ignition system malfunctions.

Ignition failures are easy to isolate:

1. Rotate the engine until the points are closed.
2. Disconnect the high voltage lead from the spark plug and hold it ¼ in. away from the cylinder head. Turn on ignition. With an insulated tool, such as a piece of wood, open the points. A fat, blue-white spark should jump from the spark plug to the cylinder head. If the spark is good, clean or replace the spark plug.

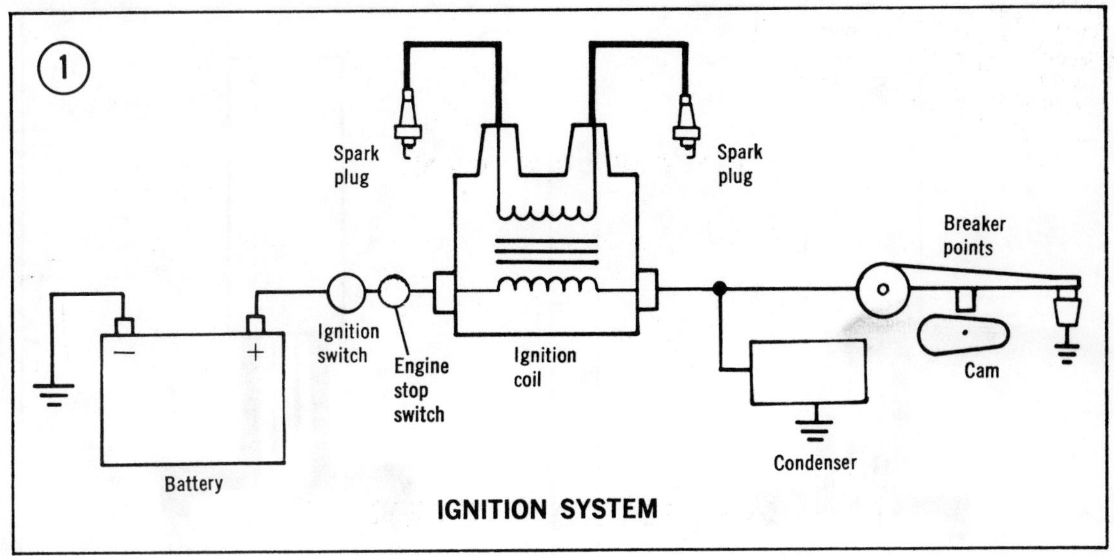

If there is no spark, or if it is thin, yellowish, or weak, continue with Step 3.

3. Connect the leads of a voltmeter to the wire on the points and to a good ground. Turn on the ignition switch. If the meter indicates more than ⅛ volt, the problem is defective points. Replace them.

4. Open points with an insulated tool, such as a piece of wood. The voltmeter should indicate battery voltage. If not, there are 3 possibilities:

   a. Shorted points
   b. Shorted condenser
   c. Open coil primary circuit

5. Disconnect the condenser and the wire from the points. Connect the ungrounded voltmeter lead to the wire which was connected to the points. If the voltmeter does not indicate battery voltage, the problem is an open coil primary circuit. Replace the suspected coil with a known good one. If that coil does not work, the problem is in the primary wiring.

6. If the voltmeter indicates battery voltage in Step 5, the coil primary circuit is OK. Connect the positive voltmeter lead to the wire which goes from the coil to the points. Block the points open with a business card or similar piece of cardboard. Connect the negative voltmeter lead to the movable point. If the voltmeter indicates any voltage, the points are shorted. Replace them.

7. If the foregoing checks are satisfactory, the problem is in the coil or condenser. Substitute each of these separately with a known good one to determine which is defective.

Ignition Coil

The ignition coil is a form of transformer which develops the high voltage required to jump the spark plug gap. The only maintenance required is that of keeping the electrical connections clean and tight, and occasionally checking to see that the coil is mounted securely.

If coil condition is doubtful, there are several checks which may be made.

1. Measure coil primary resistance, using an ohmmeter, between both coil primary terminals (**Figure 2**). Resistance should measure approximately 4 ohms.

2. Measure coil secondary resistance between both spark plug caps (**Figure 3**). Secondary resistance should be approximately 13,000 ohms.

3. Replace the coil if either spark plug lead exhibits visible damage.

Be sure to connect all wires to their proper terminals when replacing the coil.

Condenser

The condenser is a sealed unit that requires no maintenance. Be sure that both connections are clean and tight.

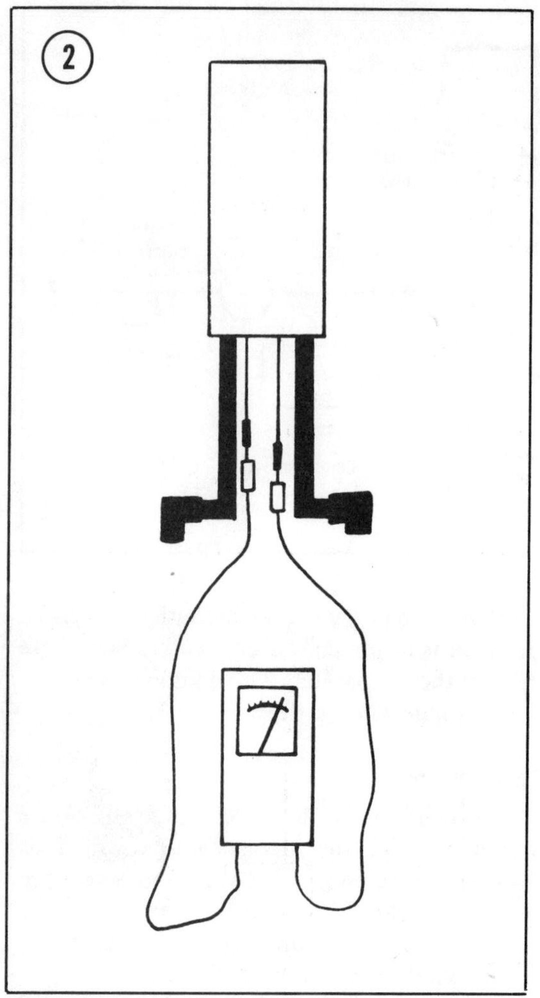

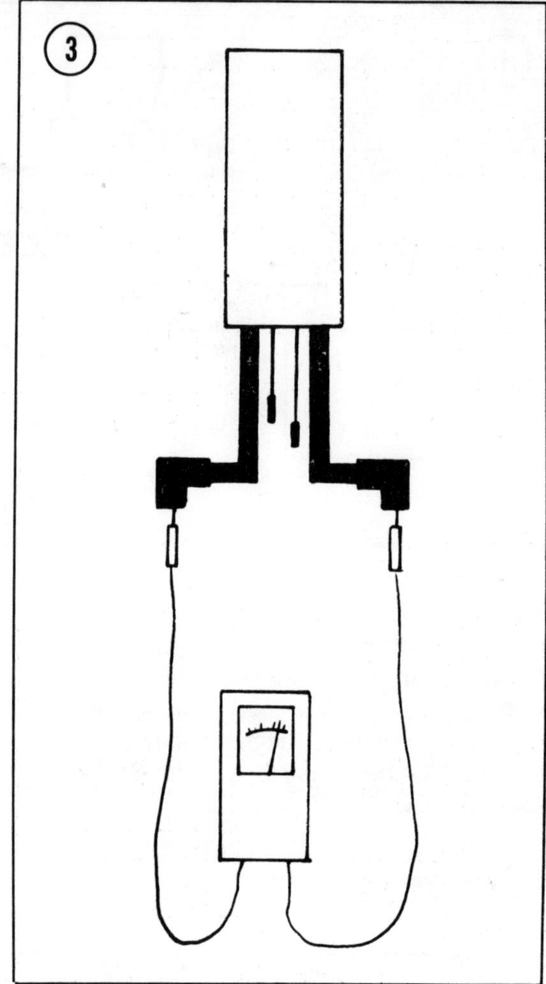

Two tests can be made on the condenser. Measure condenser capacity with a condenser tester. Capacity should be 0.20-0.24 microfarad. The other test is insulation resistance, which should not be less than 5 megohms, measured between the condenser pigtail and case.

In the event that no test equipment is available, a quick test of the condenser may be made by connecting the condenser case to the negative terminal of a 12 volt battery and the positive lead to the positive battery terminal. Allow the condenser to charge for a few seconds, then quickly disconnect the battery and touch the condenser pigtail to the condenser case. If you observe a spark as the pigtail touches the case, you may assume that the condenser is OK.

Service

Two major service items are required on battery ignition models: breaker point service and ignition timing. Both are vitally important to proper engine operation and reliability. Refer to Chapter Three for breaker point service and ignition timing procedures.

CHARGING SYSTEM

All models are equipped with 3-phase alternators, solid state rectifiers, and electromechanical voltage regulators. If charging system problems are suspected, as in the case of dim lights or a chronically undercharged battery, the following checks should isolate the problem. Before beginning any charging system tests, be sure that the battery is in good condition and that it is at or near full charge.

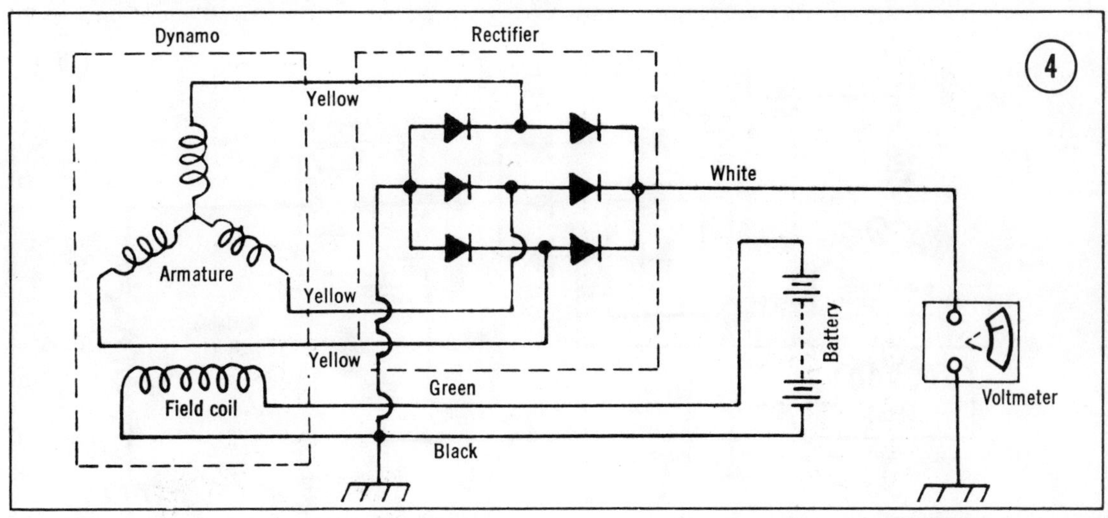

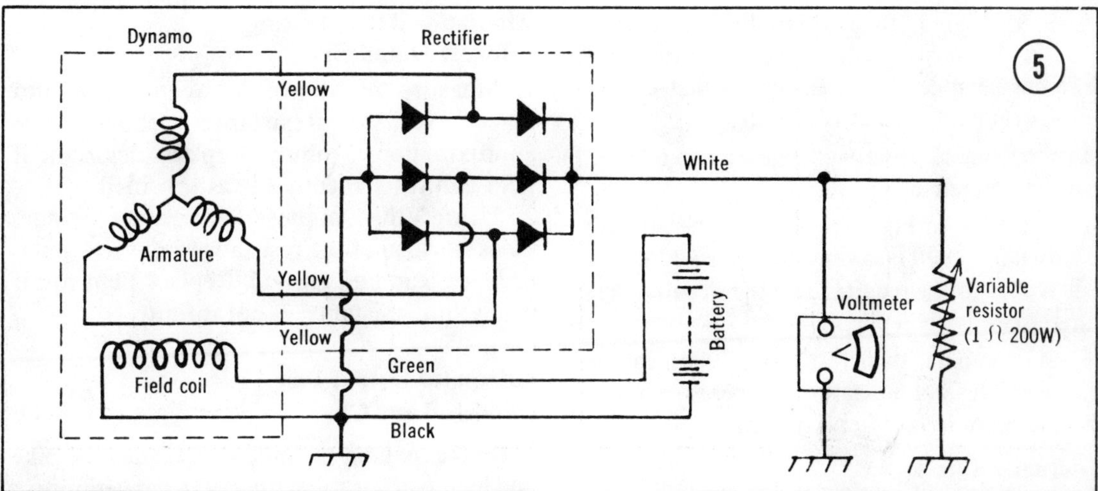

Alternator Output Test (Models D and S)

1. Remove left side cover and headlight unit.

2. Disconnect 6-pole connector from left side and 9-pole connector in headlight housing.

3. Disconnect white wire from rectifier at battery positive lead.

4. Connect the positive terminal of an accurate 0-20 DC voltmeter in the white wire which was removed. Connect the negative voltmeter terminal to a good ground.

5. Remove right side cover.

6. Disconnect green and brown leads from voltage regulator. Temporarily connect these leads together. **Figure 4** illustrates these test connections.

CAUTION

Do not allow green and brown leads to touch anything. Also, do not leave them connected for any longer than is required to make this test.

7. Start engine and run it at idling speed (1,100-1,300 rpm). Do not run it at a faster speed.

8. Observe voltmeter. If it indicates 14 volts or greater, the alternator is OK. If output voltage is less than specified, either the alternator or the rectifier is defective.

9. Stop engine. Refer to **Figure 5**. Connect a one ohm, 200 watt variable resistor, such as a commerical carbon pile, between the white wire and ground. Do not disconnect voltmeter.

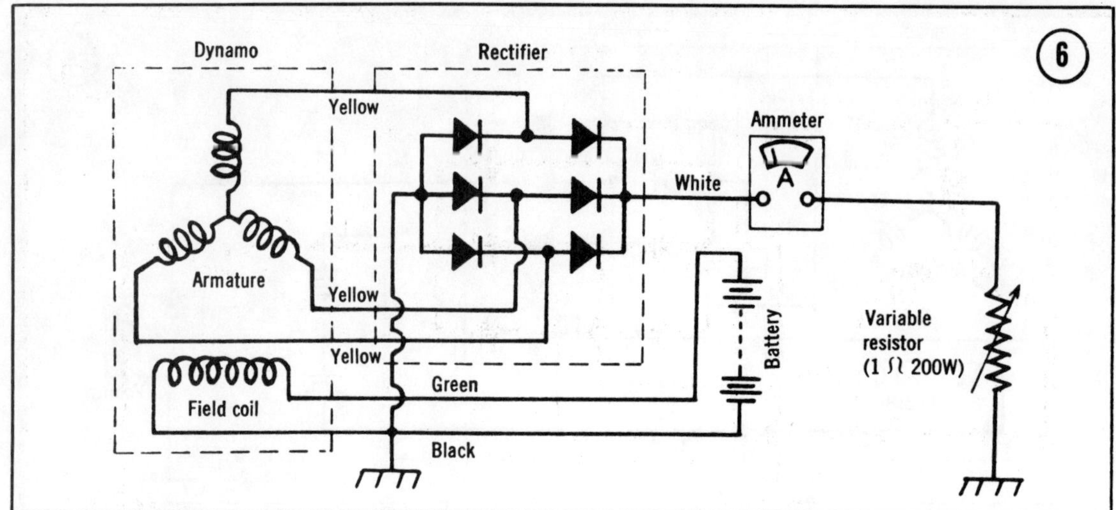

10. Start engine, then gradually increase its speed to 5,000 rpm. Adjust resistor at the same time engine speed is increasing so that output voltage is maintained at 14.5 volts.

11. Stop engine. Do not change carbon pile setting determined in Step 10.

12. Referring to **Figure 6**, connect the positive terminal of a 0-20 DC ammeter to the white wire which goes to the recitifer and the negative terminal to the carbon pile.

13. Start engine, then run it at 5,000 rpm. If ammeter does not indicate 13 amperes or more, the alternator or rectifier is defective.

Alternator Checks (Models D and S)

If the charging system failed the checks of foregoing Steps 1 through 13, the following checks should isolate any problem with the alternator.

1. Disconnect left-hand plug below voltage regulator.

2. Measure resistance between each pair of yellow wires from alternator. Resistance should be 0.4-0.6 ohm for each pair. Replace stator if any pair differs from this value.

3. Using the highest ohmmeter range, measure insulation resistance between any yellow lead and ground. Insulation resistance must be essentially infinite. Replace stator if ohmmeter indicates any continuity.

4. Disconnect white plug on right-hand side below voltage regulator.

Alternator Rotor Testing (Models D and S)

1. Measure resistance between green and black leads. Resistance should be approximately 5 ohms. Replace field coil if field coil resistance is not as specified.

2. Using the highest ohmmeter range, measure insulation resistance between green or black lead and ground. Replace field coil if insulation resistance is not infinite.

Alternator Output Test (Models B and C)

Before making the output test, start the bike and let it reach normal operating temperature.

1. Remove the engine sprocket cover as described in Chapter Four.

2. Disconnect the 2 yellow electrical leads coming from the alternator.

3. Set a voltmeter to the 250 volt DC range and connect the meter leads to the yellow alternator leads.

4. Start the engine and run at 4,000 rpm.

5. The voltage reading should be about 75 volts. If the output voltage is less than this the alternator is defective.

Alternator Stator Test (Models B and C)

Use an ohmmeter, set at R x 1, and measure the resistance between the two yellow leads

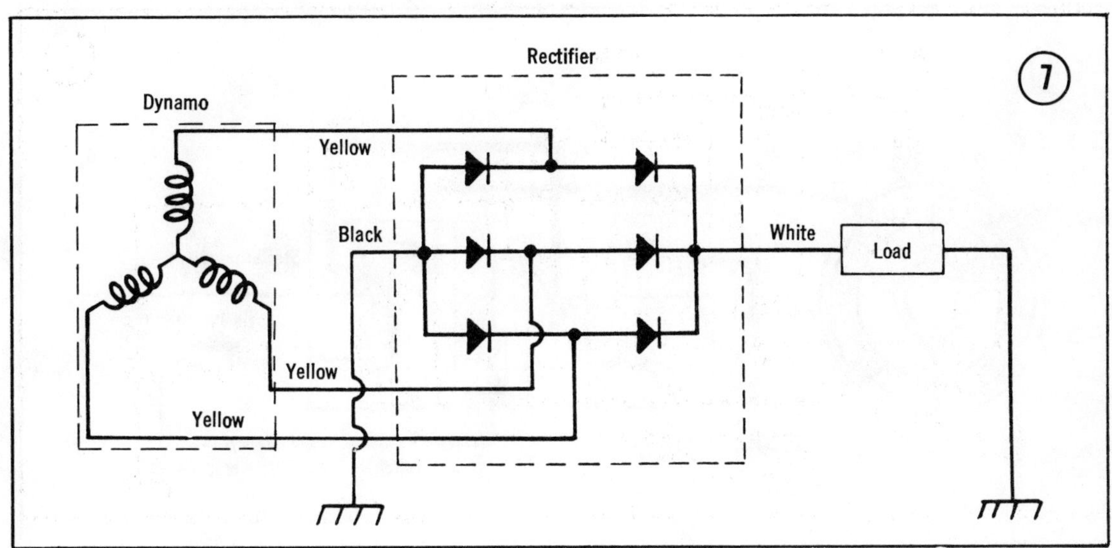

from the alternator. The value should be about 0.32 ohms. If the resistance is greater than specified or no meter reading (infinity), the stator has an open and must be replaced.

Change the ohmmeter setting to the highest range and measure the resistance between each yellow lead and the chassis (ground). The meter should read infinity; if it doesn't, this indicates a short and the stator must be replaced.

> NOTE: *If the stator winding resistance is within the specified range, but the voltage output is incorrect, the rotor has probably lost some of its magnetism and must be replaced.*

Alternator Rotor Testing (Models B and C)

The rotor is permanently magnetized and cannot be tested except by replacement with a rotor known to be good. A rotor can lose magnetism from old age or a sharp blow. If defective, the rotor must be replaced; it cannot be remagnetized.

RECTIFIER (MODELS D AND S)

The recitifer **(Figure 7)** converts 3-phase alternating current produced by the alternator into direct current, which is use to operate electrical accessories and to charge the battery.

To test the rectifier:

1. With engine not running, remove left side cover, then disconnect white wire from rectifier at battery.
2. Remove right side cover. Disconnect left-hand white plug below voltage regulator.
3. Measure and record resistance between each yellow lead and white lead.
4. Reverse ohmmeter leads, then repeat Step 3. Each pair of measurements must be high with the ohmmeter connected one way and low when the ohmmeter leads are connected the other way. It is not possible to specify exact meter indications, but each pair of measurements should differ by a factor of not less than 10.
5. Repeat Steps 3 and 4, but make measurements between each yellow lead and the black lead.
6. Replace the rectifier if it fails any check of Steps 3, 4, or 5.

VOLTAGE REGULATOR (MODELS D AND S)

Varying engine speeds and electrical system loads affect alternator output. The voltage regulator controls alternator output by varying its field current.

Voltage Regulator Tests

Before making any voltage regulator test, be sure that the battery is in good condition and is at or near full charge.

6

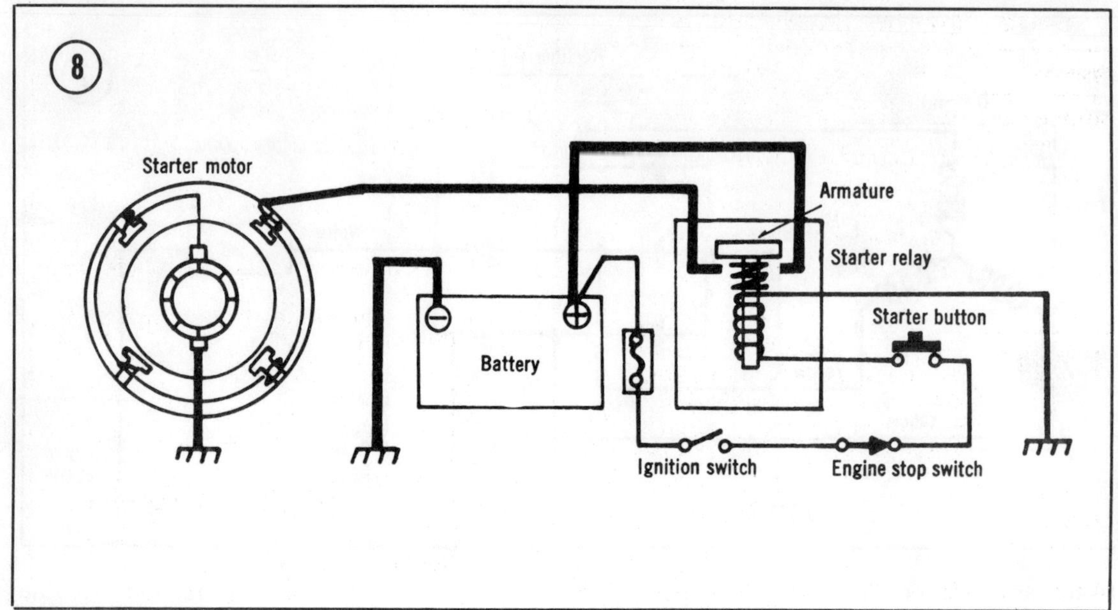

1. Remove left side cover and headlight unit.
2. Remove 6-pole connector from left side of motorcycle and 9-pole connector from headlight housing.
3. Connect an accurate 0-20 DC voltmeter across battery terminals.
4. Start engine and run it at 1,600 rpm. Voltmeter should indicate 14.0-15.0 volts.
5. Gradually increase the engine speed to 4,000 rpm. Voltmeter should again indicate 14.0-15.0 volts. Do not allow engine speed to decrease until second measurement is made.

It is suggested that a defective voltage regulator be replaced rather than repairs attempted. It may be possible to clean any corrosion from its contacts with emery cloth.

VOLTAGE REGULATOR/RECITIFER (MODELS B AND C)

Voltage Regulator Test

1. Remove the right-hand side cover; turn the ignition switch to the OFF position.
2. Disconnect the electrical connector containing 3 wires — 2 yellow and 1 black.

CAUTION

Do not short circuit the voltage regulator when connecting the test leads or it will be damaged.

3. Use an ohmmeter set at R x 1, and measure the resistance between each yellow lead and the black one. Attach the ohmmeter positive (+) lead to the yellow leads and the ohmmeter negative lead (−) to the black lead. The value should be less than 20 ohms.
4. Reset the ohmmeter at R x K ohm. Attach the ohmmeter positive (+) lead to the black lead and the negative (-) ohmmeter lead to the yellow leads. Their value should be more than 100 ohms.
5. If any two leads are too high or too low in both directions the voltage regulator/rectifier must be replaced.

Voltage Regulator Performance Test

Connect a voltmeter to the battery terminals. Start the engine and let it idle; increase engine speed until the voltage going to the battery reaches 14.0-15.0 volts. At this point, the voltage regulator must divert the current to ground. If this does not happen, the voltage regulator/rectifier must be replaced.

ELECTRIC STARTER

The starter circuit includes the starter button, starter relay, battery, and starter motor. When the button is pressed, a small amount of current

Table 2 STARTER TROUBLESHOOTING

Symptom	Probable Cause	Remedy
Starter does not work	Low battery Worn brushes Defective relay Defective switch Defective wiring or connection Internal short circuit	Recharge battery Replace brushes Repair or replace Repair or replace Repair wire or clean connection Repair or replace defective component
Starter action is weak	Low battery Pitted relay contacts Worn brushes Defective connection Short circuit in commutator	Recharge battery Clean or replace Replace brushes Clean and tighten Replace armature
Starter runs continuously	Stuck relay	Replace relay
Starter turns; does not turn engine	Defective starter clutch	Replace starter clutch

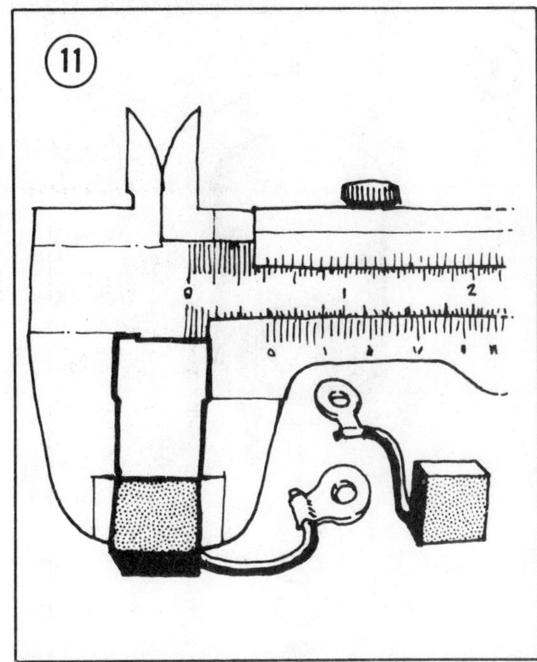

flows through the switch and through the relay coil. This current magnetizes the relay core, which then pulls the armature to it and closes the relay contacts. The closed contacts complete a current path for the starter motor, and the motor turns. The reason for using a relay instead of using the switch to turn on the starter directly is the high current requirement of the starter motor. It is not practical to put a heavy switch on the handlebars and have large wires running to it, so the starter switch is made only to carry relay coil current and heavy contacts inside the relay carry the starter motor current. **Figure 8** illustrates the starter circuit.

CAUTION

Never continue pressing the starter switch if the engine does not turn over, because excess current through the starter motor will burn out its windings.

Figures 9 and 10 illustrate starter motor construction. The field coils are wound around cores, forming the yoke. The armature windings are connected to the commutator and receive their current through the brushes. Field windings and armature windings are connected in series and if the brushes do not make good contact, no starter current will flow and the starter will not turn over. A short circuit or an open wire in either winding will also cause the starter to be inoperative. Dust from brush wear might be another cause of starter failure if it gets into bearings, making them overheat and seize.

Table 2 lists possible starter problems, probable causes, and the most common remedies.

Brushes

Worn brushes or weak brush springs can cause poor brush contact, resulting in starter motor malfunction. Measure the brushes (**Figure 11**) and replace them if they are worn to ¼ in. (6mm). Standard length for new brushes is about ½ in. (12mm).

Spring tension should normally be 18-24 ounces (500-600 grams), measured with a spring gauge. The springs can be considered serviceable if they snap the brushes firmly into position.

Commutator

A dirty or rough commutator will result in poor brush contact and cause rapid brush wear. In addition, carbon dust resulting from brush wear accumulates between commutator segments and partially shorts out starter current.

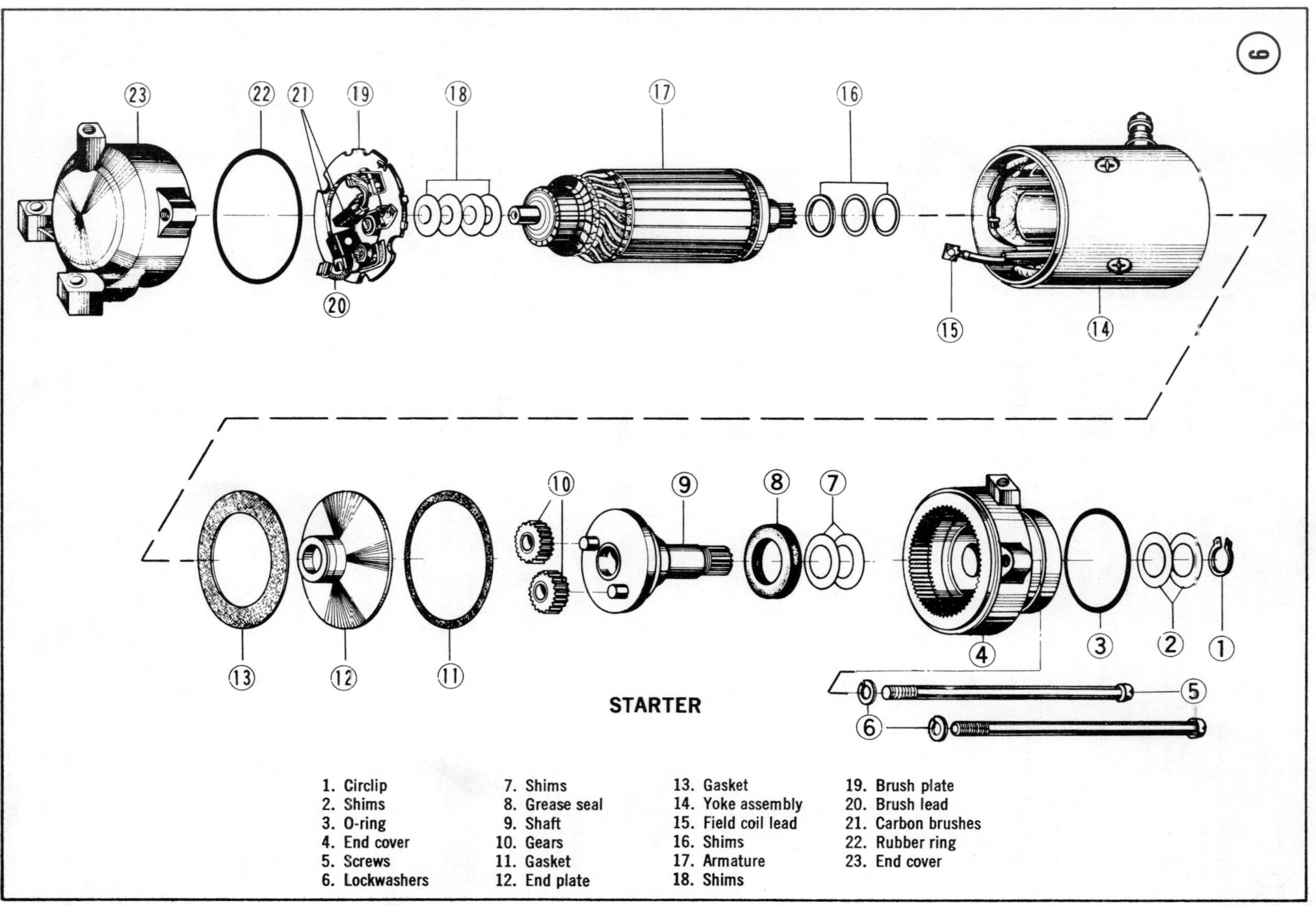
9
STARTER
1. Circlip
2. Shims
3. O-ring
4. End cover
5. Screws
6. Lockwashers
7. Shims
8. Grease seal
9. Shaft
10. Gears
11. Gasket
12. End plate
13. Gasket
14. Yoke assembly
15. Field coil lead
16. Shims
17. Armature
18. Shims
19. Brush plate
20. Brush lead
21. Carbon brushes
22. Rubber ring
23. End cover

(10)

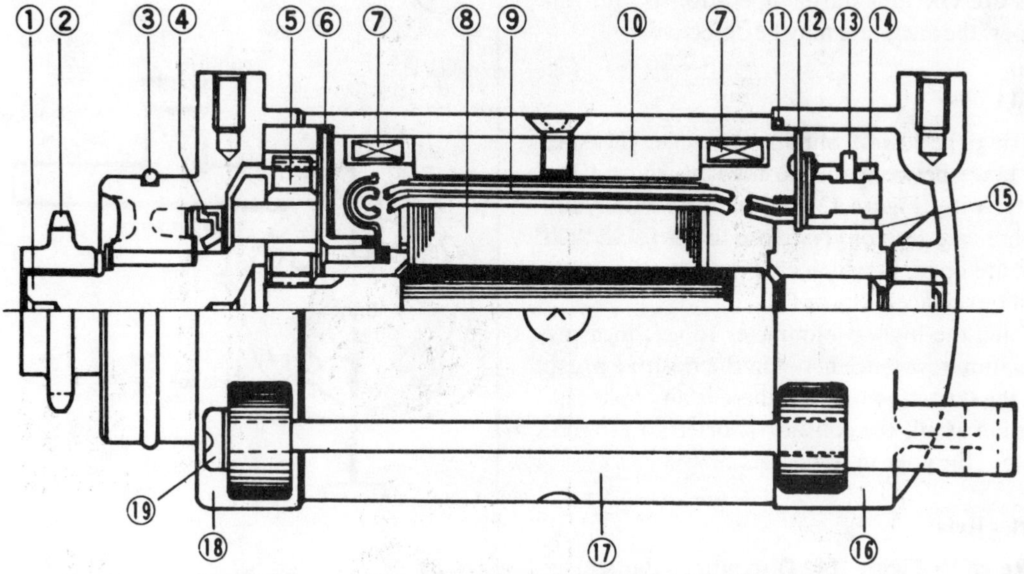

STARTER MOTOR

1. Shaft
2. Sprocket
3. O-ring
4. Grease seal
5. Gears
6. End plate
7. Field coil
8. Armature
9. Armature winding
10. Cores
11. Rubber ring
12. Brush plate
13. Spring
14. Brushes
15. Commutator
16. End cover
17. Yoke assembly
18. End cover
19. Screws

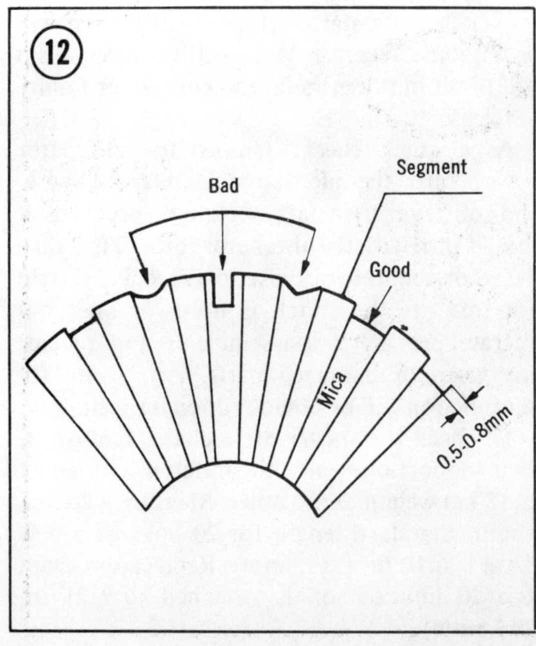

1. Clean the commutator of oil, dust, and foreign material.

2. If the commutator is rough or covered with carbon dust, polish it with fine sandpaper.

3. Refer to **Figure 12**. Replace the commutator if depth of insulator grooves between segments is less than 0.008 in. (0.2mm).

Armature

Using the lowest ohmmeter range, measure resistance between each pair of adjoining commutator segments.

If there is high resistance between any pair, or no indication at all, a wire is open, in which case the armature must be replaced. Using the highest ohmmeter range, measure insulation resistance between any commutator segment and the shaft. If there is any indication at all, replace the armature.

If the foregoing checks show the armature to be good and the following tests on the field coils are OK and starter operation is still improper, the armature may be defective.

Field Coils

Using the lowest ohmmeter range, measure resistance between the positive brush and the starter wire (**Figure 13**). If the ohmmeter does not indicate zero or very close to zero, the field coils are open, in which case the yoke assembly must be replaced.

Using the highest ohmmeter range, measure insulation resistance between the positive brush and the starter housing. If there is any meter indication at all, the coils are shorted to ground. Replace the yoke in this case.

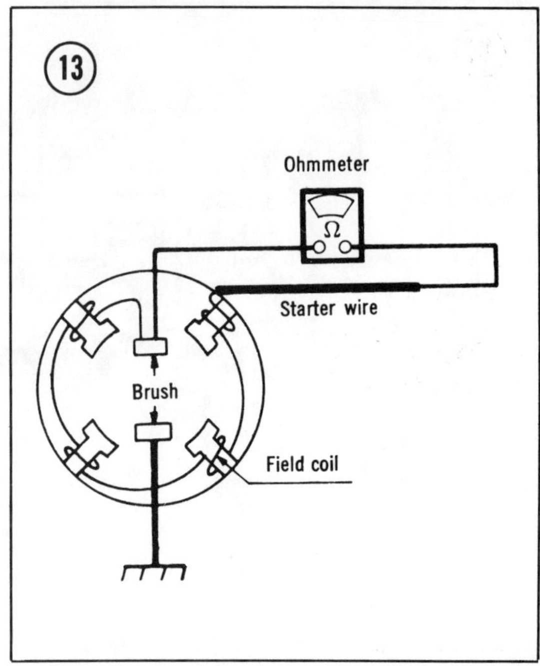

Starter Relay

1. Refer to **Figure 14**. Disconnect the starter wire from the starter relay. Connect the ohmmeter leads across the relay terminals.

2. Press the starter button. The relay should click and the ohmmeter should indicate zero resistance. If the relay clicks but the meter indicates any value greater than zero, replace relay.

3. If the relay does not click, disconnect the remaining wires, then measure resistance across the relay coil terminals. If there is not close to zero resistance, the relay coil is defective.

4. If there is close to zero resistance, the relay may be good but inoperative because no current is reaching it. Connect the positive voltmeter lead to the black wire and the negative meter lead to the black/yellow wire, then press the starter switch. If the meter indicates battery voltage, the relay is defective. If there is no voltage indication, the switch or wiring is defective.

Starter Clutch and Chain

Figure 15 is a sectional view of the starter clutch. The clutch body is attached to the alternator rotor. When sprocket (1) rotates in the direction of the arrow, rollers (3) wedge themselves between the clutch body and clutch sprocket hub, thereby locking the clutch body and clutch sprocket together. Under these conditions, starter torque is transmitted to the engine through the starter chain, starter clutch sprocket, rollers, clutch body, and alternator rotor.

When the engine starts, inertia forces the rollers back against their springs, so that they no longer wedge between the clutch body and clutch sprocket. The engine is then free to turn without driving the starter.

Usually, any starter clutch malfunction will be obvious. Wear or damage in the mechanism will result in noise, failure to engage, or failure to release.

As a quick check, remove the alternator cover, turn the alternator counterclockwise, and observe the starter clutch sprocket; it should turn with the alternator rotor. Then turn the rotor counterclockwise; the sprocket should not turn. If the clutch is noisy or does not operate properly, disassemble it and replace any worn or damaged parts. Any cause for malfunction will be obvious upon inspection.

To check the starter drive chain, remove it, then support one end and stretch it with an 11 lb. (5 kg) weight at the other. Measure a 20 link length. Standard length for 20 links of a new chain is 6.12 in. (155.5mm). Replace the chain if a 20 link section is stretched to 6.21 in. (157.8mm).

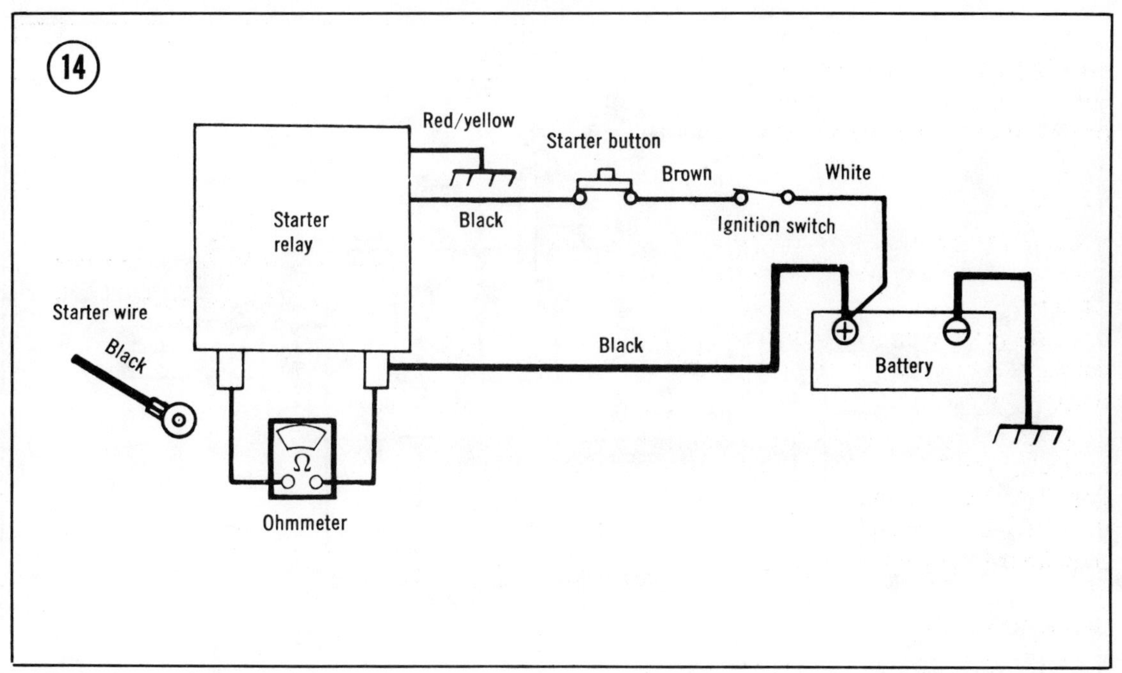

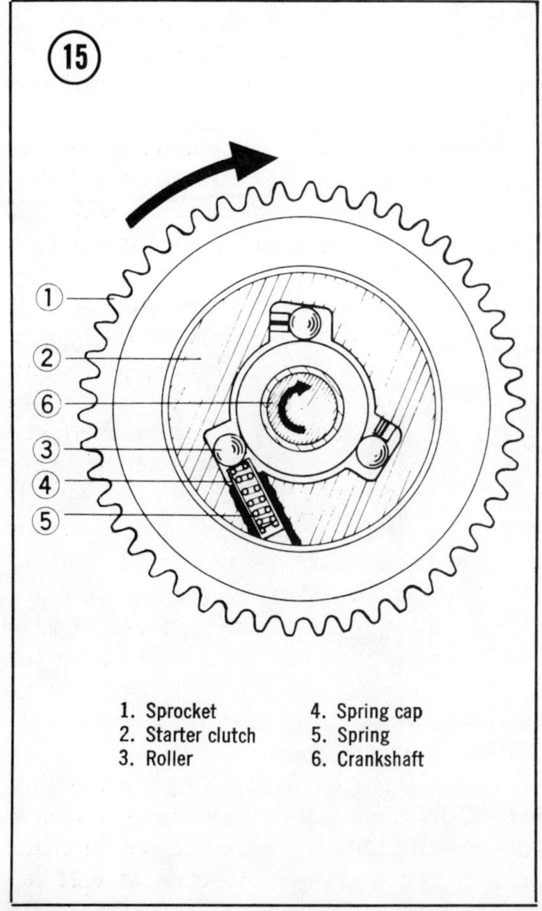

1. Sprocket
2. Starter clutch
3. Roller
4. Spring cap
5. Spring
6. Crankshaft

LIGHTS

In the event of trouble with lights, the first thing to check is the affected bulb itself. If the bulb is good, check all wiring and connections.

Headlight and Taillight

Figures 16, 17, and 18 are wiring diagrams of the headlight and/or taillight circuits. Reference to those illustrations will aid fault diagnosis.

Brake Light

Figures 19 and 20 illustrate the brake light circuits. Note that the brake light will not operate when the ignition switch is off. If either switch is defective, it must be replaced.

To check the brake light failure indicator switch:

1. Turn ignition on and apply either brake. Check that indicator lamp glows steadily.
2. With brake applied, remove brake light bulb. Indicator lamp must remain lit.
3. With brake light bulb removed, release then reapply brake. Indicator light must flash.
4. Install brake light bulb.
5. Replace the brake light failure indicator switch if it fails the foregoing checks.

(16)

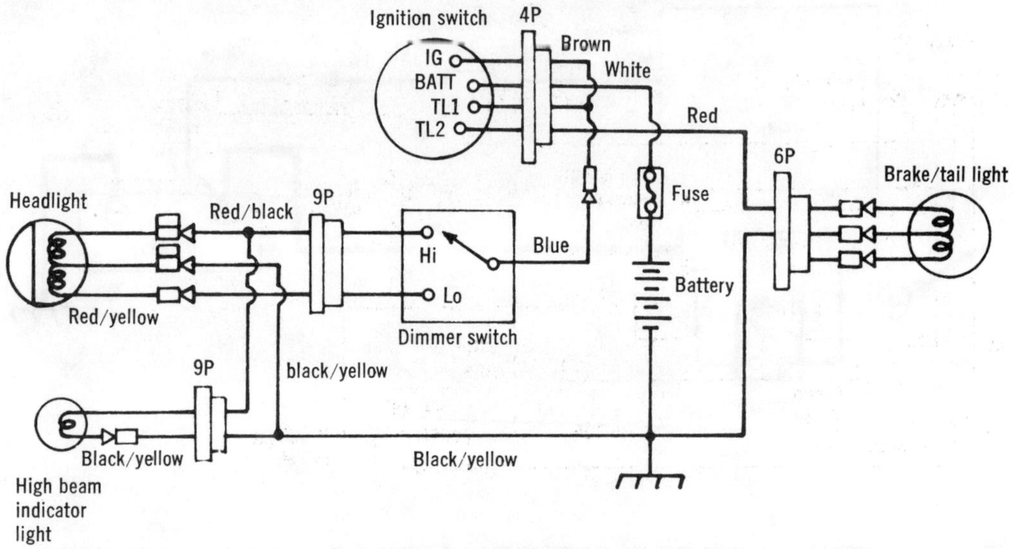

Ignition switch
4P
IG
BATT
TL1
TL2
Brown
White
Red
6P
Brake/tail light
Headlight
Red/black
9P
Fuse
Hi
Blue
Lo
Battery
Red/yellow
Dimmer switch
9P
black/yellow
Black/yellow
Black/yellow
High beam indicator light

HEADLIGHT AND TAILLIGHT CIRCUIT (MODELS D AND S)

(17)

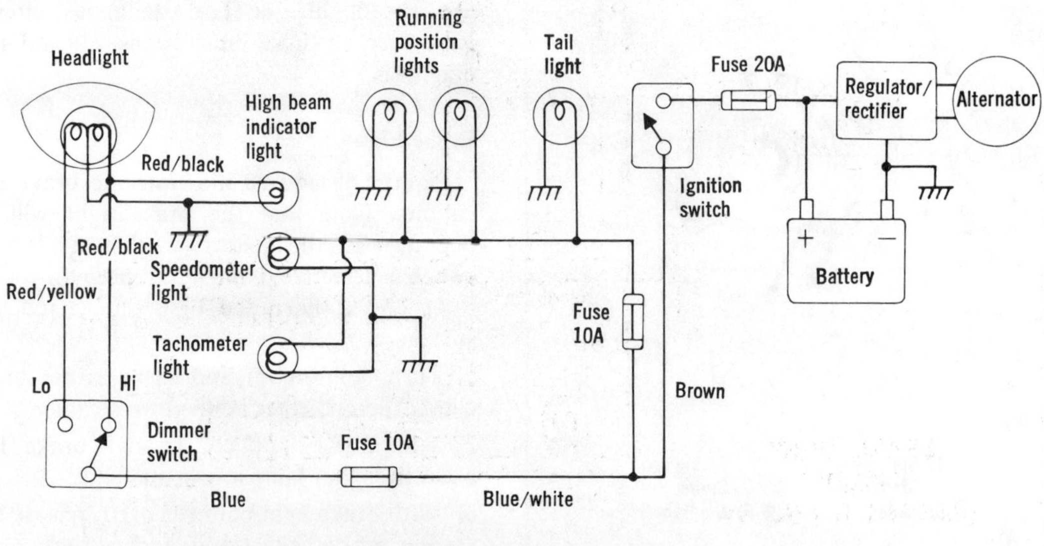

Running position lights
Tail light
Headlight
High beam indicator light
Fuse 20A
Regulator/ rectifier
Alternator
Red/black
Ignition switch
Red/black
Speedometer light
Battery
Red/yellow
Fuse 10A
Tachometer light
Lo
Hi
Brown
Dimmer switch
Fuse 10A
Blue
Blue/white

HEADLIGHT CIRCUIT (U.S. AND CANADIAN MODELS)

(18)

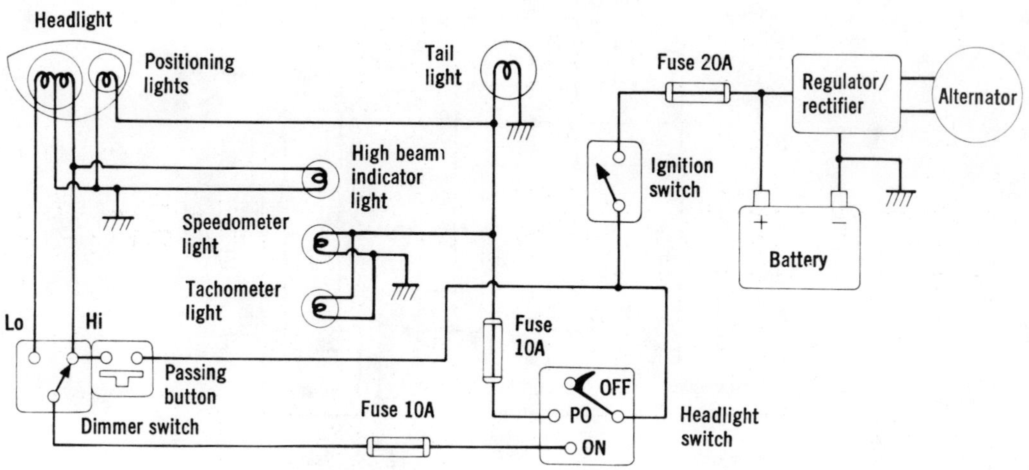

Headlight
Positioning lights
Tail light
Fuse 20A
Regulator/rectifier
Alternator
High beam indicator light
Ignition switch
Speedometer light
Battery
Tachometer light
Lo
Hi
Fuse 10A
Passing button
OFF
PO
Headlight switch
Fuse 10A
Dimmer switch
ON

HEADLIGHT CIRCUIT
(EUROPEAN MODELS)

(19)

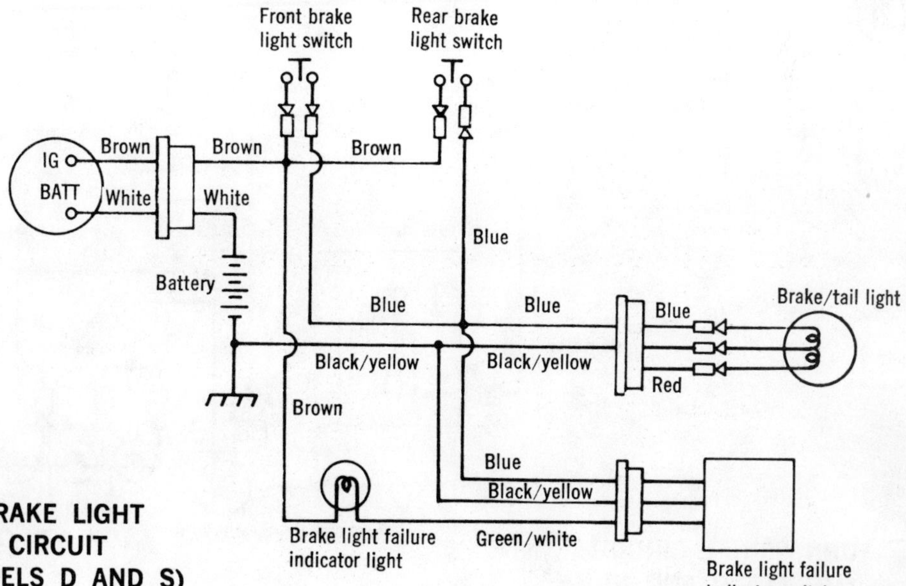

Front brake light switch
Rear brake light switch
IG
BATT
Brown
White
Brown
White
Brown
Blue
Battery
Blue
Blue
Blue
Brake/tail light
Black/yellow
Black/yellow
Red
Brown
Blue
Black/yellow
Brake light failure indicator light
Green/white
Brake light failure indicator switch

BRAKE LIGHT CIRCUIT
(MODELS D AND S)

6

(20)

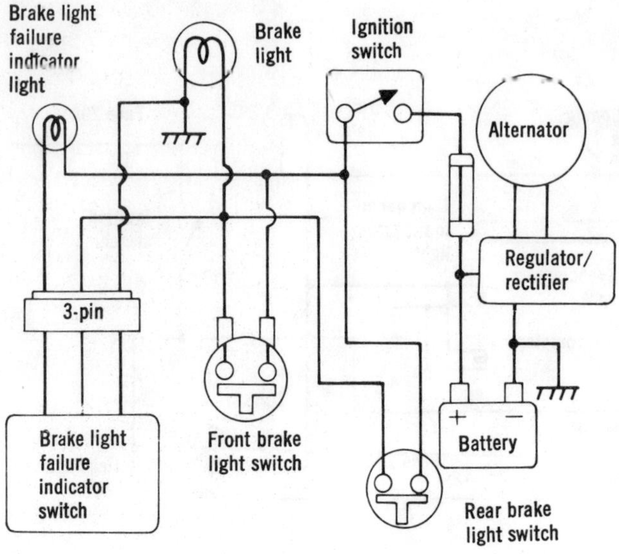

Brake light failure indicator light
Brake light
Ignition switch
Alternator
Regulator/ rectifier
3-pin
Battery
Brake light failure indicator switch
Front brake light switch
Rear brake light switch

BRAKE LIGHT CIRCUIT (MODELS B AND C)

(21)

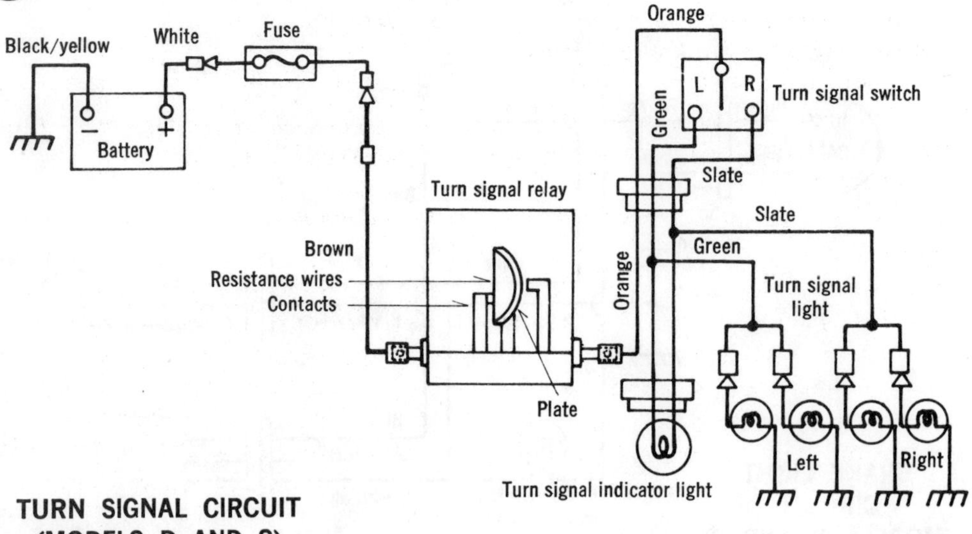

Black/yellow
White
Fuse
Battery
Orange
Green
Turn signal switch
Slate
Turn signal relay
Slate
Brown
Green
Resistance wires
Contacts
Orange
Turn signal light
Plate
Left
Right
Turn signal indicator light

TURN SIGNAL CIRCUIT (MODELS D AND S)

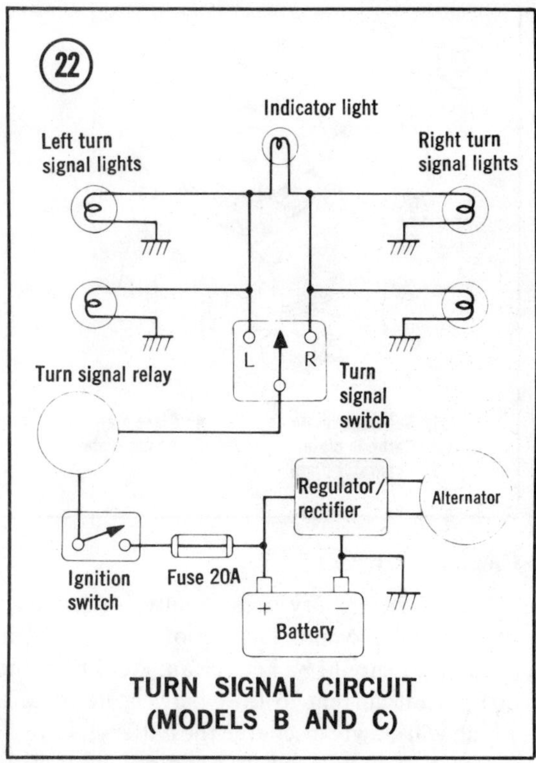

TURN SIGNAL CIRCUIT (MODELS B AND C)

Turn Signals

Figures 21 and 22 are functional diagrams of the turn signal circuit. Any malfunction in the turn signal system is usually caused by a defective relay, or the use of wrong bulbs.

If turn signals do not work at all on either side, check the system as follows:

1. Check that battery voltage is up to normal. If battery voltage is low, the turn signals will come on but not flash.
2. Disconnect relay leads.
3. Using an ohmmeter, check relay continuity. If relay resistance is not essentially zero, replace relay. Any indication of greater than one ohm can be considered cause for replacement.
4. Connect the positive terminal of a 0-20 DC voltmeter to the brown lead that was disconnected from the relay. Connect the negative meter lead to the orange wire. Turn the ignition on, then operate the turn signal switch in both "R" and "L" positions. The meter should indicate battery voltage in each position. If not, the turn signal switch, ignition switch, wiring, or fuse is at fault. Trace all wiring to isolate the malfunction.

HORN

If the horn malfunctions, the following checks should isolate the fault.

1. Check that the battery is in good condition and is at least half charged.
2. Disconnect both horn leads, then, using an ohmmeter, measure horn resistance. Any resistance greater than a few ohms means that the horn should be replaced.
3. Connect the positive terminal of a 0-20 DC voltmeter to the brown lead which was disconnected from the horn and the negative terminal to the black lead. Press the horn pushbutton. The meter must indicate battery voltage. If not, check back through the horn wiring circuit.
4. If the meter indicated battery voltage in Step 3, and turning the horn adjustment screw does not cure the problem, replace the horn.

NOTE: *Do not loosen the armature mounting screw. Doing so will result in altered armature position and probably the necessity of horn replacement.*

BATTERY

The KZ400 motorcycles are equipped with lead-acid storage batteries, smaller in size but similar in construction to batteries used in automobiles.

WARNING
*Read and thoroughly understand the section on **Safety Precautions** before doing any battery service.*

Safety Precautions

When working with batteries, use extreme care to avoid spilling or splashing electrolyte. This electrolyte is sulphuric acid, which can destroy clothing and cause serious chemical burns. If any electrolyte is spilled or splashed on clothing or body, it should immediately be neutralized with a solution of baking soda and water, then flushed with plenty of clean water.

Electrolyte splashed into the eyes is extremely dangerous. Safety glasses should always be worn when working with batteries. If electrolyte is splashed into the eye, force the eye open, flood with cool clean water for about 5 minutes, and call a physician immediately.

If electrolyte is spilled or splashed onto painted or unpainted surfaces, it should be neutralized immediately with baking soda solution and then rinsed with clean water.

When batteries are being charged, highly explosive hydrogen gas forms in each cell. Some of this gas escapes through the filler openings and may form an explosive atmosphere around the battery. *This explosive atmosphere may exist for several hours.* Sparks, open flame, or a lighted cigarette can ignite this gas, causing an internal explosion and possible serious personal injury. The following precautions should be taken to prevent an explosion:

1. Do not smoke or permit any open flame near any battery being charged or which has been recently charged.
2. Do not disconnect live circuits at battery terminals, because a spark usually occurs where a live circuit is broken. Care must always be taken when connecting or disconnecting any battery charger; be sure its power switch is off before making or breaking connections. Poor connections are a common cause of electrical arcs which cause explosions.

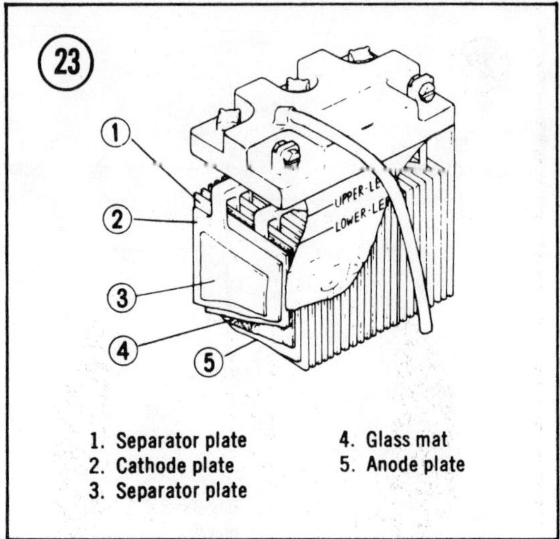

1. Separator plate
2. Cathode plate
3. Separator plate
4. Glass mat
5. Anode plate

Electrolyte Level

Battery electrolyte level should be checked regularly, particularly during hot weather. Most batteries are marked with electrolyte level limit lines (**Figure 23**). Always maintain the fluid level between these lines, using distilled water as required for replenishment. Distilled water is available at almost every supermarket. It is sold for use in steam irons and is quite inexpensive.

Overfilling leads to loss of electrolyte, resulting in poor battery performance, short life, and excessive corrosion. Never allow the electrolyte level to drop below the top of the plates. That portion of the plates exposed to air may be permanently damaged, resulting in loss of battery performance and shortened life.

Excessive use of water is an indication that the battery is being overcharged. The most common causes of overcharging are high battery temperature or high voltage regulator setting. It is advisable to check the voltage regulator if this situation exists.

Cleaning

Check the battery occasionally for presence of dirt or corrosion. The top of the battery, in particular, should be kept clean. Acid film and dirt permit current to flow between terminals, which will slowly discharge the battery.

For best results when cleaning, wash first with diluted ammonia or baking soda solution, then flush with plenty of clean water. Take care to keep filler plugs tight so that no cleaning solution enters the cells.

Battery Cables

To ensure good electrical contact, cables must be clean and tight on battery terminals. If the battery or cable terminals are corroded, the cables should be disconnected and cleaned separately with a wire brush and baking soda solution. After cleaning, apply a very thin coating of petroleum jelly to the battery terminals before installing the cables. After connecting the cables, apply a light coating to the connection. This procedure will help to prevent future corrosion.

Battery Charging

WARNING

Do not smoke or permit any open flame in any area where batteries are being charged or immediately after charging.

Motorcycle batteries are not designed for high charge or discharge rates. For this reason,

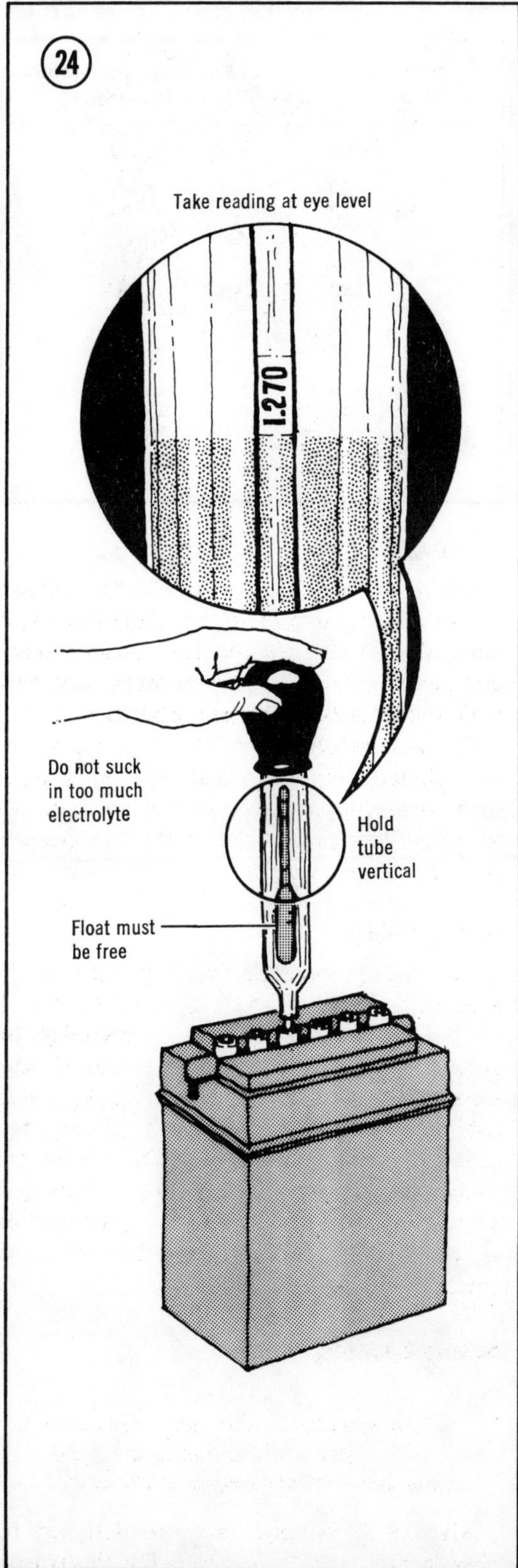

it is recommended that a motorcycle battery be charged at a rate not exceeding 10 percent of its ampere-hour capacity. That is, do not exceed 1.2 amperes for a 12 ampere-hour battery. This charge rate should continue for 10 hours if the battery is completely discharged, or until specific gravity of each cell is up to 1.260-1.280, corrected for temperature. If, after prolonged charging, specific gravity of one or more cells does not come up to at least 1.230, the battery will not perform as well as it should, but it may continue to provide satisfactory service for a time.

Some temperature rise is normal as a battery is being charged. Do not allow the electrolyte temperature to exceed 110°F (43°C). Should temperature reach that figure, discontinue charging until the battery cools, then resume charging at a lower rate.

Testing State of Charge

A hydrometer is an instrument which measures specific gravity, which is related to state of charge. To use this instrument, place its suction tube into the filler opening and draw in just enough electrolyte to lift the float (**Figure 24**). Hold the instrument in a vertical position and read specific gravity on the scales, where the float stem emerges from the electrolyte.

Specific gravity of the electrolyte varies with temperature change, so it is necessary to apply a temperature correction to the reading so obtained. For each 10°F (5.5°C) that battery temperature exceeds 80°F (26.6°C) add 0.004 to the indicated specific gravity. Likewise, subtract 0.004 from the indicated value for each 10° that battery temperature is below 80°F.

Repeat this measurment for each battery cell. If there is more than 0.050 difference (50 points) between cells, battery condition is questionable.

State of charge may be determined from **Table 3**. Do not measure specific gravity immediately after adding water. Ride the motorcycle a few miles to ensure thorough mixing of the electrolyte.

It is most important to maintain batteries fully charged during cold weather. A fully charged battery freezes at a much lower

Table 3 STATE OF CHARGE

Specific Gravity	State of Charge
1.110 - 1.130	Discharged
1.140 - 1.160	Almost discharged
1.170 - 1.190	One-quarter charged
1.200 - 1.220	One-half charged
1.230 - 1.250	Three-quarters charged
1.260 - 1.280	Fully charged

temperature than does one which is partially discharged. **Table 4** illustrates the relationship between specific gravity and battery freezing temperature.

Table 4 BATTERY FREEZING TEMPERATURE

Specific Gravity	Freezing Temperature (Degrees F)
1.100	18
1.120	13
1.140	8
1.160	1
1.180	—6
1.200	—17
1.220	—31
1.240	—50
1.260	—75
1.280	—92

NOTE: If you own a 1980 or later model, first check the Supplement at the back of the book for any new service information.

CHAPTER SEVEN

CHASSIS

This chapter discusses service operations on wheels, brakes, suspension components, and related items.

WHEELS AND TIRES

Except for removal and installation, service on front and rear wheels is generally similar. **Figure 1** is an exploded view of typical wheel and tire assemblies.

Front Wheel Removal

1. Support motorcycle so that front wheel is clear of ground.
2. Refer to **Figure 2**. Remove shaft clamp pinch nuts, then remove clamp.
3. On models with internal expanding (drum) brakes, refer to **Figure 3**. Remove brake cable at brakè lever (A). Also disconnect the torque link (B).
4. Disconnect speedometer cable.
5. Remove cotter pin, shaft nut, and washer.
6. Pull out shaft, then roll front wheel out from motorcycle.

Front Wheel Installation

Reverse the removal procedure to install the front wheel. Observe the following notes.

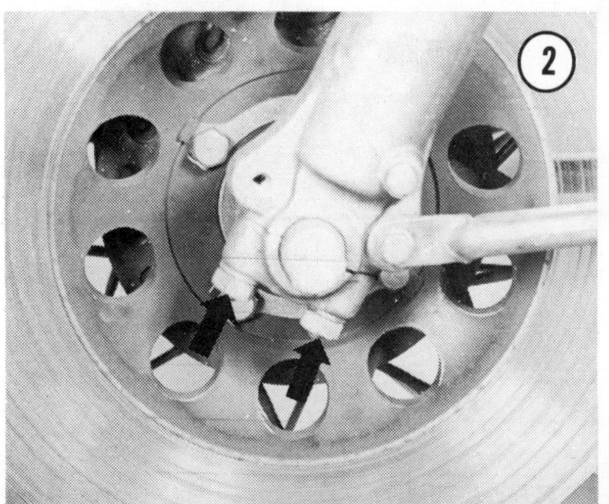

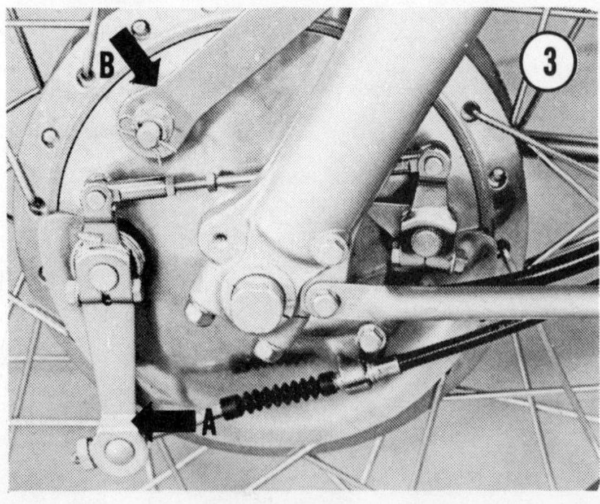

7

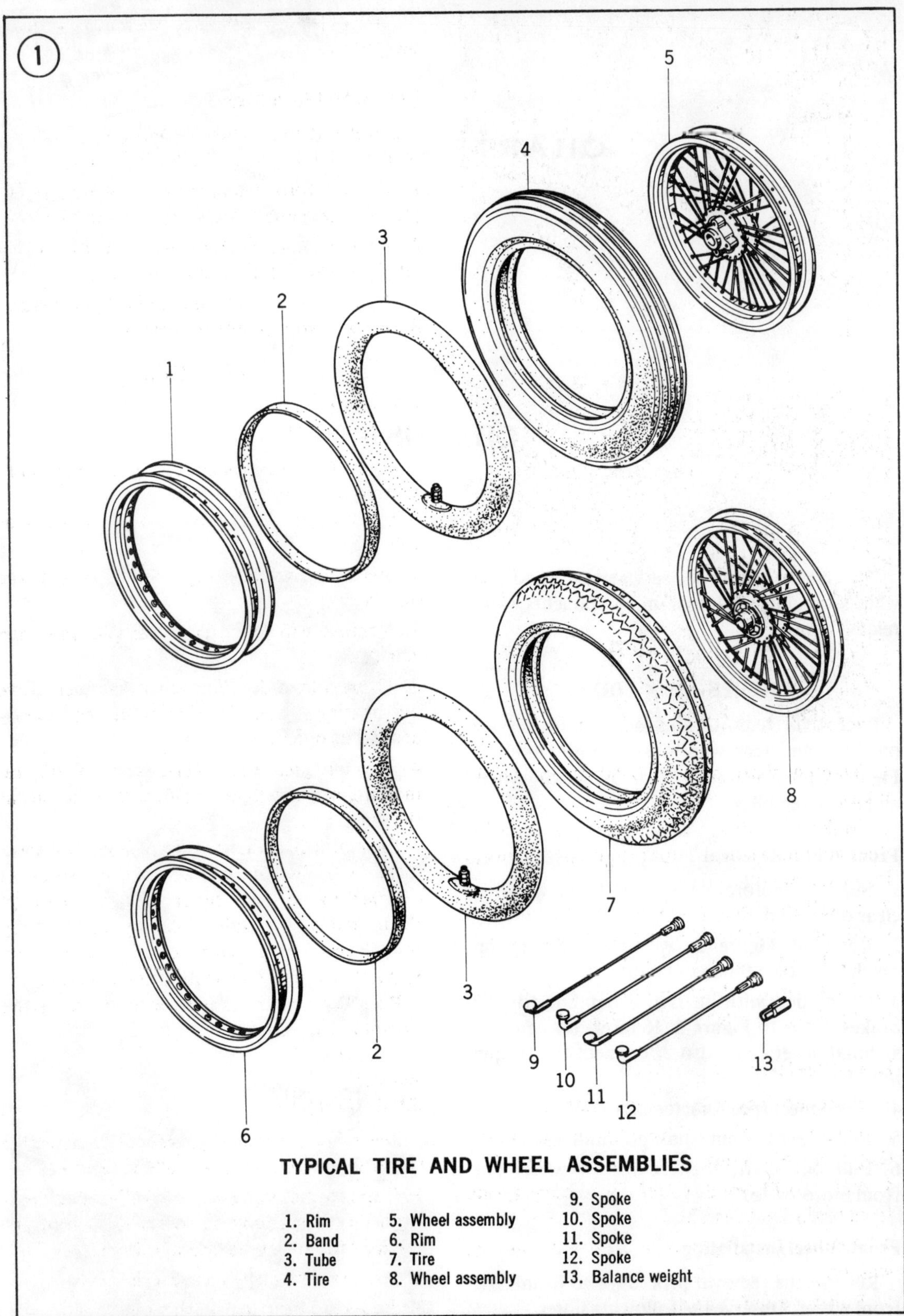
1
1
2
3
4
5
6
7
8
2
3
9
10
11
12
13
TYPICAL TIRE AND WHEEL ASSEMBLIES
1. Rim
2. Band
3. Tube
4. Tire
5. Wheel assembly
6. Rim
7. Tire
8. Wheel assembly
9. Spoke
10. Spoke
11. Spoke
12. Spoke
13. Balance weight

1. Tighten shaft nut to 72-94 ft.-lb. (10-13 mkg).

2. Make sure that speedometer gear housing does not move as shaft nut is tightened. Always install a new cotter pin.

3. Install shaft clamp so that arrow points forward. First, tighten front nut to 13-14.5 ft.-lb. (1.8-2.0 mkg), then repeat with rear nut.

4. On models with drum brakes, adjust front brake. Refer to Chapter Three for details.

Rear Wheel Removal

1. Place motorcycle on its centerstand.

2. Disconnect torque link (A) at rear brake (**Figure 4**). Also remove brake adjuster nut (B).

3. Refer to **Figure 5**. Carefully remove spring from brake light switch.

4. Remove cotter pin, rear axle nut, and its washer.

5. Pull out axle from left side.

6. Work rear wheel free, then roll it from motorcycle.

Rear Wheel Installation

Reverse the removal procedure to install the rear wheel. Observe the following notes.

1. Tighten torque link bolt to 19.5-22 ft.-lb. (2.7-3.0 mkg) and be sure to replace its clip.

2. Tighten axle nut to 94-116 ft.-lb. (13-16 mkg). Always install a new cotter pin.

3. Adjust rear brake and brake light switch. Refer to Chapter Three for details.

FRONT HUB

Disassembly (Model D and S)

Figure 6 is an exploded view of a typical front hub. Refer to it during service.

To disassemble the front hub, proceed as follows.

1. Remove disc retaining bolts (2) and brake disc (5).

2. Remove cap (4), grease seal (7), and snap ring (8).

3. Using a long drift and small hammer, drive out bearing (9) on disc side by tapping evenly around its outer race.

4. Pry out grease seal (11), then tap out remaining bearing. Spacer (10) will come out at the same time.

Clean bearings thoroughly in solvent. Inspect them carefully for galling, pitting, signs of overheating, or any other defects. Then oil them lightly and spin them by hand. They should spin easily, with no noise or binding. Replace any defective bearing immediately.

Pack bearings thoroughly with grease before assembling the front hub.

Assembly (Model D and S)

Reverse the removal procedure to assemble the front hub. Observe the following notes.

1. Tap bearings into place carefully. If no bearing driver is available, a socket wrench of appropriate diameter may be substituted.

2. Always install new grease seals.

3. Be sure to bend lockwasher tabs.

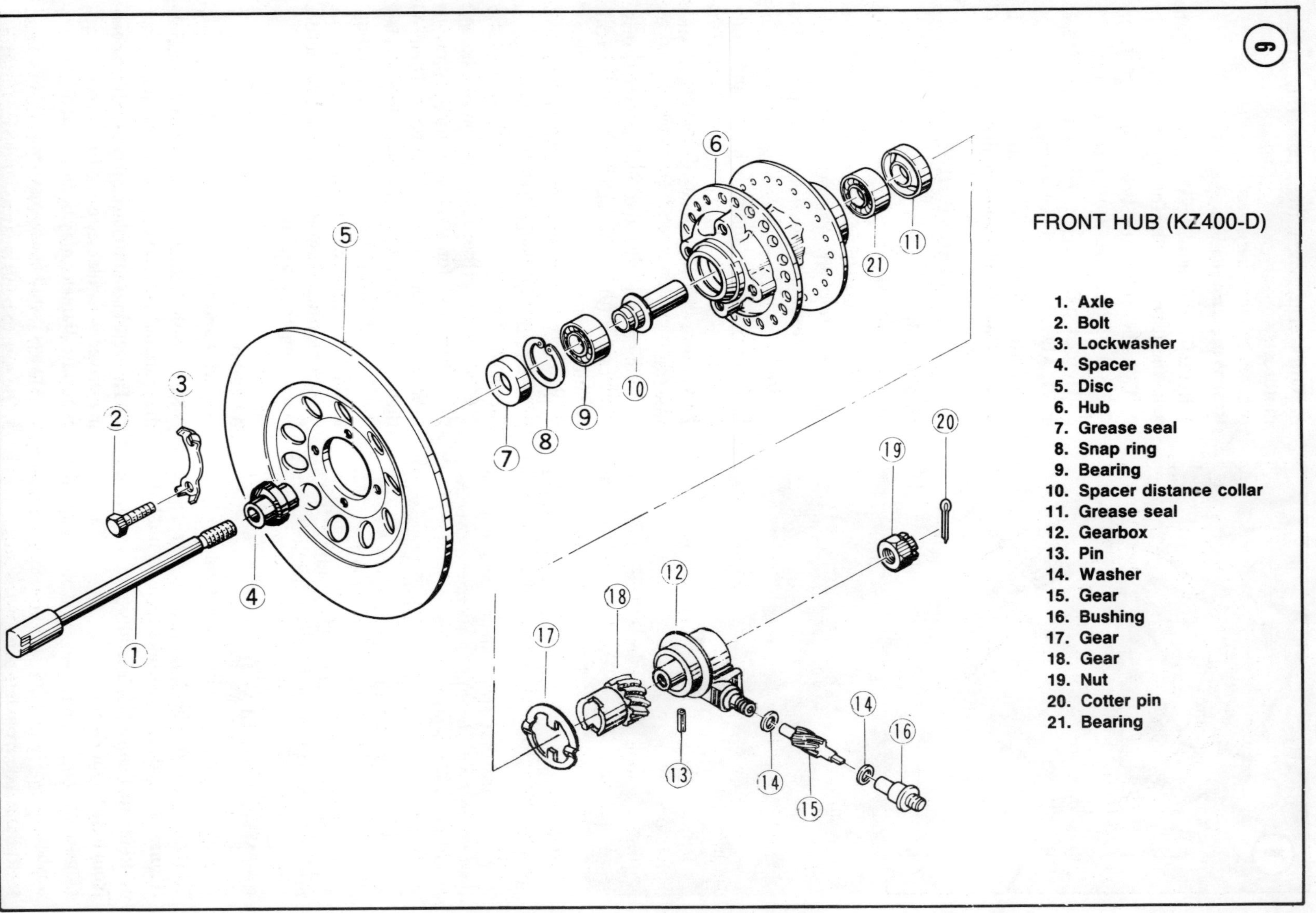
6
FRONT HUB (KZ400-D)
1. Axle
2. Bolt
3. Lockwasher
4. Spacer
5. Disc
6. Hub
7. Grease seal
8. Snap ring
9. Bearing
10. Spacer distance collar
11. Grease seal
12. Gearbox
13. Pin
14. Washer
15. Gear
16. Bushing
17. Gear
18. Gear
19. Nut
20. Cotter pin
21. Bearing
1
2
3
4
5
6
7
8
9
10
11
12
13
14
14
15
16
17
18
19
20
21

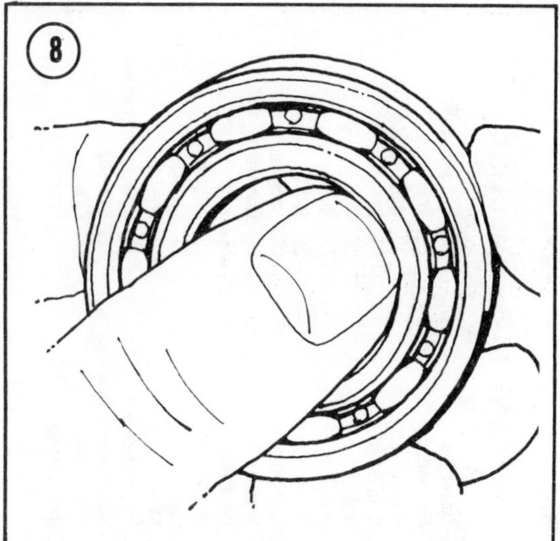

Disassembly (Model C)

Refer to **Figure 7** for this procedure.

1. Pull the brake panel assembly up and out of the hub.
2. Remove the grease seal (21) from the right-hand side.
3. Insert a long drift punch from the right-hand side and remove the left-hand bearing (17). Tap evenly around the inner race so the bearing will not get cocked in its bore. The distance collar (18) will come out at the same time.
4. Turn the wheel over and repeat Step 3 to drive out the right-hand bearing (20).
5. To remove the grease seal (16), first remove the speedometer gear (15) with a gear puller, then pull the grease seal out with a hook.
6. Clean the bearings thoroughly in cleaning solvent. Inspect them carefully for galling, pitting, signs of overheating, or any other defects. Turn each bearing by hand (**Figure 8**); make sure it turns smoothly. Replace any defective bearing immediately.
7. Pack bearings thoroughly with grease before installing them into the front hub.

Assembly (Model C)

Reverse the removal procedure to assemble the front hub. Observe the following notes.

1. Tap bearings into place carefully. If no bearing driver is available, a socket wrench of appropriate diameter may be substituted.
2. Always install new grease seals.
3. After installing the speedometer gear, stake it in 2 places, where it is flush with the hub/drum, to lock it in place.

Disassembly (Model B)

Refer to **Figure 9** for this procedure.

1. Remove the speedometer gear housing (4) and collar (26).
2. Remove the 2 screws securing the cap (23) and remove it.
3. Straighten the locking tabs on the double lockwashers (10) and remove the 4 bolts, double lockwashers and speedometer gear drive (7) and disc (1).
4. Pull out the grease seal (22) and remove the circlip (21).
5. Insert a long drift punch from the right-hand side and remove the left-hand bearing (12). Tap evenly around the inner race so the bearing will not get cocked in its bore. The distance collar (18) will come out at the same time.
6. Turn the wheel over and repeat Step 5 to drive out the right-hand bearing (20).
7. Clean the bearings thoroughly in cleaning solvent. Inspect them carefully for galling, pitting, signs of overheating, or any other defects. Turn each bearing by hand (**Figure 8**); make sure it turns smoothly. Replace any defective bearings immediately.
8. Pack the bearings thoroughly with grease before installing them into the front hub.

Assembly (Model B)

Reverse the removal procedure to assemble the front hub. Observe the following notes.

1. Tap bearings into place carefully. If no bearing driver is available, a socket wrench of appropriate diameter may be substituted.
2. Always install new grease seals.
3. Always install new double lockwashers and bolts. Tighten the bolts to 29 ft.-lb. (40 mkg).

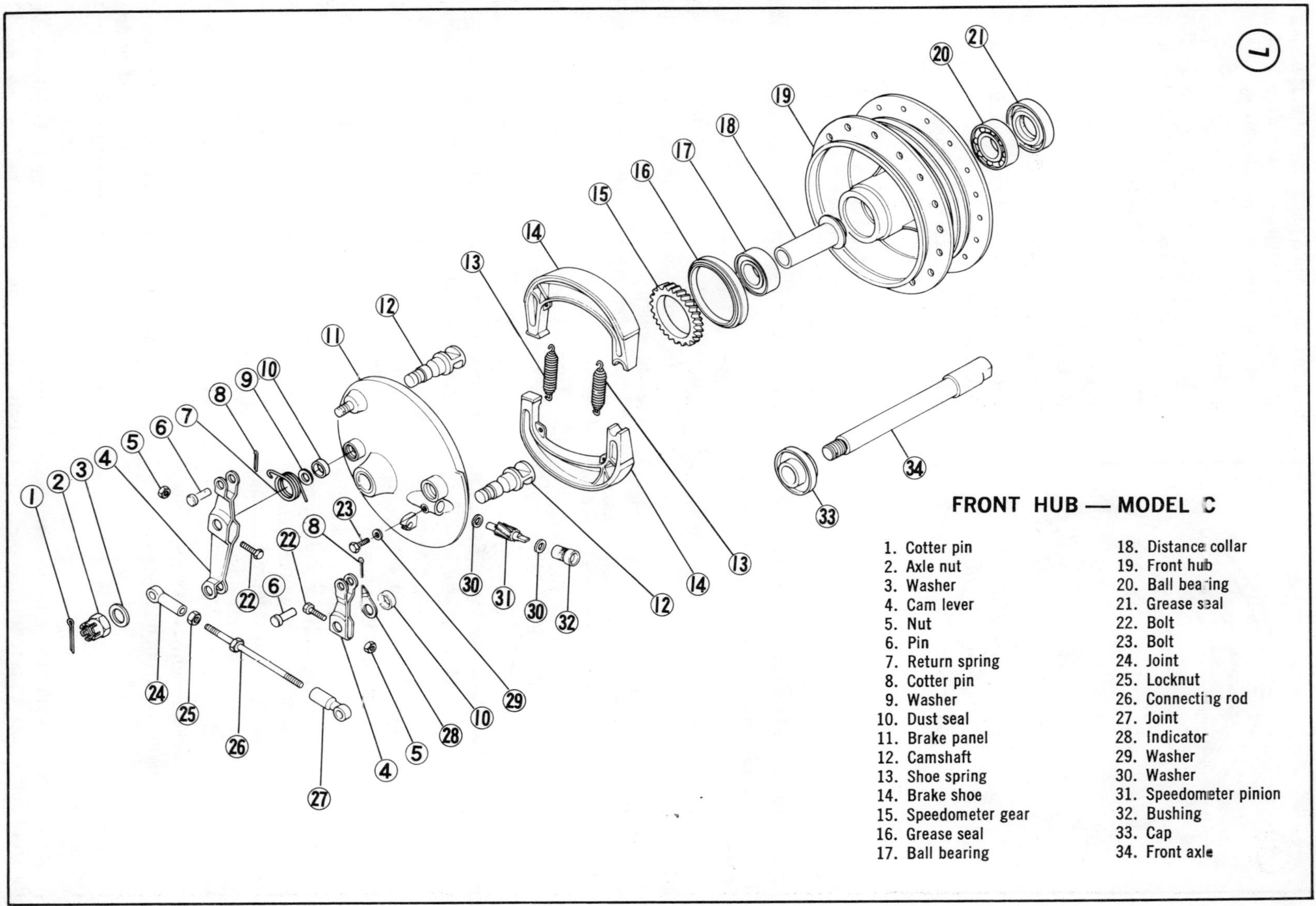

7

FRONT HUB — MODEL C

1. Cotter pin
2. Axle nut
3. Washer
4. Cam lever
5. Nut
6. Pin
7. Return spring
8. Cotter pin
9. Washer
10. Dust seal
11. Brake panel
12. Camshaft
13. Shoe spring
14. Brake shoe
15. Speedometer gear
16. Grease seal
17. Ball bearing
18. Distance collar
19. Front hub
20. Ball bearing
21. Grease seal
22. Bolt
23. Bolt
24. Joint
25. Locknut
26. Connecting rod
27. Joint
28. Indicator
29. Washer
30. Washer
31. Speedometer pinion
32. Bushing
33. Cap
34. Front axle

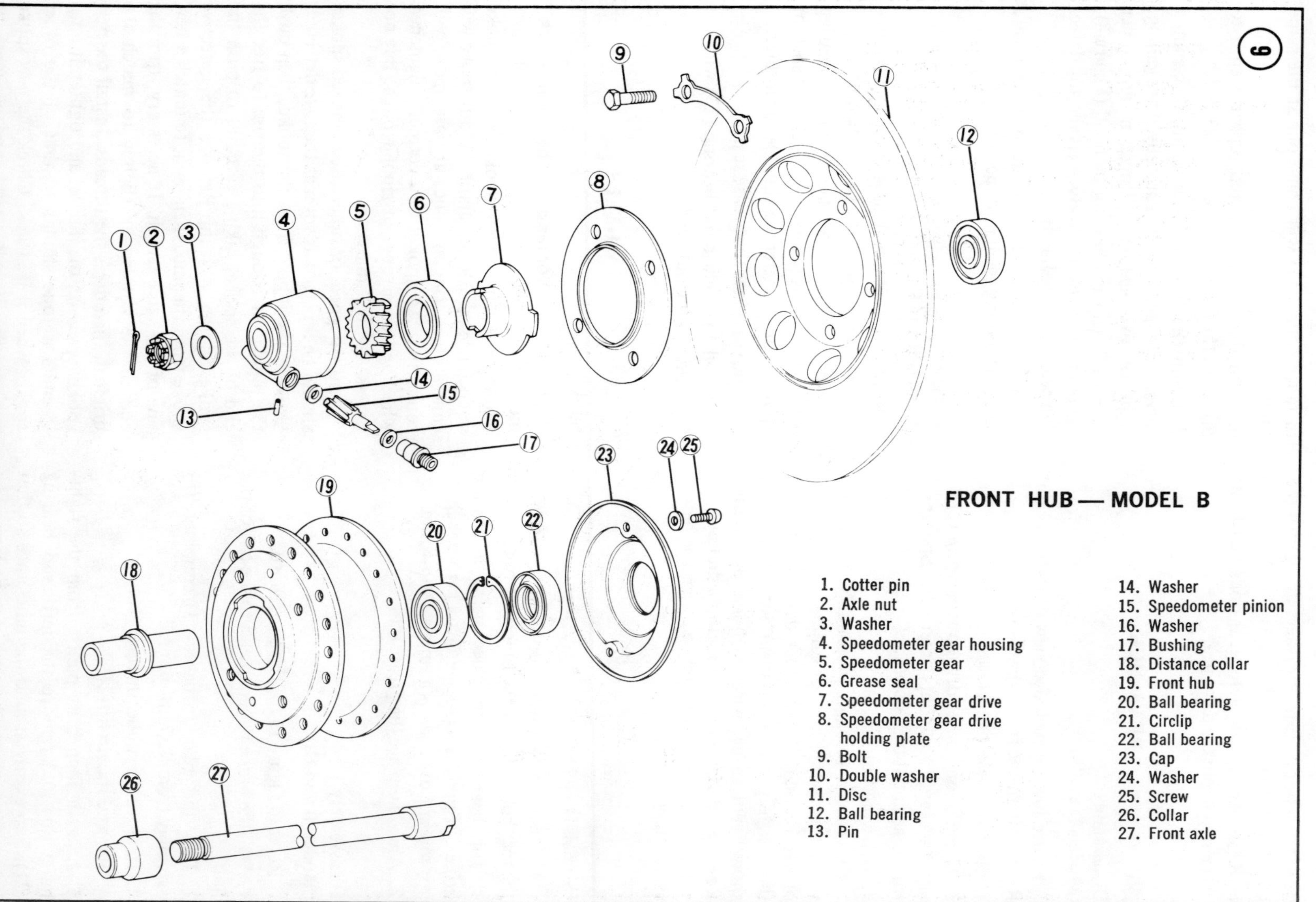
9
FRONT HUB — MODEL B
1. Cotter pin
2. Axle nut
3. Washer
4. Speedometer gear housing
5. Speedometer gear
6. Grease seal
7. Speedometer gear drive
8. Speedometer gear drive holding plate
9. Bolt
10. Double washer
11. Disc
12. Ball bearing
13. Pin
14. Washer
15. Speedometer pinion
16. Washer
17. Bushing
18. Distance collar
19. Front hub
20. Ball bearing
21. Circlip
22. Ball bearing
23. Cap
24. Washer
25. Screw
26. Collar
27. Front axle

Bend the tabs on the lockwashers up against the sides of the bolts.

4. Be sure the speedometer gear housing fits into the notches in the drive gear.

REAR HUB

Disassembly (Models D and S)

Figure 10 is an exploded view of the rear hub. Refer to it during rear hub service.

1. Remove brake panel (30).
2. Using a long drift, drive out bearing (2) by tapping evenly around its outer race. Spacer (3) will come out at the same time.
3. Drive out bearing (5).

Clean both bearings thoroughly in solvent. Inspect them carefully for galling, pitting, signs of overheating, or any other defects. Then oil them lightly and spin them by hand. They should spin easily, with no noise or binding. Replace any defective bearing immediately.

Pack bearings thoroughly with grease before assembling the rear hub.

Assembly (Models D and S)

Reverse the removal procedure to assemble the rear hub. Observe the following notes.

1. Tap bearings into place using a bearing driver. If none is available, a socket wrench of appropriate diameter is a suitable substitute.
2. Always replace the grease seal.

Disassembly (Models B and C)

Refer to **Figure 11** for this procedure.

1. Pull the brake panel up and to the left of the hub.
2. Pull the rear sprocket (3)/coupling (8) assembly from the hub.
3. Remove the rubber damper (10).
4. Remove the circlip (24).
5. Insert a long drift punch from the right-hand side and remove the left-hand bearing (21). Tap evenly around the inner race so that the bearing will not get cocked in its bore. The distance collar (11) will come out at the same time.
6. Turn the wheel over and repeat Step 5 to drive out the right-hand bearing (23).
7. Clean the bearings thoroughly in cleaning solvent. Inspect them carefully for galling, signs of overheating, pitting, or any other defects. Turn each bearing by hand (**Figure 8**); make sure it turns smoothly. Replace any defective bearing immediately.
8. Pack the bearings thoroughly with grease before installing them into the hub.

Assembly (Models B and C)

Reverse the removal procedure to assemble the rear hub. Observe the following notes.

1. Tap bearings into place using a bearing driver. If none is available, a socket wrench of appropriate diameter is a suitable substitute.
2. Always replace the grease seal.
3. Install the right-hand bearing (23) with the flush side facing outward.

WHEELS

Spokes

Check spokes for tension. The "tuning fork" method for checking tension is simple and works well. Tap each spoke with a spoke wrench or screwdriver shank. A taut spoke will emit a clear, ringing tone; a loose spoke will sound flat. All spokes in a correctly tightened wheel will emit tones of similar pitch, but not necessarily the same tone.

Bent, stripped, or otherwise damaged spokes should be replaced as soon as they are detected. Unscrew the nipple from the spoke, then push the nipple far enough into the rim to free the end of the spoke, taking care not to push the spoke all the way in. Remove the defective spoke from the hub, then use it to match a new one of the same length. If necessary, trim the end of the new spoke slightly to match the original, then dress the threads. Install the new spoke, screw on the nipple, and tighten it until it emits a tone similar to that of the other spokes when it is struck. Check the new spoke periodically; it will stretch and so must be

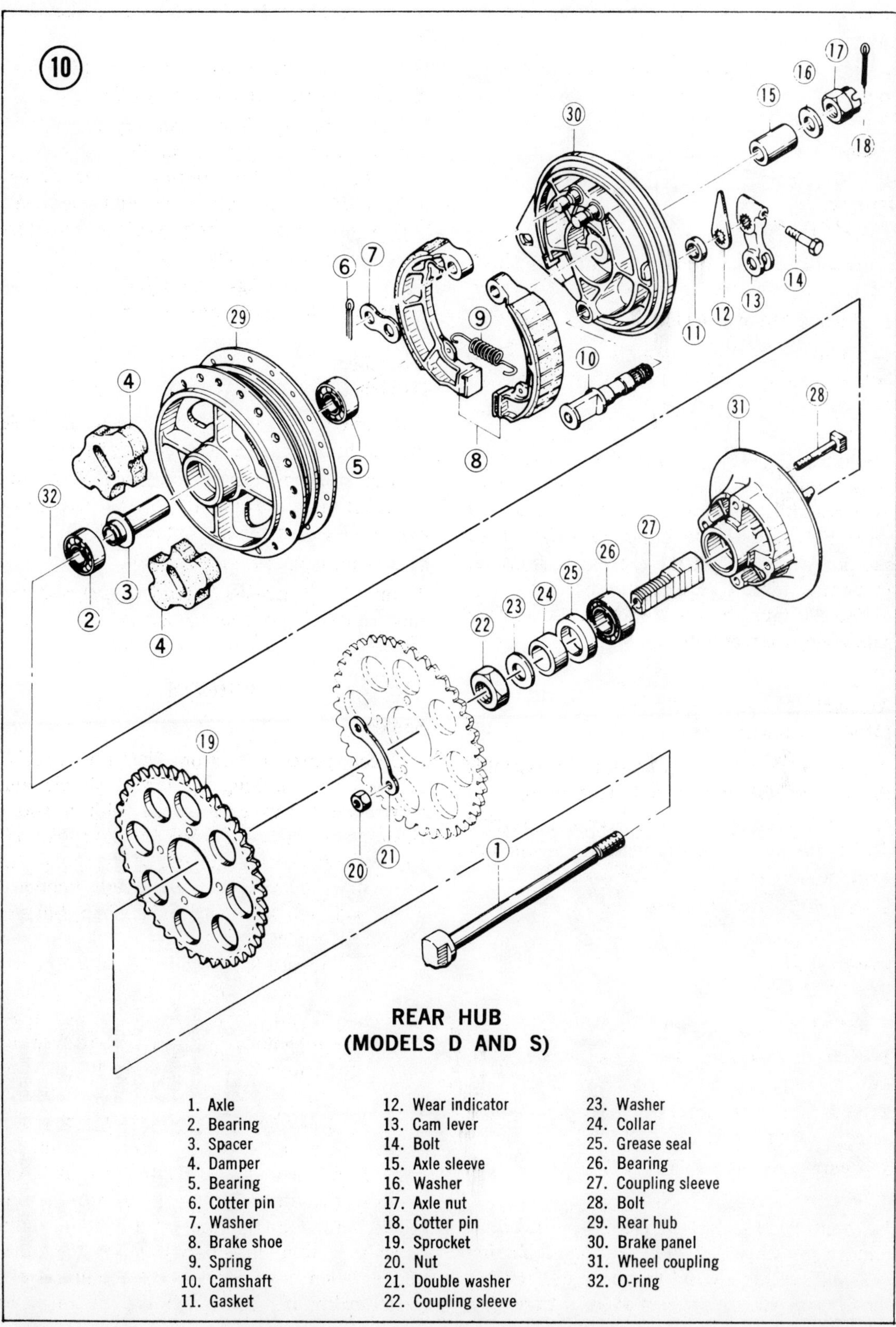

10

REAR HUB (MODELS D AND S)

1. Axle
2. Bearing
3. Spacer
4. Damper
5. Bearing
6. Cotter pin
7. Washer
8. Brake shoe
9. Spring
10. Camshaft
11. Gasket
12. Wear indicator
13. Cam lever
14. Bolt
15. Axle sleeve
16. Washer
17. Axle nut
18. Cotter pin
19. Sprocket
20. Nut
21. Double washer
22. Coupling sleeve
23. Washer
24. Collar
25. Grease seal
26. Bearing
27. Coupling sleeve
28. Bolt
29. Rear hub
30. Brake panel
31. Wheel coupling
32. O-ring

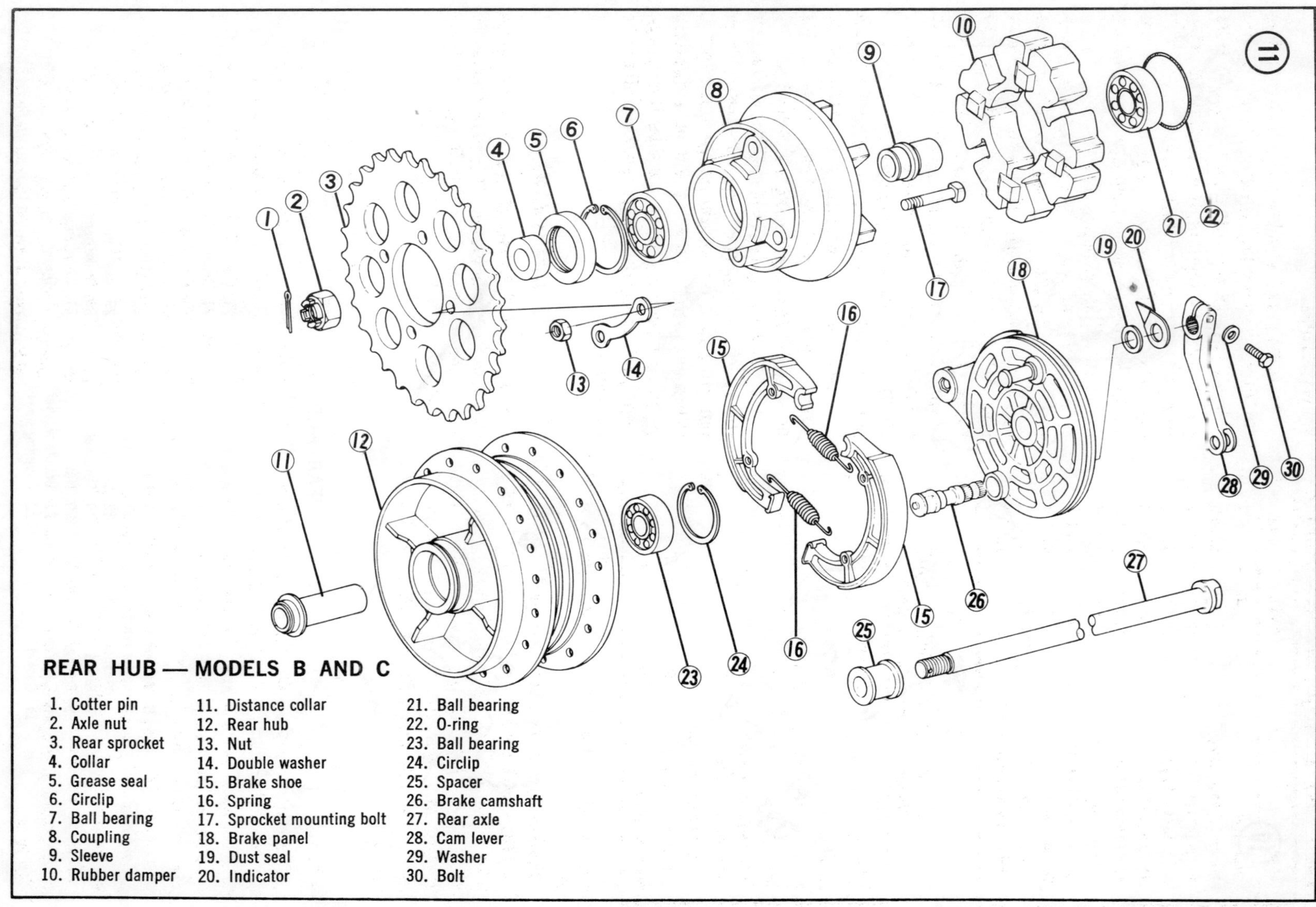
11
REAR HUB — MODELS B AND C
1. Cotter pin
2. Axle nut
3. Rear sprocket
4. Collar
5. Grease seal
6. Circlip
7. Ball bearing
8. Coupling
9. Sleeve
10. Rubber damper
11. Distance collar
12. Rear hub
13. Nut
14. Double washer
15. Brake shoe
16. Spring
17. Sprocket mounting bolt
18. Brake panel
19. Dust seal
20. Indicator
21. Ball bearing
22. O-ring
23. Ball bearing
24. Circlip
25. Spacer
26. Brake camshaft
27. Rear axle
28. Cam lever
29. Washer
30. Bolt

Table 1 BRAKE TORQUE VALUES — MODEL D

Item	Ft.-lb.	Mkg
Brake lever	3.7-5.0	0.5-0.7
Master cylinder clamp	3.8-6.5	0.6-0.9
Banjo fittings	19-23	2.5-3.3
Metal tube fittings	12-13	1.7-1.8
Three-way connector	3.7-4.1	0.5-0.6
Front brake switch	11-14.5	1.5-2.0
Caliper shafts	22-26	3.0-3.6
Caliper mounting bolts	19-23	2.5-3.3
Bleeder valve	6-7	0.8-1.0
Disc mounting bolts	11.5-16	1.6-2.2
Brake lever adjuster locknut	13-16.5	1.8-2.3

Table 2 DISC BRAKE TORQUE VALUES — MODELS B AND C

Item	Ft.-lb.	Mkg
Brake lever	4.3	0.6
Master cylinder clamp	4.3	0.6
Banjo fittings	22	3.0
Three-way connector	4.3	0.6
Front brake switch	20	2.8
Caliper mounting bolts	29	4.0
Disc mounting bolts	29	4.0
Bleeder valve	5.7	0.8

retightened several times until it takes its final set.

Spokes tend to loosen as the machine is used. Retighten each spoke one turn, beginning with those on one side of the hub, then those on the other side. Tighten the spokes on a new machine after the first 50 miles of operation, then at 50-mile intervals until they no longer loosen.

Rims

Check rims periodically for runout and out-of-round; also check for bends or dents following a collision or hard spill. Severe rim damage is difficult to repair successfully, and it is generally wiser and safer to replace the rim in such cases. The rubber rim band, which covers the spoke nipples and prevents them from chafing the inner tube, should be checked carefully each time the tire is removed. If the rim band is torn, exposing a spoke, replace it or repair it with tape.

Wheel Balance

An unbalanced wheel results in unsafe riding conditions. Depending on the degree of unbalance and speed of the motorcycle, the rider may experience anything from a mild vibration to a violent shimmy which may even result in loss of control. Balance weights may be installed on spokes on the light side of the wheel to correct this condition.

Before attempting to balance wheels, check to be sure that the wheel bearings are in good condition and properly lubricated. Also make sure that brakes do not drag, so that wheels rotate freely. With the wheel free of the ground, spin it slowly and allow it to come to rest by itself. Add balance weights to the spokes on the light side as required, so that the wheel comes to rest at a different position each time it is spun. Balance weights are available in weights of 10, 20, and 30 grams. Remove the drive chain before balancing rear wheels.

If more than one ounce is required to balance the wheel, add weight to adjacent spokes; never put more than one weight on the same spoke. When the wheel comes to rest at a different point each time it is spun, consider it balanced and tightly crimp the weights so they will not be thrown off.

DISC BRAKE

Kawasaki KZ400 Models B and D are equipped with disc front brakes. Disc brake service is not difficult, but be sure to follow instructions carefully.

WARNING

Use only isopropyl alcohol, ethyl alcohol, or disc brake fluid for cleaning disc brake components which are exposed to brake fluid. Do not allow oil or grease to come into contact with the brake disc or pads. If any does get on, remove it at once with cleaning solvent. If brake pads cannot be cleaned, replace them immediately. Always bleed the system whenever any connection has been opened. Brake malfunction may occur if fasteners are not tightened to the proper torque. ***Tables 1 and 2*** *specify proper tightening torque for each fastener. Refer to them as necessary.*

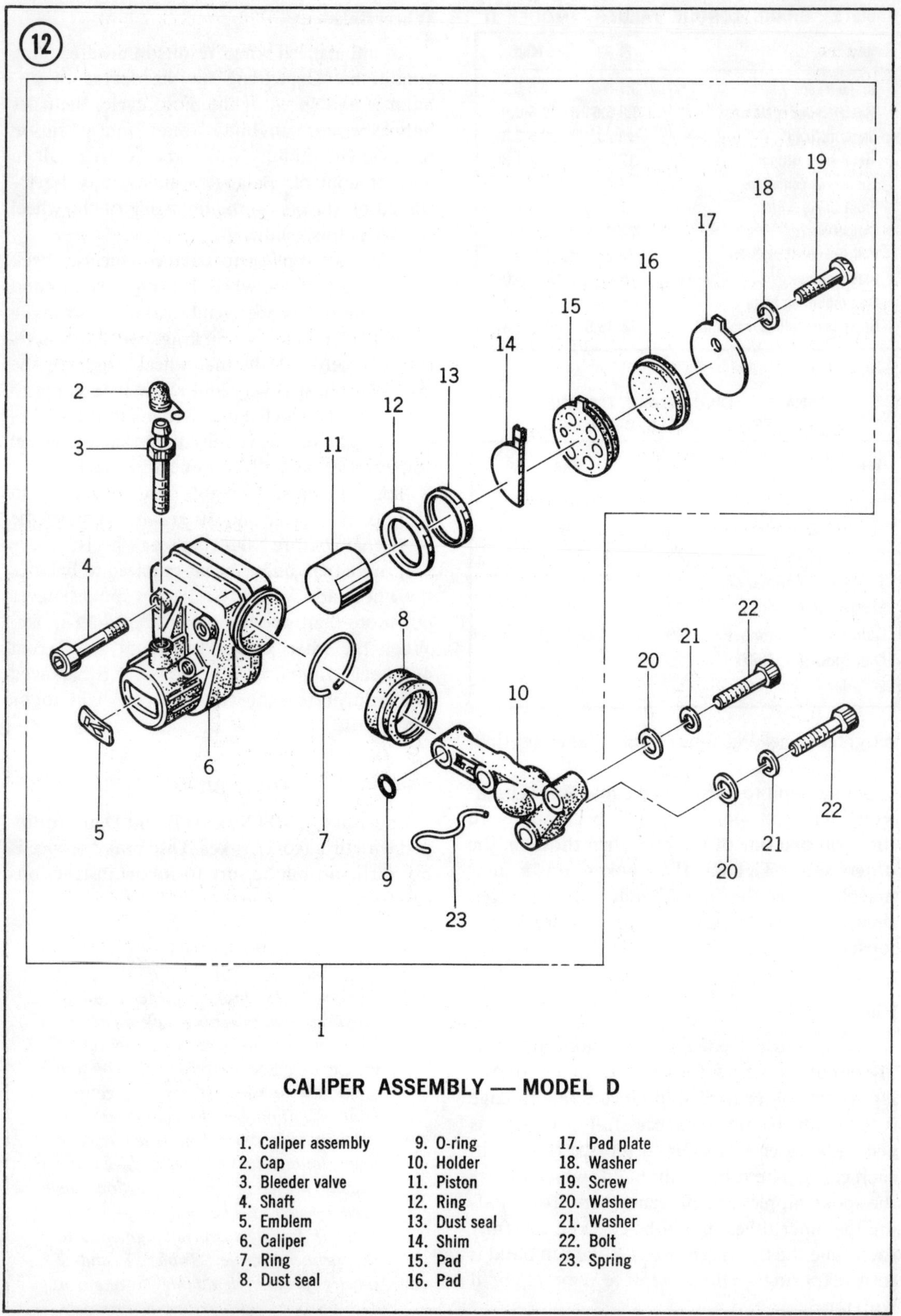

CALIPER ASSEMBLY — MODEL D

1. Caliper assembly
2. Cap
3. Bleeder valve
4. Shaft
5. Emblem
6. Caliper
7. Ring
8. Dust seal
9. O-ring
10. Holder
11. Piston
12. Ring
13. Dust seal
14. Shim
15. Pad
16. Pad
17. Pad plate
18. Washer
19. Screw
20. Washer
21. Washer
22. Bolt
23. Spring

BRAKE PAD

Replacement (Model D)

Refer to **Figure 12** for this procedure.

1. Remove front wheel.
2. Remove screw (19), lockwasher (18), plate (17), and pad (16).
3. Operate brake hand lever several times to force out pad (15).
4. Remove cover (2) from bleeder valve (3). Open valve slightly.
5. With valve open, push in piston (11) fully. Close valve (3) and install cover (2).

CAUTION
Brake fluid will attack painted surfaces. Wipe up any spills immediately.

6. Align projection on replacement pad (15) with that on shim (14).
7. Insert pad and shim into caliper (6).
8. Install replacement pad (16) and plate (17). Apply thread locking cement to screw (19).
9. Check reservoir, and add brake fluid as required.

WARNING
Use only brake fluid marked DOT 3 on its container. Use only fluid from sealed containers. Never reuse old brake fluid.

10. Operate hand lever to take up brake pad clearance, then recheck fluid level. Replenish it if necessary.

Replacement (Model B)

Refer to **Figure 13** for this procedure.

1. Remove the 2 caliper mounting bolts,

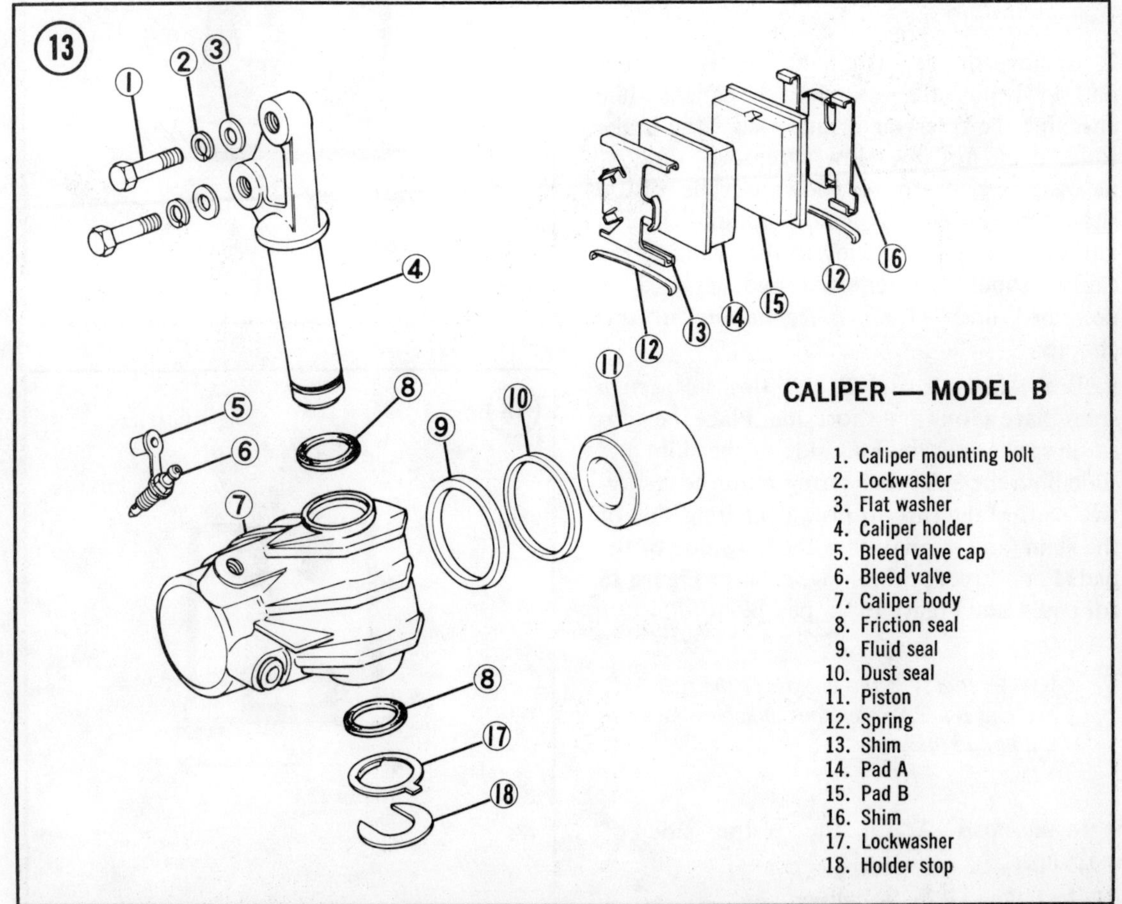

CALIPER — MODEL B

1. Caliper mounting bolt
2. Lockwasher
3. Flat washer
4. Caliper holder
5. Bleed valve cap
6. Bleed valve
7. Caliper body
8. Friction seal
9. Fluid seal
10. Dust seal
11. Piston
12. Spring
13. Shim
14. Pad A
15. Pad B
16. Shim
17. Lockwasher
18. Holder stop

7

lockwashers, and washers (A, **Figure 14**). Carefully slide the caliper assembly off the disc.

2. Push pad B (15) toward the piston then remove it from the caliper opening.
3. Slide pad A (14) toward the piston and remove it.
4. Slide the shim off of each pad. The anti- rattle spring will come out at the same time.
5. Clean the pad recess and end of the piston with a soft brush. Do not use solvent, wire brush, or any hard tool which would damage the cylinder or the piston.
6. Lightly coat the end of the piston and the backs of the new pads (not the friction material) with disc brake lubricant.

NOTE: *Check with your dealer to make sure the friction compound of the new pads is compatible with the disc material. Remove any roughness from the backs of the new pads with a fine cut file and blow them clean with compressed air.*

7. Remove the cap from the master cylinder and slowly push the piston into the caliper while checking the reservoir to make sure the brake fluid does not overflow. Remove fluid if necessary, prior to overflowing. The piston should move freely. If it does not and there is any evidence of it sticking in the cylinder, the caliper should be removed and serviced as described under *Caliper Rebuilding* in this chapter.
8. Brake pads A and B and their respective shims have a long and short side. Place the anti-rattle spring into the long side of the shim and slide both the shim and spring onto the respective pad. Make sure to install the long side of the shim (and spring) onto the long side of the pad. For correct positioning, refer to **Figure 15** for pad A and **Figure 16** for pad B.

NOTE: *Pad A is the thicker of the two and pad B has a notch that indicates the usable pad thickness.*

9. Install pad A on the piston side of the caliper.
10. Install pad B in the caliper.

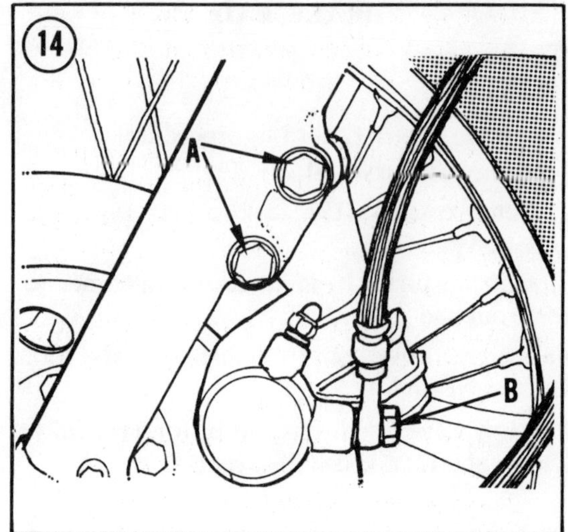

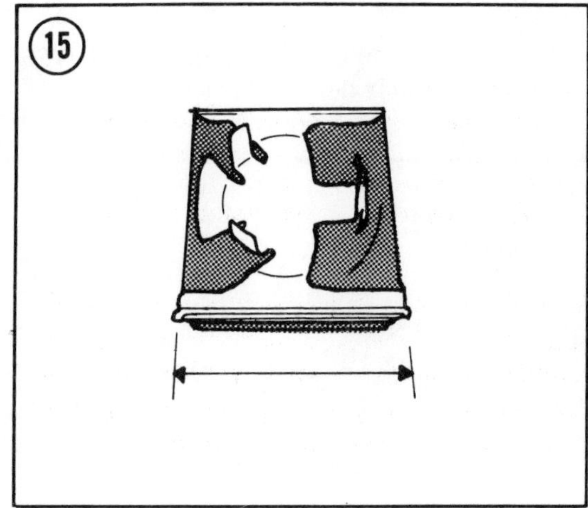

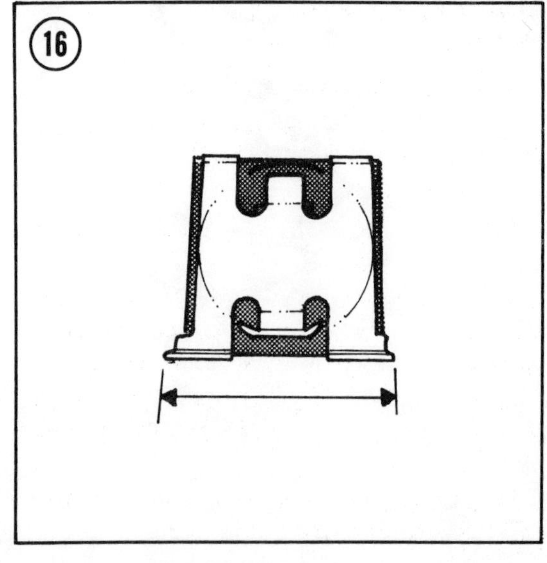

11. Carefully install the caliper assembly onto the disc and install the caliper mounting bolts, flat washers, and lockwashers. Tighten the bolts to 29 ft.-lb. (4.0 mkg).

12. Block the motorcycle up so that the front wheel is off the ground. Spin the front wheel and activate the brake lever for as many times as it takes to refill the cylinder in the caliper and correctly locate the pads.

13. Refill the fluid in the reservoir if necessary and replace the top cap.

WARNING

Use brake fluid clearly marked DOT 3 only. Others may vaporize and cause brake failure. Always use the same brand name; do not intermix, as many brands are not compatible.

WARNING

*Do not ride the bike until you are sure that the brake is operating correctly with full hydraulic advantage. If necessary, bleed the brakes as described under **Bleeding Front Brake** in this chapter.*

14. Bed the pads in gradually for the first 50 miles by using only light pressure as much as possible. Immediate hard applications will glaze the new friction material and greatly reduce the effectiveness of the brake.

BRAKE CALIPER

Removal/Inspection/Installation (Model D)

Refer to **Figure 12** for this procedure.

1. Disconnect brake line at caliper cap end of tube to prevent loss of brake fluid.

2. Loosen bolts (4).

3. Take out bolts (22) to remove caliper assembly from bike.

4. Inspect pads for wear. Replace both pads if either is worn down to its stepped portion. Replace both pads if either is oily or greasy.

5. Measure piston outside diameter. If its diameter is less than 1.492 in. (37.90mm), replace it.

6. Measure cylinder bore. If it measures more than 1.503 in. (38.17mm), replace it.

7. Replace seal (12) if it leaks, if brakes overheat, if it adheres to piston (11), or if there is a marked difference between wear of both pads. Replace dust seal (13) if seal (12) is replaced.

8. Reverse the removal and disassembly procedure to install the caliper assembly. Observe the following notes:

   a. Tighten mounting bolts (22) to 19-23 ft.-lb. (2.5-3.3 mkg).

   b. Tighten caliper shaft bolts (4) to 22-26 ft.-lb. (3.0-3.6 mkg).

   c. Bleed front brake. Refer to *Bleeding Front Brake*.

Removal/Installation (Model B)

1. Remove the banjo bolt securing the brake hose to the caliper (B, **Figure 14**). To prevent the loss of brake fluid, tie up the end of the brake hose to the front forks. Tape the end of the hose to prevent the entry of moisture and dirt.

2. Remove the 2 bolts, flat washers, and lockwashers (A, **Figure 14**) securing the caliper assembly to the fork and carefully slide it off the disc.

3. Install by reversing these removal steps. Tighten the caliper mounting bolts to 29 ft.-lb. (4.0 mkg). Be sure to install new washers on each side of the brake hose fitting and tighten the banjo bolt to 22 ft.-lb. (3.0 mkg).

4. Bleed the brakes as described under *Bleeding Front Brake* in this chapter.

WARNING

Do not ride the bike until you are sure that the brake is operating properly.

Caliper Rebuilding (All Models)

If piston leaks, the caliper should be rebuilt. If the piston sticks in the cylinder, indicating severe wear or galling, the entire unit should be replaced. Rebuilding a leaky caliper requires special tools and experience.

Caliper service should be entrusted to your Kawasaki dealer or brake specialist. Considerable expense can be saved by removing the caliper yourself and taking it in for repair.

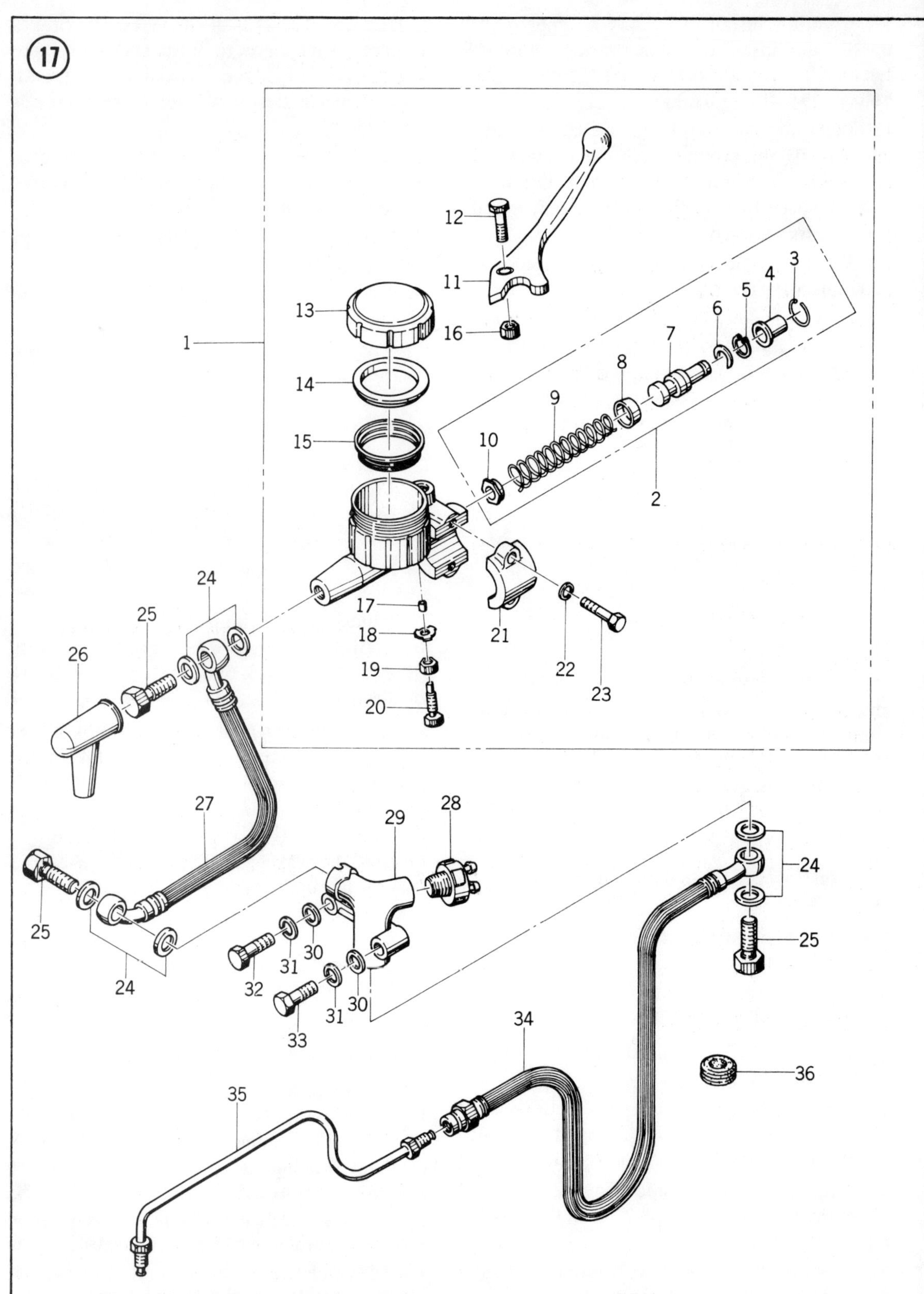
17
1
2
3
4
5
6
7
8
9
10
11
12
13
14
15
16
17
18
19
20
21
22
23
24
25
26
27
28
29
30
31
32
33
34
35
36

MASTER CYLINDER (MODEL D)

1. Master cylinder assembly
2. Repair kit
3. Dust cover stopper
4. Dust cover
5. Snap ring
6. Stopper
7. Piston
8. Primary cup
9. Spring
10. Check valve
11. Lever
12. Bolt
13. Cap
14. Plate
15. Diaphragm
16. Nut
17. Tube
18. Lockwasher
19. Nut
20. Bolt
21. Clamp
22. Washer
23. Bolt
24. Washer
25. Bolt
26. Dust cover
27. Hose
28. Switch
29. Joint
30. Washer
31. Washer
32. Bolt
33. Bolt
34. Hose
35. Tube
36. Brake hose grommet

MASTER CYLINDER

Disassembly/Inspection/Assembly (Model D)

Refer to **Figure 17** for this procedure.

1. Remove right rear view mirror.
2. Pull back dust cover (26), then disconnect brake line at banjo bolt (25).
3. Take out mounting bolts (23) to remove master cylinder.
4. Remove cap (13), then pour out and discard brake fluid.
5. Remove brake lever (11).
6. Remove dust seal stop (3). A special tool is available for this job, but a piece of welding rod or heavy wire may be bent to do the job.
7. Remove dust seal (4).
8. Remove snap ring (5), stop (6), piston (7), primary cup (8), spring (9), and check valve (10).

CAUTION

Do not remove secondary cup from piston. Doing so will result in damage to it.

9. Clean all parts in alcohol or brake fluid.
10. Be sure that relief port is open. If this port is plugged, the brake pads will not release properly.
11. Check that primary and secondary cups are not worn, damaged, or deteriorated. Better yet, replace the primary cup and piston at this time.
12. Check that there are no scratches, pits, or signs of corrosion on the piston or in the master cylinder bore. Replace either component if its condition is doubtful.
13. Measure master cylinder bore. Replace it if it measures more than 0.554 in. (14.08mm).
14. Measure piston diameter. Replace it if it measures less than 0.547 in. (13.90mm).
15. Measure primary cup diameter. Replace primary cup if it measures less than 0.571 in. (14.50mm).
16. Measure secondary cup diameter. Replace piston and secondary cup as an assembly if it measures less than 0.571 in. (14.50mm).
17. Measure free length of spring. Replace it if it measures less than 1.89 in. (48.0mm).

18. Check that the dust seal is not damaged. Replace it if there is any doubt about its condition.

Disassembly (Model B)

Refer to **Figure 18** for this procedure.

1. Remove the 4 screws and remove the cap (8), plate (7) and diaphragm (6). Pour out the brake fluid and discard it — *never* reuse brake fluid.

2. Remove the bolt and nut securing the brake lever (11) and remove it.

3. Use a small bladed screwdriver and press it on the locking tabs on the liner (19) and remove it.

4. Remove the dust seal (18), piston stop (17), piston assembly (16) and spring.

Inspection (Model B)

1. Clean all parts in denatured alcohol or fresh brake fluid. Inspect the cylinder bore and piston contact surfaces for signs of wear or damage. If either part is less than perfect, replace it.

2. Check the end of the piston for wear caused by the hand lever and check the pivot bore in the front-hand lever. Replace the piston if the secondary cup requires replacement.

3. Make sure the passages in the bottom of the brake fluid reservoir are clear. Check the reservoir cap and diaphragm for damage and deterioration and replace as necessary.

4. Inspect the condition of the threads in the bore for the brake line.

5. Check the front-hand lever pivot lug for cracks.

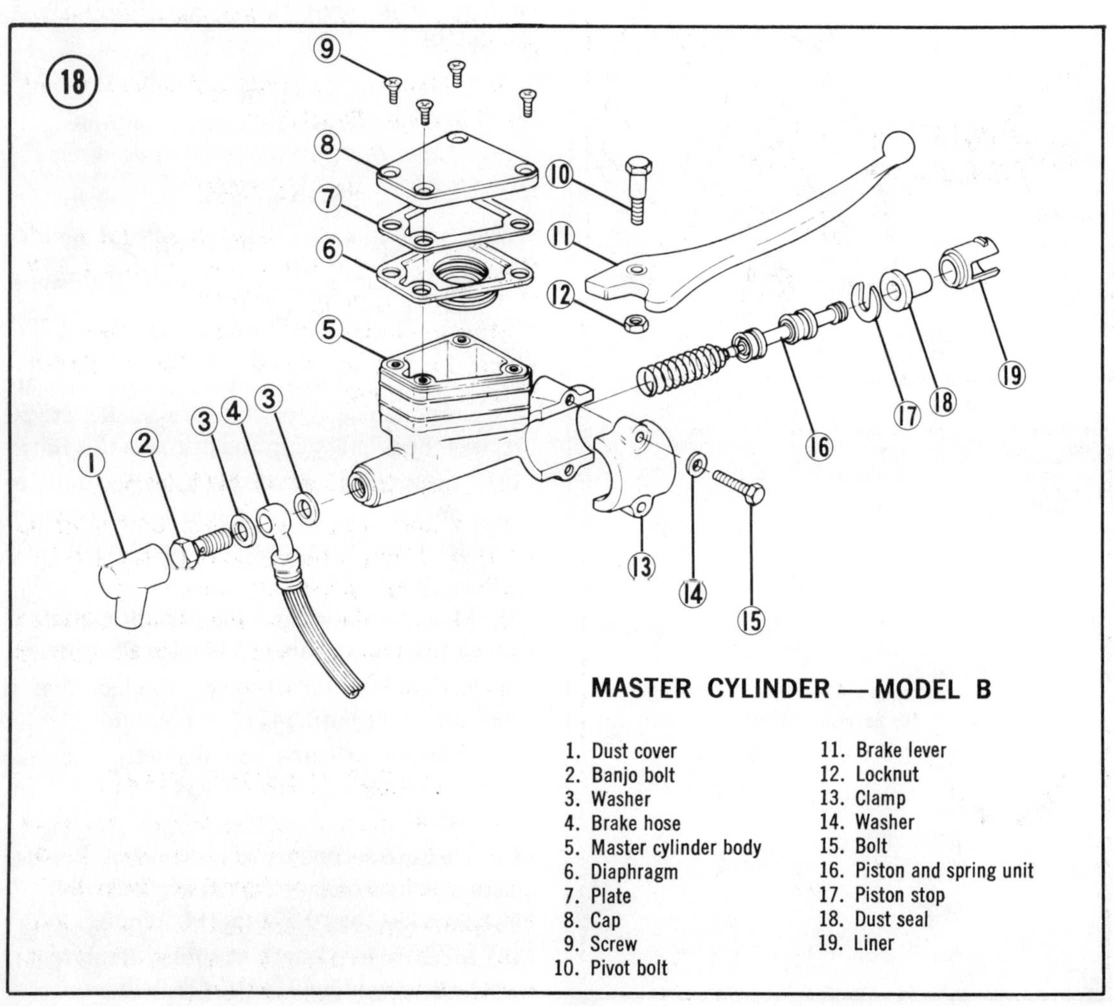

MASTER CYLINDER — MODEL B

1. Dust cover
2. Banjo bolt
3. Washer
4. Brake hose
5. Master cylinder body
6. Diaphragm
7. Plate
8. Cap
9. Screw
10. Pivot bolt
11. Brake lever
12. Locknut
13. Clamp
14. Washer
15. Bolt
16. Piston and spring unit
17. Piston stop
18. Dust seal
19. Liner

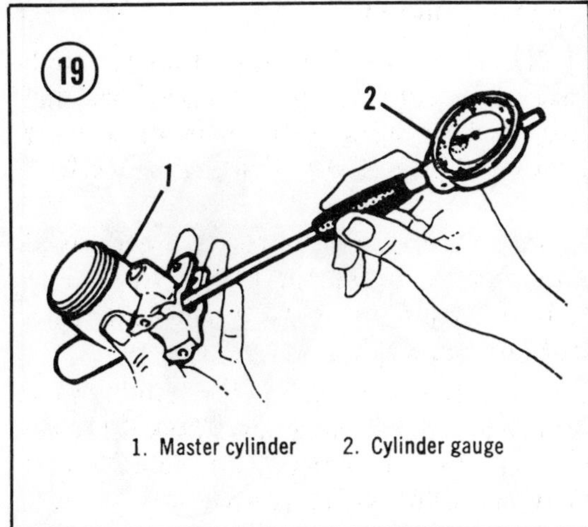

1. Master cylinder 2. Cylinder gauge

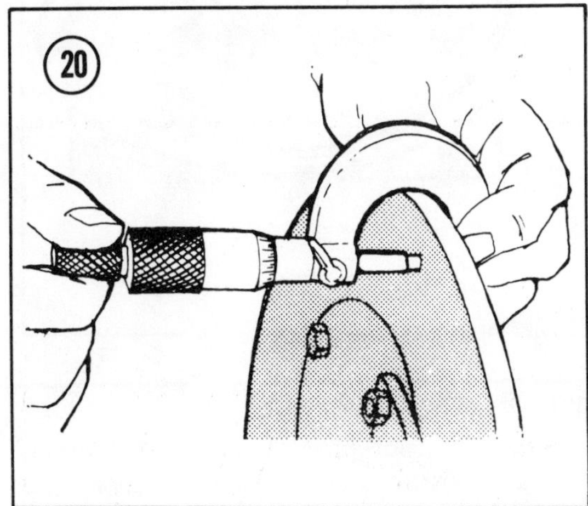

6. Measure the cylinder bore (**Figure 19**). The cylinder bore must not exceed 0.554 in. (14.08mm). The master cylinder body must be replaced if this dimension is exceeded.

7. Measure the outside diameter of the piston. It must not exceed 0.547 in. (13.90mm). Replace piston if this dimension is exceeded.

Assembly (Model B)

1. Soak the new cups in fresh brake fluid for at least 15 minutes to make them pliable. Coat the inside of the cylinder with fresh brake fluid prior to installation of parts.
2. Install the spring with the closer wound coils facing out, toward the piston.
3. Install the piston assembly, piston stop, dust seal, and liner.
4. Install the diaphragm, plate, and top cap.
5. Install the brake lever and install the master cylinder.
6. Bleed the brakes as described under *Bleeding Front Brake* in this chapter.

BRAKE DISC

Measure brake disc wear at several points (**Figure 20**). If it is worn to less than 0.216 in. (5.5mm) at any point, replace it.

Measure brake disc runout as shown in **Figure 21**. Replace the disc if runout exceeds 0.012 in. (0.3mm).

TUBING AND FITTINGS

Bend and twist the flexible brake tubing while examining it for cracks or bulges. Replace it at once if any defects are evident.

Be sure that the metal tubing is not corroded and that its plating is intact. Check all pressure fittings carefully for leaks.

BLEEDING FRONT BRAKE

Air enters the hydraulic system whenever any fluid connection is opened. After such an occurrence, all air must be bled from the system.

1. Remove reservoir cap. Add sufficient brake fluid to fill reservoir. Use only brake fluid from sealed containers marked DOT 3.

2. With reservoir cover removed, operate brake lever slowly several times, until no more bubbles come from bottom of reservoir.

3. Install reservoir cap.

4. Connect one end of a 12 in. (30 cm) clear plastic tube to bleeder valve (**Figure 22**). Submerge other end of tube in a vessel containing a small quantity of brake fluid.

5. Operate brake lever several times, until resistance is felt. Lever may feel spongy at this time. Hold lever in brake-applied position.

6. Quickly open bleeder valve, then close it.

7. Repeat Steps 5 and 6 until no more air comes out, and brake lever operation is firm. Replenish reservoir if necessary during Steps 5 and 6.

8. Replenish reservoir, install its cap, and install rubber cover on bleeder valve.

DRUM (INTERNAL EXPANDING) BRAKE

KZ400 Models B, C, and D are equipped with drum type rear brakes and Models C and S are equipped with drum type front brake. Service procedures are similar and where differences occur they are identified.

WARNING

Do not allow any grease to get onto brake shoes or drums during brake service. Serious brake malfunction may occur.

Disassembly (Models D and S)

Refer to **Figure 23**.

1. Remove brake panel (6).

2. Mark position of cam lever on camshaft so that it may be installed at same angle.

3. Remove cam lever, wear indicator (13), and gasket (12).

4. Remove cotter pin (7) and washer(8).

5. Protect brake shoes with clean rags, then remove brake shoes (9), spring (10), and camshaft (11) as an assembly from brake panel.

6. Twist brake shoes apart to separate them from camshaft.

7. Remove spring.

Inspection (Models D and S)

1. Examine inside of brake drum for scoring. As a general rule, any scoring deep enough to catch a fingernail is cause to have the brake drum turned. If turning is necessary, do not exceed 7.12 in. (180.75mm).

2. Measure brake drum inside diameter. Replace the drums if its diameter at any point exceeds 7.12 in. (180.75mm). If diameter measurements differ, turn the drum, but do not exceed 7.12 in. (180.75mm).

3. Measure brake lining thickness. If brake lining on either shoe is worn to 0.098 in. (2.5mm), replace both shoes.

4. If brake shoes are serviceable, remove any particles on their friction surfaces with a wire brush.

5. Check brake linings for any oil or grease deposits. If any exist, replace both shoes.

6. Measure free length of brake shoe spring between its hooks. If free length exceeds 2.28 in. (58mm), replace the spring.

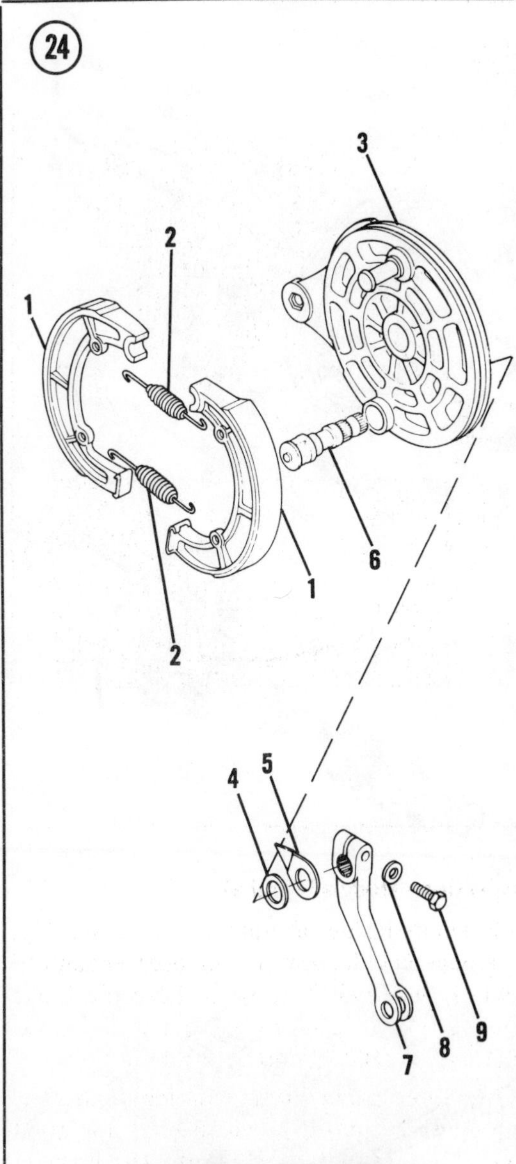

INTERNAL EXPANDING DRUM BRAKES (MODELS B AND C)

1. Brake shoes
2. Springs
3. Brake panel
4. Dust seal
5. Brake lining wear indicator
6. Camshaft
7. Cam lever
8. Washer
9. Bolt

7. Measure camshaft diameter, where it passes through brake panel. If it measures less than 0.663 in. (16.83mm), replace the camshaft.

8. Measure inside diameter of camshaft hole in brake panel. If it measures greater than 0.676 in. (17.18mm), replace brake panel.

Assembly (Models D and S)

Brake reassembly is the reverse of disassembly. Observe the following notes:

1. Apply a small quantity of grease to brake camshaft, cam pivot points and/or pins, and spring ends. Fill camshaft groove with grease.
2. Adjust brake. Refer to Chapter Three for details.

Disassembly (Models B and C)

Refer to **Figure 24** for this procedure.

1. Remove brake panel assembly from hub.
2. Wrap the linings with a clean shop cloth and remove both shoes (1) by pulling up on the center of the linings (**Figure 25**).
3. Remove springs (2) and separate the 2 shoes.
4. Mark the position of the cam lever (7) on the camshaft (6) so that it will be installed at the same angle.
5. Remove the cam lever (7), brake lining wear indicator (5), dust seal (4), and camshaft (6).

Inspection (Models B and C)

1. Examine each brake drum for scoring. As a general rule, any scratch deep enough to catch a fingernail is cause to have the brake drum turned. If turning is necessary, do not exceed 7.12 in. (180.75mm) for the front drum and 6.33 in. (160.75mm) for the rear.
2. Measure the inside diameter of the drum (**Figure 26**). Replace the drum(s) if its inside diameter at any point exceeds 7.12 in. (180.75mm) for the front and 6.33 in. (160.75mm) for the rear. If the measurements differ within the drum, have the drum turned but do not exceed the preceding minimum inside diameter.
3. Measure brake lining thickness (**Figure 27**). If brake lining on either shoe is worn to 0.098 in. (2.5mm) for the front brake and 0.079 in. (2.0mm) for the rear, replace both shoes.

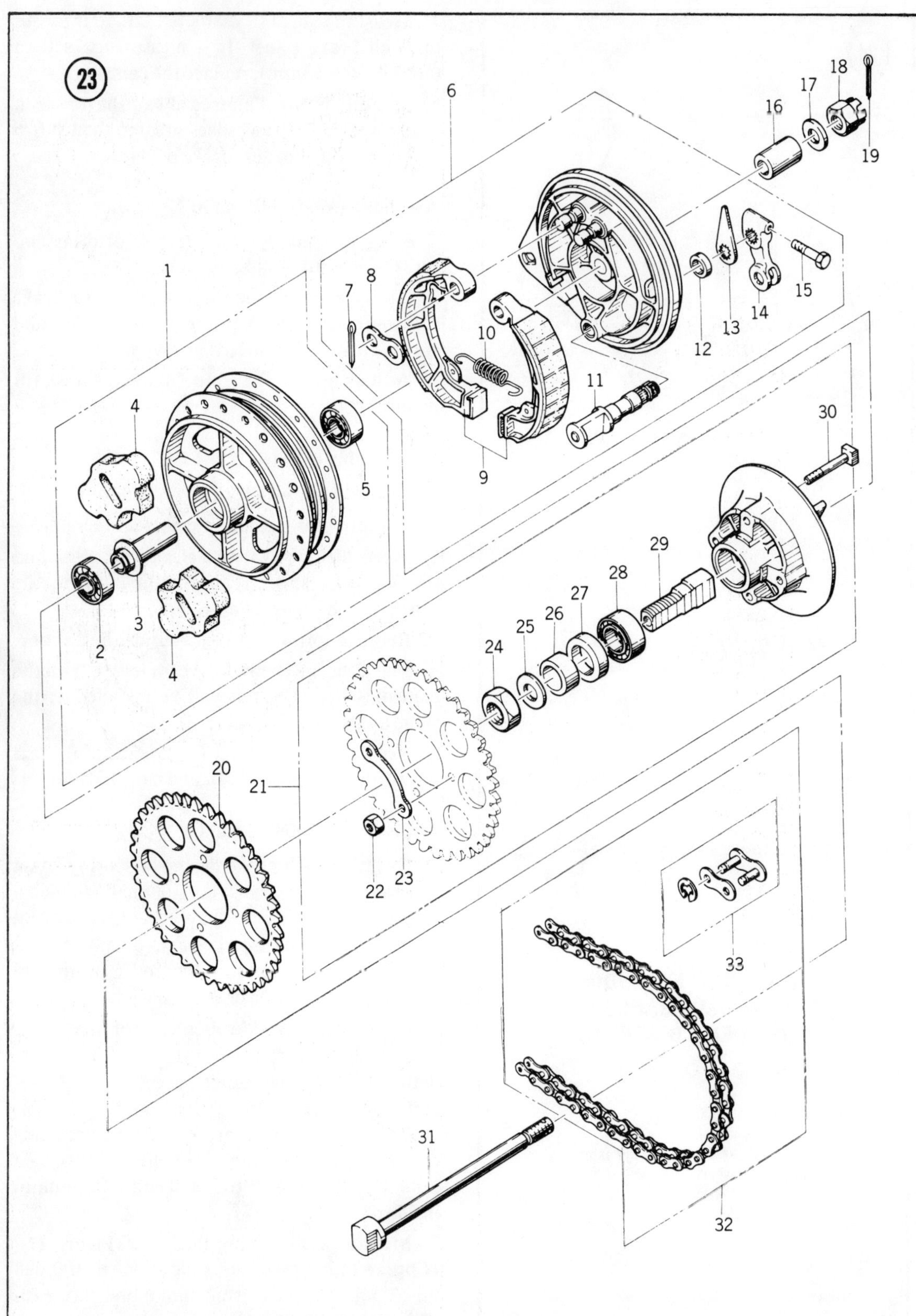

23
1
2
3
4
4
5
6
7
8
9
10
11
12
13
14
15
16
17
18
19
20
21
22
23
24
25
26
27
28
29
30
31
32
33

INTERNAL EXPANDING DRUM BRAKES (MODELS D AND S)

1. Rear brake drum assembly
2. Bearing
3. Spacer
4. Damper
5. Bearing
6. Brake panel assembly
7. Cotter pin
8. Washer
9. Brake shoe
10. Spring
11. Camshaft
12. Dust shield
13. Indicator
14. Lever
15. Bolt
16. Spacer
17. Washer
18. Nut
19. Cotter pin
20. Sprocket
21. Coupling
22. Nut
23. Lockwasher
24. Nut
25. Washer
26. Spacer
27. Oil seal
28. Bearing
29. Sleeve
30. Bolt
31. Axle
32. Chain
33. Master link

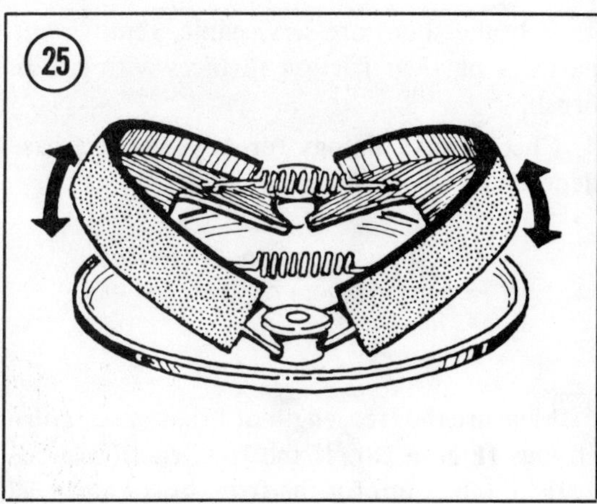

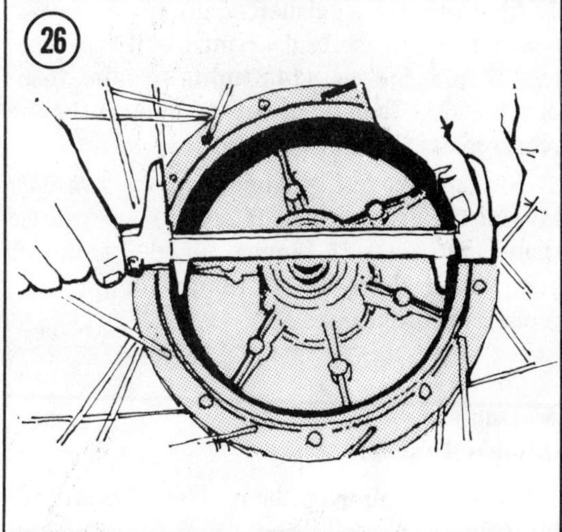

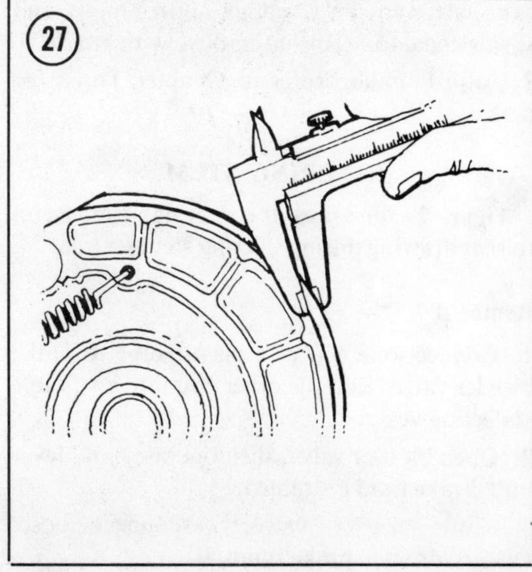

4. If brake shoes are serviceable, remove any particles on their friction surfaces with a wire brush.

5. Check brake linings for any oil or grease deposits. If any exist, replace both shoes.

> NOTE: *Always replace both shoes as a set — never replace only one shoe of a set at a time.*

6. Measure the free length of brake shoe return springs (**Figure 28**). If the free length exceeds 1.91 in. (48.5mm) for the front brake and 1.97 in. (50mm) for the rear, replace the spring.

7. Measure the camshaft diameter where it passes through the brake panel. If it measures less than 0.584 in. (14.83mm) for the front brake or less than 0.663 in. (16.83mm) for the rear, replace the camshaft.

8. Measure the inside diameter of the camshaft hole in the brake panel. If it measures greater than 0.598 in. (15.18mm) for the front or greater than 0.676 in. (17.18mm) for the rear, replace the brake panel.

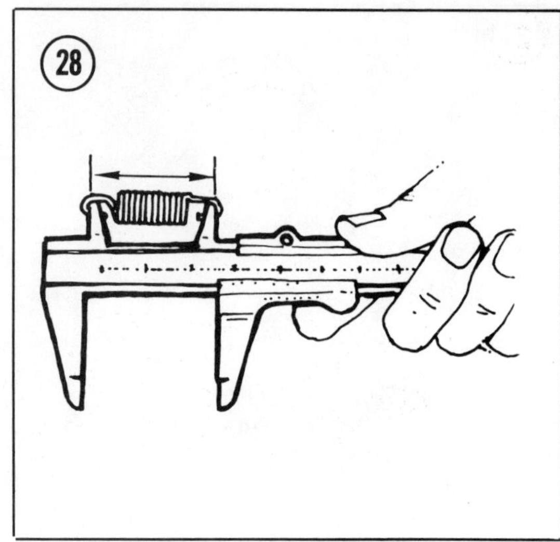

Assembly (Models B and C)

Brake reassembly is the reverse of disassembly. Observe the following:

1. Apply a small quantity of grease to brake camshaft, cam pivot points and/or pins, and spring ends. Fill camshaft groove with grease.

2. Adjust brake. Refer to Chapter Three for details.

STEERING STEM

Figure 29 illustrates the steering stem. Refer to that drawing during steering stem service.

Removal

1. Connect one end of a plastic tube to brake bleeder valve. Run the other end into a suitable collection vessel.

2. Open bleeder valve, then operate hand lever until brake fluid is drained.

3. Close bleeder valve. Disconnect hose. Discard drained brake fluid.

4. Remove front wheel.

5. Remove master cylinder.

6. Remove brake caliper assembly.

7. Remove front fender.

8. Loosen front fork pinch bolts, then slide both fork legs downward to remove them.

9. Disconnect cable at tachometer.

10. Disconnect leads at front brake light switch.

11. Remove 3-way fitting.

12. Remove headlight assembly from its housing.

13. Disconnect gray and black/yellow turn signal wires and main wire harness plugs inside headlight housing.

14. Remove headlight housing.

15. Remove instrument cluster.

16. Remove stem head bolt (1), stem head bolt clamp (4), and washers (2 and 3).

17. Tap bottom of stem head lightly with a plastic mallet until fork covers and turn signal lamps can be removed.

18. Continue tapping bottom of stem head until it is free of steering stem. Let stem head and handlebar hang clear of work area.

19. Push upward on stem base, then remove locknut (5).

> NOTE: *As steering stem is removed, a number of steel balls may fall out. Be prepared to catch them.*

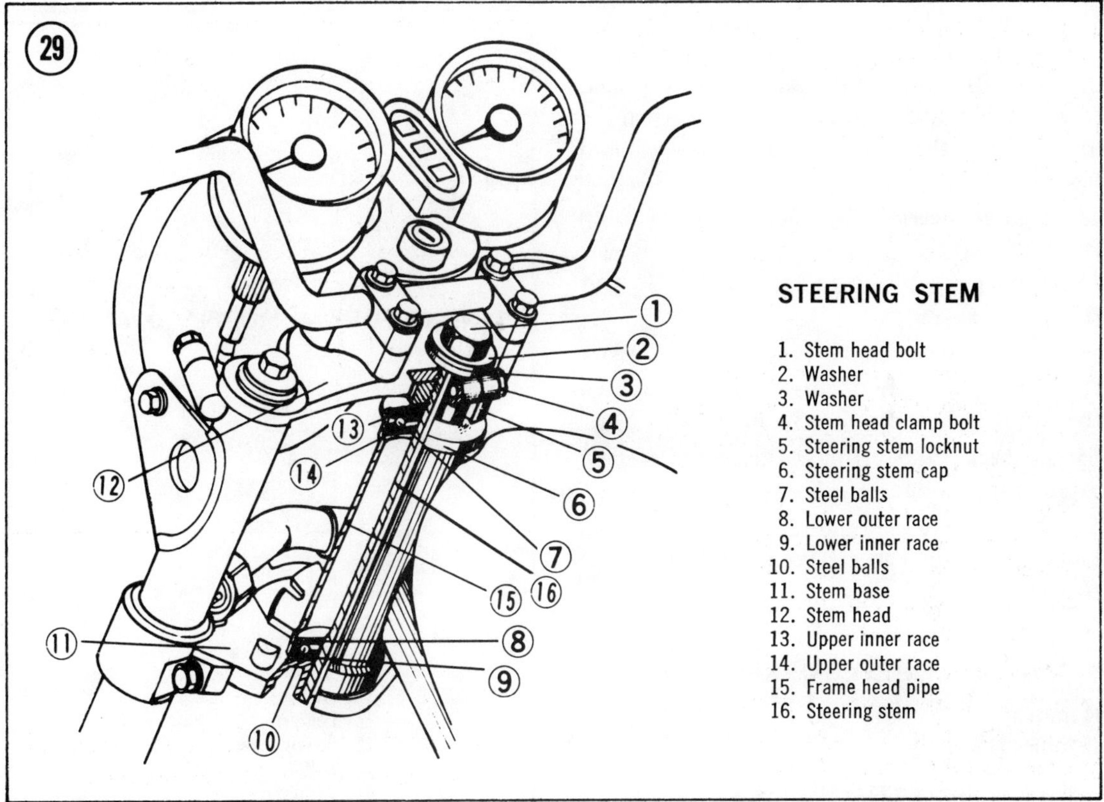

STEERING STEM

1. Stem head bolt
2. Washer
3. Washer
4. Stem head clamp bolt
5. Steering stem locknut
6. Steering stem cap
7. Steel balls
8. Lower outer race
9. Lower inner race
10. Steel balls
11. Stem base
12. Stem head
13. Upper inner race
14. Upper outer race
15. Frame head pipe
16. Steering stem

20. Remove steering stem and stem base as a unit. Remove all balls which still adhere.

21. Remove steering stem cap (6), upper inner race (13), and upper balls.

> NOTE: *Keep these balls separate from those removed from lower bearing.*

Inspection

Check that the steering stem is not bent or cracked. It if is damaged or defective, replace it.

Check bearings and races for wear, chips, galling, or other defects. If any bearing component is defective, replace both races and all associated balls as a set. Do not use any combination of new and used parts in either bearing.

Installation

Reverse the removal procedure to install the steering stem. Observe the following notes:

1. Apply grease liberally to the upper and lower races, and hold the balls in place with grease during assembly. Install 19 balls in each bearing.
2. Tighten steering stem locknut to 19.5-22 ft.-lb. (2.7-3.0 mkg) as an initial adjustment.
3. Tap stem head partway into place.
4. Install left fork leg first, so that its upper end is flush with upper surface of stem head. Tighten upper clamp bolts (only) to 12-13 ft.-lb. (1.6-1.8 mkg).
5. Repeat Step 3 with right fork leg.
6. Tap stem head until it is fully in place.
7. Install washers (2 and 3). The thicker washer goes uppermost. Install stem head bolt (1). Do not tighten in yet.
8. Install stem head clamp bolt (4). Do not tighten it yet.
9. Tighten stem base clamp bolts to 14.5-22 ft.-lb. (2.0-3.0 mkg).
10. Complete installation of all parts which were removed.

7

11. Tighten or loosen steering stem locknut (5) until entire front end assembly continues moving under its own momentum when it is pushed to either side, and no play can be felt when the lower ends of the forks are pushed forward and backward.

12. Tighten steering stem head bolt (1) to 40 ft.-lb. (5.5 mkg).

13. Tighten stem head clamp bolt (4) to 12-13 ft.-lb. (1.6-1.8 mkg).

14. Loosen lower clamp bolts to allow front fork tubes to reseat themselves, then tighten them to 14.5-22 ft.-lb. (2.0-3.0 mkg).

15. Recheck the steering adjustment. Repeat Steps 11 through 15 as necessary.

16. Replenish brake fluid reservoir, then bleed front brake. Refer to foregoing *Bleeding Front Brake*.

FRONT FORKS

Removal (Models D and S)

Refer to **Figure 30** for this procedure.

1. Remove front wheel.
2. Remove front fender.
3. Remove brake caliper. Support it so that tube to it is not bent.
4. Loosen but do not remove fork cap bolts (2).
5. Loosen upper and lower clamp bolts (4 and 16).
6. Twist and pull fork legs downward to remove them.

Disassembly (Modes D and S)

Refer to **Figure 30** for this procedure.

1. Remove top bolt (2).
2. Pull out spring (18).
3. Obtain a suitable drain pan, then invert fork leg to drain oil. Pump it to assist draining.
4. Pull off dust seal (24).
5. Hold cylinder (29), then remove bolt (32).
6. Pull fork tubes apart.
7. Remove cylinder (29) and spring (28) together.

FRONT FORK — MODELS D AND S

1. Front fork assembly
2. Bolt
3. O-ring
4. Bolt
5. Washer
6. Bolt
7. Steering stem head
8. Nut
9. Cap
10. Cover
11. Bearing cone
12. Guide
13. Washer
14. Damper
15. Steering stem
16. Bolt
17. Washer
18. Spring
19. Tube
20. Cover
21. Outer tube
22. Bolt
23. Gasket
24. Dust shield
25. Clip
26. Oil seal
27. Piston ring
28. Spring
29. Cylinder
30. Tube
31. Gasket
32. Bolt
33. Clamp
34. Stud
35. Nut
36. Steering lock
37. Key set
38. Screw
39. Cylinder base

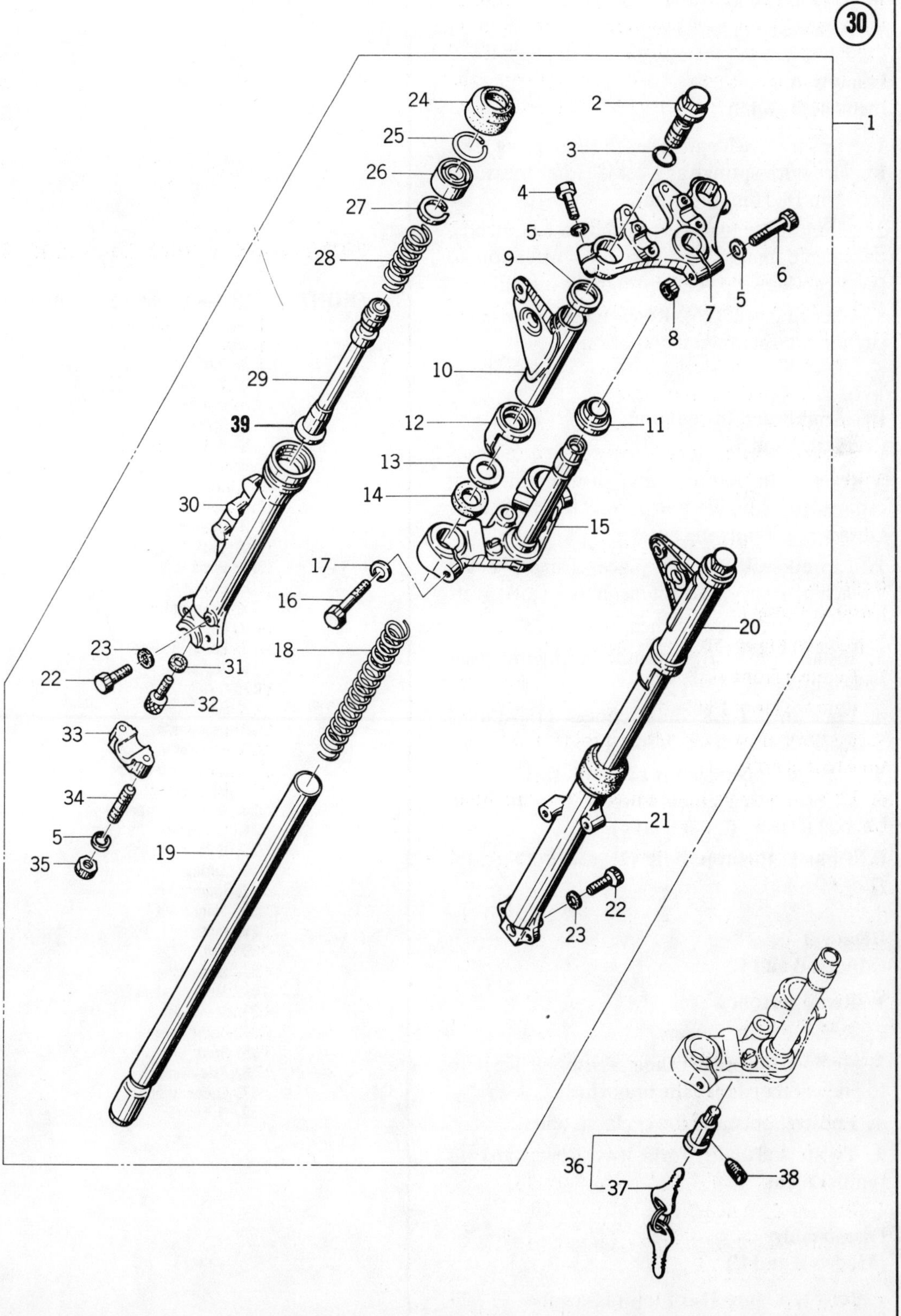
30
1
2
3
4
5
6
7
8
9
10
11
12
13
14
15
16
17
18
19
20
21
22
23
24
25
26
27
28
29
30
31
32
33
34
35
36
37
38
39

8. Remove clip (25) and oil seal (26).
9. Remove cylinder base (39).

Inspection
(Models D and S)

1. Measure free length of each fork spring (18). Replace both springs as a set if either measures less than 18.31 in. (465mm).
2. Check inner tube (19) for corrosion, bends, or other damage. Pay particular attention to the area where it passes through the oil seal.
3. Check oil seal (26). Replace it if there is the slightest doubt about it condition.

Reassembly and Installation
(Models D and S)

Reverse the removal and disassembly procedures to assemble and install the fork legs. Observe the following notes:

1. Tap oil seal (26) into place, using a socket wrench of appropriate diameter as a seal driver.
2. Apply thread lock cement to bolts (32).
3. Install spring (18) so that the end with closer coils is upward.
4. Pour in 5.1-5.8 fluid ounces (150-170cc) SAE 5W-20 oil into each fork leg.
5. Tighten upper clamp bolts to 12-13 ft.-lb. (1.6-1.8 mkg). Tighten lower clamp bolts to 14.5-22.0 ft.-lb. (2.0-3.0 mkg).
6. Tighten the top bolt (2) to 18-22 ft.-lb. (2.5-3.0 mkg).

Removal
(Models B and C)

1. Remove front wheel.
2. Remove front fender.
3. Remove the brake caliper assembly. Tie it up to prevent damage to the brake hose.
4. Loosen upper and lower clamp bolts.
5. Twist and pull fork legs downward to remove them.

Disassembly
(Models B and C)

Refer to **Figure 31** for this procedure.

1. Remove cap (14) from the inner tube (27).

FRONT FORK — MODELS B AND C

1. Dust seal
2. Retainer
3. Oil seal
4. Spacer
5. Piston ring
6. Piston and cylinder unit
7. Spring
8. Cylinder base
9. Outer tube
10. Gasket
11. Drain screw
12. Gasket
13. Allen bolt
14. Cap
15. Retaining ring
16. Top plug
17. O-ring
18. Bolt
19. Lockwasher
20. Fork cover
21. Stem base cover
22. Damper ring
23. Rubber damper
24. Lockwasher
25. Bolt
26. Spring
27. Inner tube
28. Stem head
29. Bolt
30. Nut
31. Lockwasher
32. Steering stem
33. Stem base
34. Outer tube
35. Stud
36. Axle clamp
37. Lockwasher
38. Nut

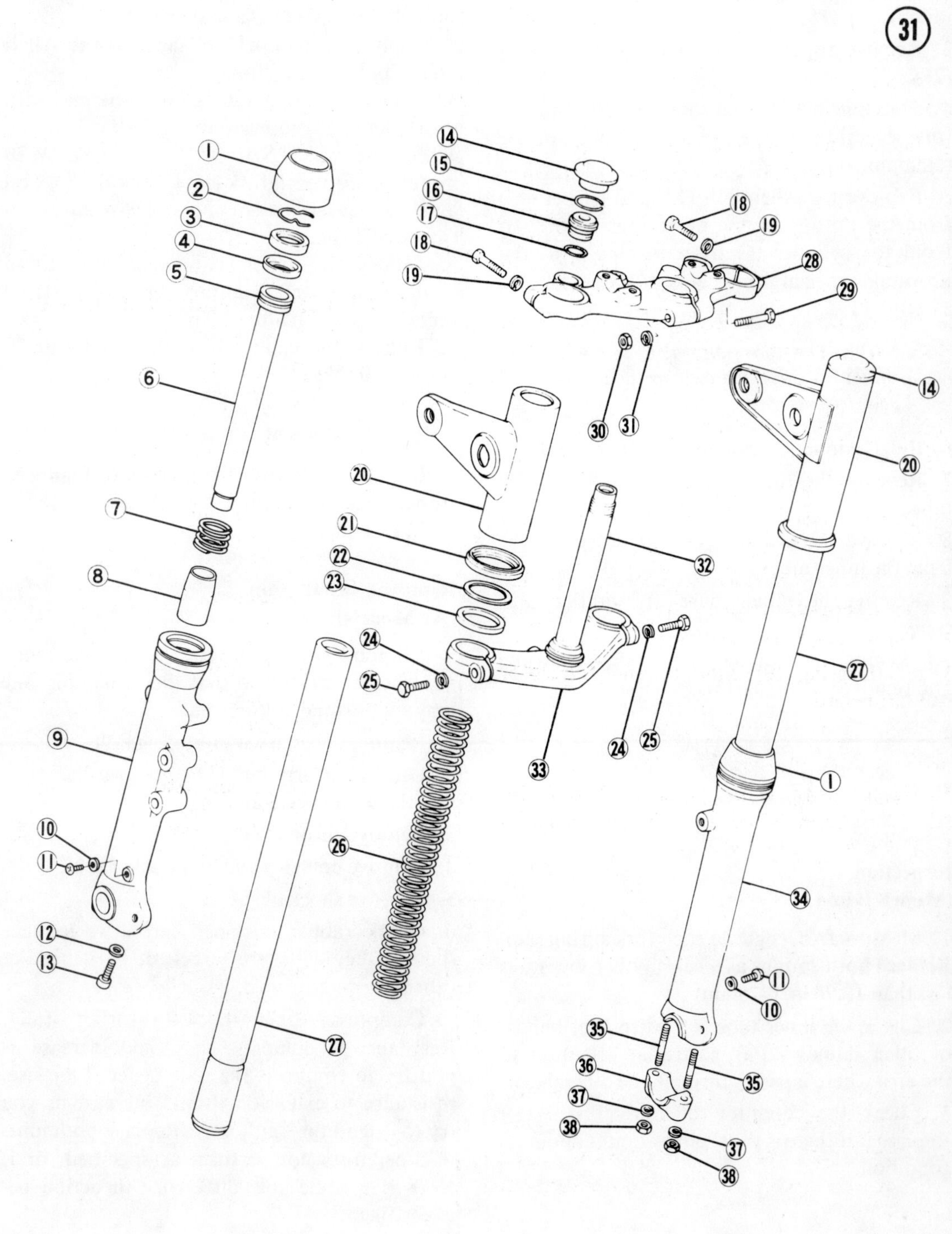
31

2. Depress the top plug (16) and remove the retaining ring (15).

3. Remove top plug and pull out the spring (26).

4. Pour the oil out and discard it. Pump the fork several times by hand to expel most of the remaining oil.

5. Remove the Allen bolt (13) and gasket (12) from the bottom of the outer tube (9 or 34). Hold the cylinder (6) from turning with the Kawasaki special tools Nos. 57001-183 and 57001-1-11.

> NOTE: *The Allen bolt may be removed without holding the cylinder if an impact driver is used.*

6. Pull the inner tube out of the outer tube.

7. Remove the dust seal (1) from the outer tube.

8. Remove the cylinder (6) and its spring (7) from the inner tube.

9. Remove the cylinder base (8) from the outer tube.

10. Remove the retainer (2) from the outer tube and remove the oil seal (3).

> NOTE: *It may be necessary to slightly heat the area around the seal on the outer tube prior to removal.*

Inspection (Models B and C)

1. Measure free length of each fork spring (26). Replace both springs as a set if either measures less than 18.70 in. (475mm).

2. Check the inner tube for corrosion, bends, or other damage. Pay particular attention to the area where it passes through the oil seal (3).

3. Check the condition of the oil seal (3). Replace it if there is the slightest doubt about its condition.

Assembly and Installation (Models B and C)

Reverse the removal and disassembly procedures to assemble and install the fork legs. Observe the following notes:

1. Tap the oil seal (3) into place, using a suitable size socket as a seal driver.

2. Apply Loctite Lock 'N' Seal to the Allen bolt prior to installation.

3. Install the spring (26) so that the end with the closer coils is upward in the fork.

4. Pour about 5 U.S. oz. (150cc) of SAE 5W20 motor oil into each fork leg. Check the fork oil level as described in *Fork Oil Change* in Chapter Three.

5. Tighten the upper clamp bolts (18) to 13 ft.-lb. (1.8 mkg). Tighten the lower clamp bolts (25) to 22 ft.-lb. (3.0 mkg).

6. Tighten the caliper mounting bolts to 29 ft.-lb. (4.0 mkg).

SHOCK ABSORBERS

Refer to shock absorber portion of **Figure 32** for removal/installation. This relates to Models B, C, D, and S.

Removal/Installation (All Models)

It is good practice to remove only one shock absorber at a time, so that the remaining one may support the motorcycle.

1. Remove chrome bar mounting bolts.

2. Remove acorn nut (11), lockwasher (12), and flat washers (13 and 14).

3. Remove chrome bar.

4. Remove bolt (17) and lockwasher (12).

5. Remove shock absorber.

6. Check rubber bushings carefully. Replace them if they are worn, cracked, hardened, or otherwise deteriorated.

7. Compress each shock absorber fully. Resistance to compression should increase as you try to compress the unit faster. Likewise, resistance to extension should increase as you try to extend the unit faster. Replace both units if either does not perform as specified, or if there is a noticeable difference in action between them.

8. Check each unit for oil leakage. Replace both units if either of them leaks.

Reverse the removal procedure to install the shock absorbers. Take care not to damage the threads on bolt (17).

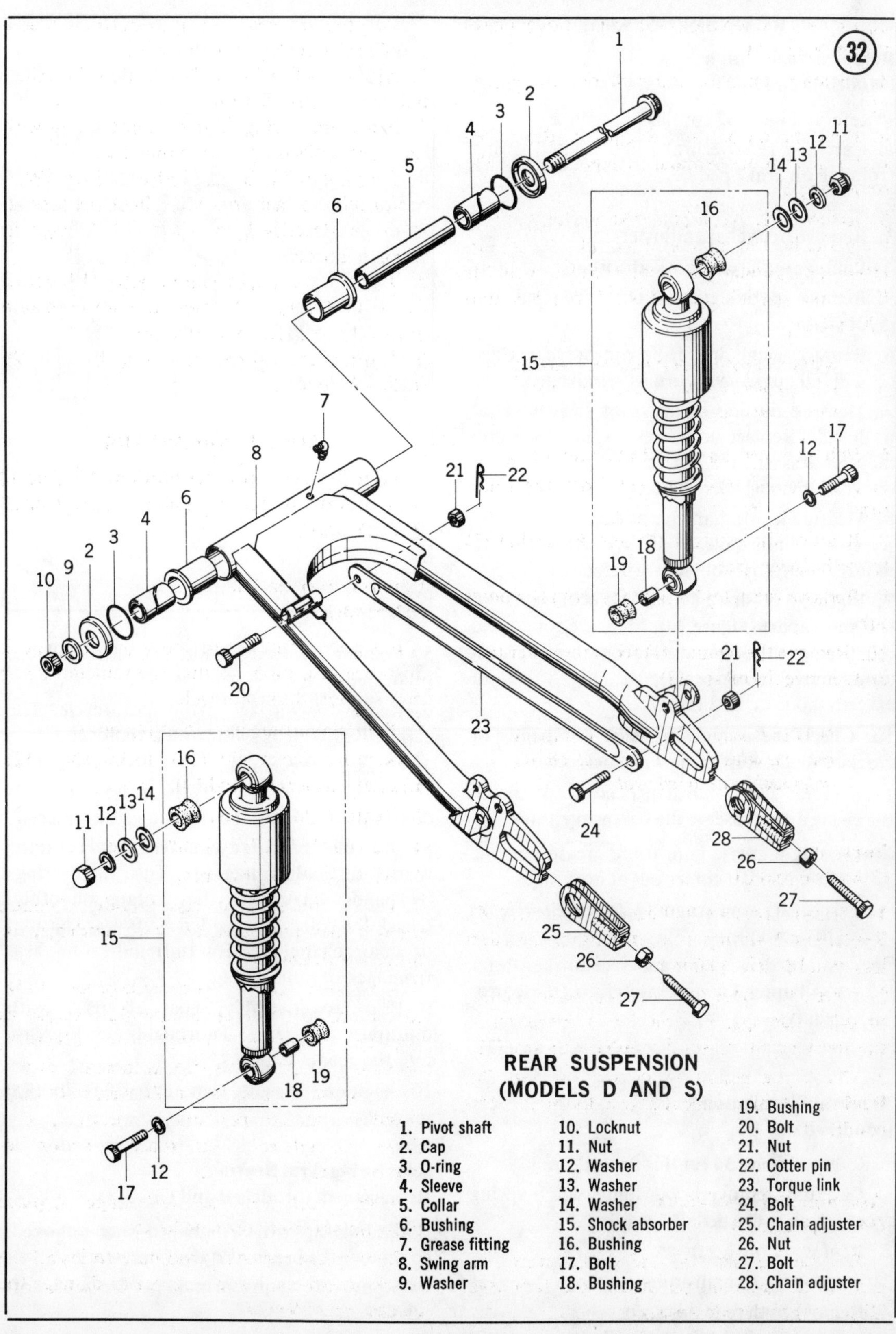

32

REAR SUSPENSION (MODELS D AND S)

1. Pivot shaft
2. Cap
3. O-ring
4. Sleeve
5. Collar
6. Bushing
7. Grease fitting
8. Swing arm
9. Washer
10. Locknut
11. Nut
12. Washer
13. Washer
14. Washer
15. Shock absorber
16. Bushing
17. Bolt
18. Bushing
19. Bushing
20. Bolt
21. Nut
22. Cotter pin
23. Torque link
24. Bolt
25. Chain adjuster
26. Nut
27. Bolt
28. Chain adjuster

REAR SWING ARM

Removal/Installation (Models D and S)

Refer to **Figure 32** for this procedure.

1. Carefully remove brake light switch spring from tab on brake pedal.
2. Remove rear wheel.
3. Remove both chain adjusters.
4. Remove both rear shock absorbers.
5. Remove pivot shaft nut (10), then pull out pivot shaft.
6. Remove swing arm from motorcycle. Caps (2) will fall out as swing arm is removed.
7. Measure outside diameter of sleeves (4) at both ends. Replace both sleeves if any measurement is less than 0.864 in. (21.95mm) or if either is obviously defective.
8. Measure inside diameter of each bushing (6). Replace both bushings if either is worn to 0.876 in. (22.26mm) or is obviously defective.
9. Place pivot shaft (1) in V-blocks set 4 in. (100mm) apart (**Figure 33**). Measure total bend by turning the shaft through several revolutions. Straighten or replace the shaft if runout exceeds 0.008 in. (0.2mm).
10. Check the swing arm itself for bends or cracked welds. Replace it if it is defective.
11. Reverse the removal procedure to install the swing arm. Observe the following notes:
    a. Using a grease gun, force grease into the fitting until it comes out at both sides.
    b. Tighten swing arm nut (10) to 72-94 ft.-lb. (10-13 mkg).
    c. Adjust drive chain and rear brake. Refer to Chapter Three for details of these procedures.

Removal/Installation (Models B and C)

Refer to **Figure 34** for this procedure.

1. Carefully remove brake light switch spring from tab on brake pedal.
2. Remove rear wheel.
3. Remove both chain adjusters.
4. Remove both rear shock absorbers.

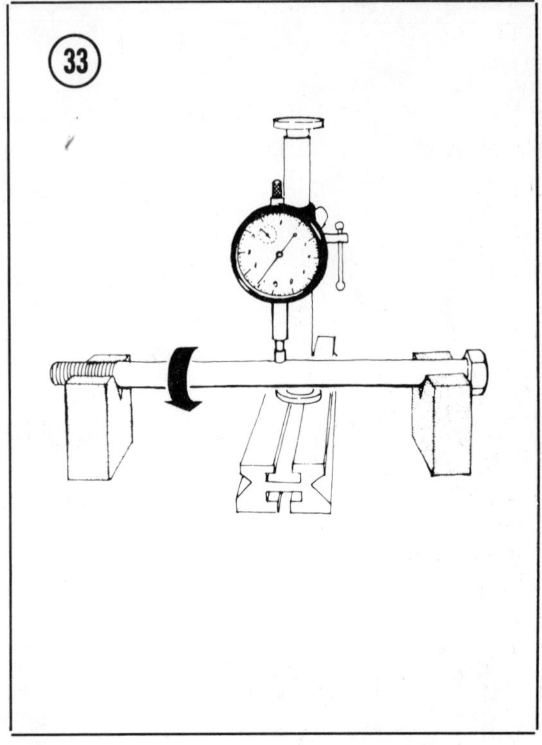

5. Remove pivot shaft nut (1), then pull out pivot shaft (7).
6. Remove swing arm from motorcycle. The caps will fall out as swing arm is removed.
7. Measure the runout of the pivot shaft as shown in **Figure 33**. If the runout exceeds 0.0055 in. (0.14mm) the shaft must be replaced.
8. The roller bearings wear very slowly and the wear is difficult to measure. Turn the bearings by hand; make sure they rotate smoothly. Check the rollers for evidence of wear, pitting, or color change (bluish tint) indicating heat from lack of lubrication.
9. Prior to assembly, coat all parts with multipurpose grease. Thoroughly work grease into the needle bearings.
10. Tighten the swing arm nut to 58 ft.-lb. (8.0 mkg).

Rear Swing Arm Bearing Replacement (Models B and C)

The bearings will be damaged when removed, so remove the bearings only if necessary.

1. Secure the swing arm in a vise with soft jaws.

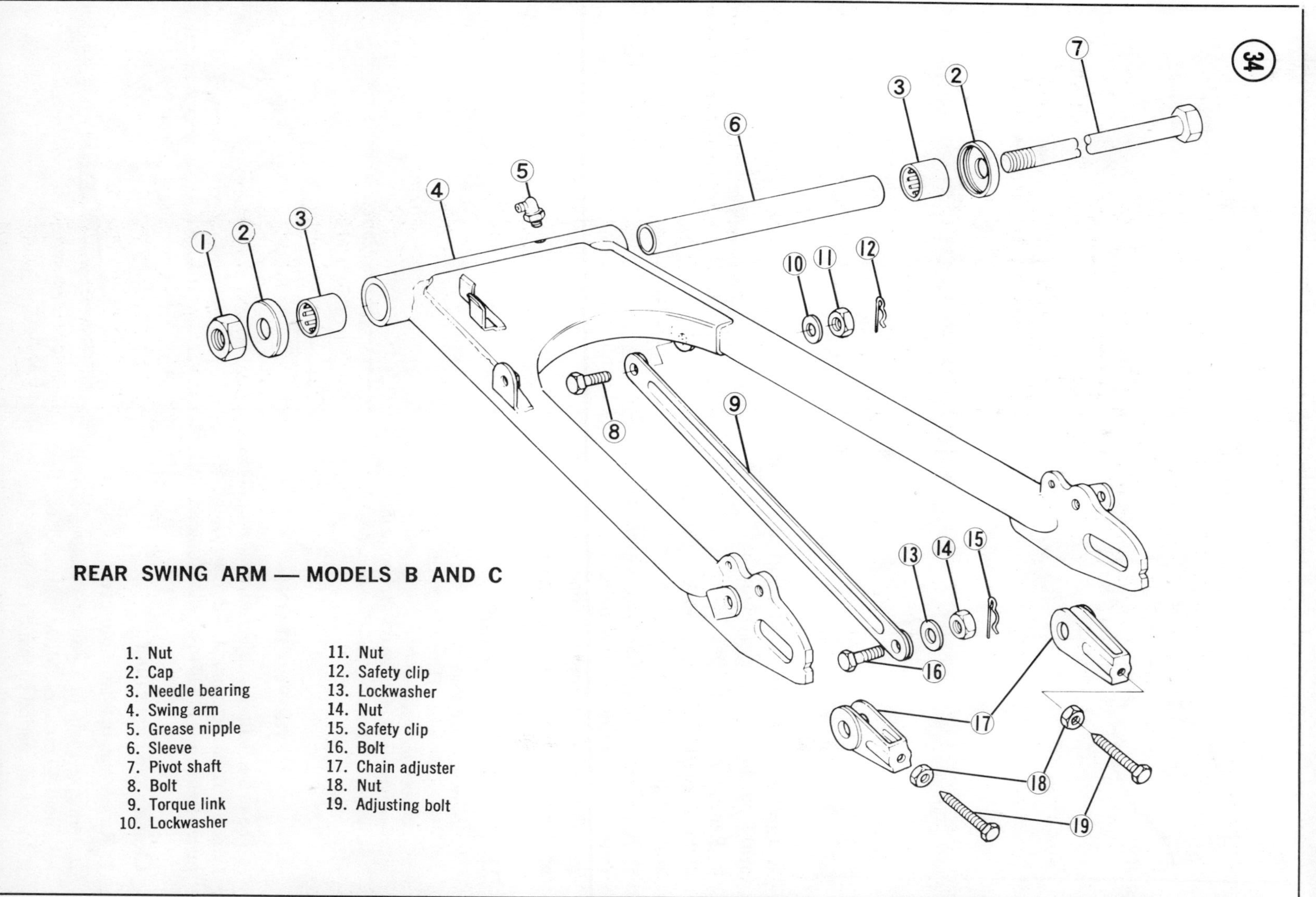

REAR SWING ARM — MODELS B AND C

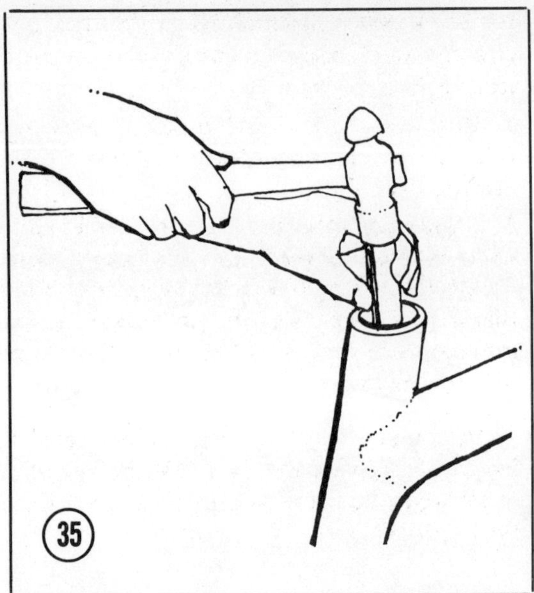

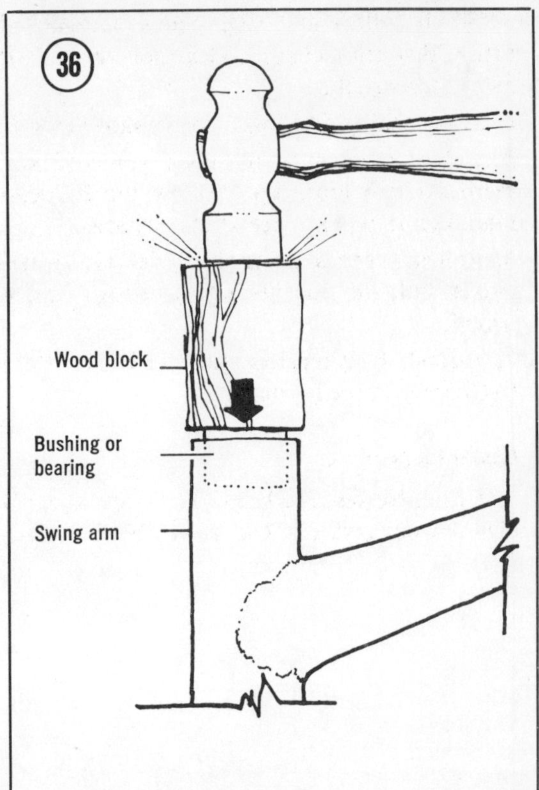

2. Tap the bearing out with a soft aluminum drift from the opposite end (**Figure 35**).

3. Repeat for the other end.

4. Thoroughly clean out the inside of the swing arm with solvent and dry with compressed air.

5. Apply oil to the inside and outside of the roller bearing prior to installation.

6. Tap the new bearing into place slowly and squarely with a wood block (**Figure 36**). Make sure they are properly seated.

CAUTION

Never reinstall a needle bearing that has been removed. During removal it is slighly damaged and no longer true to alignment. If installed it will damage the sleeve and create an unsafe riding condition.

DRIVE CHAIN

The drive chain is subject to wear and abrasion and must be cleaned, lubricated, and adjusted frequently if it is to provide long service.

Cleaning and Lubrication

1. Remove chain from motorcycle.

2. Immerse chain in a pan of cleaning solvent for about 30 minutes. Move it around and flex it during this period so that dirt between its pins and rollers may work its way out.

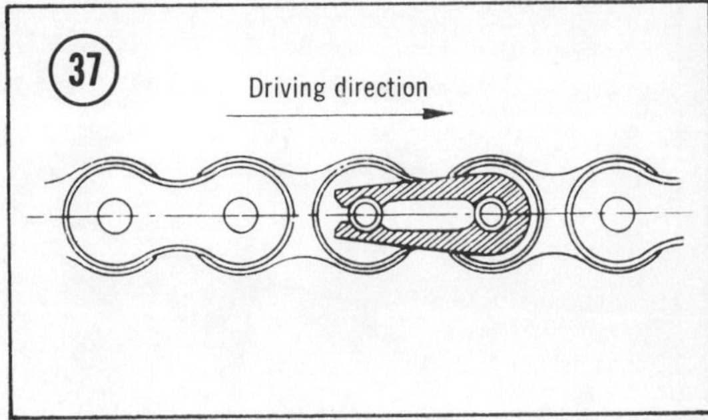

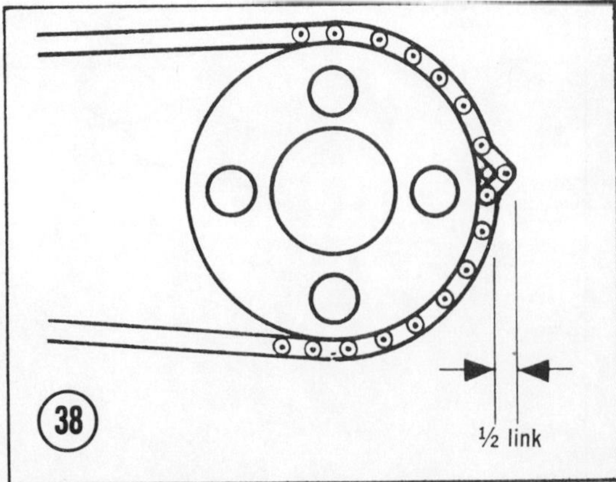

3. Scrub rollers and side plates with a stiff brush, then rinse chain in clean solvent to carry away loosened dirt.

4. Hang chain and allow it to dry thoroughly.

5. Lubricate chain with a good grade of commercial chain lubricant. Follow the lubricant manufacturer's application instructions.

6. Reinstall chain on motorcycle. Use a new master link clip and install it as shown in **Figure 37**.

7. Adjust chain tension and rear brake. Refer to Chapter Three for details.

Chain Inspection

1. Check for binding links. To do so, hang the chain by one end. If there are any binding links, the chain will exhibit a kink at that point. If cleaning and lubrication do not solve the problem, replace the chain.

2. Rust results in rapid wear of pins and rollers. If rust is present, clean and lubricate the chain at once.

3. The best method for measuring chain wear is to stretch the chain with an 11 lb. (5 kg) weight, then measure length of a 20 link section. Make this measurement between pin centers. If this measurement exceeds 12.72 in. (323mm), replace the chain.

As a quick check of chain wear, refer to **Figure 38**. Replace the chain if it can be pulled away from the rear sprocket by more than ½ the length of a link.

SUPPLEMENT

1980 AND LATER SERVICE INFORMATION

This supplement provides service procedures unique to these 1980 and later models:

a. 1980 KZ440-A1, -B1, -C1 and -D1.
b. 1981 KZ440-A2, -B2, -C2, -D2 and -D3.
C. 1982 KZ440-A3 (LTD, Standard and European), -D4 (belt-driven LTD), -G1 (belt-driven standard) and -H1 (European).

Other service procedures remain the same as described in the basic book. The chapter headings in this supplement correspond to Chapters One through Seven of this book. If a chapter is not referenced in this supplement, there are no changes affecting that chapter; follow the procedures described for the comparable KZ400-B/C model in the basic book.

The Chapter Eight section of this supplement describes the KZ440-D/G belt-drive inspection, its adjustment and removal/installation.

CHAPTER THREE

LUBRICATION, MAINTENANCE, AND TUNE-UP

SCHEDULED MAINTENANCE

See **Table 1**. The maintenance schedule for KZ440 models is similar to that for KZ400-B/C models, with these major exceptions:

a. No cam chain tensioner adjustment is required. The KZ440 has an automatic cam chain tensioner. See the Chapter Four section of this supplement for repair.
b. The belt-drive models require drive belt adjustment and wear inspection at the initial 500 mile (800 km) service and at each regular 3,000 mile (5,000 km) service interval. See the Chapter Eight section of this supplement.
c. 1981 and later models have transistorized ignition. No periodic inspection of ignition timing is required. There are no contact breaker points in this system. See the Chapter Six section of this supplement for repair.
d. Kawasaki recommends replacing the disc brake master cylinder and wheel caliper fluid and dust seals every 2 years, regardless of mileage. See the Chapter Seven section of this supplement.
e. Kawasaki recommends replacing the brake hoses and fuel hose every 4 years, regardless of mileage. See the Chapter Seven section of this supplement for brake hose replacement.

The following maintenance procedures are new for the 440cc models.

AIR FILTER

An oiled foam air filter element is used on models other than the KZ440-A and -B. Kawasaki recommends replacing the foam air filter element after cleaning it 5 times, because the cleaning process enlarges the pores of the filter.

1. Lift the seat for access to the air cleaner (**Figure 1**).
2. Remove the air filter housing and pull out the filter (**Figure 2**).

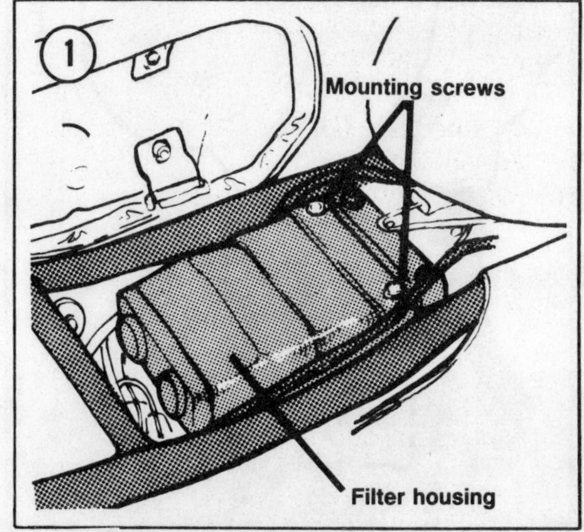

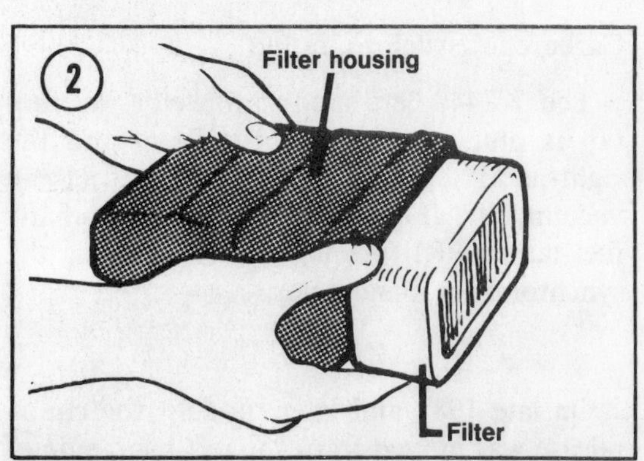

8

3. Pull the foam element off its frame. Clean the element in solvent and let it dry. Inspect the element and replace it if it has any holes or tears.
4. Soak the foam element with SAE 30 motor oil, then wrap it in a rag and carefully squeeze it as dry as possible.
5. When installing filter element, seat the filter against the back of the still air box (**Figure 3**). Make sure the filter element doesn't crimp or slip off its frame when you install it and be certain the bottom ridge of the housing fits in the still air box groove (**Figure 3**).

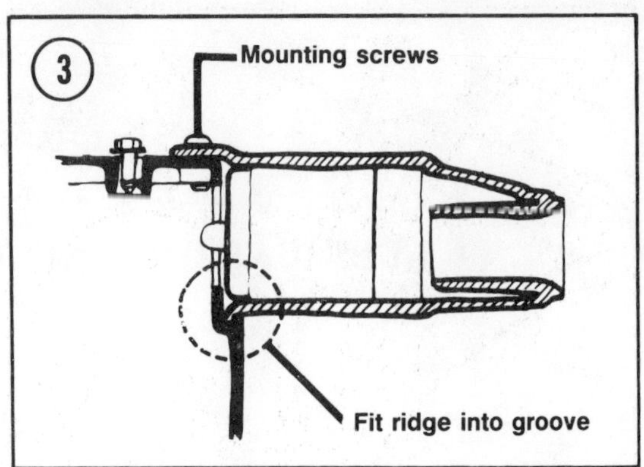

FUEL SYSTEM

When cleaning the fuel system, note that there is no drain screw on the fuel tap and that to drain the float bowls you need only *loosen* the float bowl drain screws 1 or 2 turns (**Figure 4**). Any accumulated water will flow out of the attached overflow hoses.

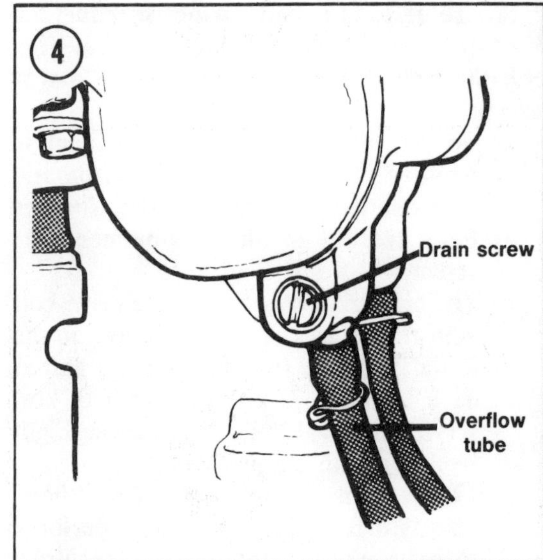

Throttle Cable Play

A single throttle cable is used, simplifying adjustment. Specified cable play remains at about 1/8 in. (2-3 mm).

Idle Speed

The KZ440 throttle stop screw is between and under the carburetors (**Figure 5**). The specified idle speed is 1,200 rpm.

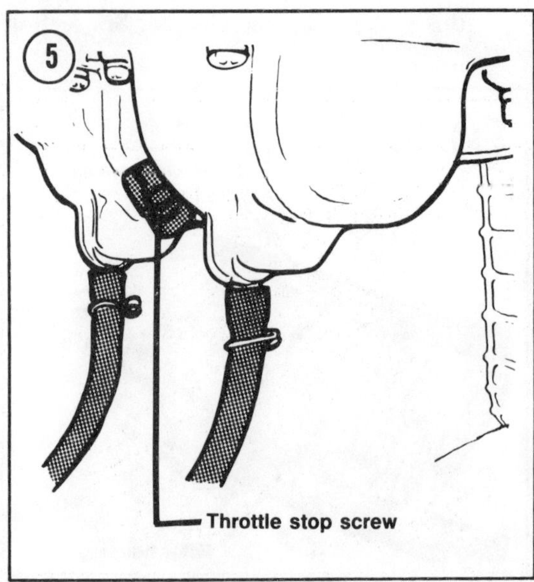

Idle Mixture

On 1980 and later U.S. models, the idle mixture screw is set and sealed at the factory and requires no adjustment.

Carburetor Synchronization

The KZ440 left-hand carburetor vacuum tap is plugged with a rubber cap and the right-hand tap is attached to the fuel tap vacuum line (**Figure 6**). Turn the automatic fuel tap to PRI (prime) after connecting the synchronizing manometer.

CLUTCH

On late 1981 and later models, the clutch release was moved from the left-hand side of

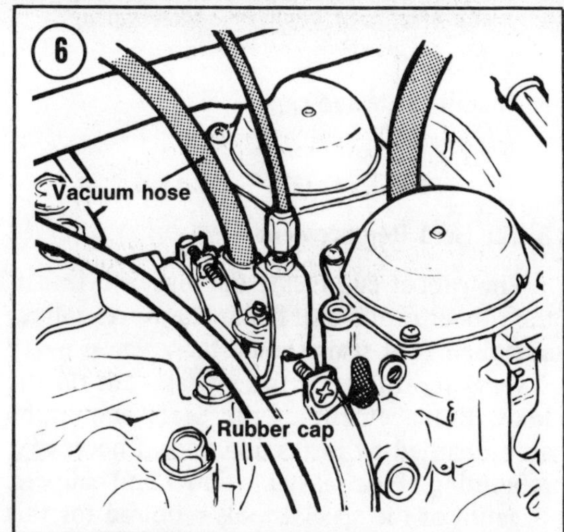

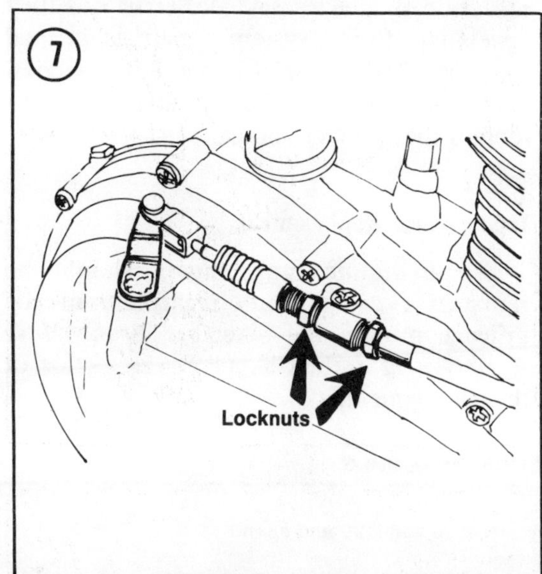

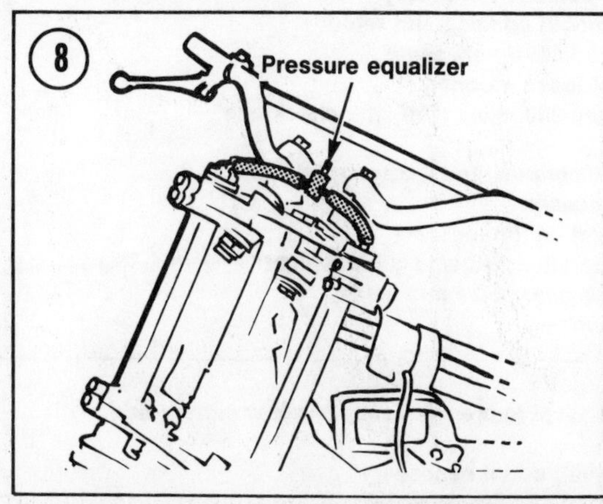

the engine to the right side (**Figure** 7). When adjusting the clutch on these models, make your adjustments at the hand lever as described in the basic book, take up all play at the bottom end of the cable, then tighten the locknuts and adjust play at the hand lever. Check the clutch action before you ride the bike; readjust if necessary.

DRIVE CHAIN

On 1982 and later models, the drive chain adjusters use an adjuster nut and locknut instead of an adjuster bolt and locknut. The procedure remains the same as for earlier models.

SWING ARM

The swing arm grease fitting was deleted in 1981. To lubricate the swing arm bearings, remove the swing arm; see *Removal/ Installation (Models B and C)* in Chapter Seven of the basic book.

FRONT FORKS

Fork Oil Capacity

The fork oil capacity and level was changed for 1982 models; see **Table 2**.

Fork Air Pressure

Air pressurized forks are standard equipment on some models. Both the fork springs and air pressure support the motorcycle and rider. Air pressure should be measured with the forks at room temperature.

The air pressure can be varied to suit the load and your ride preference, but it is very important to have the same pressure in both forks to prevent an unbalanced suspension with poor handling. You may want to install an accessory pressure equalization line between the forks (**Figure 8**). The maximum allowable air pressure difference between the forks is 1.5 psi, so be very careful when adding or bleeding air from the forks. Don't use a high-pressure hose or air bottle to pressurize the forks; a tire pump is a lot closer to the scale you need. Keep the following points in mind when adjusting the front forks.

a. Increase air pressure for heavy loads.

b. If the suspension is too hard, reduce air pressure.
c. If the suspension is too soft, increase air pressure.
d. Occasional bottoming of the forks shows that you are taking good advantage of all their travel. Severe or frequent bottoming should be avoided by increasing air pressure.

1. Support the bike with the front wheel off the ground.
2. Remove the air valve caps.
3. Connect a pump to the valve and pump the forks up to about 25 psi.

CAUTION
Do not exceed 36 psi or the fork seals will be damaged.

4. Slowly bleed off the pressure to reach the desired value. The standard pressure is 8.5 psi (60 kPa). The usable range is 7-10 psi (50-70 kPa). Kawasaki recommends balancing light fork air pressure with light rear shock preload; heavy fork air pressure with heavy rear shock preload.

NOTE
Each application of a pressure gauge bleeds off some air pressure merely in the process of applying and removing the gauge.

5. Install the valve caps.

FRONT DISC BRAKE

Brake Seal Replacement

The rubber cup inside the master cylinder, the rubber piston seal inside the wheel caliper and their dust seals should be replaced every 2 years regardless of the mileage put on the bike. Replacement of the seals should be accompanied by inspection and, if necessary, rebuilding of the master cylinder and calipers. Because of the special tools required for this kind of work, we recommend you have the job done by a Kawasaki dealer or qualified specialist. Brake system repair is critical work; see *Brakes* in the Chapter Seven section of this supplement before attempting to rebuild the cylinder and calipers.

Brake Hose Replacement

The hydraulic brake hoses should be replaced every 4 years regardless of the mileage put on the bike; see *Brake Hose Replacement* in the Chapter Seven section of this supplement.

Table 1 MAINTENANCE SCHEDULE

Weekly/Gas Stop Maintenance	
	•Check tire pressure cold; adjust to suit load and speed •Check brakes for a solid feel •Check brake lever play; adjust if necessary (1974-1977 models) •Check brake pedal play; adjust if necessary •Check throttle grip for smooth opening and return •Check clutch lever play; adjust if necessary •Check for smooth but not loose steering •Lubricate drive chain every 200 miles (300 km); check and adjust play if necessary •Check axles, suspension, controls and linkage nuts, bolts and fasteners; tighten if necessary •Check engine oil level; add oil if necessary •Check lights and horn operation, especially brake light •Check for any abnormal engine noise and leaks •Check kill switch operation
Monthly/3,000 Mile (5,000 km) Maintenance	
	•Check battery electrolyte level (more frequently in hot weather); add water if necessary •Check disc brake fluid level; add if necessary

Table 1 MAINTENANCE SCHEDULE (CONTINUED)

6-Month/3,000 mile (5,000 km) Maintenance	
	•All above checks and the following •Clean or replace air filter •Drain float bowls; clean fuel tap •Clean spark plugs, set gap; replace if necessary •Adjust cam chain tension (1974-1979 models) •Clean contact breaker points, adjust gap; replace if necessary (breaker-point models) •Check ignition timing; adjust if necessary (breaker-point models) •Check valve clearance; adjust if necessary •Check and adjust carburetor cable play, idle speed mixture; synchronize •Change engine oil and filter (filter at every other check) •Lube cables, levers, pedals, pivots and throttle grip •Adjust clutch release •Check tire wear •Check drive chain wear •Check brake lining wear •Check steering play; adjust if necessary •Check suspension •Check drive belt tension, adjust if necessary; inspect for wear (belt-driven models)
Yearly/6,000 Mile (10,000 km) Maintenance	
	•All above checks and the following •Change air filter element •Change disc brake fluid •Change fork oil •Lubricate ignition advance •Check and tighten all nuts, bolts and fasteners •Grease swing arm pivot
2-Year/12,000 Mile (20,000 km) Maintenance	
	•All above checks and the following •Grease speedometer gear housing •Grease wheel bearings •Grease steering bearings
2-Year Maintenance	
	•Grease drum brake camshaft •Replace disc brake master cylinder cup and dust seal •Replace disc brake caliper piston seal and dust seal
4-Year Maintenance	
	•Replace brake hoses •Replace fuel hoses

Table 2 KZ440 STANDARD FORK OIL

Model	Dry Capacity U.S. fl. oz. (cc)	Wet Capacity U.S.fl. oz. (cc)	Oil Level* SAE 5W20 Inch (mm)
1982 G, H	5.1 (150)	4.4 (130)	18.5 (470)
1982 A, D	5.9 (175)	5.1 (150)	16.8 (426)
1980-1981 B, C	5.1 (150)	4.2 (125)	17.1 (435)
1980-1981 A, D	5.1 (150)	4.2 (125)	18.7 (475)

* Fork oil level is checked with forks fully extended and the fork spring removed

8

CHAPTER FOUR

ENGINE, TRANSMISSION AND CLUTCH

The KZ440 engine is essentially the same as the 1978-1979 KZ400-B/C engine, with the following major changes:

a. Bore increases from 64 mm to 67.5 mm bringing displacement up from 398cc to 443cc.
b. Compression ratio is down from 9.5:1.0 to 9.2:1.0.
c. Automotive type cam chain replaces roller type cam chain.
d. Automatic cam chain tensioner is adopted.
e. Kickstarter is deleted.

See **Table 3** for engine wear limits new for the KZ440. See **Table 4** for engine fastener torque specifications new for the KZ440. All other specifications remain as described in the basic book. Follow the procedures described for models B and C in Chapter Four of the basic book, noting the following exceptions.

Engine Removal/Installation

Some KZ440's have shims at the engine mounting bolts to take up play resulting from manufacturing variations. When installing the engine in the frame, check all mating surfaces after you torque the engine mounting bolts. If there is a gap between the engine and frame, add shims to take up any slack and provide a rigid engine/frame assembly.

CAM CHAIN TENSIONER

The KZ440 uses an automatic cam chain tensioner that is continually self-adjusting (**Figure 9**). Special attention to tensioner installation is required during camshaft and cylinder head removal and installation.

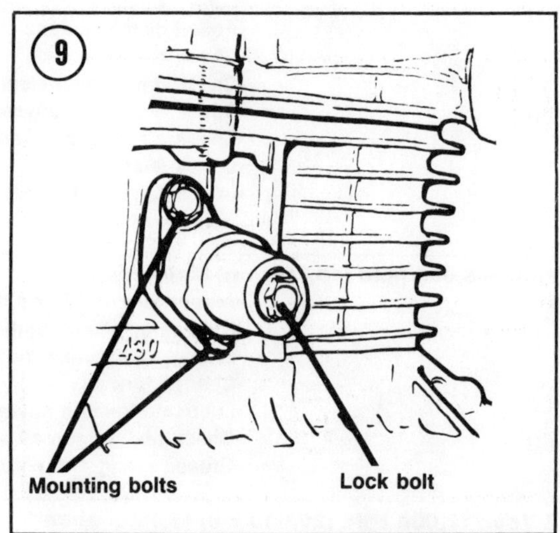

The bolt on the end of the tensioner is used only to lock the tensioner during engine disassembly/assembly. During normal operation, this lock bolt doesn't touch the tensioner pushrod. The pushrod is free to move inward, but can't move out because of a one-way ball and retainer assembly.

Removal

1. Loosen the lock bolt several turns to make sure the tensioner pushrod is free.
2. Remove the 2 tensioner mounting bolts and the tensioner assembly.

CAUTION
Do not loosen the tensioner mounting bolts without removing, resetting and locking the tensioner. If you don't reset the tensioner, the pushrod will overextend and lock, damaging the cam chain when the mounting bolts are tightened.

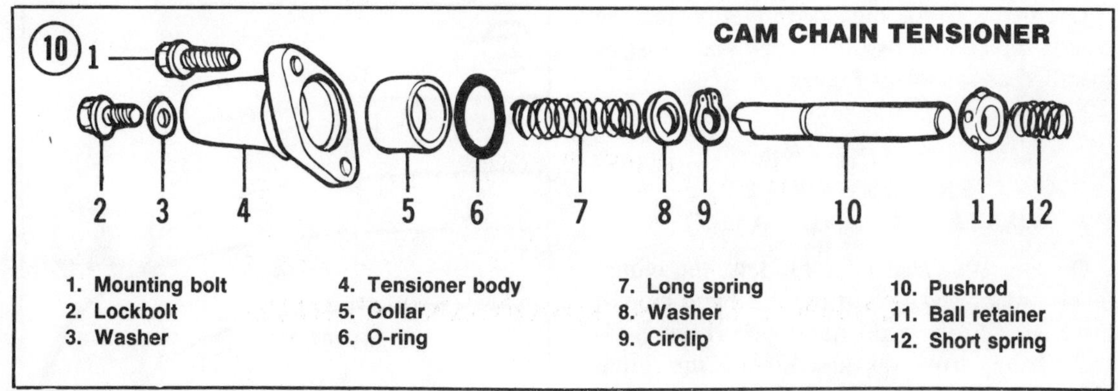

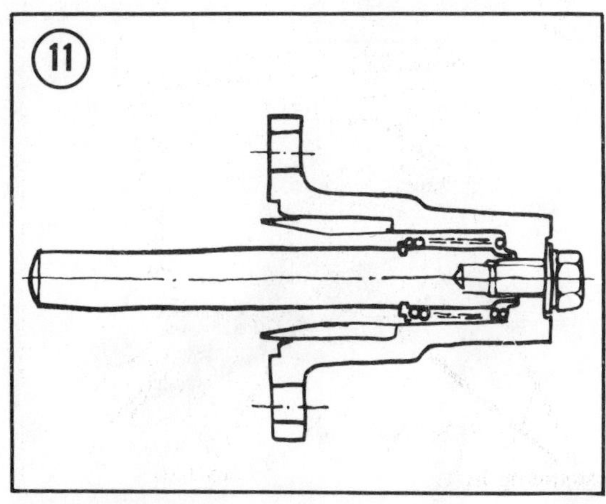

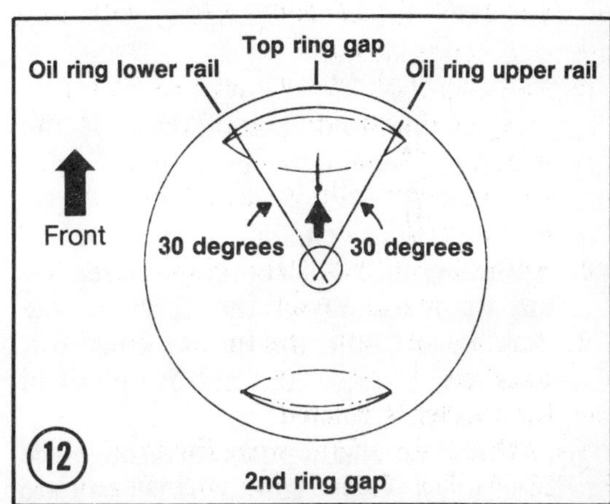

Resetting and Installation

1. See **Figure 10**. Loosen the lock bolt a few turns.
2. Put the long spring and flat washer on the pushrod, then push the pushrod into the tensioner body, compressing the spring and aligning the flats on the end of the rod with the recess in the body. Thread the lock bolt into the pushrod to keep it in the compressed position **(Figure 11)**.

WARNING

Do not loosen the lock bolt before installing the tensioner. The pushrod could spring out forcefully.

3. Hold the tensioner rod up and drop the retainer and ball assembly onto the pushrod, then install the short spring.
4. Install the locked tensioner assembly and O-ring on the cylinder block. Tighten the mounting bolts.
5. Listen carefully as you loosen the lock bolt. You should hear the tensioner rod spring out against the cam chain and take up the chain slack.
6. Tighten the lock bolt; it should turn freely all the way until the bolt head seats against the tensioner body. If it doesn't, you must remove, reset and re-install the tensioner as explained in this section of the supplement.

PISTON RINGS

The KZ440 uses a 3-piece oil control ring, consisting of 2 flat rails with an expander in between.

WARNING

The rails of a 3-piece oil contol ring can be very sharp. Be careful when handling them to avoid cut fingers.

When installing a 3-piece oil control ring, offset the rail openings about 30° to either side of the front (**Figure 12**).

On the KZ440, the second compression ring is tapered on its outer edge and must be installed as shown in **Figure 13**.

13

Top ring

Second ring

CLUTCII AND PRIMARY DRIVE (LATE 1981 AND LATER)

On late 1981 and later models, the clutch release was moved from the left-hand side of the engine to the right-hand side (**Figure 14**) and a ball bearing was added inside the clutch pressure plate.

14

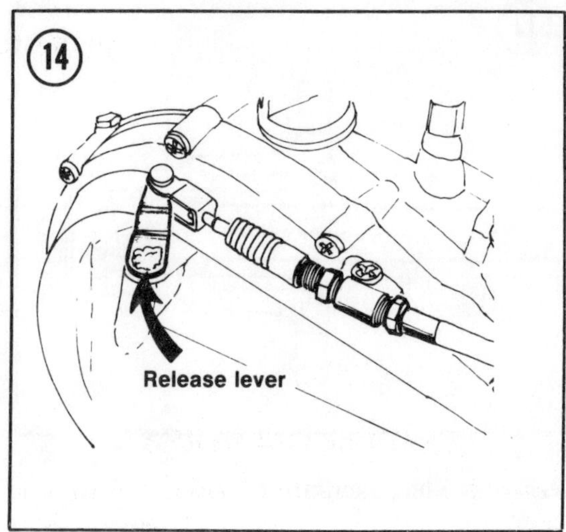

Clutch Removal/Installation

Clutch removal and installation are the same as described in the basic book, with these exceptions:

a. Remove the clutch release before removing the right crankcase cover. To do this, disconnect the cable at the bottom end, turn the release lever so it points to the rear and pull it up out of the cover.
b. The clutch release pushrod through the transmission shaft and the steel ball are eliminated.
c. The pressure plate lifter acts against a ball bearing inside the pressure plate.

Table 3 KZ440 ENGINE WEAR LIMITS

Component	Inch	mm
Cam chain (20 link length)	5.07	128.8
Cam chain guide rubber wear		
Front	0.14	3.6
Rear	0.18	4.5
Cam chain tensioner spring free length	1.57	40
Clutch plate warp	0.012	0.3
Crankshaft journal/bearing clearance	0.003	0.08
Cylinder ID	2.661	67.60
Piston OD	2.650	67.30
Piston/cylinder clearance (standard)	0.0014-0.0024	0.035-0.062

Table 4 KZ440 ENGINE TORQUES

Fastener	Ft.-lb.	Mkg
Cam chain tensioner lock bolt	87 in.-lb.	1.0
Connecting rod big end nuts	27	3.7
Engine mounting bracket bolts	18	2.5
Rocker shafts	30	4.0

CHAPTER FIVE

FUEL SYSTEM

CARBURETOR SERVICE

The KZ440 carburetor is similar to the one used on earlier models. **Table 5** lists specifications for KZ440 carburetors; high altitude pilot and secondary main jets are available for 1982 models. Refer to **Figure 15** for disassembly and assembly. Note that the idle mixture screw is mounted on top and is sealed on U.S. models.

IDLE MIXTURE SCREW (U.S. MODELS)

Removal/Installation

The idle mixture screw is sealed at the factory. When disassembling the carburetors for overhaul, the bonding agent and cover must be removed for access to the screw, O-ring and spring.

1. Carefully scrape out the bonding agent from the recess in the carburetor body.

2. Punch and pry out the plug with a small screwdriver or awl.

3. Carefully screw in the mixture screw until it seats *lightly*. Count and record the number of turns so it can be installed in the same position during assembly.

4. Remove the mixture screw, O-ring and spring from the carburetor body.

5. Repeat for the other carburetor; keep each carburetor's parts separate.

6. Inspect the O-ring and the end of the mixture screw; replace if damaged or worn.

7. Install the mixture screws in the same position as noted during removal.

8. Install new plugs.

NOTE
Apply only a small amount of bonding agent. Too much may close off the air passageway.

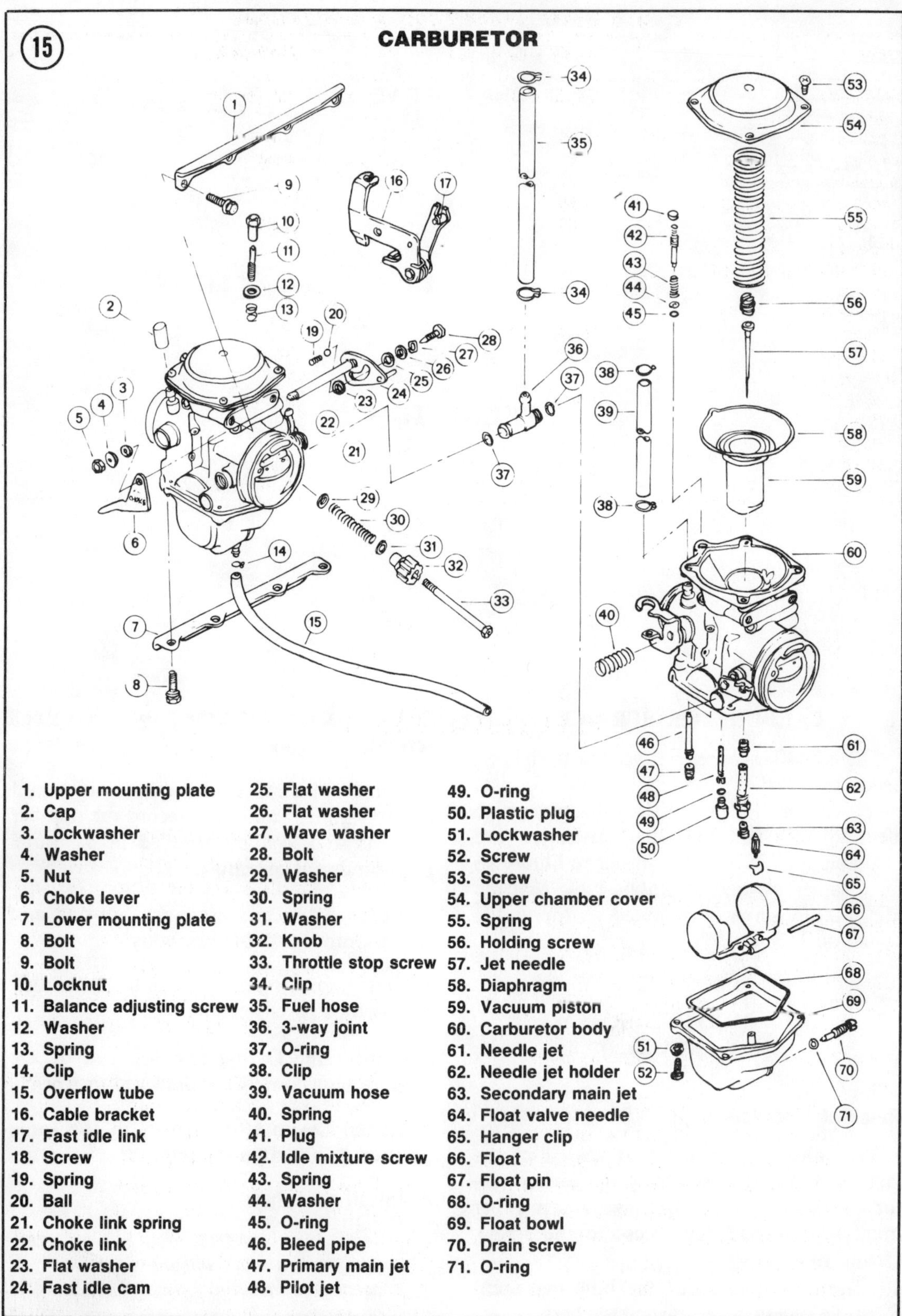
15
CARBURETOR
1. Upper mounting plate
2. Cap
3. Lockwasher
4. Washer
5. Nut
6. Choke lever
7. Lower mounting plate
8. Bolt
9. Bolt
10. Locknut
11. Balance adjusting screw
12. Washer
13. Spring
14. Clip
15. Overflow tube
16. Cable bracket
17. Fast idle link
18. Screw
19. Spring
20. Ball
21. Choke link spring
22. Choke link
23. Flat washer
24. Fast idle cam
25. Flat washer
26. Flat washer
27. Wave washer
28. Bolt
29. Washer
30. Spring
31. Washer
32. Knob
33. Throttle stop screw
34. Clip
35. Fuel hose
36. 3-way joint
37. O-ring
38. Clip
39. Vacuum hose
40. Spring
41. Plug
42. Idle mixture screw
43. Spring
44. Washer
45. O-ring
46. Bleed pipe
47. Primary main jet
48. Pilot jet
49. O-ring
50. Plastic plug
51. Lockwasher
52. Screw
53. Screw
54. Upper chamber cover
55. Spring
56. Holding screw
57. Jet needle
58. Diaphragm
59. Vacuum piston
60. Carburetor body
61. Needle jet
62. Needle jet holder
63. Secondary main jet
64. Float valve needle
65. Hanger clip
66. Float
67. Float pin
68. O-ring
69. Float bowl
70. Drain screw
71. O-ring

Table 5 KZ440 CARBURETOR SPECIFICATIONS

Item	Models A, D, G, H	Models B, C
Size and type	CV, 36 mm	CV, 36 mm
Primary main jet		
1981-on	# 65	# 68
1980	# 62	# 68
Secondary main jet		
1982 U.S. high-altitude	# 85	
Others	# 88	# 90
Pilot jet		
1982 U.S. high-altitude	# 32	
Others	# 35	# 35
Jet needle		
1982	N02A	
1980-1981	N02A	N03A
Mixture screw		
U.S.	preset	preset
Others		
1982	2 3/4	
1980-1981	2 1/4	2 1/4
Fuel level	0.16 in. (4 mm)	0.16 in. (4 mm)

CHAPTER SIX

ELECTRICAL SYSTEM

TRANSISTORIZED IGNITION

Transistorized ignition is used on 1981 and later models. The ignition system consists of 2 spark plugs, one ignition coil, an IC igniter unit and a timing pickup unit. **Figure 16** is a diagram of the transistorized ignition circuit. The Kawasaki transistorized ignition system is similar to the earlier contact breaker point ignition system. It works much the same, with these differences:

a. Mechanical contact points are replaced by a magnetic triggering pickup coil. The elimination of contact breaker points means that periodic adjustment of point gap and ignition timing are no longer required. Once set properly, initial timing should not require adjustment for the life of the motorcycle.
b. An intermediate electronic switch, the battery powered IC igniter, receives the weak signals from the pickup coil and uses them to turn the ignition coil primary current ON and OFF.
c. The ignition coil has a special low-resistance primary winding that helps it produce a powerful spark at high rpm.
d. The transistorized ignition system's dwell angle *increases* slightly as engine speed increases. This is a characteristic of the magnetic pickup coil.
e. Ignition timing is *not* adjustable.

Ignition takes place every 360° of crankshaft rotation. One of the spark plugs fires (harmlessly) on the exhaust stroke.

Because the ignition coil fires through 2 spark plugs wired in series, if one of the plugs fails to fire, so will the other. If one plug develops a weak spark, so will the other.

The ignition coil primary current is normally OFF until the ignition timing rotor cam approaches the pickup coil. As the rotor cam approaches the pickup coil, a pickup coil signal builds to a level that turns the IC igniter ON, allowing primary current to flow through the ignition coil. As the rotor cam passes the pickup coil, the trigger signal reverses polarity and turns the IC igniter OFF. The sudden stoppage of current through the ignition coil primary winding causes the magnetic field to collapse. When this occurs, a very high voltage (up to about 20,000 volts) is induced in the secondary winding of the ignition coil. This high voltage is sufficient to jump the gap at the spark plug, causing the plug to fire.

IGNITION TIMING

Transistorized ignition initial timing is very stable and once it is set properly it should last the life of the motorcycle without adjustment. This optional procedure is provided in case of suspected trouble.

The ignition advance mechanism is a mechanical device that must be lubricated according to the maintenance schedule (**Table 1**). If not maintained properly, the advance mechanism could stick and cause low power, overheating, spark knock or detonation.

Transistorized ignition can not be checked statically. It must be inspected dynamically (engine running) with a strobe timing light.

1. Remove the timing cover and gasket from the lower right side of the engine.
2. Hook up a stroboscopic timing light to either spark plug lead according to the manufacturer's instructions.
3. Start the engine and allow it to idle. Check that the idle speed is within specification before inspecting dynamic timing; a very high idle speed will begin the ignition advance process and give a faulty reading.
4. Shine the timing light at the timing inspection marks. The "F" mark on the advancer should align with the index mark at idle (**Figure 17**).
5. If the "F" mark does not align at idle, stop the engine and remove and inspect the ignition advance assembly; see *Ignition Advance Unit* in Chapter Four of the basic book. Recheck the timing.
6. Increase the engine speed to 4,000 rpm and check that the index mark falls between the double line advance mark (**Figure 17**). If the advancer does not work correctly, refer to *Ignition Advance Unit* in Chapter Four of the basic book.

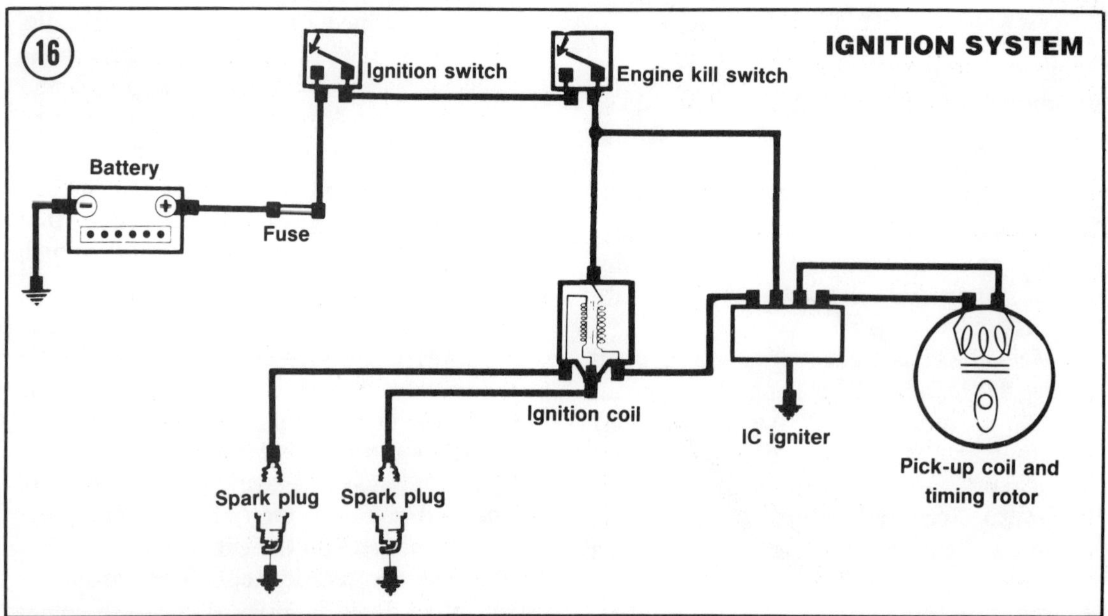

7. Stop the engine and install the timing cover and gasket.

IGNITION COIL

Removal/Installation

The ignition coil is under the fuel tank and the IC igniter is mounted next to it (**Figure 18**).

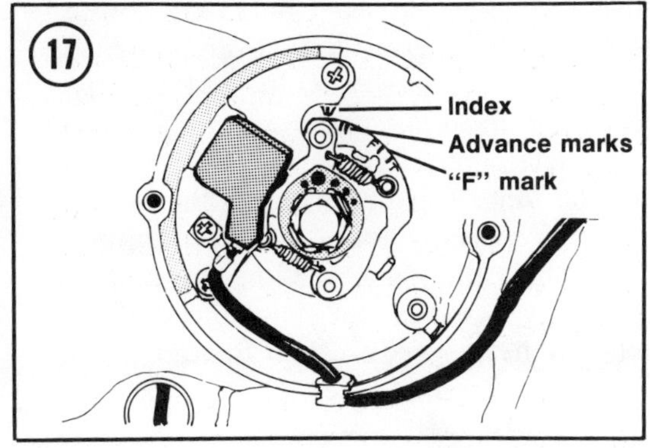

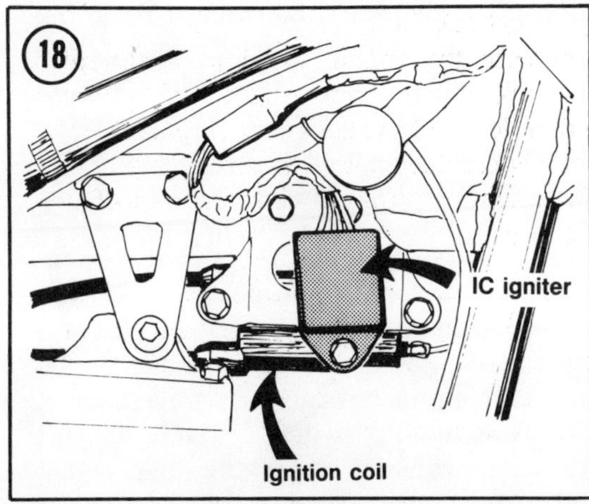

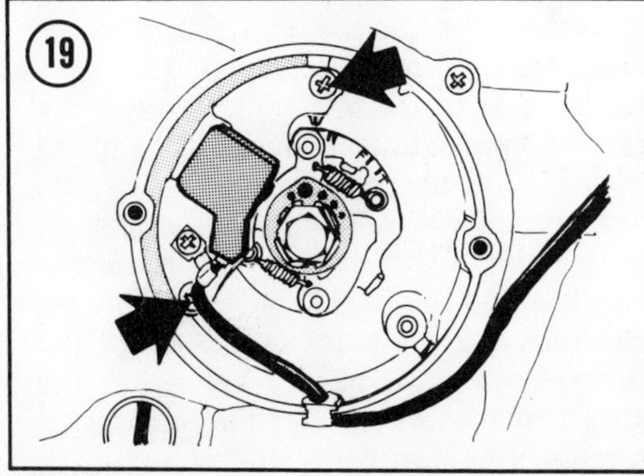

Testing

1. If the coil condition is doubtful, there are several checks which can be made. Disconnect the coil wires before testing. Measure coil primary resistance, using an ohmmeter set at R x 1. The resistance should be *about* 2.3 ohms.
2. Measure coil secondary resistance; remove the resistor-type plug caps from the leads and measure between the secondary leads. The resistance should be *about* 13,000 ohms when the coil is at room temperature.
3. Measure the resistance between either coil primary lead wire and ground (coil core) and between the coil secondary lead and ground (coil core). The resistance should be infinite. A reading of continuity indicates a short circuit.
4. If a coil does not meet these resistance values, it should be replaced. If the coil exhibits visible damage, it should be replaced.

PICKUP COIL

Inspection

1. Remove the fuel tank and disconnect the 2-pole pickup coil/IC igniter connector.
2. With an ohmmeter set at R x 100, measure the resistance between the black and blue leads. The resistance should be about 360-540 ohms.
3. Set the ohmmeter at its highest scale and check the resistance between either lead and chassis ground. The reading should be infinite.
4. If the pickup coil fails either of these tests, check the wiring to the coil. Replace the coil if the wiring is okay.

Removal/Installation

The pickup coil is under the timing cover on the right-hand side of the engine.

1. Remove the fuel tank and disconnect the 2-pole pickup coil/IC igniter connector.
2. Remove the 2 timing cover screws, the cover and gasket.
3. Remove the 2 timing plate screws and the plate with the pickup coil (**Figure 19**).
4. To install, reverse these steps.

IC IGNITER

To check the operation of the IC igniter (**Figure 18**), remove one spark plug, ground it against the cylinder head while the plug lead is connected, turn the ignition ON and touch a screwdriver to the pickup coil core. If the IC igniter is good, the plug will spark.

Remember that the IC igniter is battery-powered and will not function if the battery is dead. The following IC igniter test can be made on the motorcycle.

1. Remove one spark plug and ground it against the cylinder head while its plug wire is connected.
2. Disconnect the 2-pole connector from the pickup coil.
3. Turn the ignition ON. Connect a positive (+) 12 volt source to the black lead and a negative (-) 12 volt source to the blue lead. As the voltage is connected, the plug should spark.
4. If the IC igniter fails these tests, install a new one. If the IC igniter passes these tests but you still have an ignition problem that can't be traced to any other part of the ignition system, substitute an IC igniter that you know is good and see if that solves the problem. Some transistorized ignition troubles just won't show up on your workbench.

TURN SIGNAL CANCELLING SYSTEM

Some models are equipped with an automatic turn signal cancelling system that turns off the turn signals after 4 seconds have passed and after the bike has traveled 50 meters. **Figure 20** is a schematic diagram of the system.

The distance sensor is a switch in the speedometer that opens and closes as the front wheel turns. The turn signal control unit counts 4 seconds after you push the turn signal switch ON, then it electrically counts the number of front wheel revolutions detected by the distance sensor. After both time and distance conditions have been met, the turn signal control unit energizes a solenoid in the turn signal switch body that pushes the switch OFF.

Troubleshooting

1. In case of trouble with the system, check all wiring and connectors first.
2. If the wiring is okay, check the distance sensor. Remove the headlight and disconnect the red and light green leads from the sensor. Connect an ohmmeter to the red and light green leads from the speedometer. Disconnect the speedometer cable at its lower end and turn the inner cable by hand. If the distance sensor is working properly, the ohmmeter should show the sensor making and breaking continuity 4 times per revolution; if not, install a new speedometer. Reconnect the wires.
3. If the distance sensor is okay, check the solenoid in the turn signal switch body. Remove the fuel tank. Disconnect the 6-pin connector from the turn signal switch. Push the turn signal switch ON. Momentarily apply 12 positive (+) volts to the white/green lead from the switch, using a wire connected to the positive (+) battery terminal. If the solenoid is okay, it will push the switch OFF; if not, install a new turn signal switch. Reconnect the 6-pin connector.
4. If the solenoid is okay, open the turn signal switch at the handlebar and clean the switch contacts. No replacement parts are available.
5. If cleaning the switch contacts doesn't solve the problem, check the turn signal control unit. Open the turn signal switch at the handlebar. Set a voltmeter at 25 volts DC and connect the positive (+) probe to the white/green solenoid terminal (not the grounded side of the solenoid). Connect the negative (-) probe to the grounded side of the solenoid. With the ignition switch ON and the turn signal selector set at "A" (automatic), push the turn signal switch ON. Raise the front wheel and spin it at least 30 revolutions. If the turn signal control unit is okay, the voltmeter will show battery voltage as the control unit tries to energize the solenoid; if not, replace the turn signal control unit.

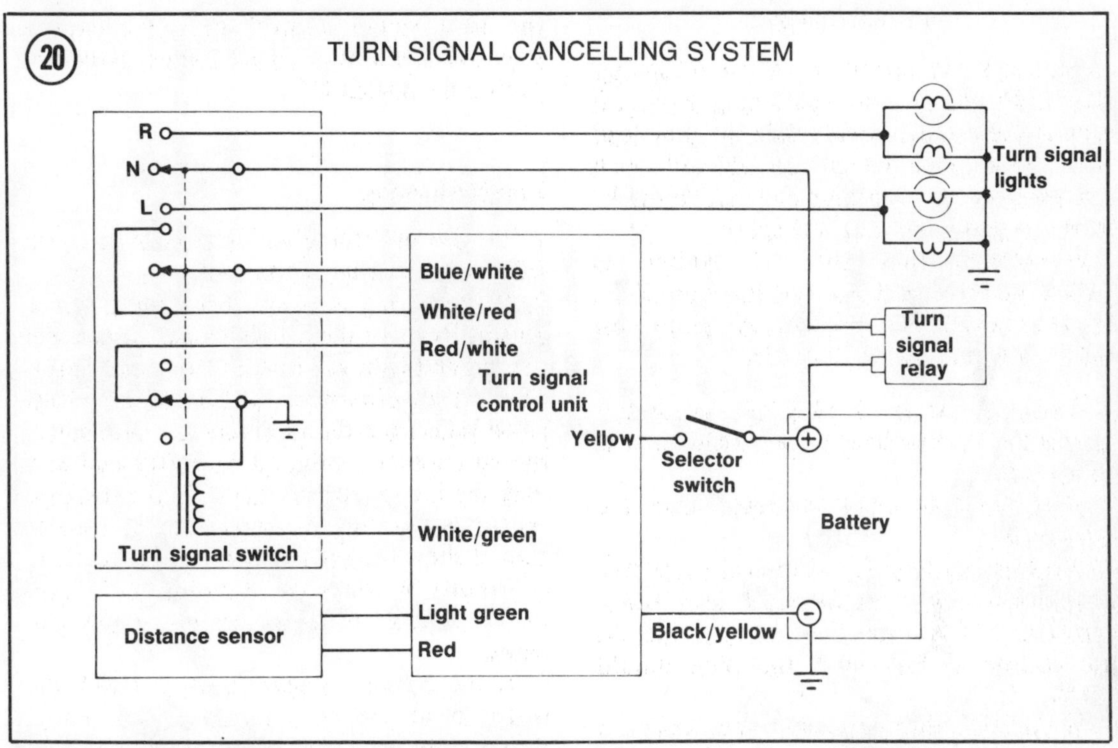

CHAPTER SEVEN

CHASSIS

See **Table 6** for new KZ440 chassis fastener torque specifications. Follow the procedures described for models B and C in Chapter Seven of the basic book, noting the following exceptions.

WHEELS AND TIRES

Some models have one-piece cast aluminum wheels. Removal and installation is the same as for wire-spoked wheels. See **Table 7** for tire sizes and pressures new for KZ440 models.

FRONT HUB

Disassembly/Assembly

Refer to **Figure 21** for front hub disassembly/assembly. Note that 2 types of speedometer gear drives have been used.

NOTE

When installing semi-sealed wheel bearings, be sure the sealed side faces out.

WHEEL INSPECTION

Check the cast aluminum wheels for cracks, bends or warping. If a wheel is damaged or cracked, replace it. Repair is not possible.

8

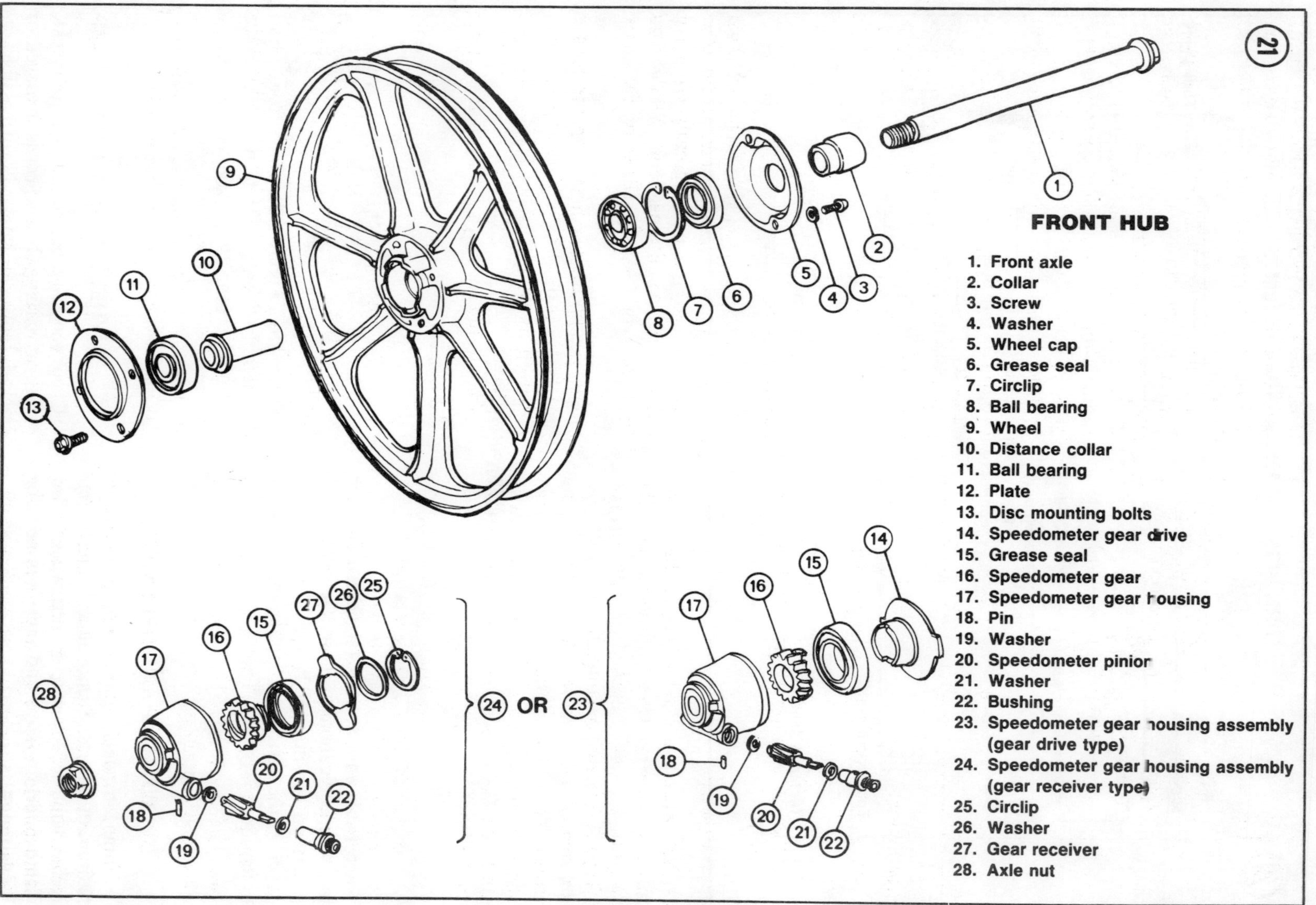
21
FRONT HUB
1. Front axle
2. Collar
3. Screw
4. Washer
5. Wheel cap
6. Grease seal
7. Circlip
8. Ball bearing
9. Wheel
10. Distance collar
11. Ball bearing
12. Plate
13. Disc mounting bolts
14. Speedometer gear drive
15. Grease seal
16. Speedometer gear
17. Speedometer gear housing
18. Pin
19. Washer
20. Speedometer pinion
21. Washer
22. Bushing
23. Speedometer gear housing assembly (gear drive type)
24. Speedometer gear housing assembly (gear receiver type)
25. Circlip
26. Washer
27. Gear receiver
28. Axle nut
OR

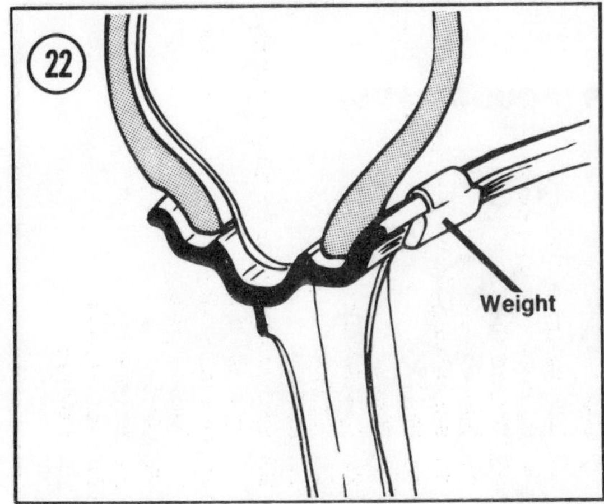

Rim Runout

Wheel rim run-out tolerance on cast wheels is:

a. Axial (side-to-side): 0.02 in. (0.5 mm).
b. Radial (up-and-down): 0.03 in. (0.8 mm).

Wheel Balance

Cast wheels are balanced in the same manner as wire spoked wheels, but the weights are not attached to the spokes. "Tape-A-Weight" or similar adhesive weights are available at motorcycle or auto supply stores. These kits contain test weights and strips of adhesive backed weights that can be cut to the desired length and attached directly to the rim.

NOTE
*Kawasaki offers weights that can be crimped on the aluminum rims (**Figure 22**). You may have to let some air out of the tire to install this type of weight.*

DISC BRAKE

See **Table 8** for KZ440 brake wear limits. See **Table 9** for KZ440 disc brake system torque specifications.

BRAKE HOSE REPLACEMENT

A brake hose should be replaced whenever it shows cracks, bulges or other damage. The deterioration of rubber by ozone and other atmospheric elements may require hose replacement more often than every 4 years.

1. Before replacing a brake hose, inspect the routing of the old hose carefully, noting any guides and grommets the hose may go through.
2. Drain the brake fluid from the system as described in *Bleeding Front Brake* in Chapter Seven of the basic book.
3. Disconnect the banjo bolts securing the hose at either end and remove the hose with banjo bolt and 2 washers at both ends.
4. Install a new hose with 2 new washers at each banjo bolt.
5. Torque the banjo bolts as specified in **Table 9**.
6. Fill the reservoir and bleed the system as described in *Bleeding Front Brake* in Chapter Seven of the basic book.

BRAKE PAD

Replacement

There is no recommended mileage interval for changing the friction pads in the disc brake. Pad wear depends greatly on riding habits and conditions. See *Brake Pad Inspection* in Chapter Three of the basic book.

There is no wear indicator on the KZ440 disc brake pads. Replace both pads when either one is worn to about 1/16 in. (1 mm) thickness.

Always replace all pads (2 per disc) at the same time.

Round Pads Removal

1. See **Figure 23**. Remove the 2 caliper mounting bolts and lift the caliper off the brake disc.
2. Remove the screw, lockwasher and plate securing the inboard pad.
3. Remove the inboard pad.
4. Slide the caliper holder toward the bleed valve and remove the outboard pad.

NOTE
If the pad won't come out, squeeze the brake lever a few times until the piston pushes the pad out.

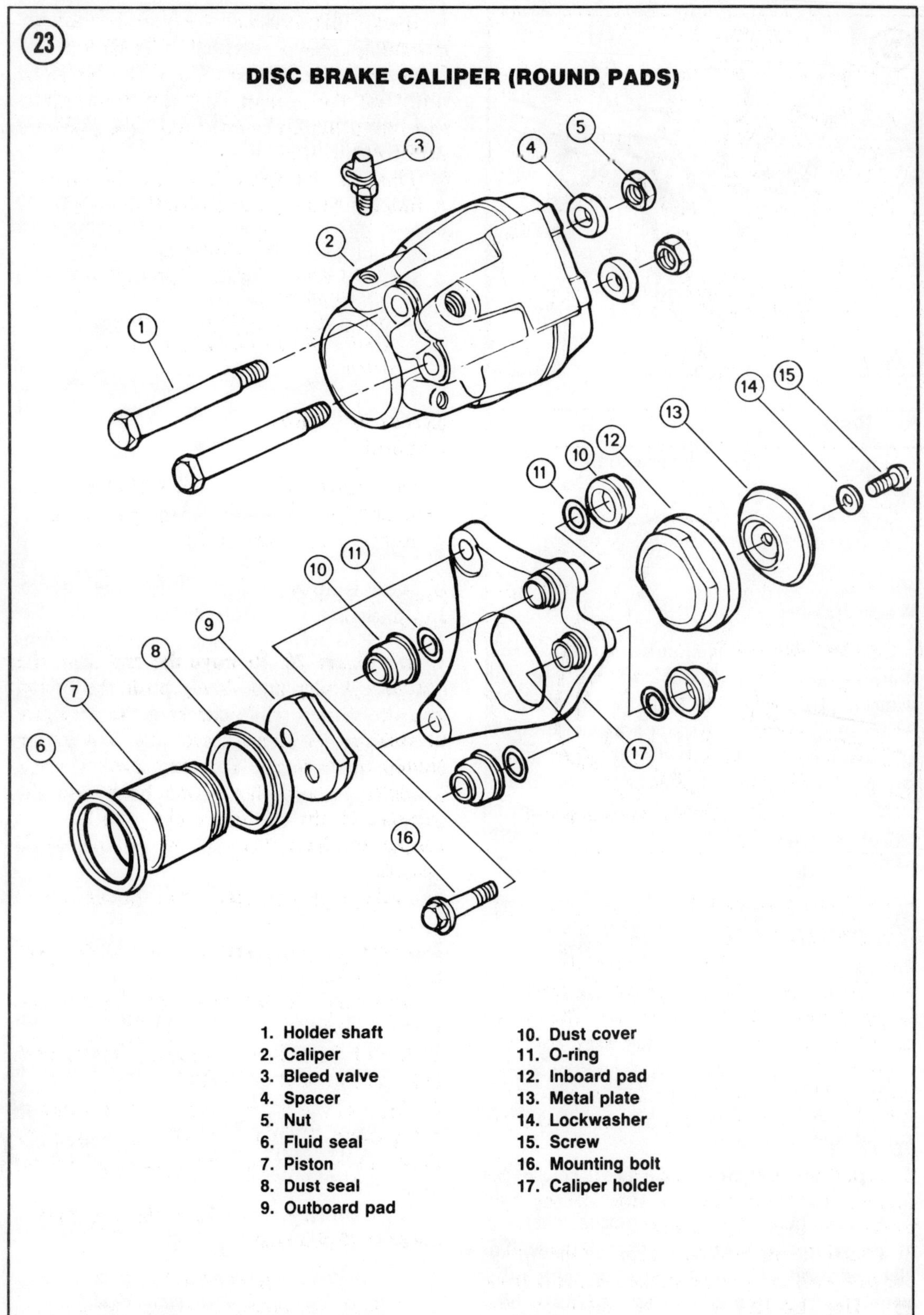
23
DISC BRAKE CALIPER (ROUND PADS)
1
2
3
4
5
6
7
8
9
10
11
12
13
14
15
16
17
10
11
1. Holder shaft
2. Caliper
3. Bleed valve
4. Spacer
5. Nut
6. Fluid seal
7. Piston
8. Dust seal
9. Outboard pad
10. Dust cover
11. O-ring
12. Inboard pad
13. Metal plate
14. Lockwasher
15. Screw
16. Mounting bolt
17. Caliper holder

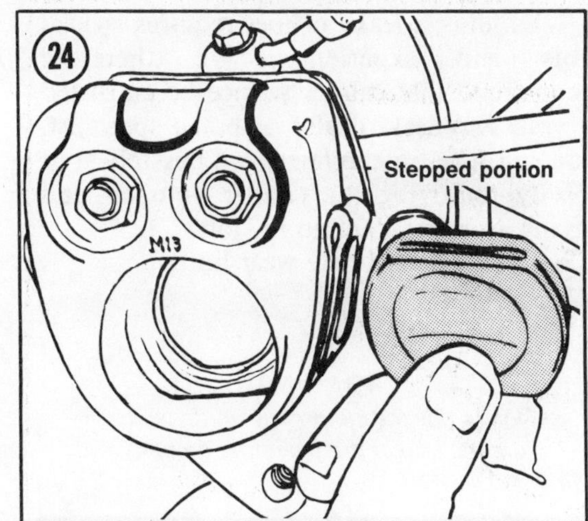

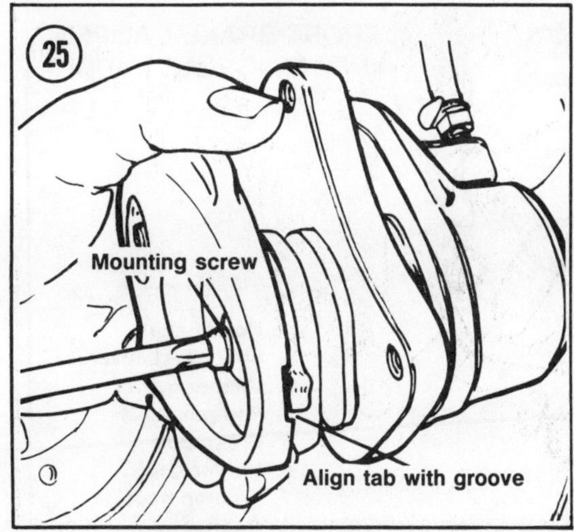

Round Pads Installation

1. See **Figure 23**. Remove the cap from the master cylinder and slowly push the piston into the caliper while checking the reservoir to make sure it doesn't overflow. The piston should move freely. You may need to use a C-clamp to push the piston back into the caliper. If the piston sticks, remove the caliper and have it rebuilt by your Kawasaki dealer.
2. Install the outboard pad against the caliper piston, with the stepped side of the pad toward the disc (**Figure 24**).
3. Install the inboard pad, aligning the tab on the pad with the groove in the caliper (**Figure 25**). Use Loctite Lock N' Seal on the mounting screw threads.
4. Install the caliper. Torque the caliper mounting bolts as specified in **Table 9**.
5. Support the motorcycle with the front wheel off the ground. Spin the front wheel and pump the brake lever until the pads are seated against the disc.
6. Top up the fluid level in the master cylinder if necessary and install the cover.

WARNING
Do not ride the motorcycle until you are sure the brakes are working with a solid feel. If necessary, bleed the brakes to remove any accumulated air from the system.

Rectangular Pads
Removal

1. See **Figure 26**. Remove the 2 caliper shaft bolts and lift the caliper off the pad holder.
2. Remove the brake pads.

Rectangular Pads
Installation

1. See **Figure 26**. Remove the cap from the master cylinder and slowly push the piston into the caliper while checking the reservoir to make sure it doesn't overflow. The piston should move freely. You may need to use a C-clamp to push the piston back into the caliper. If the piston sticks, remove the caliper and have it rebuilt by your Kawasaki dealer.
2. Make sure the brake pad guides are in place.
3. Install the pads with the friction material toward the disc.
4. Make sure the anti-rattle spring is installed in the caliper.
5. Install the caliper. Torque the caliper shaft bolts as specified in **Table 9**.
6. Support the motorcycle with the wheel off the ground. Spin the wheel and pump the brake until the pads are seated against the disc.
7. Top up the fluid level in the master cylinder if necessary.

WARNING
Do not ride the motorcycle until you are sure the brakes are working with a solid

feel. If necessary, bleed the brakes to remove any accumulated air from the system.

BRAKE CALIPERS

Rebuilding

See **Figure 23** or **Figure 26**. If the caliper leaks, it should be rebuilt. If the piston sticks in the cylinder, indicating severe wear or galling, the entire unit should be replaced. The factory recommends that the piston fluid seal and dust cover be replaced every 2 years or every other time the pads are replaced.

Rebuilding a leaky caliper requires special tools and experience. We therefore recommend that caliper service be entrusted to your Kawasaki dealer or brake specialist. You will save time, money, and possibly your life by removing the caliper yourself and having a professional do the job.

See **Table 8** for brake wear limits.

WARNING
Do not ride the motorcycle until you are sure the brakes are operating properly.

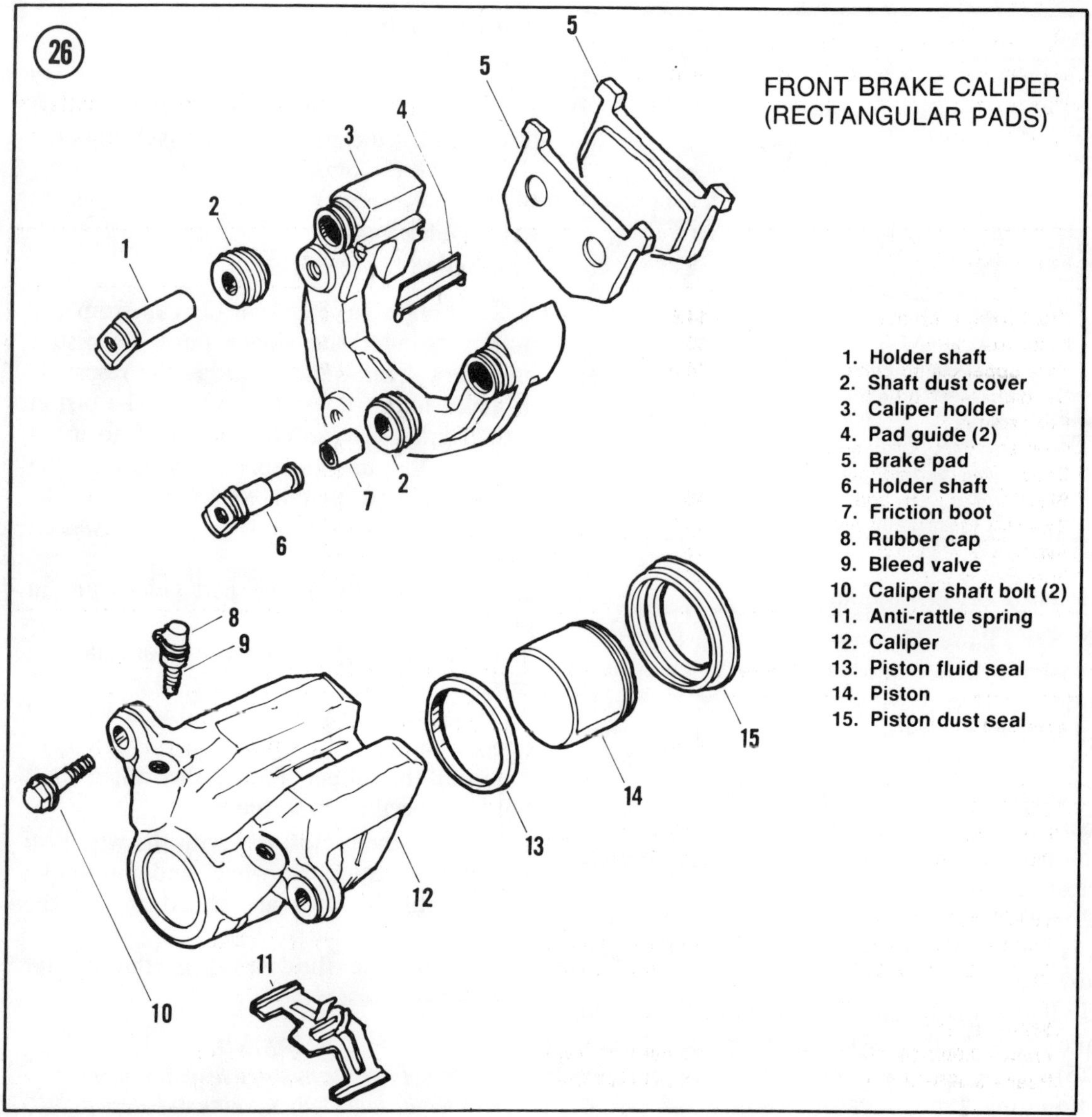

Front Caliper Removal/Installation

Remove the calipers and disconnect the brake hoses as described in *Brake Pad Replacement* and *Brake Hose Replacement.*

Install the calipers as described in *Brake Pad Replacement* and reconnect the brake hoses as described in *Brake Hose Replacement.*

BRAKE DISCS

Installation

On the 1981 and later KZ440-C, the brake disc must be mounted so the side marked with the minimum thickness faces away from the wheel hub.

FRONT FORKS

Air Pressurized Forks

On models with air pressurized front forks, be sure to release any fork air pressure before disassembling the fork legs. See the Chapter Three section of this supplement for fork pressure recommendations.

WARNING
Release all fork air pressure before removing the fork caps. Air pressure and spring preload may eject the caps forcibly.

Inspection

See **Table 10** for minimum free length of KZ440 fork springs.

Table 6 KZ440 CHASSIS TORQUES

Fastener	Ft.-lb.	Mkg
Front axle pinch nuts	14.5	2.0
Front axle nuts	45	6.5
Fork upper clamp bolts	14.5	2.0
Handlebar clamp bolts	15	2.1
Rear axle nut	55	7.5
Rear sprocket/pulley nuts	25	3.3
Shock absorber mounts	25	3.3
Steering head top bolt	40	5.5
Steering head clamp bolt	14.5	2.0
Swing arm pivot nut	65	9.0
Torque link nuts	25	3.3

Table 7 KZ440 TIRES AND TIRE PRESSURE

Model/Tire Size	Pressure @ Load	
	0-215 Lb. (0-97.5 Kg)	Over 215 Lb. (Over 97.5 Kg)
1982 G, H		
Front - 3.60S-19 4PR	25 psi (175 kpa)	25 psi (175 kpa)
Rear - 4.10S-18 4PR	28 psi (200 kpa)	32 psi (225 kpa)
1980-82 A, D		
Front - 3.25S-19 4PR	25 psi (175 kpa)	25 psi (175 kpa)
Rear - 130/19-16 67S	21 psi (150 kpa)	25 psi (175 kpa)
1980-81 B, C		
Front - 3.00S-18 4PR	25 psi (175 kpa)	25 psi (175 kpa)
Rear - 3.50S-18 4PR	28 psi (200 kpa)	36 psi (250 kpa)

Table 8 KZ440 DISC BRAKE WEAR LIMITS

Item	Inch	mm
Caliper/Disc		
Caliper ID	1.690	42.92
Caliper piston OD	1.683	42.75
Disc runout	0.012	0.3
Disc thickness (front)	0.177	4.5
Pad thickness	0.040	1.0
Master Cylinder		
Cylinder ID	0.554	14.08
Piston OD	0.547	13.90
Primary cup OD	0.555	14.1
Secondary cup OD	0.571	14.5
Spring free length	1.60	40.7

Table 9 KZ440 DISC BRAKE TORQUES

Item	Ft.-lb.	Mkg
Banjo bolts	22	3.0
Bleed valve	70 in.-lb.	0.80
Brake lever pivot bolt	25 in.-lb.	0.30
Brake lever pivot locknut	50 in.-lb.	0.60
Caliper holder shaft bolts		
Rectangular pads	13	1.8
Caliper holder shaft nuts		
Round pads	20	2.6
Caliper mounting bolts		
Rectangular pads	22	3.0
Round pads	30	4.0
Disc mounting bolts		
Rectangular pads	16.5	2.3
Round pads	25	3.3
Master cylinder clamp bolts	80 in.-lb.	0.90

Table 10 KZ440 FORK SPRING MINIMUM LENGTH

Model	Inch	mm
A, D	20.1	510
B, C	18.7	475
G, H	19.7	501

CHAPTER EIGHT

BELT DRIVE SYSTEM

The belt-driven KZ440-D/G is basically the same machine as the chain-driven KZ440-A/H, with the substitution of a toothed rubber belt for the drive chain. Cast aluminum pulleys with side plates are used instead of chain sprockets.

The belt requires no lubrication. The only maintenance required is belt tension inspection, adjustment and inspection of the belt and sprockets for wear.

DRIVE BELT TENSION

The drive belt has a milky-colored nylon lubricant coating. Do not apply any lubricants.

Belt Tension Inspection

The final drive belt stretches very little after the first 500 miles, but belt tension *must* be adjusted at the scheduled maintenance intervals (**Table 1**) and any time the rear wheel is removed. Proper alignment of the belt and sprockets is critical to long belt life.

NOTE

*Some models come with a special belt tension gauge in the bike's tool kit (**Figure 27**). If you have such a gauge, follow the instructions provided in your Owner's Manual. The procedure given here applies to all models and can be used if the gauge has been lost or damaged.*

1. Put the motorcycle up on its centerstand.
2. Apply a 10 lb. (4.5 kg) force to the middle of the bottom belt run. Deflection of the belt should be 3/8-5/8 in. (8.5-17 mm). See **Figure 28.**
3. Turn the wheel a little and recheck belt deflection. It should be within specification at the tightest and loosest parts of the belt.
4. If the belt deflection is not within specification as the belt is rotated, adjust the belt tension.

Belt Tension Adjustment and Alignment

When adjusting the drive belt, you must also maintain rear wheel alignment. A misaligned rear wheel can cause poor handling and pulling to one side or the other, as well as rapid belt, pulley and tire wear. If both adjusters are moved an equal amount (equal turns of the nuts), the rear wheel should be aligned correctly.

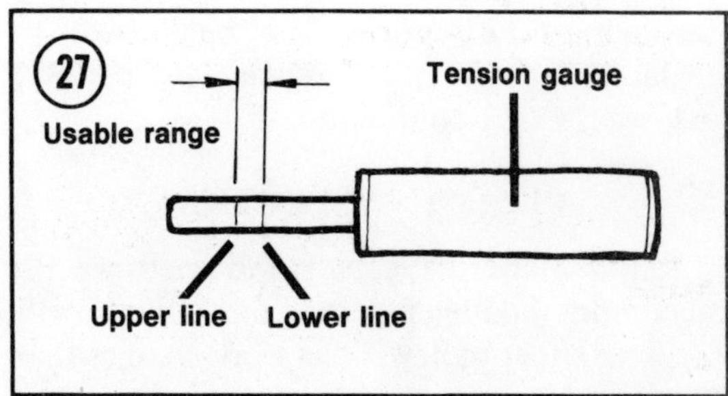

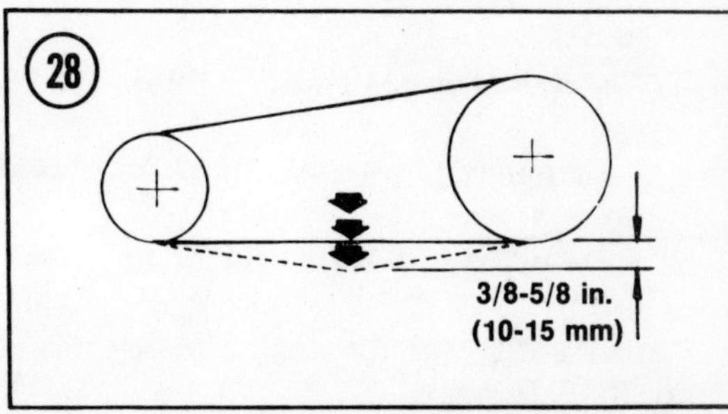

8

1. Loosen the rear torque link nut and the axle nut.
2. Loosen the locknuts on both belt adjusters.
3. *If the belt was too tight*, back out both adjuster bolts an equal amount and kick the rear wheel forward until the belt is too loose.
4. Turn both adjuster bolts in an equal amount until belt tension is within specification. The notch in each adjuster should be positioned the same distance along the swing arm alignment marks on both sides. If you are using the special Kawasaki tension gauge, remove and insert the gauge again to be sure the tension is correct.
5. When belt tension is correct, tighten the axle nut *partially*, spin the wheel and stop it forcefully with the brake pedal, then torque the axle nut to 55 ft.-lb. (7.5 mkg). This centers the brake shoes in the drum and prevents a "spongy" feeling rear brake.
6. Tighten the belt adjuster locknuts and the rear torque link nut.
7. Recheck belt tension.
8. Adjust the rear brake, if required. See *Rear Brake Adjustment* in Chapter Three.

BELT WEAR INSPECTION

At each regular service interval, inspect the belt for wear. When the nylon facing of the belt teeth is worn through so that the underlying urethane compound is showing through at any point, the belt must be replaced. Whenever you replace a drive belt, inspect the belt pulleys too.

PULLEY INSPECTION

Remove the drive belt and measure the maximum diameter across the pulley teeth. Replace either pulley if it is worn smaller than these limits.

a. Engine pulley (22 teeth): 3.74 in. (95.0 mm).
b. Engine pulley (24 teeth): 4.09 in. (103.9 mm).
c. Rear pulley (60 teeth): 10.39 in. (264.0 mm).
d. Rear pulley (65 teeth): 11.27 in. (286.3 mm).

Proper torque for the engine pulley nut is 60 ft.-lb. (9.0 mkg).

BELT REMOVAL/INSTALLATION

1. Mark the side of the belt so you will know which side faces out. Reversal of the belt will greatly shorten its service life.
2. Remove the rear wheel and swing arm as described for models B and C in Chapter Seven of the basic book.
3. Remove the engine pulley cover.
4. On 1980 to early 1981 models, pull out the clutch pushrod (**Figure 29**).
5. Remove the drive belt.
6. To install a new drive belt, reverse the removal procedure. Note the following.
   a. The drive belt is made by Gates. On 1980 to early 1981 models, the drive belt dimensions are 14 mm x 25.4 mm x 125 teeth. On late 1981 and later models, the drive belt dimensions are 14 mm x 32 mm x 129 teeth.
   b. Install new belts with the white paint marked edge in, toward the rear wheel. New belts have been broken in with this orientation.
   c. On 1980 to early 1981 models, install the clutch pushrod with the narrow end pointing out (**Figure 29**).
   d. Clean and lubricate the swing arm bearings. Inspect them for wear.
   e. Adjust drive belt tension and alignment initially and after 500 miles of use, then according to the maintenance schedule (**Table 1**).

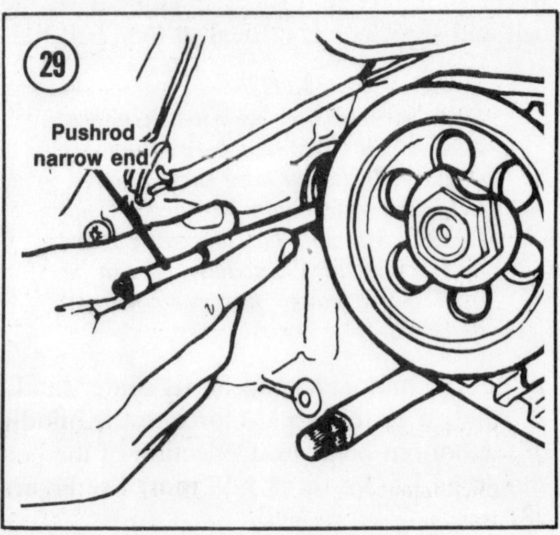

INDEX

9

E

F

G

H

I

K

L

M

9

1974-1977 KZ400, S & A – U.S. & 1978 KZ400A – U.S.

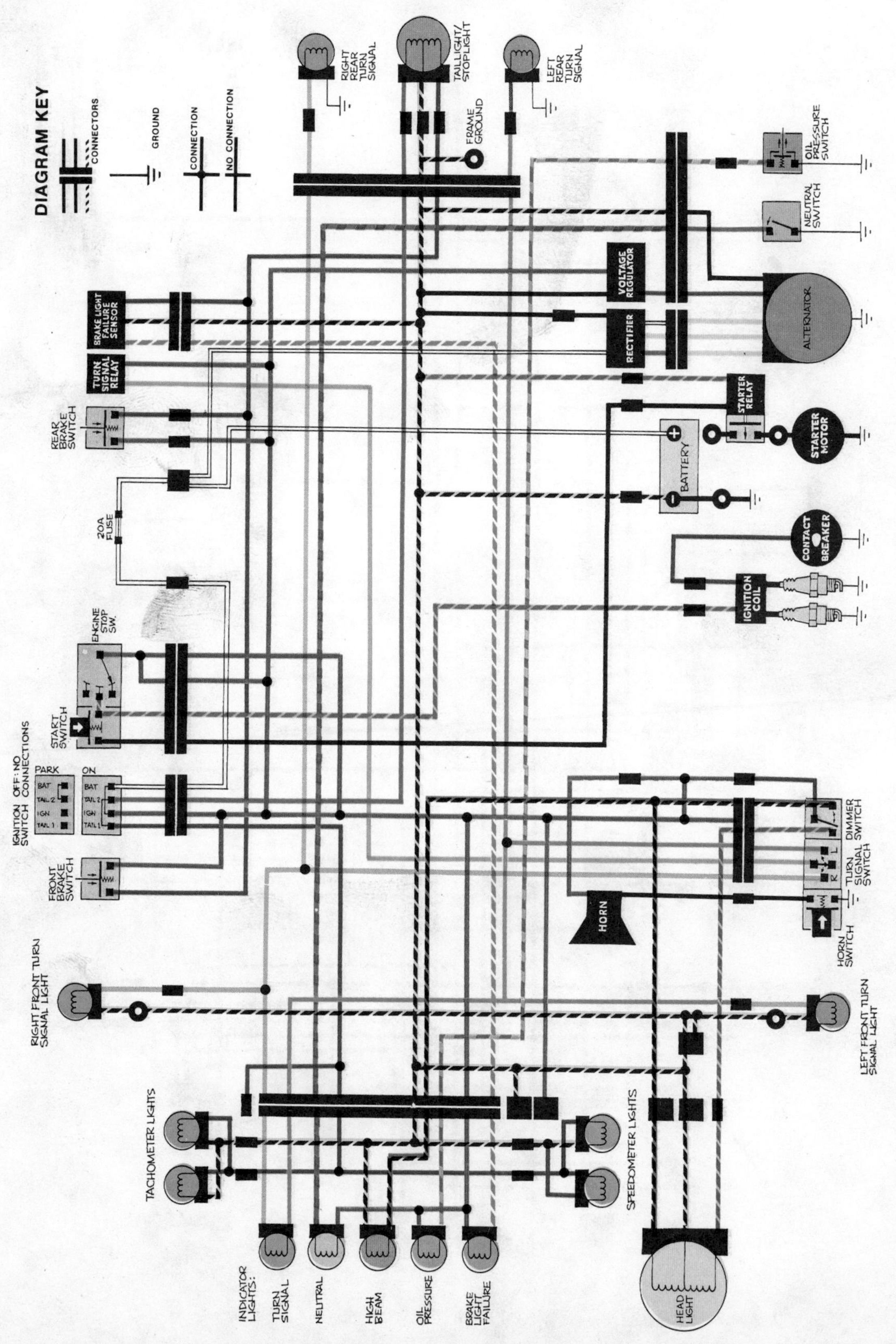

1978-1979 KZ400B – U.S. & Canada

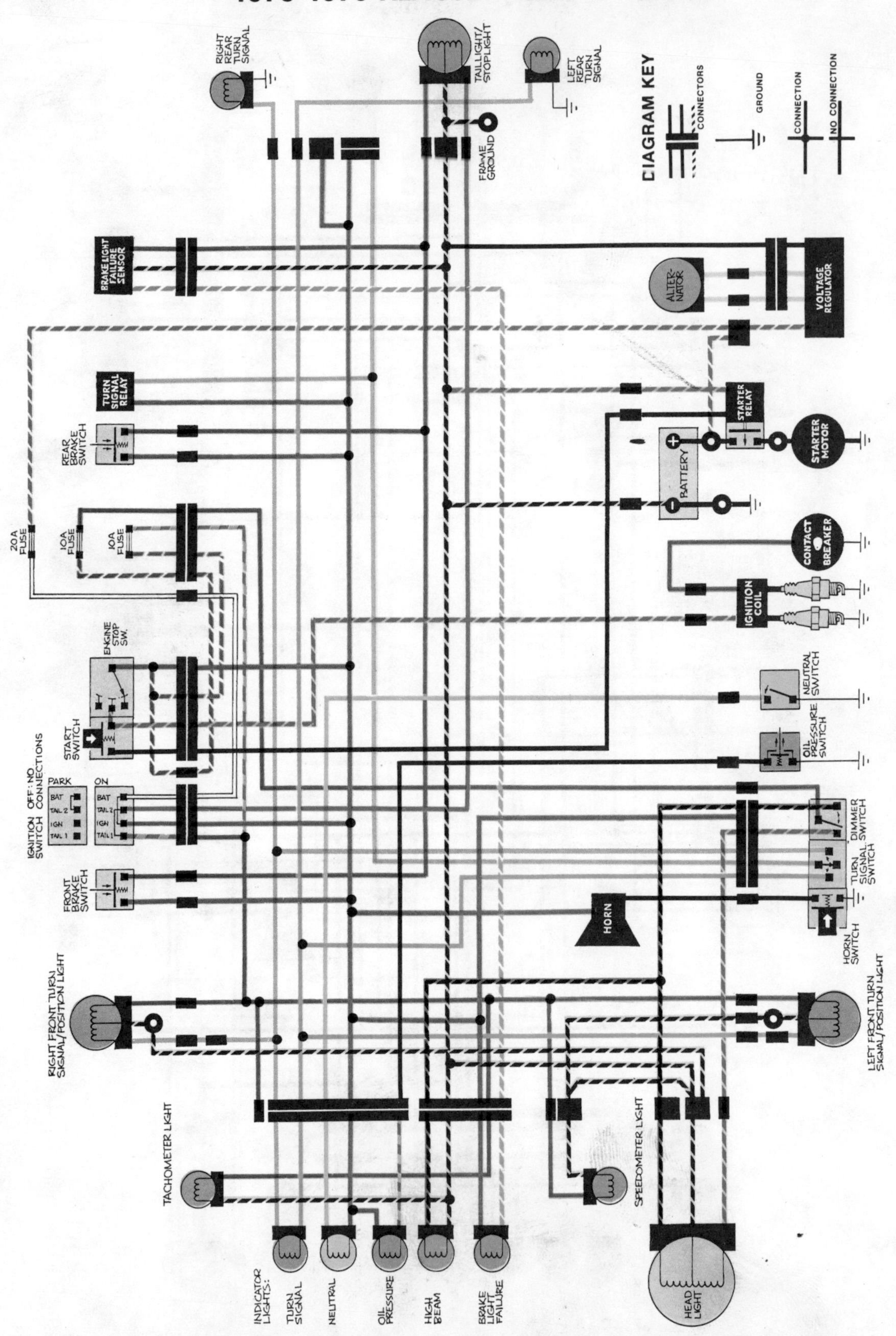

1978-1979 KZ400B – Europe

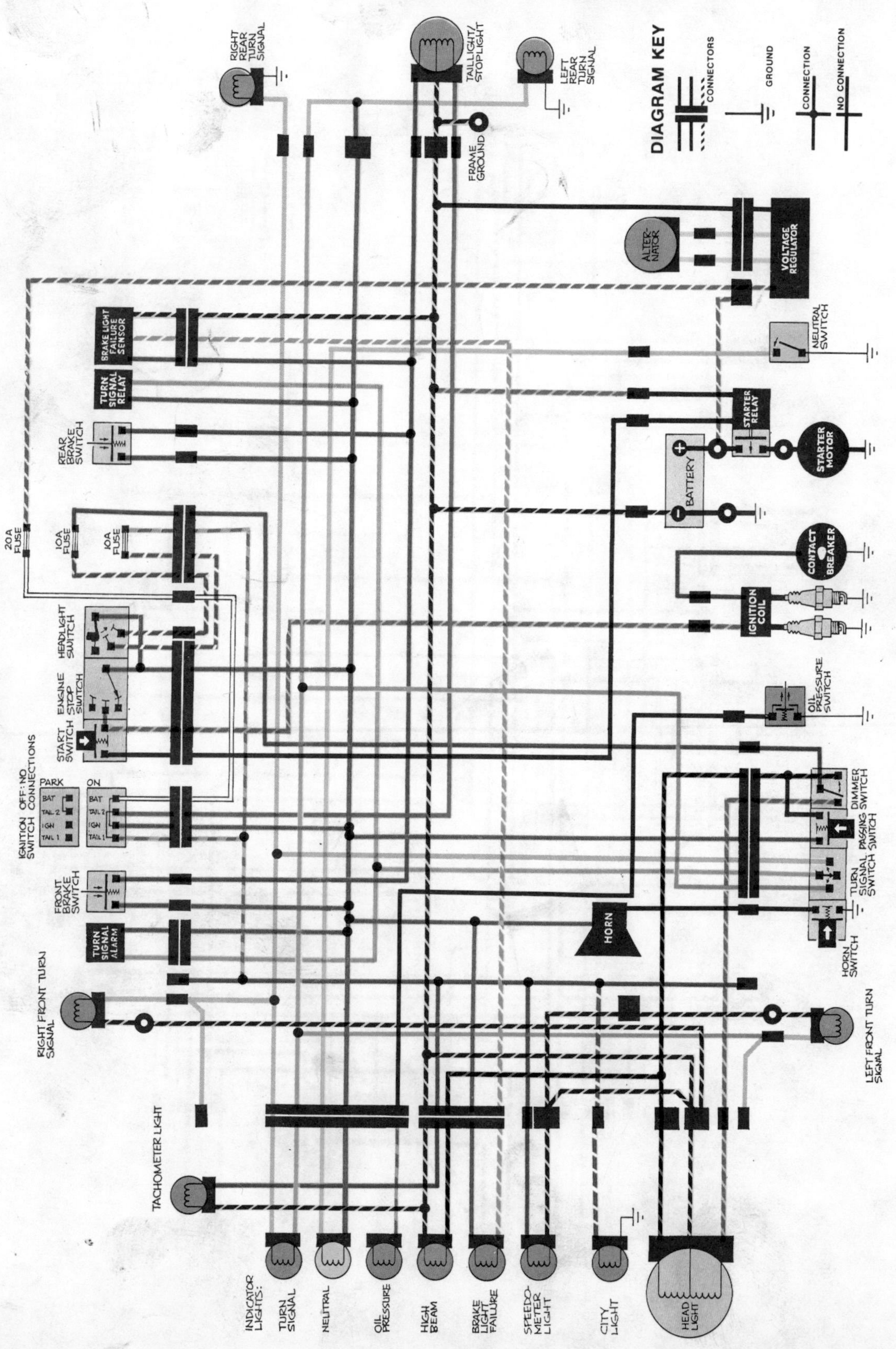

1978 KZ400C – U.S.

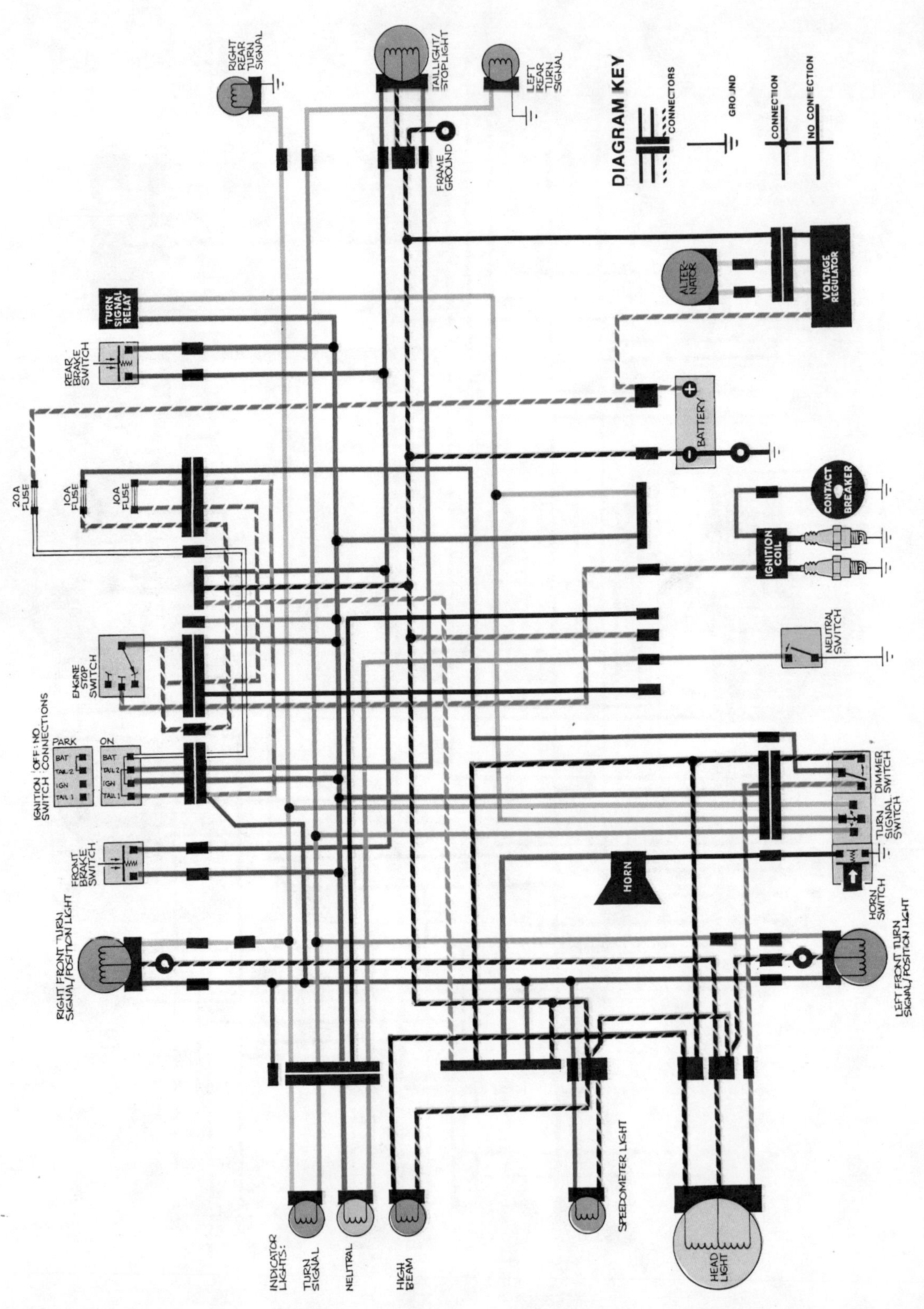

1979 KZ400H (LTD)
& 1980 KZ440A & D – U.S. & Canada

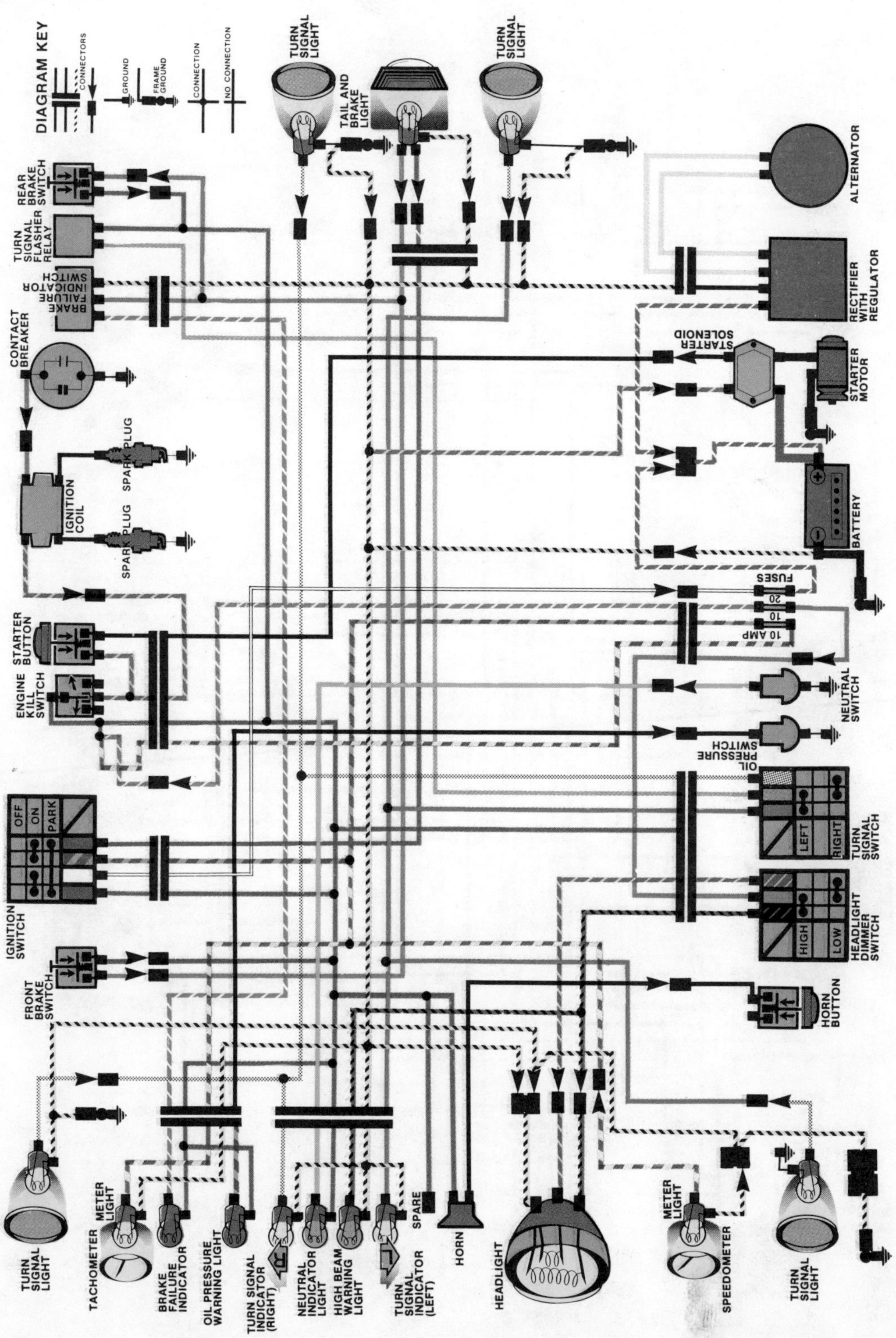

1980 KZ440B – U.S. & Canada

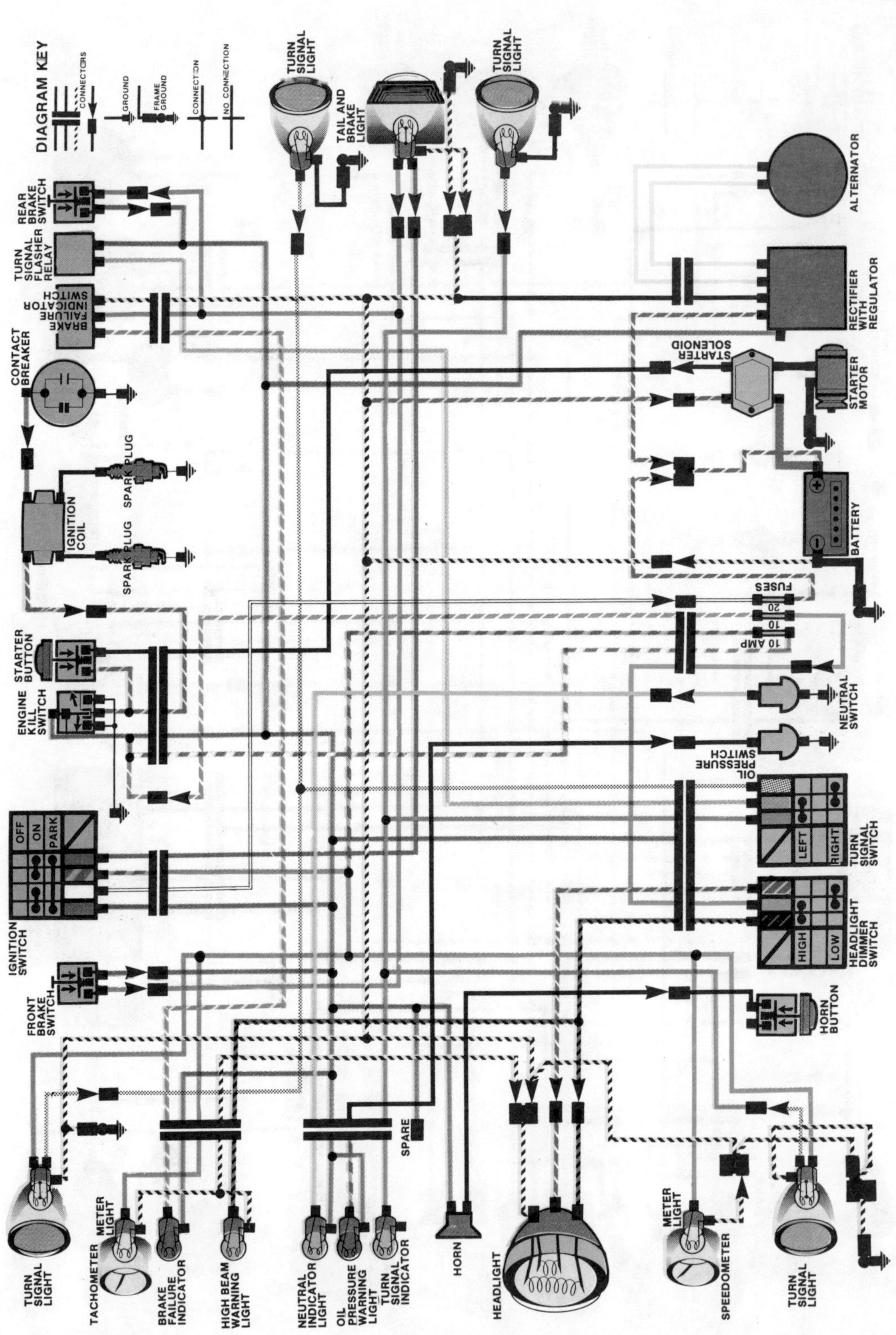

1980 Z440A – Europe

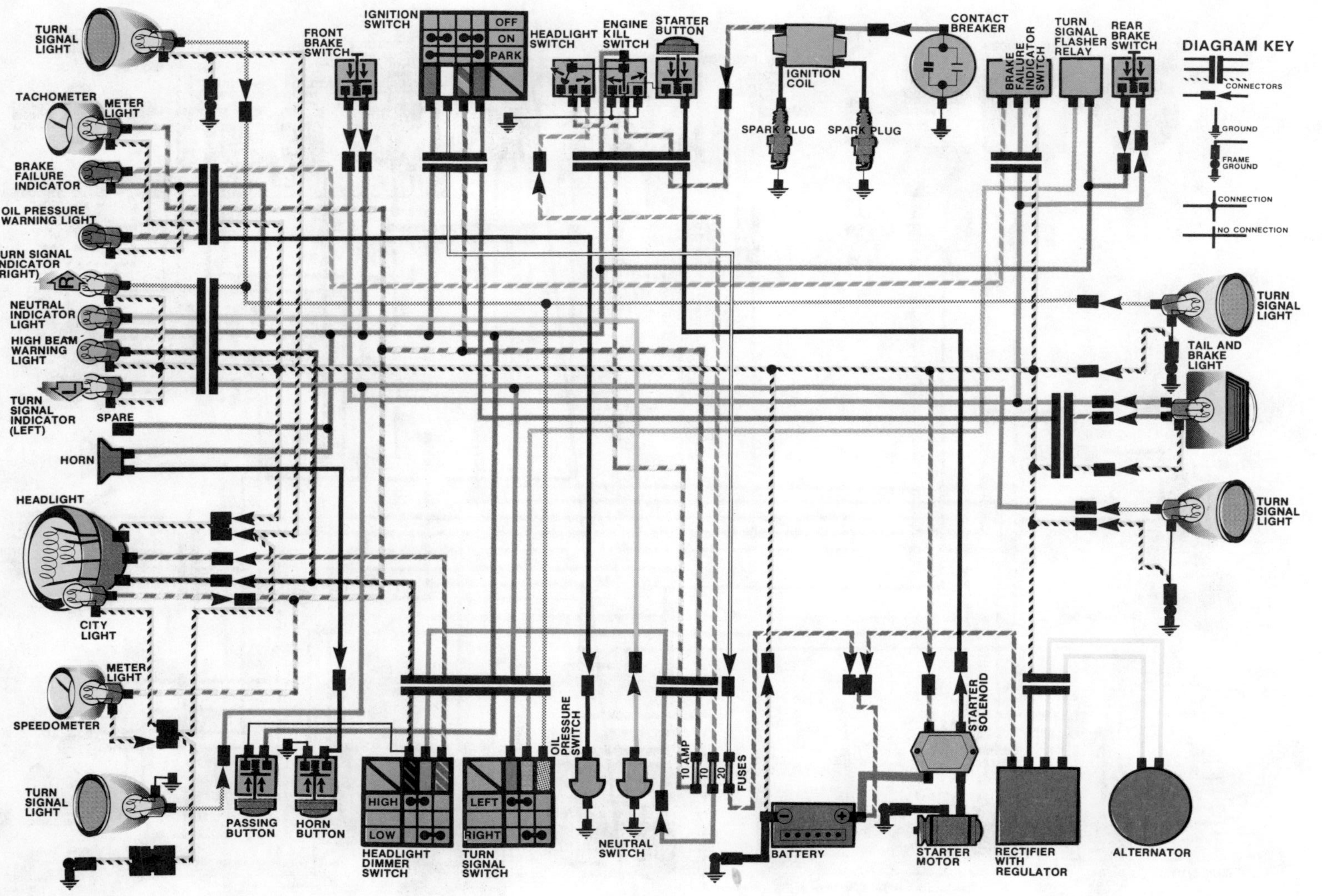

1980 Z440C – Europe

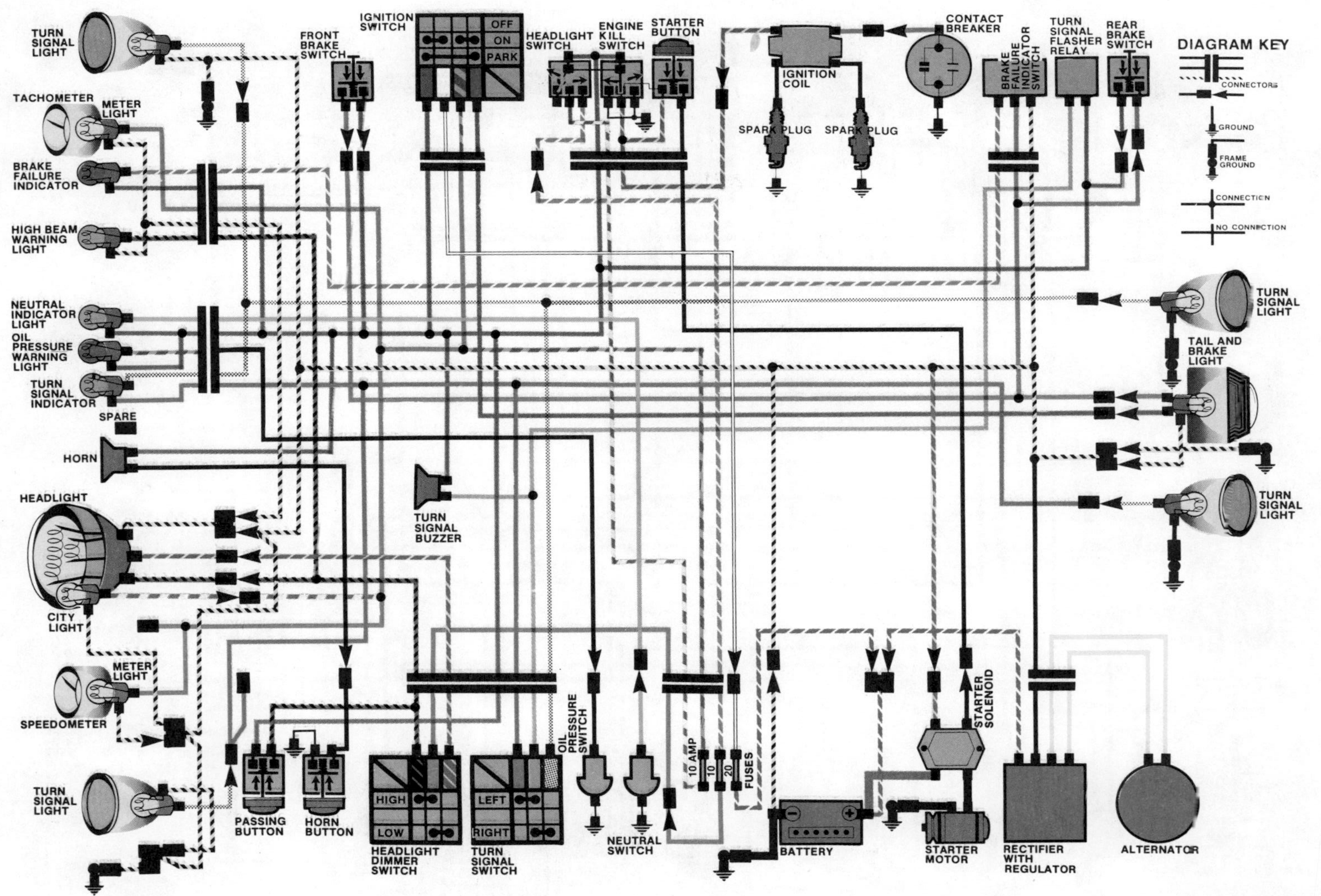

1981 KZ440A & D – U.S. & Canada

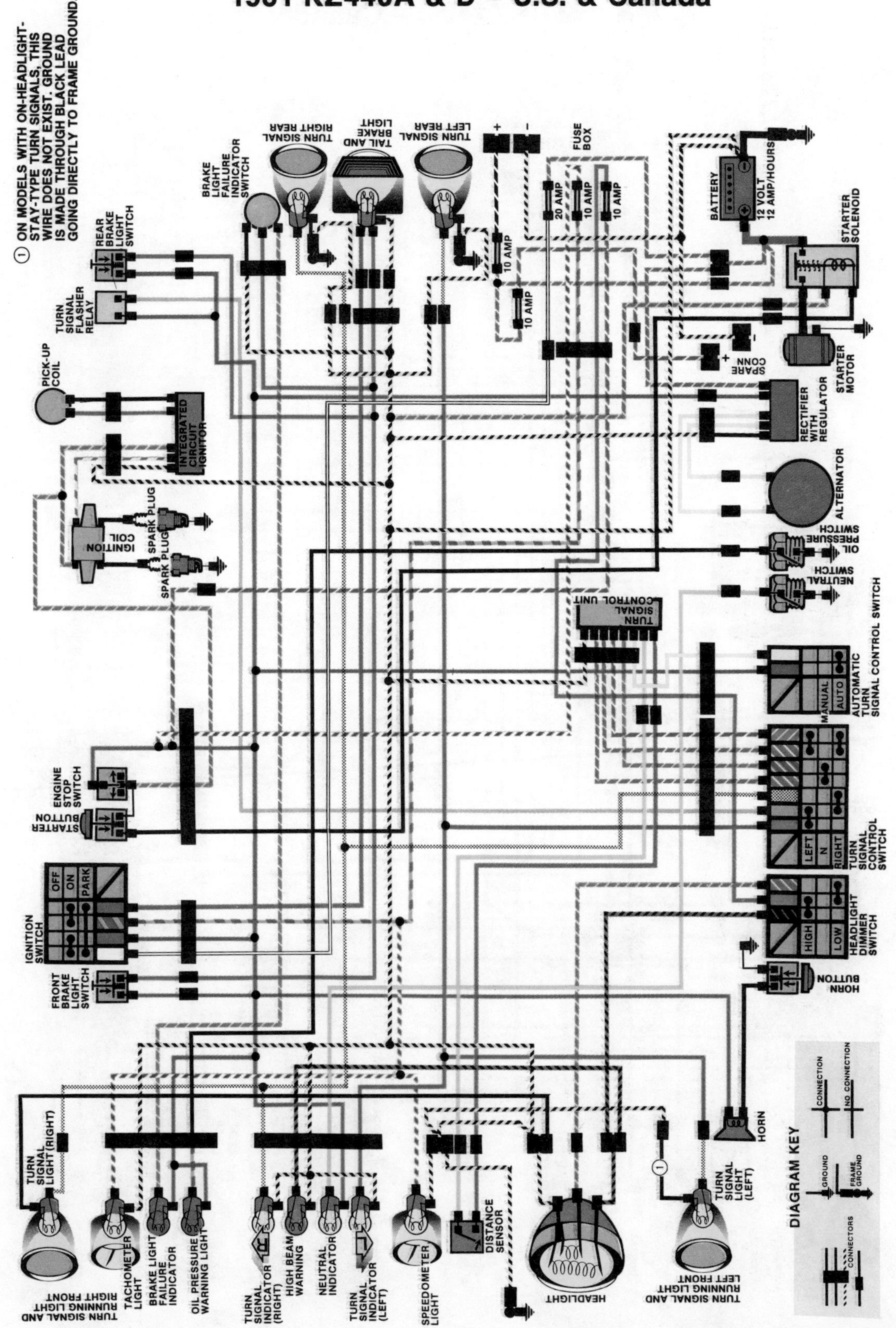

1981 KZ440B – U.S. & Canada & 1981 KZ440C – Canada

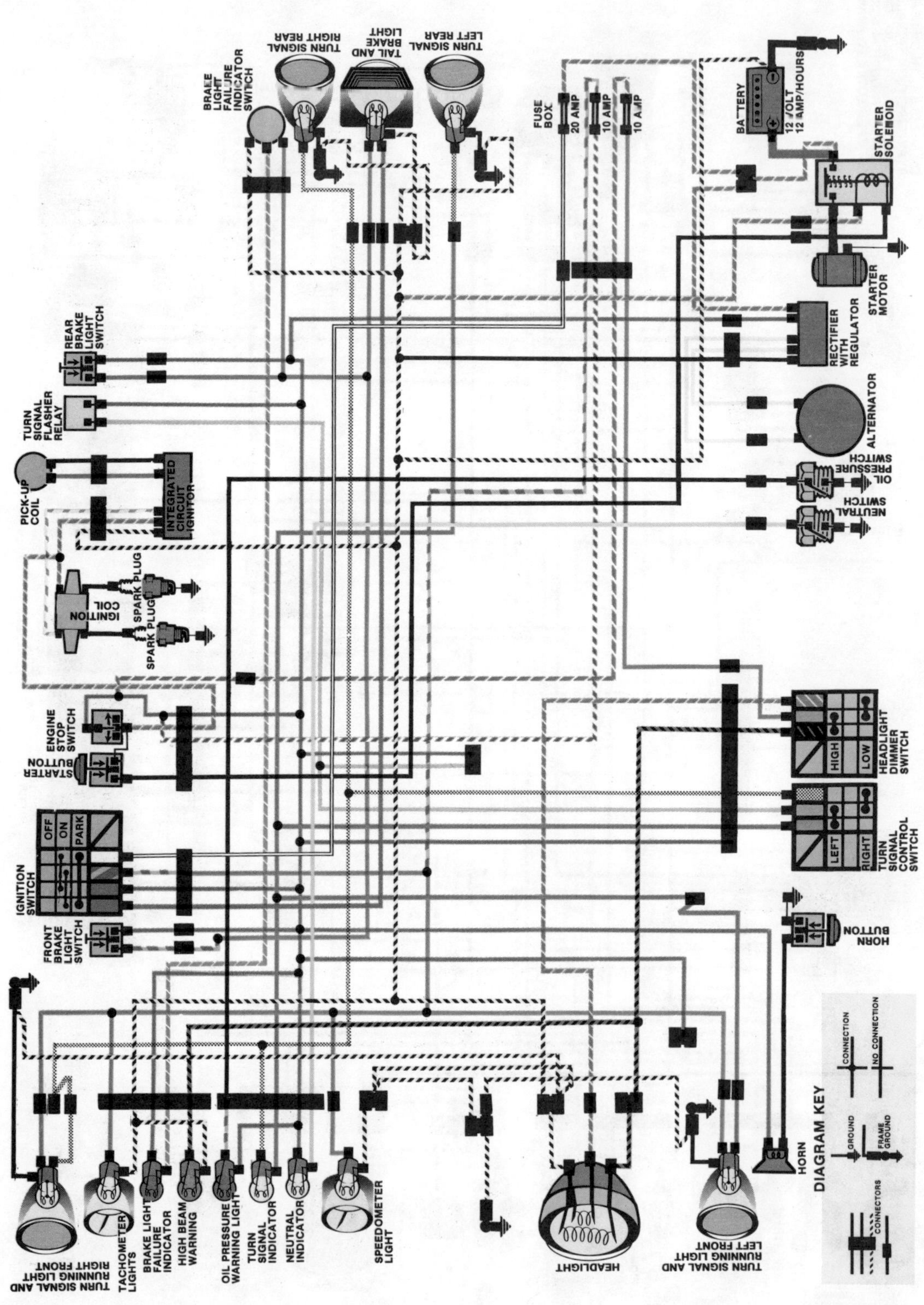

1981 Z440C – Europe

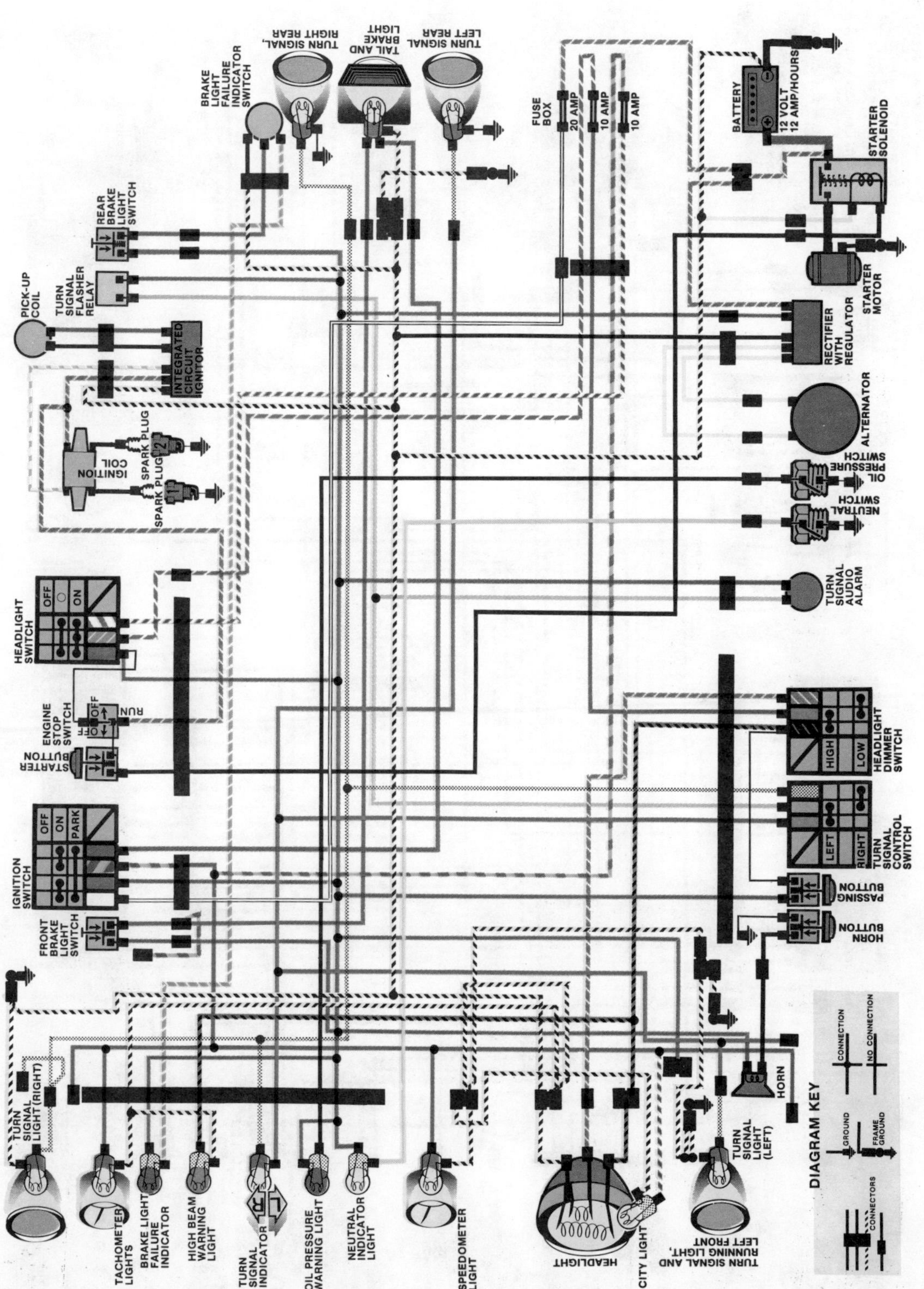

1981-1982 Z440A & D – Europe

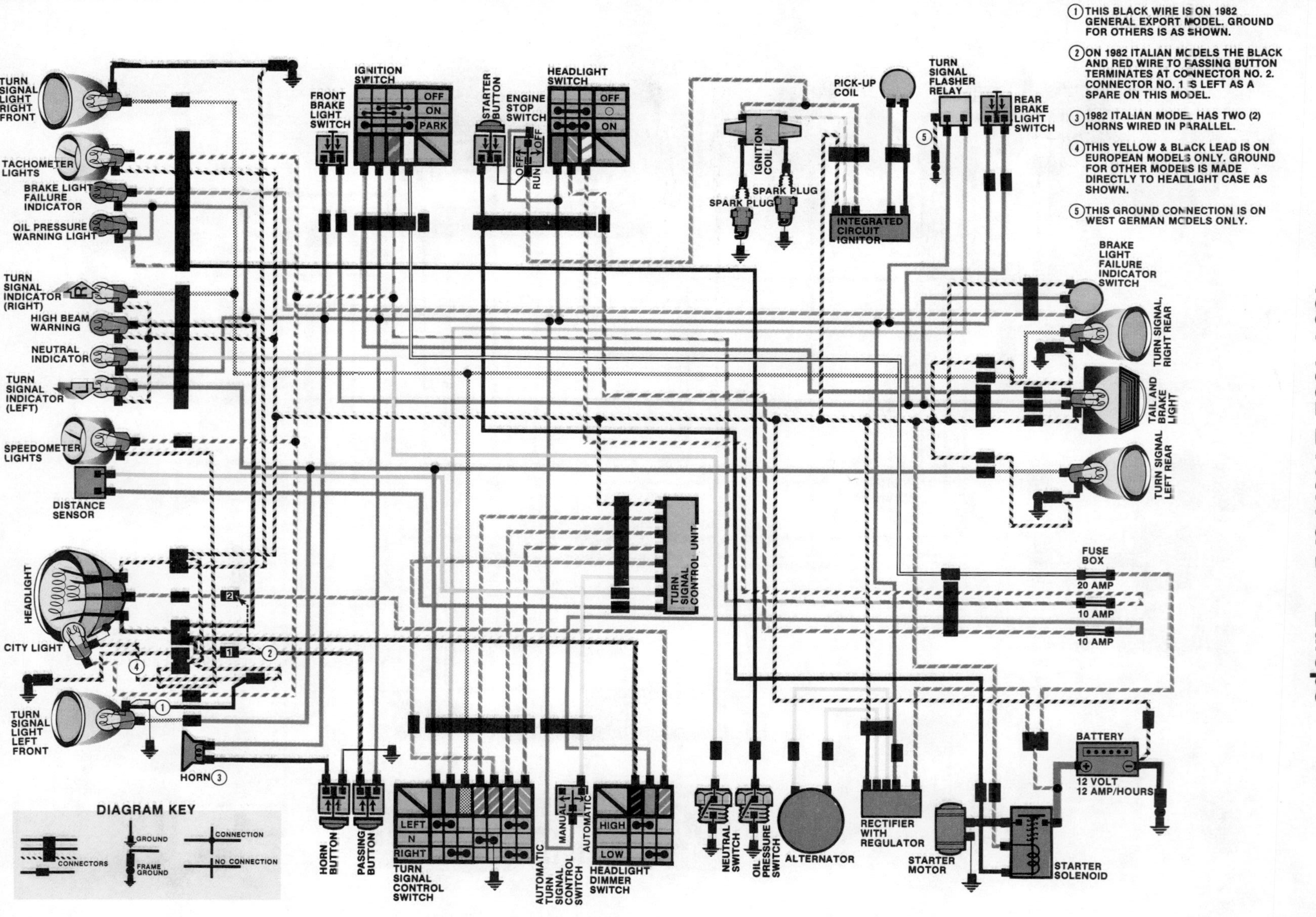

1982 KZ440A & D – U.S. & Canada

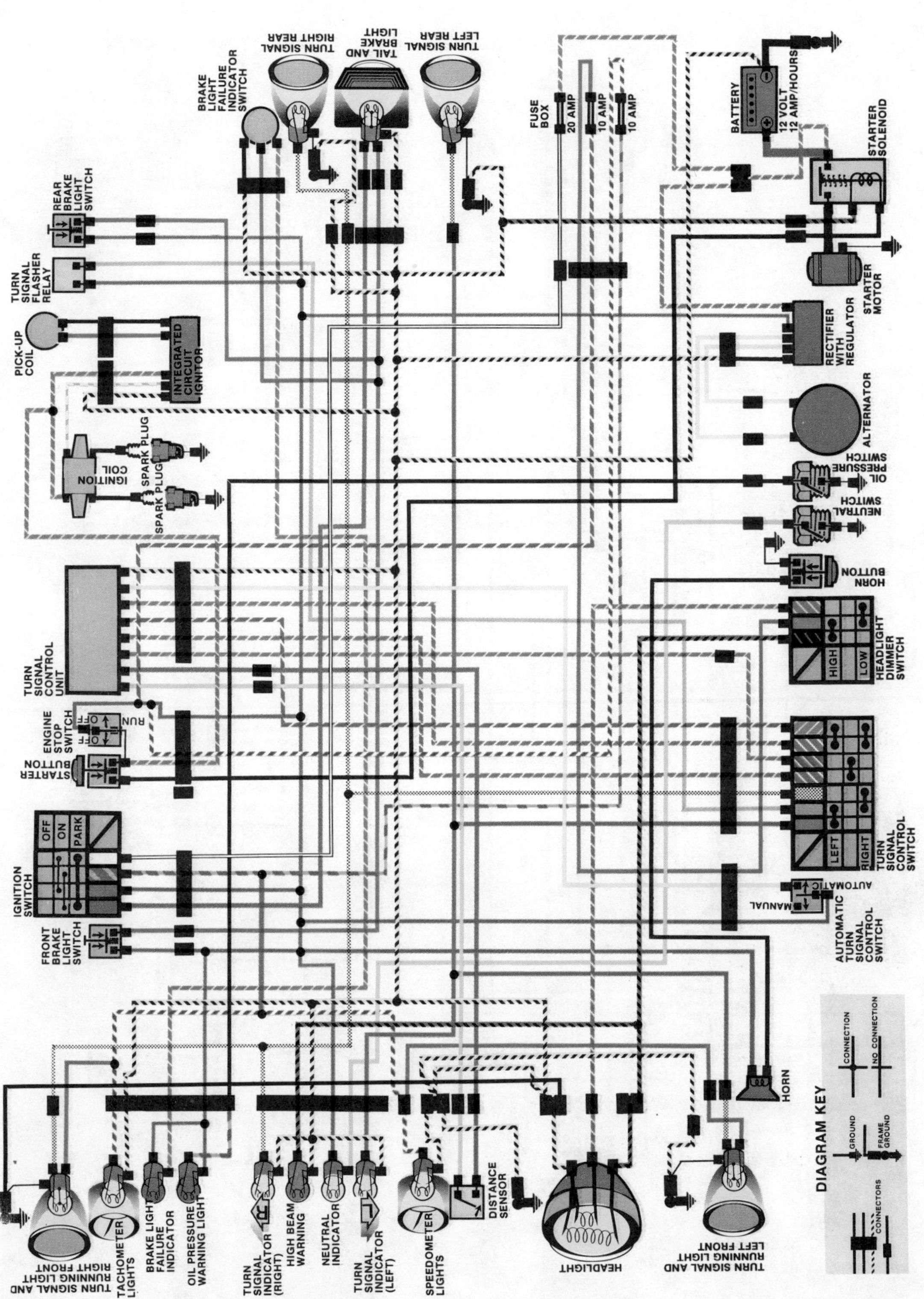

1982 KZ440G – U.S. & Canada

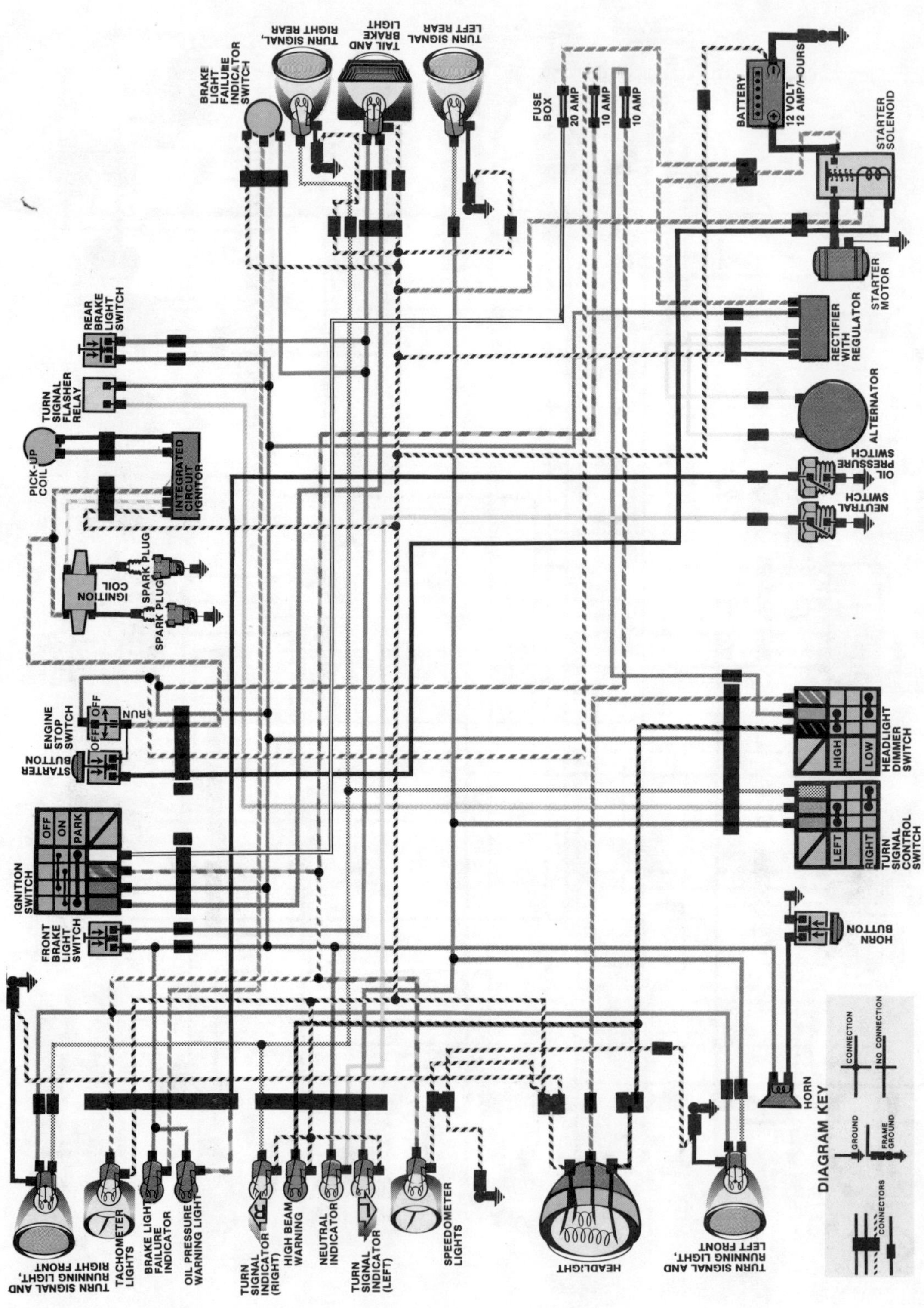

1982 KZ440H – Europe

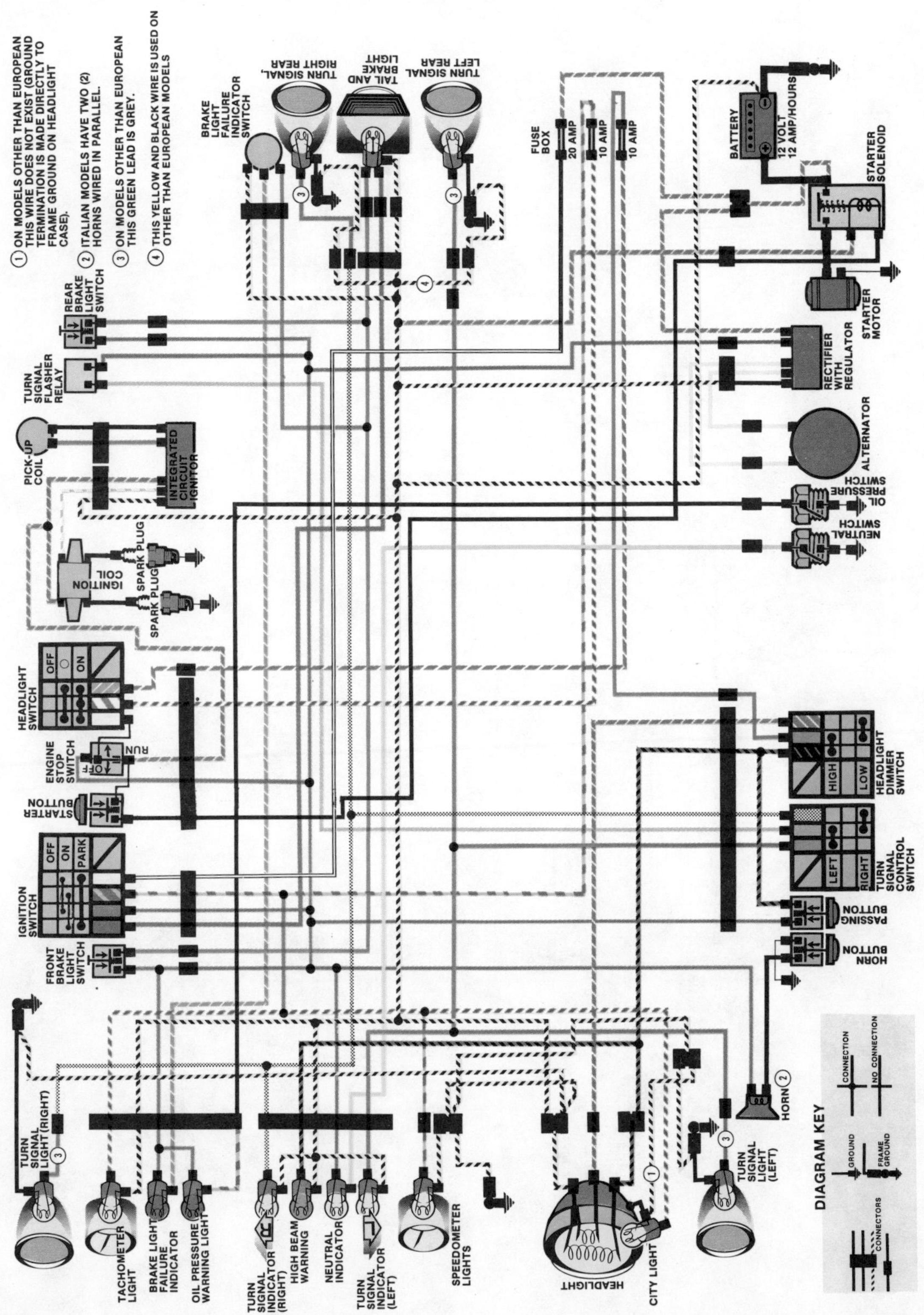